I0797565

The First World War in the Baltic Sea

Volume 1: Essen's triumph, 1914 to February 1915

Mark Harris

Helion & Company

To Mandy – for love and grammar

Helion & Company Limited
Unit 8 Amherst Business Centre
Budbrooke Road
Warwick
CV34 5WE
England
Tel. 01926 499619
Email: info@helion.co.uk
Website: www.helion.co.uk
X (formerly Twitter): @Helionbooks
Facebook: @HelionBooks
Visit our blog at https://helionbooks.wordpress.com/

Published by Helion & Company 2025
Designed and typeset by Mach 3 Solutions (www.mach3solutions.co.uk)
Cover designed by Paul Hewitt, Battlefield Design (www.battlefield-design.co.uk)
Text and maps © Mark Harris 2025
Illustrations © as individually credited

Every reasonable effort has been made to trace copyright holders and to obtain their permission for the use of copyright material. The author and publisher apologise for any errors or omissions in this work, and would be grateful if notified of any corrections that should be incorporated in future reprints or editions of this book.

ISBN 978-1-804519-10-3

British Library Cataloguing-in-Publication Data.
A catalogue record for this book is available from the British Library.

All rights reserved. No part of this publication may be reproduced, stored in a retrieval system, or transmitted, in any form, or by any means, electronic, mechanical, photocopying, recording or otherwise, without the express written consent of Helion & Company Limited.

For details of other military history titles published by Helion & Company Limited, contact the above address, or visit our website: http://www.helion.co.uk

We always welcome receiving book proposals from prospective authors.

Contents

Acknowledgements

Thanks are due to the following for their kind permissions for the use of archive images: Alex Franke, webmaster of <http://www.theFrankes.com>, Eesti Meremuuseum (EM), Library of Congress (LC), Naval History and Heritage Command of the U.S. Navy (NH), Europeana, Satakunnan Museo (SM), United States National Archives (USNA) and Wien Museum online archive (WM).

The research to complete the book would not have been possible without the work of the staff of the various archives that have made their material accessible, especially the Bundesarchiv, Russian State Archives of the Navy and UK National Archives.

Most of all my thanks go to my wife Mandy.

Glossary, notes and reference maps

Airship: Any lighter than air aircraft using hydrogen for buoyancy. Includes non-rigid types operated by all combatants and the rigid types, which includes zeppelins, operated by Germany.

Destroyer: sea-going fast torpedo craft also carrying significant gun armament. The term is contemporary but also applies to the German Grosse-Torpedoboot or Hochsee-Torpedoboot and Russian Eskadrennyye Minonostsy.

GRT: Gross Register Tonnage. This was the standard measure used to represent the capacity of a merchant ship based on its total internal volume, with one ton of capacity equal to 100 cubic feet (2.83 cubic metres). All GRT figures quoted are as per Lloyd's Register of Shipping.

Knot: one nautical mile per hour. Approximately 1.15 land miles per hour, or 1.85 kilometres per hour.

Mile: a nautical mile, the international measure of distance at sea. Traditionally one minute of latitude; about 2,025 yards or 1,852 metres.

Torpedo Boat: small coastal torpedo craft, with limited range and sea-going abilities, including smaller Russian Minonostsy.

Location names are those used at the time, by the country in which they were located. Romanisation of Russian names and ranks uses the BGN/PCGN convention. For example, Либава is Libava, not the germanised Libau, which is modern day Liepāja in Latvia. Administrative place names in the Grand Duchy of Finland were Swedish, transliterated into Cyrillic for Russian language documents. To avoid the confusion caused by transliterating back, the underlying Swedish is used. So for example, Гельсингфорс is Helsingfors, not the literal Gel'singfors, modern day Helsinki. Refer to the following three maps for locations mentioned in the text. Note that since 1918 many have been re-named.

All translations into English are by the author.

All times for Baltic operations are GMT+2, as used by British and Russian naval forces. This is one hour ahead of CET, used by German naval forces. Times quoted in translations of German sources are adjusted by adding an hour, to avoid confusion. Another source of confusion is that contemporary dates in Russian sources use the Julian calendar, which was 13 days behind the Gregorian calendar. These dates are therefore translated as their Gregorian equivalent.

BALTIC THEATRE OF OPERATIONS
LULEÅ
GULF OF BOTHNIA
SUNDSVALL
RÄFSÖ
MÄNTYLUOTO
BJÖRNEBORG
NORWAY
SWEDEN
RAUMO
FINLAND
ÅLAND ISLANDS
GÄVLE
ÅBO
KRONSHTADT
HELSINGFORS
PORKALA-UDD
MARIE-HAMN
ÅLAND SEA
STOCKHOLM
EKENÄS
GULF OF FINLAND
LAPPVIK
PAPONVIK
UTÖ
HANGÖ
NARGEN
BOGSKÄR
ODENSKHOL'M
REVEL'
SUROP
PETROGRAD (SANKT PETERBURG)
NARVA
OXELÖSUND
DAGERORT
DAGO
MOON SOUND
RUSSIA
GOTSKA SANDÖN
KIL'KOND
SKAGERRAK
EZEL'
FÅRÖ
GULF OF RIGA
GOTLAND
ÖSTERGARN
VINDAVA
RIGA
KATTEGAT
ÖLAND
HOBURG
STEYNORT
LIBAVA
KARLSKRONA
DENMARK
POLANGEN
KØBENHAVN
MALMÖ
CHRISTIANSØ
KURISCHEM LAGOON
MEMEL
FALSTERBO
STOLPE BANK
DANZIG BAY
TILSIT
MØN
BORNHOLM
RIXHÖFT
HELA
GEDSER
STILO
BRUSTERÖRT
K. BAY
ARKONA
SCHOLPIN
PUTZIG
KÖNIGSBERG
SASSNITZ
PILLAU
RÜGEN
STOLP-MÜNDE
DANZIG
OSTPREUSSEN
KIEL
KOLBERG
NEUFAHRWASSER
LÜBECK
WARNEMÜNDE
WOLLIN
GERMANY
SWINEMÜNDE
STETTIN
0 25 50 75 100
NAUTICAL MILES
© Mark Harris 2025
All rights reserved

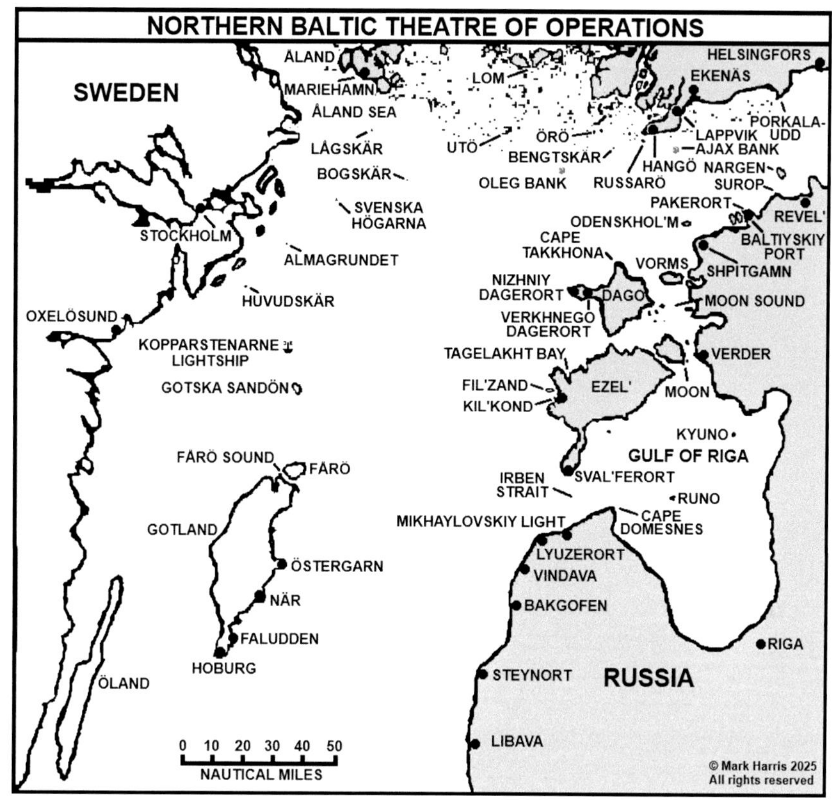
NORTHERN BALTIC THEATRE OF OPERATIONS
SWEDEN
ÅLAND
MARIEHAMN
ÅLAND SEA
LOM
HELSINGFORS
EKENÄS
PORKALA-UDD
LAPPVIK
AJAX BANK
LÅGSKÄR
UTÖ
ÖRÖ
BENGTSKÄR
HANGÖ
NARGEN
BOGSKÄR
OLEG BANK
RUSSARÖ
SUROP
SVENSKA HÖGARNA
PAKERORT
REVEL'
ODENSKHOL'M
BALTIYSKIY PORT
STOCKHOLM
CAPE TAKKHONA
ALMAGRUNDET
VORMS
SHPITGAMN
NIZHNIY DAGERORT
DAGO
MOON SOUND
HUVUDSKÄR
VERKHNEGO DAGERORT
OXELÖSUND
KOPPARSTENARNE LIGHTSHIP
TAGELAKHT BAY
VERDER
GOTSKA SANDÖN
FIL'ZAND
EZEL'
MOON
KIL'KOND
KYUNO
FÅRÖ SOUND
FÅRÖ
GULF OF RIGA
IRBEN STRAIT
SVAL'FERORT
RUNO
CAPE DOMESNES
MIKHAYLOVSKIY LIGHT
GOTLAND
LYUZERORT
ÖSTERGARN
VINDAVA
NÄR
BAKGOFEN
FALUDDEN
RIGA
HOBURG
ÖLAND
STEYNORT
RUSSIA
0 10 20 30 40 50
NAUTICAL MILES
LIBAVA
© Mark Harris 2025
All rights reserved

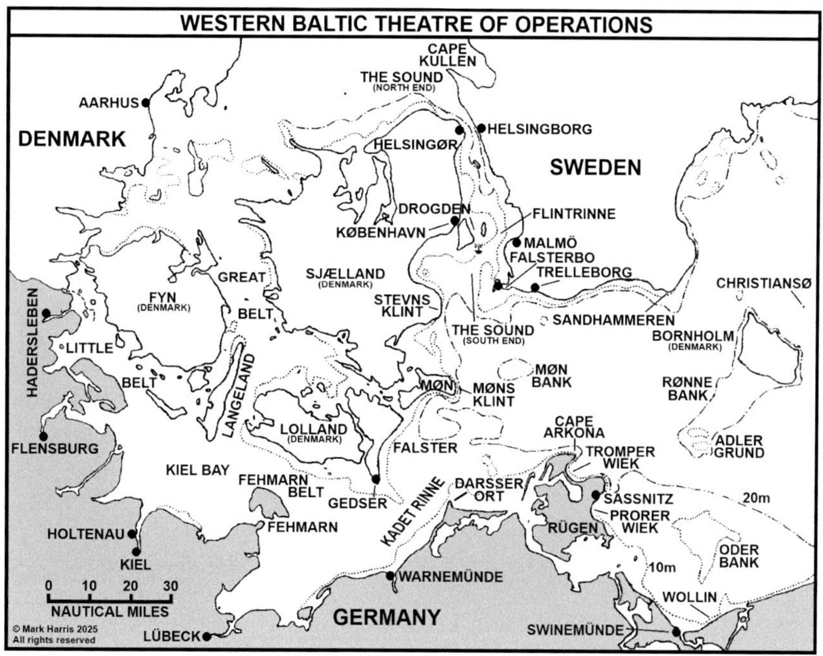
WESTERN BALTIC THEATRE OF OPERATIONS
CAPE KULLEN
THE SOUND (NORTH END)
AARHUS
HELSINGBORG
DENMARK
HELSINGØR
SWEDEN
DROGDEN
FLINTRINNE
KØBENHAVN
MALMÖ
FALSTERBO
TRELLEBORG
GREAT
SJÆLLAND (DENMARK)
CHRISTIANSØ
FYN (DENMARK)
STEVNS KLINT
BELT
SANDHAMMEREN
HADERSLEBEN
THE SOUND (SOUTH END)
BORNHOLM (DENMARK)
LITTLE
MØN BANK
BELT
MØN
MØNS KLINT
RØNNE BANK
LANGELAND
CAPE ARKONA
LOLLAND (DENMARK)
ADLER GRUND
FLENSBURG
FALSTER
TROMPER WIEK
KIEL BAY
FEHMARN BELT
DARSSER ORT
SASSNITZ
20m
GEDSER
KADET RINNE
PRORER WIEK
FEHMARN
RÜGEN
HOLTENAU
ODER BANK
KIEL
10m
WARNEMÜNDE
0 10 20 30
NAUTICAL MILES
WOLLIN
GERMANY
© Mark Harris 2025
All rights reserved
LÜBECK
SWINEMÜNDE

1

The opposing fleets in the Baltic and their plans

The Baltic Sea was the scene of a decisive naval conflict between the German and Russian empires in the First World War. Trade routes criss-crossed it to carry goods and raw materials that sustained the war effort of both sides in the conflict. A loss of control over the Baltic could become a decisive factor in the war. This led the British to send forces to support the outnumbered fleet of their embattled ally. The conflict ebbed and flowed in unexpected ways as strategic priorities changed and naval tactics evolved. Reputations rose and fell. Both fleets had their successes and failures.

The northern Baltic freezes in the winter, stopping conflict until the spring thaw. The first campaign that ended with the winter freeze in February 1915 had an outcome that few, if any, would have predicted in August 1914. This remarkable outcome arose from strategy and tactics, but above all personalities and preconceptions of those on the opposing sides. The lessons revealed have a timeless relevance.

Russian naval policy 1880-1914

The conflict grew out of the complex web of alliances and imperial ambitions that came to a head in the summer of 1914. Both Russia and Germany had been on a path to conflict for many years. The empires shared a long border. Both sought to expand their influence and interests in the Balkans and the Near East. When an expansionist Germany concluded an alliance with Austria-Hungary in 1879, this conflict of interest came into sharp focus.

Whilst both Germany and Russia were pre-eminently land powers, Russia had historically maintained a considerable fleet in the Baltic. Finland and the Baltic provinces were important for Russian trade and controlled the gateway to the capital of Sankt Peterburg in the Gulf of Finland. The fleet needed to be able to dominate the other navies in the Baltic, especially that of the traditional enemy, Sweden. It also needed to be available to defend Russian interests anywhere in the world. However, the focus from 1880 onwards shifted to Germany. This, in turn, inevitably brought Russia and France together against a common enemy. By 1894, this led to a Franco-Russian military alliance aimed at countering Germany and her Austro-Hungarian ally. A Russian fleet also faced another traditional enemy, the Ottoman Empire, across the Black Sea. A new threat emerged when Japan established herself as a naval power in the Far East

Novik, in September 1913. Armed with 4x10.2cm high velocity guns and 8x45cm torpedo tubes in twin mounts, all capable of engaging to either side. Rails for 60 mines and an outstanding speed of 36 knots. (EM:SA MMF4815)

following her victory over China in 1895. The need to counter growing Japanese and German fleets at the turn of the century proved an impossible task. The funds available were unable to expand Russia's industrial base rapidly enough to build all the ships required. War with Japan in 1904–5 then brought disaster. At the Battle of Tsushima, the Japanese fleet largely destroyed the Baltiyskiy Flot (Baltic Fleet), when it arrived in the Far East. Even worse, Germany then embarked on an accelerated programme of naval construction.

This disastrous situation focussed minds. The Baltiyskiy Flot had to adopt a purely defensive posture. Ships already designed and funded during the recent war filled out the fleet as they were completed. This included two new battleships, four armoured cruisers, a large number of destroyers and a small force of short-range submarines. However, their construction only partially absorbed the lessons learned from the war. In 1906, a step change in the size, speed and armament of naval vessels followed the advent of the British battleship *Dreadnought*. This meant early obsolescence for all of the battleships and armoured cruisers now joining the fleet.

Meanwhile, a new Russian Naval General Staff set out to learn the lessons of the recent war, focussing on solving strategic problems, systematically rebuilding the fleet and developing its bases. In 1907, they proposed a plan for a relatively modest new force of heavy ships. These would counteract any incursion into the Gulf of Finland, protected by minefields and supported by coastal batteries and torpedo craft covering these narrow waters. War experience proved that mines and torpedoes were a powerful defensive force multiplier. A 10-year plan of construction would deliver the ships required.

Money to build the planned new fleet and naval bases did not materialise. Construction only began on four modern battleships and the prototype for a new type of fast, heavily armed destroyer in 1909. Work proceeded slowly. Finally, in 1912, there was a major allocation of funds, allowing orders for four battle cruisers, four light cruisers, 36 of the new destroyers and 12 submarines capable of long-range patrol.

War came before the programme bore fruit. Only the prototype destroyer, *Novik*, had joined the fleet, but the four battleships were in the final stages of fitting out. New submarines were some way from completion. The destroyers were even further behind and at widely varying stages of construction. The battle cruisers and light cruisers were only in the earliest stages of construction.[1]

German naval policy 1880-1914

The future architect of the Imperial German Navy, Albert von Tirpitz, summed up German naval policy in the 1880s as being, 'to prepare a strong coastal defence for the next war against Russia and France.' The fleet therefore needed to be able to cover both the North Sea, threatened by the French fleet, and the Baltic, threatened by that of Russia. Baltic trade was critical to the German economy, in particular the supply of iron ore from Sweden, which fuelled German industrial output. Denmark added further complications. Its fortifications, and a small but capable fleet, sat across the channels between the North Sea and the Baltic. It had lost territory in a war with Prussia in 1864 and might side with Germany's enemies.

Funds to challenge the powerful French fleet were not available. However, the Triple Alliance, concluded in 1882 with Austria-Hungary and Italy, was relied on to tie down a large part of the French naval forces in the Mediterranean. The navy aimed to retain a margin of supremacy over the Russian fleet, focussing on bold offensive action in co-operation with the army to seize a base in the Gulf of Riga in a war with Russia alone, despite this being an increasingly unlikely scenario. In contrast, the army planned largely for a war against both France and Russia, posing a much greater challenge. The resulting war on two fronts precluded making troops available for co-operation with the navy against Russia. The army focussed exclusively on this scenario from 1896 onwards. It also led to the construction of the Kaiser Wilhelm Canal between Kiel in the Baltic and Brunsbüttel on the Elbe in the North Sea. Warships could respond to threats in either sea quickly and safely, without the long detour around a hostile Denmark. Construction took eight years and it opened in 1895.

Wilhelm II had ascended the throne in Germany in 1888. He saw a powerful sea-going navy as an essential part of a growing German Empire, and reversed a recent decline in large warship construction. However, his direct interest had negative consequences for the co-ordination of policy, operational planning and fleet command. These had all fallen under the Kaiserliche Admiralität (Imperial Admiralty). Wilhelm replaced this with three functions reporting directly to him: the Oberkommando der Marine (Naval High Command), responsible for operational planning and fleet command, the Reichs-Marine-Amt (Imperial Naval Office), responsible for construction and administration and finally the Kaiserliches Marine-Kabinett (Imperial Naval Cabinet), which dealt with promotions and appointments.

1 Михаил Александрович Петров, *Подготовка России к мировой войне на море* (Москва Ленинград: Государственное издательство РСФСР, 1926), pp.25–65; N. B. Pavlovich, (Translated C. M. Rao), *The Fleet in the First World War (Flot v Pervoi Mirovoi Voine) Volume 1: Operations of the Russian Fleet* (New Delhi: Amerind Publishing Co. Pvt. Ltd., 1979), pp.1–33.

Armoured cruiser *Prinz Adalbert* representing the Kaiser's naval ambitions at the coronation of King Haakon VII of Norway, Trondheim, 22 June 1906. A future Baltic flagship, facing navies represented in the background by British cruiser *Talbot* and Russian imperial yacht *Polyarnaya Zvezda*. (Norsk Maritimt Museum)

The relatively hostile relations that Britain had with France and Russia meant that Germany had always counted on British neutrality in the event of war with either. This was vital, as Britain had the most powerful fleet in the world. There were even discussions of an alliance from time to time. However, relations soured in the late 1890s as Germany sought to expand its power and influence outside Europe, particularly over German support for the Boer Republics against Britain. This led to a new policy from 1897 onwards under the influence of Staatssekretär des Reichs-Marine-Amts (Secretary of State of the Imperial Naval Office), Alfred von Tirpitz. To obtain control over policy, he needed to end the rivalry that had developed between the Oberkommando and the Reichs-Marine-Amt. He had the Kaiser dissolve the Oberkommando in 1899. The Admiralstab, which was responsible for planning and operational direction, together with all of the individual formation and base commanders, now reported directly to the Kaiser. The result was a mire of competing interests. A major point of contention was that Tirpitz emphasised building ships in quantity for maximum political impact, whilst the fleet commanders pushed back on their quality and the level of preparedness for war.

Tirpitz used his office to initiate a wave of new naval construction to build a fleet to match German imperial ambition. This embodied his idea of the 'riskflotte'. This constituted a fleet capable of seriously weakening the British fleet in battle, in order to leave it vulnerable to the other great powers. This would allow Germany to use the fleet as a tool to force political concessions from an isolated Britain. This backfired in 1904 when France and Britain concluded a rapprochement, the Entente Cordiale. Britain made a similar agreement with Russia in 1907. Despite this, Tirpitz pressed ahead with an escalating naval arms race aimed at building a fleet that would eventually be a credible challenge to that of Britain. As a result, in 1912, the French and British governments came to an understanding, which allowed the British fleet to concentrate in home waters against Germany, whilst the French fleet concentrated in the Mediterranean. In 1913, the staff of the two navies concluded a co-operation agreement, defining arrangements if the two countries were at war with Germany, although there was no formal alliance.

Even if Britain remained neutral in a war with Russia and France, German naval planning came to require the bulk of the fleet to be reserved for action with Britain. A 1909 report by the Admiralstab concluded that, 'one has to reckon that if Germany becomes involved in any war the British Fleet will join the enemy either immediately or at the appropriate opportunity.' However, with the Russian fleet beginning to recover after the disasters of 1905, the navy planned for an offensive posture in the Baltic by significant forces. The campaign would open with an attack to destroy the flotillas based in the forward Russian base at Libava, as it was free of ice all year round and had become a particular source of concern. Demonstrations against the Russian coast would then assist the army by diverting Russian troops to coastal defence, whilst keeping the German coast open for vital trade. Ideally, the attacks would include troop landings to seize a base in the Gulf of Riga.

The navy took the plan to the army General Staff for review. Their plans did not align. The army focussed on the absolute priority of a knockout blow against France, using all available offensive forces. This gambled that Russia would be slow to mobilise. The bulk of their initially available troops would therefore have to oppose the Austro-Hungarian army. Russian troops were unlikely to land on the German coast. Russia might overrun some eastern areas of the German Empire in the early days of the war, but this risk was accepted. The army certainly had no troops available for landings in Russia. Once France was defeated in six weeks, the German army would move east to deal with Russia. Meanwhile, support from the navy would be 'appreciated', especially landing feints against Libava, but should not, 'detract from the main tasks of the navy', namely being ready to take the offensive against Britain, whose army was expected to support the French. The failure to agree consistent assumptions for policy and planning was symptomatic of a fragmented command structure.

Revised planning by the Admiralstab for war against Russia, France and Britain in 1912 finally acknowledged the growth in the Russian fleet. It accepted that there were inadequate resources for extensive offensive operations in the Baltic. The Russians were assumed to be planning offensive operations to block German forces in Danzig and then attack points as far west as Rügen Island. German offensive plans were limited to raids on Libava and other points on the coast, using only light forces spared from the North Sea. There was acceptance that Russian forces might be able to penetrate as far as Kiel Bay, which might force the redeployment of vessels from the North Sea to protect it.

One thing Germany could count on was good political relations with Sweden, which had a long history of conflict with Russia. Many in the establishment and wider society were pro-German. There had even been some serious discussion over the years between the German and Swedish militaries regarding co-operation against Russia. However, the Swedish government were wary of becoming embroiled in German imperial ambitions and nothing came of this. They were also concerned that Britain might attempt to seize Swedish territory to force entry into the Baltic. The Swedish Navy therefore maintained a significant fleet focussed on coastal defence to deter any potential aggressor.[2]

The Baltiyskiy Flot

Until new vessels completed, the fleet would have to make do with the ships it had. At the heart of the seagoing fleet were the four battleships of 1st Brigada Lineynykh Korabley (Battleship Brigade) and the four armoured cruisers of 1st Brigada Kreyserov (Cruiser Brigade). The latter had *Novik* attached as a scout. A fifth armoured cruiser, *Ryurik*, which was effectively a second-class battleship, could operate with either the battleships or armoured cruisers and was the fleet flagship. These were supported by 1st Minnaya Diviziya (1st Mine Divisional Group), made up of the 20 largest and most modern destroyers, organised into 2½ Divizions (Divisions). Minnaya is a term that embraces both torpedoes and mines. Indeed, most Russian destroyers could carry contact mines when required, in addition to their conventional torpedo armament.

There were 11 submarines in the Brigada Podvodnykh Lodok (Submarine Brigade), although three of these were of very limited capability, from the training unit. Only one submarine could operate at significant distance from the coast. The Morskaya Partiya Traleniya (Minesweeping Group), with 20 minesweepers, was available to sweep the channels used by the fleet. It was a mixture of old torpedo boats, purpose built minesweepers and adapted commercial vessels.

The second echelon of the fleet focussed on the defence of the entrance to the Gulf of Finland. The 2nd Minnaya Diviziya had four Divizions of destroyers and torpedo boats, with a total strength of 31 boats. Six minelayers of the Otryad Zagraditeley (Minelaying Detachment) were available to lay defensive minefields.

A second cruiser brigade would activate in the event of war, to reinforce the seagoing fleet. It was composed of four ageing cruisers, drawn from reserve and training duties. There were six gunboats available from the same sources. The latter were especially suited for the shallow Finnish coastal waters and the Gulf of Riga. Reservists had to be mobilised to bring the crews for all of these vessels up to strength. Once they were completed, the new battleships would form a second brigade. The remaining vessels of the fleet were obsolete vessels performing support roles away from the front line, or useful only as floating batteries. Appendix I gives the full fleet organisation.

Whilst most of the ships were old, work had gone into updating their armaments based on the lessons learned in the war against Japan. Mines and torpedoes had allowed minor, relatively inexpensive vessels to have a disproportionate impact on the battle space. Since the war, Russia had become a leader in the area of mine warfare. Newly developed mines were destructive, reliable, and stockpiled in significant numbers. Large capacity minelayers could lay extensive defensive fields in home waters quickly. Destroyers received minelaying rails to allow them to carry these mines into enemy waters. Many of the destroyers could also sweep for mines alongside the specialised minesweeper units.

2 Ivo Nikolai Lambi, *The Navy and German Power Politics, 1862-1914* (Boston: Allen & Unwin, 1984), pp.6, 13–14, 31–32, 104–106, 113, 166–167, 347–348; Rudolph Firle, *Der Krieg zur See 1914–1918 – Der Krieg in der Ostsee Band 1* (Berlin: Mittler & Sohn, 1921), p.2; Arthur J. Marder, *From the Dreadnought to Scapa Flow, Volume 1 – The road to war 1904-1914* (London: Oxford University Press, 1961), pp.306–309; Gunnar Åselius, 'Military and Strategy (Sweden)' 1914–1918 International Encyclopedia of the First World War (2017), <https://encyclopedia.1914-1918-online.net/article/military_and_strategy_sweden>, accessed 6 August 2024.

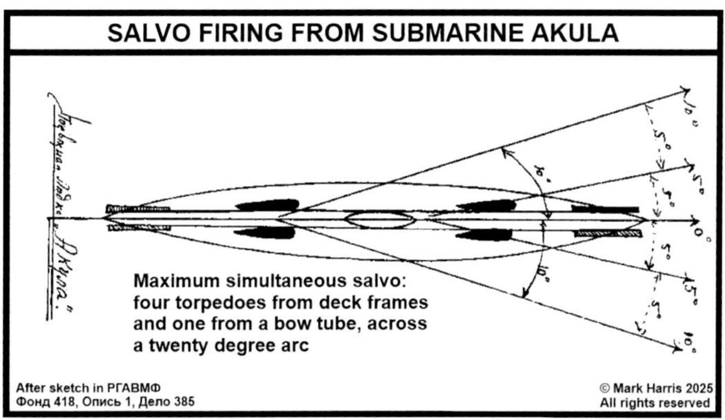

SALVO FIRING FROM SUBMARINE AKULA

Technological improvements in their engines greatly increased torpedo speeds and ranges. Older ships had old pattern torpedoes replaced. The latest torpedoes of the 1912 model on the newest ships attained ranges up to 6,000m, or speeds of up to 43 knots at shorter range. However, the technology was moving so fast that Russian torpedoes were still inferior to the latest British and German designs. The war had demonstrated that torpedo craft needed to fire a spread of multiple torpedoes to maximise the chance of a hit. New destroyers received large numbers of double and triple mountings, but to date only *Novik* was in service. Submarines received external cradles, allowing simultaneous fire on diverging courses. Nevertheless, with only one exception, *Akula*, Russian submarines lacked the range or seaworthiness for long-range operations, and were suitable only for coastal defence. Many of the destroyers in service also had limited range, restricting their ability to operate at a distance from their bases.

Gun armament also received attention. A key lesson from the war was the need for better accuracy and longer range. The hitting power of destroyers and the secondary batteries of bigger ships also needed enhancing. Enemy torpedo craft could then be driven-off, disabled or sunk before firing their torpedoes. Small calibre, largely ineffective guns were removed. Larger calibre guns replaced them on existing destroyers and torpedo boats and all new construction. This meant that Russian destroyers carried a heavier armament compared to their German adversaries.

A significant weakness was that the available battleships and armoured cruisers were constrained by their basic design. The removal of largely worthless small calibre guns was the only practical change possible. Nevertheless, the four battleships available when war broke out carried a main armament of 30.5cm guns to oppose the 28cm and 24cm guns of the German battleships of pre-Dreadnought design. The two *Imperator Pavel I* class also carried a powerful battery of 20.3cm guns. However, the Germans had greatly superior numbers of older battleships. Conversely, German armoured cruisers outgunned their Russian equivalents, especially the three *Bayan* class, which had a weak main armament. An exception was the powerfully armed *Ryurik*. A second area of weakness was the absence of any fast scouting vessels, other than *Novik*, which limited long-range reconnaissance capabilities.

However, if the Germans committed their best squadrons, these had overwhelmingly superior numbers of the most modern battleships and battlecruisers, whose speed and armament completely outclassed the Russian ships. Numerous destroyers supported them. An encounter at sea with this force could only end in disaster. The main characteristics of the vessels in the Russian fleet are summarised in Appendices II and III.

Crew of the cruiser *Oleg*. (EM:SA MMF474_5_1)

Whilst the scope to improve the armament of the large ships was limited, work was possible to improve fire control for long-range gunnery and rate of fire. There were improvements to gun breeches and shell supplies to speed up loading. Rangefinders were modernised. However, a complicating factor for fire accuracy was the mixture of main armament gun calibres on many of the battleships and armoured cruisers. This made spotting difficult at long range due to differing times of flight of the shells. The new battleships would overcome this problem with a large single calibre battery and the latest fully centralised director fire control systems. Better fuzes, bigger shells and larger bursting charges also addressed deficiencies that the war against Japan had revealed.

However, ships are nothing without their crews. The most important changes related to personnel. Officers who had weathered the disastrous war with Japan brought a fresh spirit and new thinking about strategy and tactics. Admiral Nikolay fon Essen, the commander of the Baltiyskiy Flot, was largely the one responsible for embedding this new spirit and thinking in the fleet. When war broke out, he was 53 years of age. He had acquitted himself well in the war against Japan. He gained command of the first line destroyer force of the Baltiyskiy Flot in 1906. Essen was a man of action and proved to be an inspiring leader. Under his command, the most able officers of the fleet were developed. Within two years, he took command of all of the naval forces in the Baltic. He was fearless in challenging policies and practices that got in the way of modernising the fleet. Ships were manned all year round, instead of just the summer months. The numbers of specialist seamen retained on-board was increased. He championed time spent at sea and organised extended cruises to hone seamanship skills. Exercises became more realistic and frequent. Training was reformed and expanded. He ensured that officers of proven merit received early advancement and worked to remove court favourites, although this was a monumental task and he was only partially successful. Perhaps most importantly, he revived the spirit of the fleet. One of his subordinates, Kapitan 1st Ranga Sergey Timirëv wrote, 'To him and him alone, the fleet owed the training of a number of dashing combat commanders who had been trained on destroyers. … everyone believed in Admiral Essen; I do not remember a single admiral – perhaps with the exception of Makarov – who enjoyed such popularity among the officers and crews as Essen.'[3]

Russian bases and defences

The fleet found itself in an awkward position when it came to bases from which to operate. The principal base, with its naval shipyards, was the capital at Sankt Peterburg, renamed Petrograd on 31 August 1914 to expunge the German origins of its name. This lay behind the fortifications on the island of Kronshtadt. It was unsuitable as an operational base as it lay at the eastern end of the Gulf of Finland, over 900 miles by sea from the nearest German coastline.

The strategy of having a superior offensive fleet in the Baltic led to a decision in 1888 to focus efforts on developing and fortifying a major naval base at Libava. This was the only Russian port free of ice throughout the winter, when the northern part of the sea freezes over. It was a controversial decision. Whilst well placed for a fleet acting against the German coast, it was only 35 miles from the border. A dissenter on the decision-making commission, General-Leytenant Georgiy Bobrikov, wrote that, 'The Libava fortress from a naval perspective will become a trap for the fleet … from a land perspective we are meeting the wishes of the enemy, creating an object of critical importance on the very border. … the catastrophic destruction of our fleet in Libava will be so attractive to our enemies that they will not only direct all the efforts of their invading army here, but this will perhaps serve as their greatest incentive for a breakthrough.' It proved to be an accurate insight, as neutralising the naval base at Libava became a central aim of German Baltic naval strategy.

A new plan put forward by the Naval Staff in 1903 acknowledged the growing gap between strategy and the reality of a larger German fleet. It proposed a switch to a defensive strategy centred on the Gulf of Finland and the Gulf of Riga, making Libava redundant as a wartime base. However, nothing happened to develop new bases and modern fortifications beyond modernising the existing Kronshtadt defences. The fact that fortifications fell under the budget and jurisdiction of the Army was a major complicating factor. With the fleet in the Baltic all but eliminated after the war with Japan, the revised 1907 plan resulted in the abandonment of the Libava fortifications and removal of all gun batteries. The defences and port installations were to be prepared for demolition in the event of war, to ensure their denial to the enemy. Libava continued in use only as a peacetime base for the fleet to allow year round exercising, free of the Baltic ice.

The situation languished until 1911 when a decision was finally made to build a fortified line in the Gulf of Finland at its narrowest point, running from the Surop Peninsula, west of the port of Revel', through the island of Nargen to the Porkala-Udd Peninsula, just west of the port of Helsingfors. The navigable passage was only 25 miles wide at this point. In the event of war, defensive minefields would block it, covered by batteries in the fortifications. The aim was to prevent the enemy from

3 Pavlovich, *Operations*, pp.34–35, 45–50; Контръ-Адмиралъ С.Н. Тимиревъ, *Воспоминанія Морского Офицера Балтійскій Флотъ Во Время Войны И Революціи (1914 – 1918 Г.Г.)* (Нью Іоркъ: American Society for Russian Naval History, 1961), p.3

breaking in to reach the area around the capital. The fleet would be free to manoeuver and engage any enemy forces from behind the minefield and battery line, should they attempt to sweep it. The fleet would have a new operational base at Revel', with a subsidiary base at Helsingfors. This defensive system became known as the Central Position. Another year went by without agreement on funding. Essen then demanded that the navy receive control of all coastal fortifications and their funding. The Tsar agreed and work began on the newly designated naval fortress Imperatora Petra Velikago (Emperor Peter the Great), with work scheduled to complete in 1917.

Essen overhauled the plan for around thirty coastal gun batteries. These covered the Central Position and the Finnish skerries off the northern shore of the Gulf of Finland as far west as Hangö. The skerries were a multitude of small islands, with narrow, shallow, winding channels running between them. They were notoriously difficult to navigate. Anchorages south of Ekenäs and immediately west of the Porkala-Udd peninsula offered positions in which shallow draught gunboats could operate. From them, torpedo craft could launch raids on any enemy forces in front of the Central Position. Since his appointment, Essen had insisted that his destroyer captains learn to navigate these waters. They had previously been dependant on Finnish pilots to do so. The skerries would be inaccessible to the German heavy ships and dangerous to any vessels unfamiliar with them.

When war broke out only two batteries in the Central Position were complete, leaving most of the position uncovered. There were four batteries on islands covering the approaches to the skerry anchorages. Work on improving the commercial ports at Revel' and Helsingfors had started, but none of the new facilities were complete. At Revel' space was very limited and docking facilities non-existent. This left the fleet dependant on Kronshtadt for supply and repair, with Helsingfors and its antiquated fortress defences of Sveaborg as the main forward base.

An important development immediately prior to the war was the expansion of the Sluzhba Svyazi (Communications Service). In 1911, Kapitan 1st Ranga Adrian Nepenin took command. He would prove to be an outstanding intelligence officer. A chain of wireless equipped observation and communication posts, with well-trained operators, had been set up on the coast and offshore islands. A wireless interception service was in place, with a wide range of language skills to support it. In 1912 Starshiy Leytenant Ivan Rengarten, a wireless specialist working at the fleet's Mine Warfare Training School, invented a wireless direction finding device. This took time to perfect, but the first trial installation was about to be commissioned on Ezel' Island when war broke out. It promised to be an effective way to pinpoint enemy vessels when they used their wireless. A version was also in development for deployment on warships. In 1913, Nepenin had also established a naval air service for reconnaissance, although the very short range of the few dozen seaplanes available limited their use. There was a forward base near Kil'kond on Ezel' island.[4]

4 Петров, *Подготовка*, pp.34–43; Л. И. Амирханов, *Морская крепость Императора Петра Великого* (Санкт-Петербург: Иванов и Лещинский, 1995), pp.14–16, 70; Л.В. Баширова, 'Строительство Морской Крепости Императора Петра Великого (1913–1914)' in *Война и оружие, Новые исследования и материалы Труды Третьей международной научно, практической конференции, 16–18 мая 2012 года, Часть I* (Санкт Петербург: ВИМАИВиВС, 2012), p.87; Владимир Г. Кикнадзеб, *Невидимый фронт войны на море. Морская радиоэлектронная разведка в первой половине XX века* (Москва: Русский фонд содействия образованию и науке, 2011), Глава 1.3.

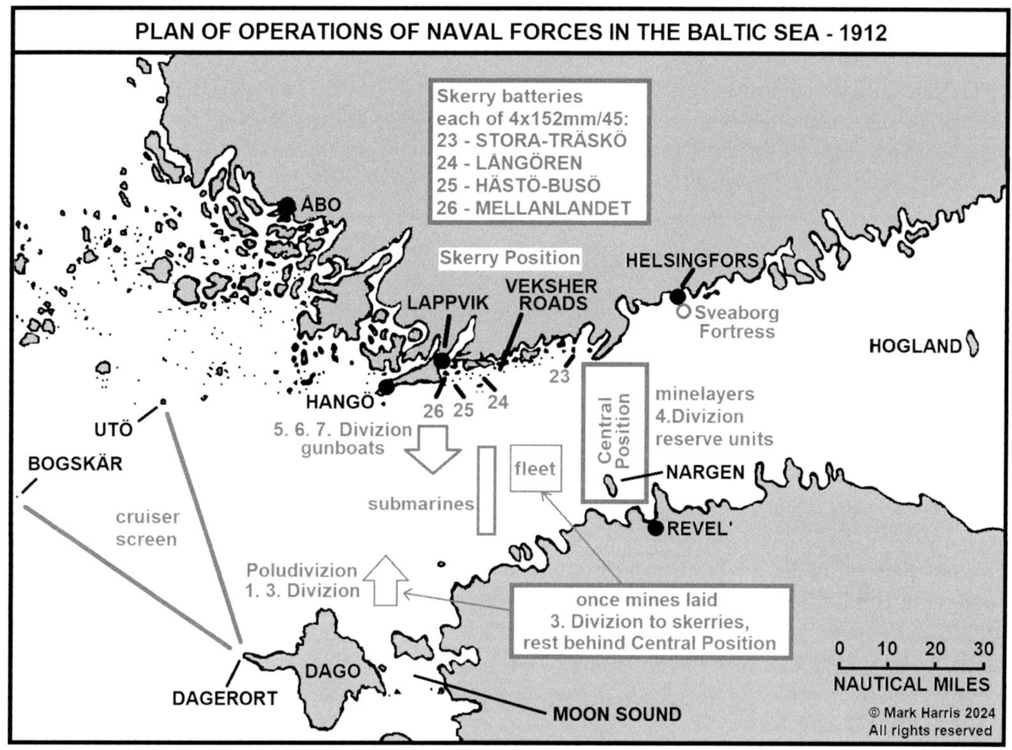

The Russian war plan

Whilst Germany's fleet heavily outnumbered the Baltiyskiy Flot, it also had to contend with France and Britain. However, the French were largely concentrated in the Mediterranean against the threat from Austria-Hungary and Italy. Whilst countering the German fleet had become a key focus of both Russia and Britain, there had been no contact on naval co-operation. In April 1914, the agreements recently concluded between Britain and France prompted the Tsar to request discussions about a similar agreement between Britain and Russia. Although it was not a universally held view, Sir Edward Grey, the British Foreign Secretary, saw, 'little if any strategic necessity or value. … To my mind, in a war against Germany, the Russian Fleet would not get out of the Baltic and the British Fleet would not get into it.' The British were wary of escalating tensions with Germany. However, he agreed with the French that it was necessary to, 'reassure Russia and keep her loyal.' A couple of initial discussions took place between the head of the British Navy, the First Sea Lord, Admiral Prince Louis of Battenberg, and the Russian Naval Attaché in London, Kapitan 1st Ranga Nikolay Volkov. The areas for consideration were essentially the same as those in the agreement with France. This included co-ordination of actions, agreeing a common signal convention, mutual use of naval ports and the sharing of technical data. The British Battle Cruiser Squadron also visited Revel' and Kronshtadt in June. This visit did help to establish good relations between the personnel of the two navies. The international crisis interrupted work before the discussion moved to any areas of substance, but the goodwill generated was to have important consequences for future events.

The latest Russian plan of operations for the Baltic dated from 1912 and essentially shared Grey's view that the Russian Fleet was on its own. Essen's staff produced it under the instructions of Vitse-Admiral Aleksandr Liven, the Chief of the Naval General Staff. It set out the strategic challenge:

> In relation to our allies, we are completely isolated in the closed Baltic theatre, and therefore … we alone will have to deal with the German fleet, with possible joint actions involving that of Sweden.
>
> Any hope of assistance from the British fleet must be completely set aside, since external communications with the Baltic Sea basin will be in the hands of our enemy.
>
> With regard to possible assistance by the British fleet, I conclude that it can only manifest itself in the diversion of the German fleet from the Baltic theatre to the North Sea theatre. However, given the sparsity of information and the difficulty of making predictions … I must conclude that we will have the entire German fleet, perhaps combined with the Swedish, facing our naval forces in the Baltic.

The key task of the fleet would be to mount the most effective defence possible of the Russian coast with the limited resources to hand. Once war broke out, Essen would be sub-ordinated to the commander of Sixth Army, which would be responsible for defending the coastline. The danger was at its greatest until the relatively poor communications network in Russia allowed Russian troops to mobilise and reach the front. The two main concerns were that the Germans could stage a landing to seize the capital at Sankt Peterburg or land in the Gulf of Riga to outflank the Russian armies, which were planning to make an early attack on the easternmost German province of Ostpreussen. Essen had to concentrate all of his limited resources on defending against the most important threat, an attack on the capital. The key to his defence was that, 'On the assumption of having to deal with the entire German fleet, I must somehow compensate for the weakness of our forces; such a mitigation is to give battle in a previously prepared position, using all the forces of underwater positional defence [mines and torpedoes] at the decisive moment.' This would, '… prevent the enemy from penetrating into the eastern part of the Gulf of Finland, beyond the meridian of Nargen Island, at least temporarily, by ensuring the mobilization of the ground forces of the Sankt Peterburg Military District, whose immediate task is to protect the capital.' However, a defensive posture was not one Essen relished:

> If, after clarifying the actual situation, it turns out that the second line forces [older warships] of the enemy are advancing on us, or if the enemy's attempt to seize the position is unsuccessful, then it will be possible to advance with our operationally capable forces and seek a battle with the enemy under favourable conditions for us. If we are dealing with all the forces of the German fleet, then we should give battle at the position, defending it to the last ship.

The paramount task in the plan was for the minelayers of the Otryad Zagraditeley to lay a minefield in the Central Position, before hostilities commenced. Eight destroyers of 4th Divizion would screen the minelayers. Laying would begin 12 hours after the announcement of mobilisation and should take six to eight hours to complete. The four cruisers of 1st Brigada Kreyserov would set up a patrol screen between Dagerort, at the western tip of Dago, and Utö or Bogskär. These three points would all have naval observation posts. Essen, with the flagship *Ryurik* and the four battleships of 1st Brigada Lineynykh Korabley, would concentrate in support of the cruisers to the west of the Central Position. *Novik* and eight destroyers of 2nd Divizion would screen the battleships. This force would prevent any enemy interference with the minelayers and delay as long as possible if attacked by superior forces.

Essen was concerned that the few available cruisers were inadequate for an effective screen, but Nepenin's intelligence service gave him confidence: 'all hope for detecting the enemy is placed by me on the surveillance service, which … under normal atmospheric conditions, already has the ability to detect the appearance of the enemy at the mouth of the Gulf.' Given how vital it was to know the location of the enemy fleet, it would have been prudent to integrate long-range covert surveillance capabilities, such as agents and wireless equipped steamers sailing under merchant flags, to increase this margin of safety. It was a criticism expressed after the war by the Russian naval staff analysis.

The rest of the destroyers would deploy to flank positions. The remainder of the 1st Minnaya Diviziya – 1st Divizion, and the Poludivizion Osobogo Naznacheniya (Special Purpose Half-Division), plus 3rd Divizion, would concentrate in Moon Sound, 20 destroyers in all. They would remove all navigation marks in this area to confuse the enemy and prepare to lay minefields blocking the entrance to the Gulf of Riga. The bulk of 2nd Minnaya Diviziya, with 5th Divizion, 6th Divizion and 7th Divizion, a total of 10 destroyers and 13 torpedo boats, would occupy the Finnish skerry position, based at Lappvik. All six of the fleet's gunboats would join them to assist in the defence. This force would prepare the skerry defences for action. All of the destroyer divisions in the flank positions were to be prepared to launch night torpedo attacks on any German forces that advanced on the Central Position.

The newest eight submarines of the Brigada Podvodnykh Lodok provided the final line of defence in front of the Central Position, based at Veksher Roads in the skerries. During the day, they would occupy fixed positions and submerge to attack German vessels that approached. The three submarines of the Uchebnyy Otryad Podvodnago Plavaniya (Submarine Training Detachment), would form a last reserve and would sortie from Revel' to attack anything entering the channel between Nargen and the mainland.

Once the minefield in the Central Position was laid, the battle fleet and the forces in Moon Sound would retire behind it, with the exception of 3rd Divizion, which would rejoin 2nd Minnaya Diviziya in the northern skerries. The cruiser and submarine screens would remain in position if possible. If things became critical the skerry forces could be pulled back to defend the Central Position through their narrow channels.

One significant weakness was that there had been no attempt to ensure that the plans of the navy and army aligned other than at a strategic level. The Tsar had agreed both, but that was as far as it went. The naval plans merely noted that the Sixth Army would concentrate its troops to defend Sankt Peterburg, east of the Central Position. This would result in a scramble to protect exposed naval bases left unprotected by troops when war broke out, such as the island of Ezel', with its seaplane base at Kil'kond, as well as Hangö and Lappvik in the Finnish skerries. Even the need to retain troops in the Revel' fortress was not explicitly provided for, an issue which only came to the fore for resolution at a planning session on 25 July.

The plan provided for an admirable concentration of force at the narrowest position in which to give battle. However, its weakness was that it only planned in detail for an expected full-scale

German attack. If events transpired differently, there were no other plans to fall back on. Essen was an Admiral who had little time for staff work, but he also had no mandate for offensive action that would have enabled any formal fall back plans to be agreed. He would simply seize any opportunity that presented itself. However, mining off the enemy coast, particularly as the nights lengthened later in the year, was an option that he had in mind, which played to the strengths of the fleet.[5]

German bases and defences

The Marinestation der Ostsee (Baltic Naval Station) at Kiel had historically been the principal German naval base. This was under the command of Vizeadmiral Gustav Bachmann and was at the far western end of the Baltic. He would be responsible for taking the initial actions required during mobilisation. As well as being a major commercial port and shipbuilding centre, it was capable of holding the entire German fleet, protected by extensive coastal fortifications and secure from submarine attack. The shift in German naval focus to the North Sea meant that the base was now principally used for trials and training. However, Kiel was 450 miles from the nearest Russian coastline and was therefore unsuitable as an offensive operational base.

At the other end of the Baltic, the fortified naval port of Pillau was only 100 miles from the Russian border. It controlled access to the commercial port of Königsberg. However, only shallow draught vessels could enter and the facilities were limited, so it was also unsuitable as an operational base. Neufahrwasser, the harbour for the port of Danzig, 50 miles to the west, was fortified against attack from the sea, but was quite open to torpedo and submarine attack. Its port and naval shipyards provided better facilities for sustaining operations, but the water depth was only 7m, preventing entry for the largest warships. Eight obsolete coastal battleships and four cruisers were laid up in reserve here for activation in the event of war, making it a potentially tempting early target for the Russians.

Swinemünde, over 150 miles to the west of Danzig, was fortified against attack from the sea and secure against torpedo and submarine attack. It controlled access to the leading Baltic port of Stettin and its naval shipyards. The water depth was similar to Neufahrwasser. However, it was 300 miles from the Russian coast; too far away to be a good operational base. There were no other ports with defensive fortifications, although a number of harbours between Swinemünde and Kiel were suitable for use by shallow draught vessels defending the outer approaches to Kiel Bay.[6]

5 Петров, *Подготовка*, pp.214–230; Marder, *Dreadnought*, pp.309–311; Виктор Новицкий, 'Критический разбор плана операций на Балтийском море', in *Военно-морская комиссия по исследованию и использованию опыта войны 1914-1918 гг. на море, Сборник № 2* (Петроград: Государственное издательство, 1922), pp.47, 63–66, 79; Д.В. Горлова, 'Установление англо-русских военно-морских связей накануне Первой мировой войны', in *Первая мировая война, Версальская система и современность* (Санкт Петербург: СПбГУ, 2014), pp.198–210; А. В. Томашевич, *Подводные лодки в операциях русского флота на Балтийском море в 1914-1915 г.г.* (Москва Ленинград: Военно-Морское Издательство, 1939), pp.15–16; Pavlovich, *Operations*, pp.51–55.

6 Firle, *Ostsee*, pp.24–28.

Battleships of 1st (bottom right) and 2nd (centre left) Geschwader, light cruisers in background, Kiel, 1912. (USNA:165-GP-3001_28-0696M)

German naval forces

The main German fleet, the Hochseeflotte (High Seas Fleet), was a formidable force with overwhelming superiority if deployed against Russia. Once mobilised, it would have six Geschwader (Squadrons) with 22 older and 21 modern battleships, with four more about to come into service. There were five Aufklärungsgruppe (Scouting Groups) with three modern battle cruisers, five armoured cruisers, four old protected cruisers and 11 light cruisers. Eight Torpedobootsflottille with 88 destroyers formed an integral part of the fleet, as did two U-Bootsflottille with 19 submarines, two light cruisers and four destroyers as leaders. Three Minensuchdivision (Minesweeping Divisions) with 40 old converted torpedo boats and three destroyers as leaders provided support. The quality of German ships, guns, torpedoes and mines reflected Germany's industrial strength. The personnel of the fleet were well educated and trained. This fleet was based in the North Sea, but units could transfer to the Baltic as required.

In contrast, there was no fleet organisation in the Baltic, and no sea-going formations of warships. There were a few vessels permanently based at Kiel in various training and evaluation units, as well as a tiny force to defend it. Only vessels not needed in the North Sea would remain there. Some were present purely by chance, such as the gunboat *Panther*, which had just completed a refit at Kiel between overseas postings, or the modern destroyers *V.25* and *V.26*, which were undergoing working up trials after completion.

No heavy sea-going warships were available. There were seven light cruisers and an ageing protected cruiser. Two of the light cruisers, *Magdeburg* and *Augsburg*, were recently constructed, modern vessels. Both could lay mines and were significantly faster than any Russian cruiser. Their peacetime roles at Kiel were as torpedo trial and gunnery training ships respectively. The rest were significantly older, unremarkable vessels held in reserve. German light cruisers were notable for a numerous, but relatively small calibre gun armament. They were no match for the Russian cruisers in a fight.

There were only 12 destroyers to hand. Three of these were fast, modern boats, carrying the latest types of torpedo, whilst the rest were of the oldest types in the fleet. German destroyers emphasised a heavy torpedo armament and carried only a light gun armament. Four submarines of types with limited capabilities, a couple of obsolete larger cruisers, *Panther*, five torpedo boats and various tenders and school vessels completed the list of vessels available. Five steam ferries would be requisitioned for use as auxiliary minelayers to supplement minelaying capabilities. Trawlers and tugs would be requisitioned for use as minesweepers. There were 12 seaplanes available for reconnaissance: ten around Kiel and two at Putzig, near Danzig.

Almost all of these vessels were not fully manned first line units. Many were in reserve. Once mobilisation began, reservists and Seewehr (naval militia) needed to join the vessels to provide or complete their crews. There were also many vessels destined for the Hochseeflotte in the North Sea in Baltic ports. All of these ships and crews would take time to prepare for combat. The Baltic would be almost devoid of any effective naval force until they were ready for battle. If the main fleet remained in the North Sea, this created a window of opportunity for the fully manned first line Russian units.[7]

The German war plans

The political situation had constantly affected war planning amidst shifting assumptions and differing views about the likelihood and timing of British participation in any conflict with Russia and France. The fact that Britain had no formal alliance with either country created strategic ambiguity. Admiral Hugo von Pohl became Chef des Admiralstabes (Chief of the Naval Staff) in early 1913. He set out his basic approach to naval planning in a memorandum later that year:

> I consider the existence of an unweakened German fleet capable of a rapid response to be both the safest and entirely necessary means of preventing a subsequent intervention by Britain in a continental war [with France and Russia]... A fleet that is ready to strike is much more important to us in this regard than the destruction of the Russian fleet, which may have to be purchased at a high price... in the event of war we will have to be content with the lesser result of neutralising the Russian fleet.

The plan for war with only France and Russia

Over the course of 1914, there were hopes that Britain would remain neutral in a European war. This led to an update of the plans for war under these conditions. The Kaiser approved it only days before war broke out, on 30 July 1914. Despite the views that he had expressed less than a year earlier, von Pohl laid out a rationale for decisive action:

7 Otto Groos, *Der Krieg zur See 1914–1918 – Der Krieg in der Nordsee Band 1* (Berlin: Mittler & Sohn, 1920), pp.3–17, Tabelle 1; Firle, *Ostsee*, p.16, Tabelle 3; Bundesarchiv (BA):RM28 Oberbefehlshaber der Ostseestreitkräfte (OdO) der Kaiserlichen Marine, Kriegstagebuch (KTB).

> If Britain remains neutral, then, despite the very important tasks in the North Sea, I am in favour of comprehensively dealing with Russia first and using as many forces, especially light ones, as are necessary for this purpose. The tasks in the North Sea will then have to be executed with the balance and those ships etc. that are later released from the Baltic Sea.
>
> The following argues against the preference for the Western theatre of war:
>
> 1. that everything must be avoided which might disturb Britain and cause her to take sides against us,
> 2. that demonstrable success can only be achieved in the Baltic Sea,
> 3. that overly weak forces in the Baltic Sea can lead to failure.

Unless continued British neutrality could be guaranteed, the modern heavy ships were not to be risked against destroyers, mines, submarines and in attacks on coastal fortifications,. The plan adhered to the principle of holding the bulk of the fleet in the North Sea theatre, but set out a range of scalable operations against the weak French forces in the Channel and Atlantic ports, up to and including a naval blockade, depending on the level of certainty attaching to British neutrality.

With regard to the Baltic theatre, the aim was to support the army by diverting the maximum number of Russian troops into defending the coast, whilst, 'the Russian Baltic Sea Fleet must be made so harmless as to make its offensive capacity impossible'. This would require sufficient force to be detached from the Hochseeflotte to accept battle with the Baltiyskiy Flot. Blockships and mines would seal off Russian harbours as soon as possible. Destroyers and submarines were to be despatched to attack forces in the Gulf of Finland. Next Libava would be destroyed, followed by surprise attacks on Helsingfors and Revel'. Eventually, an operation to destroy the Helsingfors and Kronshtadt fortifications was possible, although this was likely to result in significant losses. There was an assumption that British neutrality would guarantee that Russian naval forces would stand on the defensive.

The core of the force would be the 2nd Geschwader, under the command of Vizeadmiral Reinhard Scheer. This comprised eight of the most powerful, but nevertheless older and less valuable, pre-Dreadnought battleships. They would be supported by three even older battleships, an armoured cruiser, six light cruisers, two Torpedobootsflottille (22 destroyers), a Minensuchdivision and two minelayers. Despite receiving the approval of the Kaiser, the plan was politically naïve and full of contradictions. Direct attacks on Russian bases by 2nd Geschwader would inevitably put the battleships at risk of torpedo attack, which was supposedly to be avoided. When the new Russian battleships joined their fleet in the near future, these would massively outclass the older German battleships. Any attack on the French coast or fleet would probably have triggered Britain's obligations to France under the recent naval agreement.

The plan for war with France, Russia and Britain

The plans for war including Britain had changed little since 1912. There would be no forces allocated from the Hochseeflotte to support the weak Baltic naval forces, with the entire fleet deployed to counter an expected British blockade in the North Sea.

There was a lack of firm intelligence about Russian intentions to inform this plan. However, the basing of the destroyers of 1st Minnaya Diviziya at Libava suggested that the Russians still planned to make advances against the German coast. Essen had also been reported to have said that, 'I hope that in the future the squadron of mining ships, together with the other ships in the fleet, will move from defensive to offensive activity', during a recent inspection of the minelayers. The Admiralstab expected that the advances would involve offensive minelaying off the German coast. They expected the first attacks against Neufahrwasser, followed by a blockade of Danzig Bay. The Admiralstab considered the fortified ports capable of resisting naval attack, but the navy would be unable to support the army in defending the rest of the coast.

The main aim was to disrupt these Russian operations. Bold raids would take place as soon as war broke out. These would target vulnerable parts of the Russian coast, with Libava as the priority. Mines laid during the raids would restrict freedom of manoeuvre for Russian forces. Warships would interdict commercial traffic as opportunities arose, but strictly according to international law and the prize warfare rules of stop and search. The only real opportunities to do so were at the entrance to the Baltic. Since only eight percent of Russian Baltic trade was in Russian flagged vessels, the scope and impact would be limited.

There had been speculation in some circles about the possibility of the British fleet entering the Baltic to support a British or Russian troop landing. However, for as long as Denmark and Sweden stayed out of the conflict there were no bases from which a British fleet could operate. The Admiralstab estimated that the Russians had the capacity to transport 20,000 troops and their equipment. The army considered this improbable, but asked the navy to keep Russian harbours and coastal forces under observation for any indications of such a move.

Essentially, this plan was an aggressive bluff. The overall size of the German fleet was an unseen menace masking the threadbare nature of the actual Baltic forces. Depending on how the situation in the North Sea theatre developed, forces drawn from there might be able to support periodic operations in the Baltic. This should maintain the illusion, keeping the Russians on the defensive. Meanwhile, operations would aim to block the exits from the Gulf of Finland with mines.[8]

The strategic position in 1914

Neither side had an accurate picture of the plans of their opponents. Both assumed a more aggressive stance from their enemy.

Russia had planned a defence against an attack that would only materialise in the event that Britain remained neutral. There was potentially an opportunity to seize the initiative, threaten the German coast in support of the planned attack by the army on Ostpreussen, and strike a potentially demoralising early blow at the German naval forces. However, it would be challenging for Essen, who was subordinate to an army commander with a strictly defensive role covering the capital, to leverage this opportunity.

German concerns about immediate attacks on their coastline from Libava were also unfounded. On the contrary, Russia had left the coast outside the Gulf of Finland undefended. However, the German army's focus on France left very limited scope to exploit this, as there were no troops to co-operate with the navy, even if it diverted the necessary ships to the Baltic to exploit the opportunity presented.

8 Firle, *Ostsee*, pp.5–7; Lambi, *Politics*, pp.395–399, 420–421

2

Fighting shadows: July to August 1914

Russian mobilisation

The assassination of Archduke Franz Ferdinand of Austria-Hungary by a Serbian nationalist caused a crisis that became an unforeseen trigger for war. Serbia was a lightning rod for the clash of interests in the Balkans between Russia, Germany and her Austro-Hungarian ally. Germany offered unqualified support for Austro-Hungarian demands that undermined Serbian sovereignty, knowing this would lead to confrontation with Russia. On 23 July, Serbia received an ultimatum from Austria-Hungary, with 48 hours to respond. The Tsar and his council of ministers met the next day. The fateful decision was taken, but not announced, that the four military districts nearest the Austro-Hungarian border in the south, as well as the fleet in the Black Sea, would be mobilised, 'depending on the course of affairs.' The Tsar himself added the Baltiyskiy Flot to this list. The capital might need protection against a surprise German attack from the sea. On the 25th, the government issued a communiqué that it was, '... closely monitoring the development of the Serbian-Austrian conflict, to which Russia cannot remain indifferent.' After Austria-Hungary rejected the Serbian response to the ultimatum, the Tsar's council convened later that day and agreed that steps preparatory to full mobilisation should proceed. Admiral Ivan Grigorovich, the Head of the Naval Ministry, also met with the Tsar and agreed that active fleet units, including minelayers, shore defences and troops in the naval fortresses could be brought up to full war readiness. However, no defensive minefields were to be laid without further approval and training units would not be disbanded to reinforce the fleet. The orders went out in the early hours of 26 July, initiating a whole range of detailed logistical preparations, as well as the requisition of wireless equipped steamers to act as fleet auxiliaries.

On the previous afternoon, Essen had just arrived at Revel' from the capital. In the current political situation, he was under no illusions about the threat from the powerful German fleet. The fleet had just assembled for annual manoeuvres. Essen had scheduled a meeting of the Baltiyskiy Flot's commanders aboard *Ryurik* to review the plans. The meeting focussed instead on the war plan. Leytenant Evgeniy Vinter of Essen's headquarters staff was present: 'The Admiral was convinced of the inevitability of a war and tried to instil this conviction in the participants of the meeting, he called for full readiness for war, which could break out at any moment, and declared that, "there will be no retreat" [from the defence of the Central Position].' Essen cancelled the manoeuvres. After his own experience of Japan's surprise attack in the last war, he intended to take no chances. At midnight, *Gromoboy*, the flagship of Kontr-Admiral Nikolay Kolomeytsev, led the other three armoured cruisers and *Novik* of the Brigada Kreyserov out of Revel'. Each morning they would take up a patrol line between Odenskhol'm and Ajax Bank, from an anchorage nearby. They would inspect commercial traffic and detain any suspicious steamers, to prevent covert minelaying. On receipt of Grigorovich's instructions next morning, Essen sent out a flurry of orders. Ships were to prepare for action and be ready to repel a night attack by torpedo craft, with crews at their action stations. Initial evacuations of supplies began from Libava. Demolition teams were despatched and the seaplanes based there moved to Kil'kond. *Andrey Pervozvannyy* was in dock at Kronshtadt after hitting an underwater rock a few days previously, but the three available battleships moved from Revel' to Helsingfors to fill up with coal and ammunition. The submarines of the Brigada Podvodnykh Lodok moved to their war anchorage at Veksher Roads in the Finnish skerries and loaded their full complement of torpedoes. Tensions were high. That afternoon on the patrol line, *Admiral Makarov* spotted two suspicious vessels in the distance. Kolomeytsev despatched *Novik* to investigate, but she found nothing of concern. On the 27th the minelayers *Amur*, *Enisey*, *Ladoga*, and *Narova* concentrated off Porkala-Udd, screened by the destroyers of 4th Divizion, with mines loaded and ready to lay in the Central Position. The various attempts at mediation of the crisis were failing, but the Tsar assured Serbia that, 'Whilst there is little hope of avoiding bloodshed, all our efforts must be directed towards this goal. … [However,] In no circumstances will Russia become indifferent to the fate of Serbia.'

Admiral Nikolay Ottovich fon Essen.
(Public domain)

This assurance was immediately tested. On the 28th Austria-Hungary declared war on Serbia. Orders went out to lay the minefield protecting the approaches to Kronshtadt and fully crew the reserve and training cruisers and gunboats. Essen was increasingly unhappy with waiting passively for a seemingly inevitable and potentially overwhelming attack. Repeated requests to disband the training detachments, withdraw the submarine training unit from its exposed base at Libava and grant discretion to lay mines at the Central Position if it was threatened, had all been turned down. There was a dearth of up to date intelligence about the situation of the German fleet. Essen now lobbied Vitse-Admiral Aleksandr Rusin, the recently appointed Chief of the Naval General Staff: 'I had the idea of … blocking the entrance to Kiel Bay with mines at the right moment … provided that war is inevitable … For this purpose … purchase the most ordinary vessel for which false foreign papers should be prepared. The steamship is loaded up to its ears with timber, and inside there are compartments for the mines … [which] it lays at night'.

The aim was to slow the German fleet, forcing them to sweep ahead as they advanced. Rusin was on the hunt for commercial steamers to carry out covert long-range reconnaissance of German warship movements and identify signs of any collusion in the use of Swedish waters. Both of these ideas needed advance planning. They had no prospect of coming to fruition in a crisis.

On the 29th, Grigorovich reminded Essen that, 'The Emperor of Russia commands that since we are not at war with Germany, it is necessary to be careful not to give rise to misunderstandings and complications.' Essen wrote, 'I beg for help, the times are serious, we cannot simply follow legal provisions.' However, the diplomatic exchanges between the Tsar and the Kaiser reached an impasse that day. Orders went out to extinguish lighthouses, making a surprise night attack more difficult, and cancelling all leave. Essen finally received approval to disband the training detachments and evacuate Libava. The naval transport *Anadyr'* towed the three training submarines out, heading for Revel'. At 4pm, the Tsar approved the mobilisation from midnight of the fleets and the four districts facing Austria-Hungary, aiming to force a climb-down from the attack on Serbia. At midnight, Rusin issued the general order containing the coded signal to adopt full war readiness: 'Naval forces and ports. Smoke. Smoke. Smoke. Remain in place.' Essen had already set things in motion that evening, having been pre-warned. All vessels and fortresses opened their sealed orders for their deployment under the war plan, together with the war cyphers and codes. Everyone worked at pace to come up to full combat readiness. Essen formally assumed the role of fleet commander and raised his flag on *Ryurik*.

Next morning, the 30th, Essen received an alarming message from the Naval Staff: 'According to the information we have, Germany has declared a general mobilization today at 3 o'clock. The Admiral has received a warning that Sweden should also be considered a probable enemy to us, since according to information, an agreement was concluded between Germany and Sweden on July 25/29.' The Russian Naval Attaché in Sweden had just notified Rusin, 'The Swedish fleet left Stockholm, according to rumours, for Gotland Island.' On the 27th, Russian intelligence had de-cyphered an intercepted telegram from the Austro-Hungarian Foreign Minister, Berchtold, to their ambassador in Sankt Peterburg: '[On the 25th] The [Swedish] King indicated to the German representative that in the event of a conflict, Sweden's position on the side of the Triple Alliance was beyond doubt.' Essen was potentially facing a combined assault from both Germany and Sweden.

For Essen, it was now critical to lay the mines in the Central Position. There would be no way for the fleet to resist attack without them. He headed off to inspect the minelayers and urgently requested permission from Grigorovich. On the way back, another wireless message suggested that the German Fleet assembled in Kiel on the 29th had potentially left for Danzig. On his return, at 6pm, with no reply to his request forthcoming, he telegraphed: 'Please inform me of the political situation. If I do not receive an answer tonight, I will set up the [mine] barrier in the morning.' *Ryurik* led the three battleships out of Helsingfors, escorted by 12 destroyers. Essen anchored east of Nargen to await a reply.

The intelligence about the German fleet came from the Naval Attaché to Denmark in København: 'In Kiel on the evening of the 29th, there were 6 dreadnought [battleship]s, 6 [older] battleships, 1 battle cruiser, 10 light cruisers, 14 destroyers, all ships were loading coal and provisions.' If this fleet had left for the Gulf of Finland, a simple calculation indicated that it would arrive at mid-day. Rusin asked for an urgent audience with the Tsar. At 3:30am, he gave his permission for the minelaying. When the message arrived at 4:15am, Essen took off his cap and with the words, 'Thank God', crossed himself. Relieved of the need to act without orders,

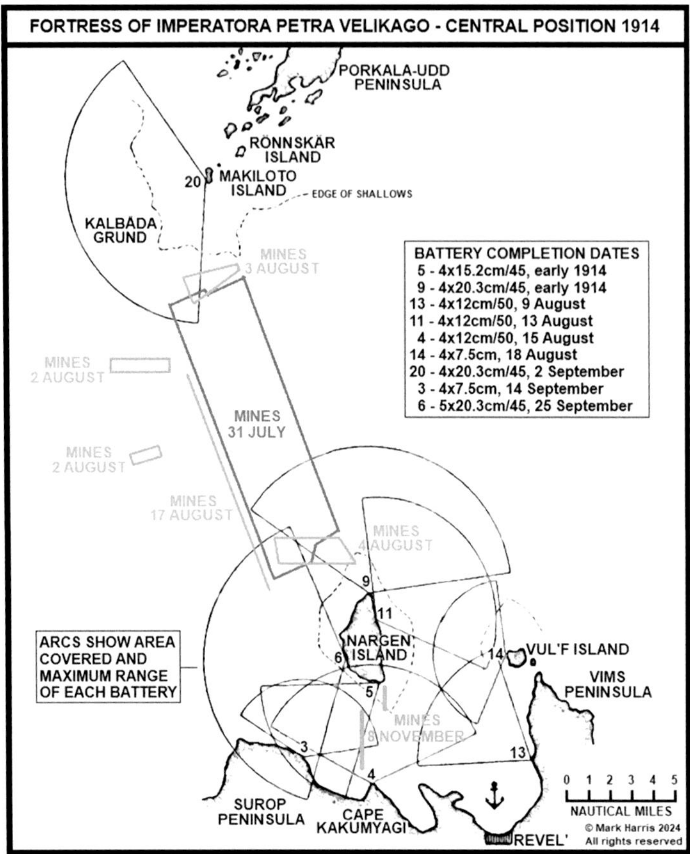

he immediately ordered laying of the minefield, instructed Kolomeytsev to detain all steamships approaching the Gulf and ordered the submarines to take up their defensive positions under the war plan. At 5:25am, Rusin issued the general order for imminent conflict: 'Fire. Fire. Fire. Naval forces and ports to begin operational actions to prepare the theatre [for war].' *Ryurik* raised the signal, 'Prepare for action.' Essen led the battleships and their destroyer escorts past Nargen to the covering position north of Cape Pakerort. The other units moved to their positions in the war plan. Coastal batteries were manned and ready. Essen expected an attack at any time, potentially preceded by covert minelaying. The cruisers on the outer screen advanced to the line off Dagerort. Their commander, Kolomeytsev, wirelessed, 'Who exactly is our enemy?' Essen replied that, 'there were no details about this, but the situation was very serious and the probable adversary was Germany and Sweden.' The four minelayers began laying just three hours later. Eight parallel lines of mines blocked the Gulf, leaving only the channel south of Nargen open. Commercial traffic would be controlled and routed through here. If enemies appeared, the minelayer *Volga* was in place to block this channel behind the retiring Russian forces. However, there was no interference. All 2,124 mines were in place before midday. The operation went smoothly. Only 11 mines exploded prematurely after laying. The battleships retired to port in Helsingfors that evening. *Anadyr'* arrived at Revel' with the submarines from Libava.

Ryurik underway off Revel'. Armed with 4x25.4cm in end turrets, and 4x20.3cm guns in two turrets on each side. Secondary armament of 10x12cm guns and a 45cm underwater torpedo tube on each side. Hull protected by 15cm armour, speed 21 knots. (EM:SA MMF4817)

That night, intelligence confirmed that the German Fleet had left Kiel, possibly for Danzig, and that the Kaiser Wilhelm Canal had closed to everything except military traffic. However, as 1 August dawned, aerial reconnaissance from Kil'kond revealed nothing. The four reserve cruisers, now the 2nd Brigada Kreyserov, arrived from Kronshtadt. The fleet was concentrated and ready to fight behind the mine barrier. The main weakness in the position was the incomplete state of the gun defences. Only batteries five and nine were finished. The day passed in tense suspense. Russia had received an ultimatum from Germany to demobilise, which expired at noon. War was now inevitable. Essen went to Revel' in the destroyer *Pogranichnik* to inspect the newly arrived cruisers. At 8:20pm, Sveaborg semaphore station passed a message to *Ryurik*: 'Germany has declared war … Grigorovich.' Essen returned to *Ryurik* from his inspection half an hour later. He raised the signal, 'Convene prayer service for the granting of victory.' After the service on the upper deck, Essen delivered a stirring address to *Ryurik*'s crew. Vinter describes the scene: 'He again proclaimed his motto: "There will be no retreat." The enthusiasm was indescribable: the incessant "Ura" [Russian cheer] turned into an ovation for the leader of the fleet, whom the crew raised on their shoulders together with the commander, Kapitan 1st Ranga [Mikhail] Bakhirev.' It was a patriotic enthusiasm that soon echoed across the nations of Europe, as war spread west across the continent. Ironically, the original protagonist, Austria-Hungary, only declared war against Russia on 6 August.[1]

1 Е. Винтер, 'Балтийский флот в период начала мировой войны', in *Военно-морская комиссия по исследованию и использованию опыта войны 1914-1918 гг. на море, Сборник № 1* (Петроград: 10-я Государственная Типография, в Главк. Адмиралтействе, 1920), pp.1–31; В. Эмме, 'Период крейсерских походов и ожидания генерального сражения, на центральной позиции', in *Сборник 2*, pp.127–138; Томашевич, *операциях*, pp.18–20; Otto Hoetzsch, *Die Internationalen*

The German path to war

The tensions over Serbia escalated at the end of July as the German fleet and the Kaiser enjoyed their customary summer cruise in Norwegian waters. They had departed when it looked like the crisis might blow over. With the news of the Austro-Hungarian ultimatum, debate between the Kaiser, the government and the navy about whether the fleet should return to Germany ebbed back and forth. The British fleet was in the midst of a test mobilisation, so there was political reluctance to recall the fleet, as this might increase tensions even further. On the evening of 25 July, the debate came to a head. The commander of the Hochseeflotte, Admiral Friedrich von Ingenohl, received a summons from the Kaiser when news of Serbian mobilisation arrived. The interview revealed a gulf between their views about where the danger lay:

> I received the order for the fleet to return verbally on board His Majesty's yacht *Hohenzollern* ... and instructions to go with the entire fleet to the Baltic Sea in order to strike the first blow against Russia if war broke out. When I urgently and earnestly suggested the high possibility, indeed definite expectation, that Britain might participate in the war, ... whereby the main part of the fleet, at least all the capital ships, had to go to the North Sea, the Kaiser replied very firmly that Britain's intervention in this war was completely out of the question. Despite repeated representations, I was only able to ensure that individual units of the fleet were sent to their home ports, on the grounds that this would make the mobilization work much easier and faster. This at least made it possible for the greater part of the capital ships and the reconnaissance forces to go to the North Sea.

The Kaiser was upending the generally accepted view that Britain would enter the war. He had also sent his brother, Prinz Heinrich von Preussen, on a diplomatic mission to speak to King George about the prospect of war. Next day the Kaiser wrote to the Reichskanzler (Imperial Chancellor, the head of the German government), Theobald von Bethmann Hollweg, who was concerned that the recall of the fleet would provoke Britain: 'There is a Russian fleet! In the Baltic five Russian destroyer flotillas are exercising right now, which in 16 hours could be positioned in whole or in part in the Belts [at the entrance to the Baltic] and block them [with mines]. Port Arthur [the Japanese surprise attack in the last war] should be a lesson for us! My fleet has orders to proceed to Kiel and there it will go!'

On the 27th, *Hohenzollern* arrived in Kiel. The Kaiser ordered Bachmann to put the port into a state of defence and institute a watch on the Fehmarn Belt, to forestall the possibility of a Russian surprise attack. This narrow stretch of international waters between Germany and Denmark formed a choke point, 50 miles east of Kiel. However, Russian vessels were not to be engaged, unless they began laying mines. The watch was composed of vessels found in the port: the old battleship *Wittelsbach*, *Panther* and the light cruisers *Magdeburg* and *Danzig*. The Hochseeflotte made the light cruiser *Rostock* and 11 destroyers of 2nd Torpedobootsflottille available. On the 29th, the fleet flagship and the battleships of the 2nd and 3rd Geschwader of the Hochseeflotte reached Kiel after returning from Norway.

Beziehungen im Zeitalter des Imperialismus, Reihe 1, Band 5 (Berlin: Reimar Hobbing G.M.B.H, 1934), pp.119, 218; Новицкий, 'Критический', pp.73–77.

Grossadmiral Prinz Heinrich von Preussen. (Public domain)

The Kaiser had been exchanging notes with the Tsar in a late attempt to find a diplomatic way out of the crisis. A telegram arrived from the Tsar in the small hours of the 30th. He had ordered Russian partial mobilisation only on the Austrian border. The note included the casual observation that he had made the decision five days previously. An incensed Kaiser commented: 'So that is almost a week ahead of us … That means I have got to mobilize as well!' He authorised the first step towards German mobilisation, placing all harbours and coastal fortifications into a state of defence.

Reports confirmed that mobilisation activity was already underway in the Russian fleet. The Russian cruisers could not be located. The Kaiser now announced the appointment of Prinz Heinrich to a newly created post, Oberbefehlshaber der Ostseestreitkräfte, or O.d.O. (Commander-in-Chief of Baltic Forces). He had recently returned from London with word from King George: '… we shall try … to stay out of this and shall remain neutral.' Heinrich was a career naval officer of 52 years age. He had risen through the ranks to command of the Hochseeflotte from 1906–1909, moving to the post of Generalinspekteur der Marine (Inspector General of the Navy) on his promotion to the highest rank of Grossadmiral. Kiel castle was both his home and place of work. Heinrich was a capable naval officer and eminently more sociable than his brother. He was an avid sailor, aircraft pilot and racer of motor cars. He was regarded as a champion of technical innovation in the area of both submarines and aviation, but lacked interest in strategy and politics.

The creation by the Kaiser of this role, whilst no doubt satisfying Heinrich's desire to play his part, was problematic for the management of the war at sea. His rank and status were vastly out of proportion with the forces available. Heinrich took command of all forces in the Baltic, but also: 'Parts of the Hochsee forces that would be sent for operations in the Baltic Sea theatre during the course of the war.' This created a command tension and potential conflict of interest with the commander of the Hochseeflotte. This was all the more important as the Chef des Admiralstabes, von Pohl, did not have any formal command responsibility over either theatre of war. This left Heinrich, who also outranked him, with a freedom of action not commensurate with the strategic significance of his command.

Next day, the 31st, Scheer, whose 2nd Geschwader would lead the Baltic forces at sea based on Pohl's most recent plans, was upbeat:

> ... this commission, which put me in a position to lead and execute the first naval enterprises independently, had a great attraction for me. ... [Prinz Heinrich's] professional knowledge, his whole mode of thought and conception of responsibility offered a guarantee that his appointment could only serve a useful purpose. ... [He] grasped and carried out in the most typical fashion the difficult and thankless task of our defensive operations in the Baltic, for which we disposed of very limited resources ...

Events now rapidly began to overshadow the focus on potential naval action in the Baltic. Reports made it clear that the British fleet was already heading to its war stations. The British government refused a request to confirm that they would remain neutral in the event of war. That afternoon, the Kaiser issued the formal order for measures preparatory to mobilisation based on an imminent danger of war. An ultimatum was despatched demanding that Russia order de-mobilisation within 12 hours. The Admiralstab sent out the order: 'Hasten the deployment of all North Sea naval forces against Britain as much as possible.' Kiel quickly began to empty over the following hours as Hochseeflotte units moved through the Kaiser Wilhelm Canal to the North Sea. Scheer's hopes of Baltic glory were dashed, as 2nd Geschwader was later ordered to join them. The dalliance with deploying parts of the fleet against Russia was over. Work began in the dockyards to activate the warships held in reserve. The forces allocated to the Baltic were finalised. There would be nothing from the Hochseeflotte. Only *Augsburg*, *Magdeburg*, *Panther*, nine destroyers, two old submarines and five torpedo boats were ready for action. Being left in a command with a handful of mostly old vessels left Kapitänleutnant Max Valentiner rather deflated: 'The students of the submarine school had scattered to the four winds, and we teachers were left behind. My mobilization assignment was sad enough: I remained commander of *U.3*, the small training boat, worn out from the many daily school trips and whose combat value was truly low. ... I felt overlooked. Sidelined. Almost demoted.'

Augsburg and *Magdeburg* left Kiel for Neufahrwasser that evening on the direct orders of von Pohl; *Augsburg* had already loaded 100 mines. The other vessels were to stand watch in Kiel Bay. The available forces were divided into the Küstenschutzdivision der Ostsee (Coastal Defence Division of the Baltic), under Heinrich, and the Hafenflottille (Harbour Flotilla) Kiel. Bachmann, previously responsible for all forces in the Baltic, retained command of both the latter and coastal fortifications. See Appendix VI for the detailed organisation and Appendices IV and V for the main characteristics of the vessels. That evening in Berlin von Pohl handed over the operational orders for the Baltic to Prinz Heinrich, who then left for Kiel to take up his duties, basing himself at the castle. Valentiner was there when he arrived: 'Suddenly the Prinz entered. Tall, very slim, with a somewhat swaying gait. He was visibly agitated. His greeting was unusual by military standards: "Gentlemen," he cried, his voice trembling, "I can give you the solemn assurance that my brother, His Majesty the Kaiser, did his utmost to prevent this war. But it was no longer possible: The others simply wanted war ...".' A partisan view tinged by fraternal loyalty, but an insight into Heinrich's state of mind and motivations for returning to active command after his failed peace mission.

August 1 was the fateful day. The German ultimatum to Russia went unanswered. As a result, that afternoon Germany declared war on Russia. However, the Baltic was virtually wide open to the Russian fleet. The Kaiser ordered full mobilisation to begin the following morning.[2]

The bombardment of Libava

Prinz Heinrich had already authorised the first spoiling attack on Libava, in line with the war plans. *Augsburg* and *Magdeburg* were 'not to wait for any further executive order to complete the task ordered following official knowledge of the outbreak of war'. However, for political reasons the German government wanted the Russians to be seen to strike the first blow. Heinrich was told that no offensive actions were to be taken without specific orders. He altered the instructions given to *Augsburg* and *Magdeburg*: 'we must first wait for a special order to proceed.'

The indecision frustrated Tirpitz. That night, he asked for written clarification from the Foreign Office as to, 'Whether operations against Russia should now begin and whether the declaration of war against Russia could be announced to the Navy accordingly.' He received a quick answer: 'As a result of Russian troops crossing our borders, we are in a state of war with Russia. I have the honour to submit to your Excellency the task of taking any military measures that may become necessary as a result.' On the 2nd, at 8:57am Russian time, Heinrich received the message. In a further illustration of muddled command accountabilities, Pohl directly instructed *Augsburg* and *Magdeburg*: 'State of war with Russia. Open hostilities. Proceed according to plan.'

Bachmann had issued the orders, before Heinrich's appointment. The cruisers were to avoid superior enemy forces on the way to the target, but were to attack any minelayers or destroyers encountered. They were to mine Libava on arrival, then bombard it. Afterwards, they were to, 'try to obtain information about the whereabouts of Russian naval forces' for as long as their coal supply lasted. Whilst returning, 'the enemy's trade must be damaged as much as possible.' The cruisers would trust to superior speed if they encountered Russian cruisers. Late on the 1st, new information caused Heinrich to amend the orders. A steamer skipper arriving in Swinemünde confirmed that Russian warships had left Libava for Revel' a few days ago, and the departure of the submarines on the 30th. He had seen the arsenal and workshops abandoned, the shipyard's coal supplies set on fire, and the military aircraft leave. The military harbour was empty apart from a few small dredgers. He sailed on the 31st, seeing no mines. With Libava apparently devoid of targets, Heinrich ordered 'that part of the 100 mines from *Augsburg* should be taken to be laid off the western exit of the Gulf of Riga instead.'

Kapitän zur See Andreas Fischer of *Augsburg* would command the operation. He had received the key points of the new intelligence along with his revised orders on the 1st. *Augsburg* and *Magdeburg* were anchored off Neufahrwasser when Fischer received an alarming warning from the Admiralstab: 'Russian attacks on the ships in Neufahrwasser cannot be ruled out tonight.'

2 BA:RM60-II Küstenschutzdivision der Ostsee der Kaiserlichen Marine, KTB; Groos, *Nordsee 1*, pp.3–24; Firle, *Ostsee*, pp.15–19, 28; Reinhard Scheer (Translated Anon), *Germany's High Sea Fleet in the World War* (London: Cassell and Company Ltd., 1920), pp.9–10; Lambi, *Politics*, p.418; Max Valentiner, *Der Schrecken der Meere: Meine U-Boot-Abenteuer* (Zürich, Leipzig, Wien: Amalthea-Verlag, 1931), pp.42–44.

He ordered the cruisers to take shelter in the port. A tense night passed without incident. The message from Pohl to commence hostilities arrived at 9:15am next morning. The cruisers left just over an hour later.

The tension rose at 6pm as the cruisers neared the Russian coast at 19 knots. This was below their top speed, but meant less coal smoke to give them away. Suddenly, smoke appeared to the southeast. Fischer signalled *Magdeburg* to be ready for action if forced to turn and engage. However, no ships appeared and the cruisers pressed on. Fischer now received a wireless message: 'Libava lightship berth [5 miles west of Libava] suspected of being mined within a radius of 5 miles.' The information had come from another steamer skipper. This warning no doubt weighed heavily on his mind. Despite the evidence that Libava had been abandoned, his plan was cautious, anticipating Russian submarines and mines, as well as fire from defending batteries. He would head to a point west-northwest of Libava, then turn toward the target, laying the mines at high speed, then finally slowing down to carry out a bombardment from over six miles off the coast. This was at the range limit of both cruiser's 10.5cm guns. *Magdeburg*, Korvettenkapitän Richard Habenicht, was to act independently, shadowing *Augsburg* whilst she laid mines, and then join the bombardment. If separated, the cruisers were to head for a rendezvous point well to the west of Libava.

At just after 8pm, *Augsburg* turned to starboard as planned. Fischer increased speed to 20 knots for the attack run, starting around 13 miles from the Russian coast. Although the sun was low in an overcast western sky, *Magdeburg* recorded that light conditions and visibility were good. *Augsburg* began laying mines a few minutes later. For 25 minutes, the cruisers steadily closed towards the coast. The sun was setting on the western horizon, when, 'in Libava, which could not be seen due to a haziness, a large cloud of smoke with flashes and little bright clouds is spotted.' Habenicht made a signal from *Magdeburg*: 'We are being fired upon.' Fischer replied, 'Wait for impacts.' With action apparently imminent, Fischer ordered the laying of all remaining mines as quickly as possible. The port was now just seven miles away. Within seven minutes the last mine had splashed into the water astern. At extreme elevation, the guns on *Augsburg* and *Magdeburg* would just reach the shore. Fischer made the planned turn to starboard, parallel with the coast, and signalled *Magdeburg* to close in and follow astern. He had assumed that Russian armoured cruisers were coming out of Libava. Fischer waited in suspense for enemy shells to plunge into the water around them. It was a false alarm: 'The enemy shots do not materialise.' The ships slowed to begin their bombardment: 'The light of a bright fire on land is selected as the target point until the city and harbour are clearly visible.' *Augsburg* fired the first shot of the naval war, with *Magdeburg* soon following suit. Fischer observed that, 'A large steamer lying in front of the harbour burns or is set on fire by gunnery. Flames soon flare up in other parts of Alexanderstadt [the military port district to the north of the residential area].' The spotting top reported that most of the shells were falling short of the target, so Fischer ordered the ships to pause firing. *Augsburg* steamed towards the shore for a few minutes to close the range. The ships then turned to port, parallel with the coast and each re-opened fire from the guns of their starboard batteries: 'The range was 11,200 to 12,600m. Large explosion on land. Hits were definitely observed in the port and on land.' The sun had set. Fischer ordered the cruisers to cease fire and made off at top speed to the north. Masthead lookouts now reported torpedo boats in the hazy light astern of *Magdeburg*, but on *Augsburg* Fischer, 'saw nothing.' The lookouts reported them again 20 minutes later. Habenicht slowed to a stop. When nothing materialised out of the gloom, *Magdeburg* returned to full speed.

Augsburg had fired 280 rounds, *Magdeburg* 140; the former's log estimates that 20 percent had fallen short in the sea.

A febrile atmosphere had developed in the naval port of Libava, as the small remaining garrison, under their commander, Kontr-Admiral Andrey Zagoryansky-Kisel', prepared the port facilities for demolition and evacuated naval stores. Trade had continued in the commercial port right up to the 1st, when the German steamer *Albatross* arrived. That morning Zagoryansky-Kisel' received orders to detain six Swedish and five German flagged steamers: *Albatross*, *Wilhelm Hemsoth*, *Düsseldorf*, *Prima* and *Saxonia*.[3] At 8:15pm, a telegram arrived from Grigorovich: 'Destroy the port, Germany has declared war.' Demolitions of dock installations, bridges and lock gates began immediately. At 4am, the German steamers were boarded and the crews removed. They were detained in an empty boarding house in the commercial port. As the day wore on, the city was full of rumours about a German Fleet off the coast. Coastal observers convinced themselves that they could see a formation of 12 large and six small vessels. Wives of the sailors accommodated in the naval port later described the chaotic results in a complaint to Grigorovich:

> Almost every hour, the port authorities considered it their duty to notify apartments by telephone and messengers: 'the docks are about to be blown up, the bridge is about to be blown up, hurry to pack, enemy destroyers have appeared, etc.' The end result was that most of us, abandoning all our property to the mercy of fate, rushed out of the port, dragging along our belongings and children.

Explosions continued to echo through the port as stocks of coal burned. The remaining naval stores were soaked in oil and set alight. Machinery was destroyed. There were three entrances in the four-mile stretch of the stout outer harbour wall, up to a mile offshore. Zagoryansky-Kisel' reported that, 'The German steamships and dredging vessels were taken to the outer harbour entrances and were partly already sunk, partly still sinking; in total, five steamships, three dredgers, three lighters and six barges with concrete and stone were sunk at the gates.' Only small, shallow gaps remained in the harbour entrances, effectively trapping the Swedish steamers and the Russian *Baltika* in the port. More port vessels were sunk to block the military canal in the inner harbour. Zagoryansky-Kisel' made a tour of the destruction at 4am. He now manifested a desire to depart as soon as possible, escaping any potential German advance before the imminent withdrawal of troops stationed in the town. At 8am, he ordered the remaining naval personnel in the port to march to the train station to board a train that he had organised. Around 50 naval personnel still engaged in sinking the vessels at the exits were still at work. The only organised forces left in the port itself were the local detachment of the Gendarmerie, whose normal responsibilities were law enforcement and state security. Zagoryansky-Kisel' states in his report that, 'everything was completed', but by his own admission the blocking work was still ongoing. The Gendarmerie were left to complete a task for which they had no expertise: 'The bridge across the canal was prepared for blasting, but it was decided to carry out its destruction only after the naval crews had left the port, entrusting this task to the Chief of the

3 *Albatross* (1893), 1,026 GRT, *Wilhelm Hemsoth* (1908) 2,017 GRT, *Düsseldorf* (1899) 901 GRT, *Prima* (1901) 1,756 GRT, *Saxonia* (1898) 967 GRT.

Gendarme Team who remained in the port.' As the afternoon wore on, the gendarmes struggled to prevent fires spreading to the abandoned private apartments and port buildings.

Such was the situation when the two German cruisers headed towards the coast. There had been no destruction in the town adjacent to the naval port. Many residents were enjoying a Sunday stroll along the beach that evening. They watched the cruisers approach in fascination. Their first salvos pitched short into the sea, but once they had closed for their second run, shells began to rain down, mainly in the naval port area. The Sankt Peterburg newspaper, *Novoye Vremya*, carried the story a few days later:

> During the shelling of Libava, approximately 300 shells were fired at the port and city. There are around 169 holes left by shell explosions in the ground.
>
> An old woman was struck by shrapnel [without serious injury]. One of the shells fell 20 paces away from a detachment of gendarmes defending the front, but the shell exploded only in its upper part … so no one was injured. Six flags with a red cross fluttered over the hospital buildings, and there were patients in the hospital itself. In all, 86 shells were aimed at the hospital. After shelling the port, German ships fired 10 shots towards the public walking along the beach.

The naval hospital was located in the main target area, along with barracks, apartments, the power plant and other buildings of the naval port. The long range and smoke from the fires made identification of targets impossible, let alone making out Red Cross flags. Fortunately, only a few seriously ill patients and essential medical personnel remained in the hospital. The buildings were dispersed in a wooded area, limiting the impact of the shelling. The small bursting charges of the 10.5cm shells failed to cause any major damage, but knocked a few holes in walls. The naval port was largely deserted and there were no deaths or serious injuries, but the gendarmes reported that the shelling: 'caused general panic and the flight of almost all civilian port guards.' The gendarmes continued to put out fires caused by the shelling. A few shells fell in the residential area and commercial docks, but there was no significant damage or casualties here either. Over the next few days, people continued to flee Libava. After the army and gendarmes marched out on the evening of the 3rd, looting of abandoned property broke out, as the coal stores continued to burn. The gendarmes later returned to restore order, but waves of panic continued amidst swirling rumours of more German ships approaching to attack.

The guards allowed out the interned German sailors on the day after the bombardment, warning that they would be subject to execution if they failed to return before darkness. However, four intrepid individuals were determined to escape. They spotted that *Saxonia* had only partially sunk and that a lifeboat was hanging from her davits. They waited for darkness, then undressed and swam over:

> They reached her unnoticed and were able to search the part of the ship above water for food and other items that could be used for their escape, but they did not find any. They only had a compass, which was welcome. The boat, sliding down from the *Saxonia*, then hit the water without making a sound. The sailors rowed back to land and got their clothes back. They stayed hidden in the harbour overnight; it was not until 11 o'clock the next morning that they had a good opportunity to leave without hindrance.

They were able to make good progress along the shore. They rowed on through the night:

> It was in the second hour when a Cossack detachment spotted the escapees and was able to identify them clearly by the light of their lanterns. Their calls and requests to come ashore were ignored; on the contrary, the four escapees redoubled their efforts to reach the open sea as quickly as possible, because the Cossacks immediately made use of their carbines and launched a sustained, albeit ineffective, but heavy, fire. After another two-hour, strenuous journey, at 4am the German border was in sight. There, the border town of Nimmersatt offered them safe refuge.

If the Libava gendarmes and the bold German escapees had risen to the occasion, others had conspicuously failed to do so. The precipitate and chaotic abandonment of the port by Zagoryansky-Kisel' came to the attention of General Pavel fon Rennenkampf, the commander of First Army, within whose operational area Libava fell. He issued his General Order Number 10 on 11 August: 'Kontr-Admiral Kisel'-Zagoryansky [*sic*] left the city of Libava the night after the bombardment [it was actually worse than that], abandoning immense amounts of property, without even informing me about it. I am removing him from the post of commander of the garrison.' He quickly retired on the grounds of ill health. However, he was not the only one whose conduct was less than exemplary.

The captains of *Augsburg* and *Magdeburg* had expected resistance, despite intelligence to the contrary. There had been a panicked assessment of the flashes and smoke resulting from the ongoing destruction. Imagination turned them into powerful forces issuing forth. Fischer had hastily laid the remaining mines, leaving none for the Gulf of Riga. The pursuing destroyers reported by Habenicht were also a fantasy. Fischer had immediately transmitted his over-hasty conclusions to Kiel: '1. Have laid mines [positions given]. 2. Bombarding Libava. 3. Libava burning. 4. Am in combat with enemy cruisers.' He later claimed that the last point was a signal error and that the wireless connection with Danzig was problematic. *Augsburg* received a request for an update from Prinz Heinrich. It apparently failed to reach the bridge. Over 13 hours later, Fischer finally reported that his cruisers were north of Kolberg. He had ignored the rest of his orders and had retired far to the west, later reporting that he intended to carry out commerce raiding around Bornholm, with the cruisers taking up billets north and south of the Danish island that night. Heinrich assumed that Fischer had retired to escape from pursuing cruisers. Late that evening, he issued new orders: 'From August 4, simultaneously alarm various points on the enemy coast. Focus on lighthouses, signal stations, no action against enemy ships. Complete with coal one ship at a time from Wednesday evening on the 5th in Danzig.' An error deciphering a wireless message from *Magdeburg* led Fischer to conclude that she was very short of coal. He ordered both cruisers to Swinemünde for coaling, rather than east to Danzig as ordered. Fischer reported to Heinrich that the ships were ready to carry out the new orders as soon as they finished, which would be late on the 4th.

The operation was audacious in conception, but lacklustre in execution, with major failures in the wireless room, jumpy lookouts, misleading reporting and questionable command judgements, whilst facing no opposition of any kind. Perhaps inevitably many had been a bit too keyed up on both sides in their first taste of war. The mines were a long way out to sea and were unlikely to cause the Russians much inconvenience. The lack of clear bearings made their

Augsburg in Swinemünde harbour on 4 August 1914, with coaling in progress. Armed with six 10.5cm guns and an underwater 45cm torpedo tube on each side. Note the gun in the open casemate. (Europeana, Sammlung Rolf Kranz)

Postcard celebrating the imaginary action between *Augsburg* and a Russian cruiser at Libava. (theFrankes.com Collection)

position somewhat indeterminate, complicating future German operations off Libava. The rumour of Russian mines around the lightship had been false. Both crews went straight into action from second line duties as school ships, and it showed. The German official history incorrectly credits the raid with prompting the Russians to destroy valuable stores, although the mistake is understandable. Material damage from the bombardment was minor. The panic temporarily created in the population of Libava was the only significant effect. The seemingly audacious raid made good newspaper copy in Germany, graced by imaginative illustrations of the cruisers under fire. The official history records that: ‘it was viewed with enthusiasm as the first act of the Navy’s new offensive spirit.’[4]

Blocking the Western Baltic

On 2 August, Kontreadmiral Robert Mischke was appointed to support Heinrich, as Chef der Küstenschutzdivision der Ostsee (Commander of the Baltic Coastal Defence Division). His

4 BA:RM92 Schwere und mittlere Kampfschiffe der Preußischen und Kaiserlichen Marine, *Magdeburg*, *Augsburg* KTB, RM28 KTB; Firle, *Ostsee*, pp.30–38; Российский государственный архив Военно-Морского Флота (РГАВМФ):Фонд 716, Морской Штаб Верховного Главнокомандующего (Ставка) (1914-1917), Опись 2, Дело 11, pp.67–69, Дело 21, pp.240–241, Опись 1, Дело 6, pp.6–8; Otto Promber, *Im Kampf uns Vaterland 1914* (Stuttgart: Loewes Verlag Ferdinand Carl, 1915), pp.1–4; Государственный архив Российской Федерации (ГАРФ):Фонд 110, Штаб отдельного корпуса жандармов, Опись 2, Дело 19860; Эмме, ‘походов’, pp.138, 141.

responsibility was to cover the narrows to the east of Kiel against Russian attack, as well as the northern approach to Kiel through the three entrances to the Baltic. The Little Belt was the westernmost. It was narrow and ran through German waters at its southern exit. The much wider Great Belt was the only channel suitable for the deepest draught vessels of the rival battle fleets. It ran through Danish waters. The more distant and easternmost entrance, the Sound, was in Danish and Swedish waters, with navigable channels in each.

Heinrich allocated all of his available vessels to Mischke, with the exception of the minelayers and the two offensive submarines, which he kept directly at his disposal. However, most of these vessels would only gradually come into service over the next two weeks (see Appendix VI for details). Initially Mischke had to use the destroyer *Sleipner* as his flagship, as no cruisers were available for action. With so few vessels, aircraft reconnaissance would be vital in giving warning of potential attack, but the force available to operate from the naval air station at Holtenau, near Kiel, was small and the pilots not yet fully trained. The commander of the Marinefliegerabteilung (Naval Flying Detachment), Fregattenkapitän Hans Gygas, began setting up improvised air bases at Hadersleben and Flensburg to allow his seaplanes to scout further north.

On 2 August, German troops invaded Luxembourg. Belgium received an ultimatum, demanding free passage for German forces. The chances of British intervention now increased. The Admiralstab warned Heinrich that surprise attacks by the British Fleet in the Baltic were a possibility as early as that night. Two destroyers went to the northern entrance of the Great Belt in order to shadow and give warning of any British warships approaching, although they were to refrain from initiating hostilities. There was patchy air reconnaissance, and the destroyers and torpedo boats covering the approaches had limited wireless capabilities. Their need to relay messages via *Panther* meant that there would be little, if any, warning of attack.

Next morning, *U.3* and *U.4* left Kiel to show themselves off the exits from the Great Belt. Heinrich hoped for a deterrent effect if the Danes spotted and reported them there. At midday, the Admiralstab warned him that, 'War could be declared by Britain at very short notice.' As minelayers became available, they were loaded with around 500 mines and stationed off the Fehmarn Belt. There were too few to block all the approaches to Kiel, but they would block the most likely routes if the British appeared. Heinrich fretted about his limited options: 'The slowness of the auxiliary mine steamers *Prinz Waldemar* and *Prinz Wilhelm*, their clumsiness in laying mines, their inexperience with wireless telegraphy, force us to make preparations prematurely and accept a decision [to lay the mines] that we will regret.' That evening Germany declared war on France. The Admiralstab informed Heinrich that Denmark had laid mines to block the entrance into the Baltic through the Sound with mines.

On the morning of the 4th, *V.186*, Kapitänleutnant Hermann Ehrhardt, reported a terrible accident on the outpost line off Gedser, reducing Heinrich's meagre force even further. The destroyer *S.143*, Oberleutnant zur See Otto Benninghoff, suffered a devastating boiler explosion at anchor that morning. *V.186* was moored alongside for crew training. Casualties were heavy, with 20 killed and 16 wounded from a crew of around 80. *V.186* was damaged in the explosion, with six crew killed and two wounded. Ehrhardt ordered the crew off the wrecked vessel and took them to Warnemünde for medical attention. He returned to attempt a tow, five hours after the explosion, just in time to see *S.143* break her back and sink in the shallow water.[5] It would take several days to repair *V.186*.

Meanwhile, German troops crossed the border into Belgium. The British issued an ultimatum demanding their withdrawal by midnight. The fast new destroyer, *V.26*, relieved the older destroyers at the outpost north of the Great Belt. There were unconfirmed reports of British vessels approaching through the Skagerrak. There was no information from air reconnaissance. That afternoon the seaplane sent up to scout the Belts crashed. Gygas informed Heinrich that, '[He] was unable to take responsibility for letting the young, yet to be fully trained pilots loose with the challenging machines.' At 6pm, he received an urgent communiqué from the Admiralstab: 'Declaration of war with Britain imminent. British ships and destroyers left Dover yesterday evening.' This prompted Heinrich to speak at length on the telephone with Pohl's deputy, Kontreadmiral Paul Behncke, who failed to give any clarity on Heinrich's critical question of blocking British access to the Baltic by mining Danish waters. He informed Heinrich that, 'A note … is to be presented to the Danish government as soon as war has been declared on us by Britain … [enquiring] whether they intend to immediately block the Great Belt effectively with mines against both belligerent parties. … It is possible the Danes will not agree … since, according to international treaties, Danish transit waters should remain open to traffic at all times. In this case, we would explain to them that for military reasons we have to reserve the right to create the defences we need in time of war by using mines and taking war measures. … In any event, it is desirable that we place our barriers to be as militarily effective as possible, but insofar as we are able, not affect the territorial sovereignty of Danish waters. This should be adhered to as a principle, as far as possible without having a military disadvantage for us. The main thing is that the mines are laid as effectively as possible and can also be defended against sweeping.' After consideration, Heinrich abandoned the planned operations against the Russian coast by *Magdeburg* and *Augsburg*, recalled them urgently to Kiel, and issued the order to lay a mine barrier to block the Great Belt in Danish and international waters, to guarantee its effectiveness. He later spoke again with Behncke, who only offered more opinions, so the order stood. That night, *Prinz Waldemar* and *Prinz Wilhelm* laid 243 mines to close the Great Belt's narrow southern exit, between the Danish island of Lolland and the southern tip of Langeland. The next morning, the 5th, destroyer *S.127* closed the narrow Little Belt with 12 mines just inside German territorial waters. *V.26* withdrew through the Sound. Mischke's force concentrated to patrol behind the mines and south of the Sound. The German government issued an expression of regret to the Danes, for action taken before receiving their reply.

The Danish government worried about the consequences of intervention by both Germany and Britain. That afternoon, the Danish Navy began closing all of the channels through Danish waters into the Baltic with mines. On the 6th, the Danish government issued a communiqué: 'Denmark will observe absolute neutrality in the German-British war. In order to maintain this neutrality and keep military operations away from Danish coastal waters, as well as to secure the connections between the provinces, the Danish government has decided to block Danish coastal waters in the Sound [the Drogden channel], Great Belt [in the narrows between Fyn and Sjælland] and Little Belt with mines.' As a result, the only channel remaining open into the Baltic was the Flintrinne, running through Swedish waters in the Sound. This was only navigable by vessels with a draught of less than 6m, and its twists and turns made it dangerous for passage at night. It was over 100 miles from Kiel, and it was impractical for Germany to block

5 *S.143* was raised and rebuilt, returning to service on 14 September 1915.

it without Swedish compliance. The Germans could also use a winding channel in their own waters to bypass the Danish minefield in the Little Belt with small, shallow draught vessels. On the 7th, Pohl directed Heinrich to avoid Danish waters in future and to set up a pilot service to pass merchant vessels through the mine barriers.

Sweden rejected German requests to restrict use of the Flintrinne out of hand. Keeping it open was vital for Swedish trade. The only concession offered was that, 'Only when warships threatened to enter the Sound would the Swedish government agree to extinguish all lights from Cape Kullen to Falsterbo in the Sound and to remove all navigation marks.'

Heinrich's fears of a surprise attack on Kiel by the British Fleet were groundless. The long shadow thrown by events in the previous conflict drove an oft-observed behaviour of assuming that events now would follow a similar pattern. The Russians had similar preoccupations.[6]

Awaiting the German attack

With the declaration of war, the Baltiyskiy Flot came under the command of Sixth Army, which was responsible for defence from the Swedish border to the Baltic coast. Their commander, General Konstantin Fan-der-Flit, confirmed the Fleet's orders, in line with the 1912 plan: 'With all ways and means to prevent a landing in the Gulf of Finland. The land forces and fortresses should provide the navy with full assistance in carrying out this task.' However, outside the Gulf, the coastline was almost undefended by Russian troops. In Hangö, there were even preparations to destroy the port and requisition a Dutch steamer to block the harbour in the event of attack. The over-riding priority was for the Baltiyskiy Flot to hold the Central Position until Sixth Army mobilised to defend the capital. Further inland, to the south, the Russian armies mobilised to launch a major overland offensive into Ostpreussen.

On the 2nd, Essen concentrated the fleet east of Nargen, and took the opportunity to practice fleet manoeuvres behind the minefield before returning to port. An overwhelming attack was still expected, but despite this morale was high. That night, 2nd Divizion patrolled to the west, responding to rumours that German destroyers were at sea, but they encountered nothing.

Work continued to strengthen the defences in the Gulf of Finland. Destroyers laid more mines. These plugged gaps north of Nargen and added a ninth line of mines in front of those in the Central Position. They also laid mines to foul the approaches to the skerries east of Hangö, as well as the port itself. Marked channels allowed vessels in and out. The two obsolete reserve battleships and *Rossiya* began giving up their 20.3cm guns to strengthen the Central Position and several additional 12cm and 7.5cm batteries were under urgent construction with guns taken from river monitors and other vessels in the fleet.

The lack of German activity since the bombardment of Libava only heightened the tense atmosphere. There were only occasional unsubstantiated reports of light cruisers and destroyers lurking off Dagerort at night. Cruisers patrolled the line between Hangö and Ajax Bank during day and destroyers by night. A double line of destroyers was in place to begin with, as well as a screen east of the minefield, as merchant vessels needed directing to pass south of Nargen. Many

6 BA:RM93 Leichte Kampfschiffe der Preußischen und Kaiserlichen Marine, *S.143*, *V.186* KTB, RM28 KTB; Firle, *Ostsee*, pp.39–52, 165; Anon., *Geheime Marine Verlustliste* (Berlin: Kaiserliche Marine, published periodically 1914-1915), *No.4*, pp.25–26.

would not be aware that a war had broken out until reaching port. The war plans had evidently been light on detail when it came to the management of commercial traffic. Rusin had recently contacted Essen: 'Please inform me urgently where you find it necessary to direct commercial vessels coming from St. Petersburg, Narva and generally eastern ports, in the event of the installation of the main barrier.' Nevertheless, the patrols were largely successful in intercepting vessels. However, on the night of 3/4 August, two Russian flagged steamers, *Berkut* and *Lembit*, coming from the west, slipped by in some fog patches.[7] Captain E. Klingenberg of the collier *Berkut*, with a cargo of coal from England for Kronshtadt, describes the consequences:

> At 10:15[pm], being at a distance of 6 miles from Nargen Island, we heard a shot and at the same time, heard an explosion at the bow of the steamer. The steamer received a heavy blow, water splashed over the side. … We heard a few more shots and shells fly over us. … in a quarter of an hour Number One hold was full; the pumps … did not draw water, apparently the pipes were damaged. … All the time we made distress signals, but there was no answer to the signals.
>
> The steamship *Lembit*, which was not far from us, sent a boat … but since they could not help us, they went back. Since the steamship was listing more and more to port, I decided to go at low speed and put the steamship on the shore. I sent off crew that were not needed in the boats and ordered them to stay close.
>
> At 3am I ordered slow ahead, but after several revolutions of the engine there was a loud explosion under the forward part of the steamer, Number One hatch flew into the air, a cloud of smoke rose in front and … the steamer immediately sank into the water up to the edge of Number Two hatch. … so everyone got into the boats and cast off from the side. We rowed with the crew to the steamer *Lembit* … [Her captain] took most of the crew … we then went back to the steamer *Berkut*. We managed to let off steam there in time to avoid a boiler explosion and returned to the steamer *Lembit*.
>
> At 5:40[am] the steamer capsized to port and sank by the bow. At 5:45[am], the steamer disappeared under water.

Battery 9 on Nargen had spotted *Berkut* approaching the mine barrier. The 20.3cm guns had briefly opened fire. It is unclear whether a shell or a mine hit *Berkut*, but the latter is more likely, as water falling on the deck indicated an explosion underwater. Fortunately, a motor launch had stopped *Lembit* before reaching the mines. *Berkut*'s attempt to reach the shore certainly resulted in striking a mine. Essen reported that the battery had sunk the steamer. Evidently, he was unaware of Klingenberg's report. Luckily, there had been no injuries. After warnings not to speak about the cause, or location of the loss, the steamer crews were released.

There were no further incidents. From the 7th onwards, the night destroyer screen reduced to a single line of vessels. Trade continued through the channel south of Nargen. Patrol and pilot vessels heavily regulated the traffic, with ships instructed to use a specific route to avoid mines, and escorted through the zone. This ensured that the skippers of neutral vessels would report the implied danger outside the narrow channel.[8]

7 *Berkut* (1905) 3,148 GRT.

8 РГАВМФ:Фонд 716, Опись 1, Дело 11, p.20 and Опись 2, Дело 21, pp.207, 213; Эмме, 'походов', pp.138–143; Новицкий, 'Критический', p.83.

The Swedish Campaign

In addition to potential German attack, Essen was concerned that the Swedes might attempt a landing in Finland. Sweden had ceded this territory to Russia after war in 1809. It was also a potential powder keg of Finnish nationalism. On the 2nd, the Russian Ambassador to Sweden communicated that, 'The Swedish fleet, with a strength of five armoured ships, sixteen torpedo boats and three submarines, has left Stockholm and, according to rumours, is in part off the island of Gotland.' On the 3rd, Sweden ordered mobilisation of the navy and partial mobilisation of the army, whilst making a declaration of neutrality. However, the Russian Naval Attaché sent another warning: 'There is reason to believe that an agreement exists between Sweden and Germany and that Sweden's intervention is dependent on the condition that Britain participates on the other side.' Next day the Russian Ambassador in London warned that 'Grey [Foreign Secretary] told me he has good reasons to fear that Germany will issue an ultimatum to Sweden to compel her to declare war on Russia.' These concerns originated from a conversation between the Swedish Foreign Minister, Knut Wallenberg, and the Russian and British Ambassadors to Sweden, as well as views expressed by the pro-German Swedish King, Gustav V.

Essen bemoaned the poor state of intelligence on the German Fleet. When the crisis first erupted, this had been relying on newspaper reports. Kapitan 1st Ranga Aleksandr Kolchak, Essen's Chief of Operations, had complained that: 'We have absolutely no information about the enemy. Our intelligence is worth zero. It does not provide anything useful.' Now a cocktail of reports was pouring in from spooked coastal observation stations and informants across the Baltic. On the 5th, Essen vented his frustration to Rusin and touched on another looming issue with fuel reserves, as a result of having to maintain high levels of fleet reconnaissance activity to compensate:

> We suffer from a lack of information about where and what the German fleet is doing, as well as the Swedish … We do not have high-speed vessels for reconnaissance. Only *Novik*, but even that is without oil – nothing but woe. … I must press you to organize covert intelligence on a large scale, otherwise we are blind and because of this there is excessive nervousness, we burn coal in vain and have no rest.

A summary received that day 'reliably' placed both the 4th and 5th Geschwader of old German battleships in the eastern Baltic, although they were actually in Kiel. Less reliable information also identified a number of armoured and light cruisers. The report highlighted the staffing of almost all of these ships by reservists. This would obviously limit their effectiveness until worked up.

Nevertheless, with the Germans apparently quiescent, the staff of the Fleet turned to the concerns about Sweden. The intelligence indicated that the British declaration of war could trigger a Swedish attack. Nepenin established a clandestine observation post, at the lighthouse on the tiny rocky outcrop of Bogskär, to give early warning of any potential advance by their fleet. They sent innocuous wireless messages in plain Swedish. For example, 'send 5 kilos of bread' meant '5 cruisers sighted'. Vinter writes on the 5th that, 'in connection with intelligence information about the concentration of the Swedish fleet at Fårö Sound [at the northern tip of Gotland] and the continuing unclear attitude of Sweden … Kolchak reported to … Essen about the need to, "resolve the Swedish question".' After debating with Kolchak and the staff, Essen decided to apply the lessons of surprise attack that he had learned at first hand in the last war and neutralise the Swedish threat before they could unite with the German Fleet. Vinter was briefed and sent to hand deliver a note detailing Essen's plan to Fan-der-Flit in Sankt Peterburg for approval. He arrived late on the 6th, having been delayed when his despatch vessel had to be replaced after hitting a rock. Fan-der-Flit was not at his headquarters. Vinter handed the note to his Chief-of-Staff, who told him the letter would be reported immediately to Fan-der-Flit, who would take it up with the Tsar.[9] He returned two hours later for the reply. He received nothing in writing, but was told, 'To clarify Sweden's position, it is planned to present a collective note from the ambassadors of the allied powers with a limited response time. In the event of an unfavourable turn of events, the Fleet Commander would be given the corresponding authorisation in a telegram, as requested in his letter (one word; "Thunderstorm"), which will indicate permission to "attack the Swedish Fleet".' Vinter returned to relay the message. In the meantime, Essen had also sent a telegraph signal, logged in the archives of the Naval General Staff in Sankt Peterburg, received at 1:40pm on the 6th: 'In view of Britain's declaration of war on Germany, it is necessary to anticipate that Sweden will declare war on us in the coming days. I request permission to send a fleet immediately to Gotland to destroy the Swedish fleet concentrated there. I request that you urgently telegraph a one word answer to this wireless signal.' Essen's plan was to present a written ultimatum to the commander of the Swedish Fleet. After describing the lack of clarity about Sweden's intentions, this remarkable document concluded:

> I appeal to you, dear sir, with a proposal to transfer the entire Swedish fleet to Karlskrona [in the far south of Sweden], with the most humble request not to leave from there during the entire duration of the war between Russia and Germany. As a military man, you will understand my order to my ships to destroy immediately any vessel of war they encounter within the Baltic Sea and its inlets. Please consider, Admiral, this statement of mine as a friendly act, eliminating the sad possibility of accidental military actions between our fleets and nations.

Refusal of such an ultimatum was almost inevitable. Essen had already prepared for the sortie. He had seen first-hand the results of Japanese minelaying during Russian advances in the last war. On the 7th, he sent out a force from Revel' to sweep for mines on the routes he planned to use. *Bogatyr'*, *Oleg* and the Poludivizion provided cover for 2nd Divizion and five boats of 7th Divizion which deployed their mine sweeps. They went as far as Tagelakht Bay on the northwest coast of Ezel'. The lookouts were jumpy. There was a major stir when *Oleg* sighted a phantom periscope. *Sibirskiy Strelok* shelled another, which turned out to be a floating pole. On the 8th, Essen imposed a communication blackout with the shore, and then left Helsingfors with the fleet. He called in the cruisers from patrol and rendezvoused with them off Nargen. That night, aboard *Ryurik*, Essen briefed all of the unit commanders and distributed the plans for the advance on Fårö Sound. The cruisers took longer to coal than expected, delaying the planned departure until the 10th.

9 Vinter does not name him. General-Leytenant Arseniy Gulevich held this post until 9 August 1914. He then moved to Ninth Army and was replaced by General-Leytenant Knyaz' (Prince) Pavel Engalychev. The changeover itself may have contributed to developments.

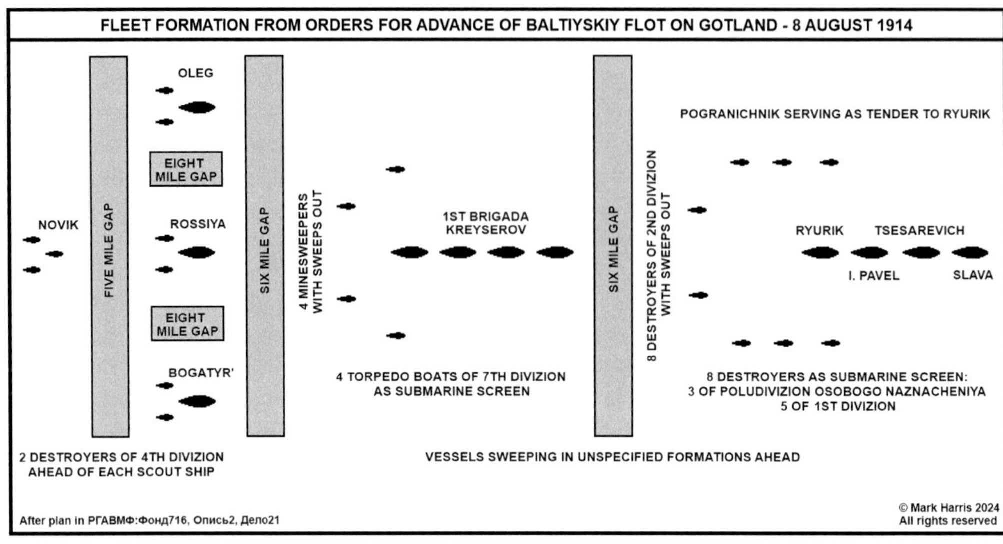

1st Brigada Lineynykh Korabley. *Tsesarevich* leading *Slava*, *Andrey Pervozvannyy* and *Imperator Pavel I* on a pre-war fleet exercise. Each had a main armament of 4x30.5cm guns, plus 7x20.3cm on each side of the two newer vessels. (Public domain)

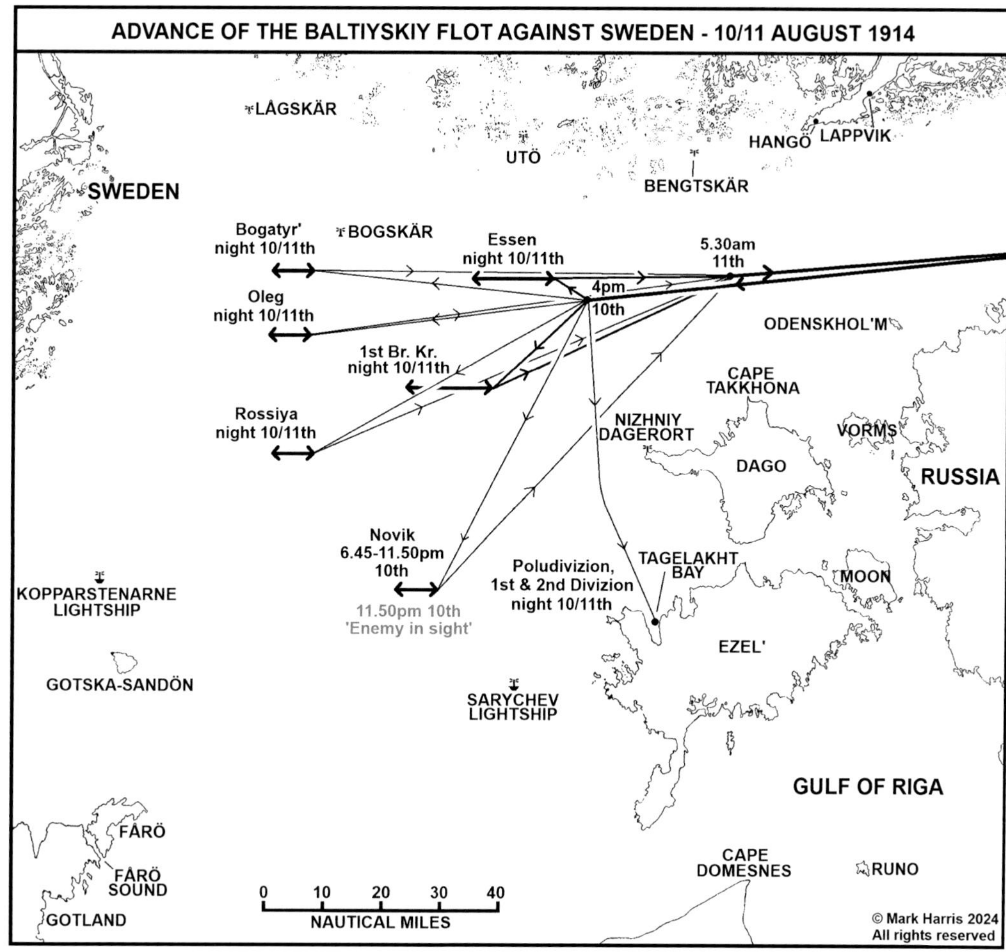

At 4am that morning, the fleet headed out with scouts ahead and screened by destroyers. The 7th and 2nd Divizions, supported by four auxiliary minesweepers, began sweeping for mines as the formation passed Odenskhol'm. They raised the mine sweeps when the fleet reached deep water. The four minesweepers and short-range torpedo boats of 7th Divizion then detached to Lappvik, in the Finnish skerries. Two destroyers from 2nd Divizion replaced them at the head of the cruisers. *Novik* headed off to port to take position well ahead of *Bogatyr'* as an advanced screen. The main body of the fleet now began exercising whilst waiting for receipt of the fateful wireless message authorising the final advance, with a clear blue sky overhead.

The plan was to move into position off Fårö Sound at 10am next morning. The orders issued on the 8th called for 1st Brigada Kreyserov, with its two minesweepers out front, to advance on the Sound from a position southeast of the main southern entrance. Essen's battleship group would closely follow them, with four sweeping destroyers out front. *Rossiya*'s group, reinforced by the last two sweeping destroyers of 2nd Divizion, would occupy a covering position west of Fårö, with *Oleg*'s group west of the Swedish island of Gotska Sandön. *Bogatyr'* and *Novik*'s groups would screen to the south of the fleet.

No message arrived. As planned, all of the destroyers with the exception of 4th Divizion headed to anchor in Tagelakht Bay, whilst 1st Brigada Kreyserov and Essen's main body steamed in formation backwards and forwards throughout the night behind the outer cruiser screen. The destroyers would rejoin in the morning. The eight destroyers of 4th Divizion took position as planned, well to the west and south of the warships that they were with, which kept underway on their positions. As night fell a near full moon rose to bathe the sea in bright moonlight. Soon after, at 11:50pm, the wireless on *Ryurik* sprang to life. The operators received the message 'GGG 84' repeatedly. This was the code for 'enemy in sight.' There was no call sign, but *Novik*'s billet was in map square 84.

Essen ordered all ships to raise steam for full speed. The wireless went silent. Calls to *Novik* went unanswered. In the absence of further information, Essen needed to concentrate the fleet. He ordered all ships at sea to meet at a position mid-way between Bengtskär and Cape Takkhona, west of the entrance to the Gulf of Finland. Essen ordered the destroyers in Tagelakht Bay to raise steam, head for the rendezvous, and attack any enemy they found off Dagerort. As the fleet concentrated, a message came in with the news that his operation was, 'considered inappropriate' by Supreme Headquarters (STAVKA). At 6:45am, Essen issued the order for the fleet to retire into the Gulf. A few hours later details followed in a message from Kapitan 2nd Ranga Vasiliy Al'tfater, the head of the Naval Directorate on Fan-der-Flit's staff:

> The Supreme Commander-in-Chief [General Grand Duke Nikolay] does not permit proactive actions during the current political impasse. The principal task of the Baltiyskiy Flot is to cover the capital, which, especially now, is achieved primarily by its position in the Gulf of Finland. When he is able to do so, the Supreme Commander-in-Chief will issue orders about where you are to go. The draft letter is considered a provocative act and an undeserved insult to the Swedes, who are currently acting with integrity towards Russia.

Vinter records that Essen was offended by the tone of the harsh rebuke and had told Rengarten, 'If we had been allowed, we would have won a brilliant victory, so necessary to strengthen the spirit of our small fleet.' Although the initiative for the operation had been Essen's, and he had kept the chain of command informed, it is surprising that he took such bold action without clear written approval. His plan was inspired by intelligence that pointed to a potential pre-emptive attack by the Swedish Fleet. However, since Essen had left Helsingfors, Sweden had moved to clarify her stance by issuing a joint declaration of neutrality in respect of all belligerents, in conjunction with Norway. The Russian Ambassador reported this on the 9th. The three allied ambassadors met with Wallenberg next day. They were now satisfied with his assurances that Sweden would keep out of the war; no ultimatum was issued. Wallenberg's assurances were not publicised, as the Swedish government feared the response of the army, which it believed might not resist an attack from Germany.

With almost no paper trail, it is impossible to confirm whom Fan-der-Flit's Chief-of Staff consulted, exactly what he told Vinter, or when the recently appointed Grand Duke became aware of the plan. No mention of a reason for the advance was included in Essen's report: 'I went out to sea, having the fleet in combat formation, and by the evening I deployed it in the northern part of the Baltic Sea.' However, there had been a serious breakdown in command control. Russian policy now focussed on ensuring that nothing provoked Sweden into siding with Germany, and normal trade relations resumed.

The intelligence about the Swedish Fleet that had given rise to the operation was flawed. The fleet commander, Viceamiral Wilhelm Dyrssen, issued orders for the annual manoeuvres, in which the 'red' attacking force was to be based in Fårö Sound. The Swedish press reported this. However, Dyrssen soon cancelled the manoeuvres, specifically to avoid aggravating the tense political situation. The fleet remained where it had gathered at the Stockholm naval base. Essen would have found no fleet in Fårö Sound.

This obscure episode is remarkable in a number of ways. Essen had positioned his fleet to deliver a surprise attack in a way directly inspired by his experiences in the last war. Neither the Germans, nor the Swedes had any inkling about what the Russian fleet was doing. The story only came out gradually many years later. Both planning and execution demonstrate Essen's audacity and offensive mindedness, but the unfortunate result was that he was now constrained from taking any offensive actions. A combination of uncoordinated pieces of flawed and often unverified intelligence, hearsay and ill-considered Swedish remarks had almost allowed Sweden and Russia to blunder into war. Shoddy staff work had then lost control of events, allowing them to develop their own momentum. The incident remains a warning for diplomats and military planners of how badly things can go wrong when the gathering, management and use of intelligence is mishandled. It exemplified the first week of operations in the Baltic. Both fleets had been reacting to fears about what their enemies might do, based on assumptions shaped by the last major naval conflict. However, the Germans were at sea as well; *Novik* had been in contact.[10]

10 РГАВМФ:Фонд 716, Опись 1, Дело 11, p.20 and Опись 2, Дело 21, pp.272–273, Фонд 418, Морской Генеральный Штаб г.Петроград (1906-1918), Опись1, Дело 3643, p.7; Эмме, 'походов', pp.141–153; Денис Ю. Козлов, 'Записка Е. Ф. Винтера о «шведском походе»', in И. А. Тихонюк (ed.), *Великая война 1914-1918: Вып. 6* (Москва: Квадрига, 2017), pp.107–118; Hoetzsch, *Beziehungen, Reihe 1, Band 5*, pp.284–5, 300, 314 and *Reihe 2, Band 6, Halbband 1*, pp.39–40; E. Björklund, 'Det Ryska anfallsföretaget mot Sverige år 1914' (Stockholm: Svensk Tidskrift, 1936); И. А. Киреев, *Траление в Балтийском море в войну 1914–1917 гг.* (Москва, Ленинград: Военмориздат НКВМФ СССР, 1939), pp.12–13; Михаил Александрович Петров, *Морская оборона берегов в опыте последних войн России* (Ленинград: Военной типографии Управления делами Наркомвоенмор и РВС СССР, 1927), p.110; Новицкий, 'Критический', pp.71–72.

3

The German offensive: August 1914

Mischke attacks the Russian coast

With the entrances to the Baltic secured, Heinrich turned his attention back to Russia. His reserve vessels would not be battle-ready until the end of August. On the 7th, the Admiralstab annoyed Heinrich by prompting him to resume coastal raids. He was waiting for his cruisers from Danzig. They arrived next day, and Heinrich ordered Mischke to resume operations, to do as much damage as possible to coastal installations, enemy ships and trade, both by direct attack and laying offensive minefields, whilst avoiding superior forces. He allocated the warships that ran the least risk operating in enemy waters, *Augsburg*, *Magdeburg* and the three modern destroyers, *V.186*, *V.25* and *V.26*, all of which had the speed to stay out of trouble.

Mischke transferred his flag to *Augsburg* and concentrated his force at a rendezvous south of Bornholm on the evening of the 9th, where he issued his orders. The first operation he planned was a raid on coastal installations and commerce, but no mining. Mischke would avoid any submarines by approaching through deep water, out of sight of land. At dawn on the 11th, he planned to bombard the signal station at Dagerort, whilst *Magdeburg* kept watch northwards. The force would then retire to the Swedish coast to consider next steps.

Mischke steamed across an almost empty Baltic, his vessels spread in a scouting line. The only sighting was an American sailing vessel, stopped and released, as her papers were in order. Intelligence placed a Russian minefield between Finland and Nargen. It placed three Russian cruisers in Revel', and one on patrol at the mouth of the Gulf of Finland. This came largely from neutral steamer skippers. As dusk approached on the 10th, the destroyers fell in behind *Augsburg*, with *Magdeburg* three miles to port. By 11:30pm, the force was heading north-northeast, steaming through the moonlit night and calm sea at 20 knots, mid-way between Gotska Sandön and Dagerort. *Magdeburg* was soon to be detached. Mischke would turn east to approach Dagerort. He was unknowingly heading directly into the outer screen of the Russian battle fleet, awaiting the order to move against the Swedes.

At 9pm, Mischke recorded that: 'Russian wireless messages are clearly audible; enemy forces assumed to be nearby'. At around 11:30pm lookouts on *Augsburg* sighted 'dim searchlights' in the distance. Mischke turned towards them, but they disappeared. *Magdeburg*'s First Officer saw them too. Minutes later, a powerful Russian wireless signal was picked-up. Almost immediately, 'a darkened vessel was spotted, the alarm sounded and reported to *Augsburg*.' The vessel made an unrecognisable challenge by signal lamp. There were now four funnels visible, implying two destroyers. *Magdeburg* wirelessed: ‘Enemy destroyers have broken through’. Mischke had ordered that: ‘Under no circumstances should an enemy reconnaissance line be broken through at night.’ Habenicht ordered *Magdeburg* to turn away and reduce speed. The enemy turned side on; the four funnels belonged to a single destroyer. As *Magdeburg* turned the destroyer disappeared behind her smoke trail, lying thickly in the still air. Habenicht ordered full speed, heading southwards to clear the smoke. *Augsburg* came into sight. *Magdeburg*’s signal prompted Mischke to order his force to reverse course.

The force had encountered *Novik*, under the command of Kapitan 2nd Ranga Pëtr Paletskiy. She was in the most advanced patrol position, slowly steaming back and forth to east and west, with only two of the six boilers lit to economise fuel. *Ispolnitel’nyy* and *Kryepkiy*, the two accompanying destroyers, were picketing to the south. At 11:45pm, *Novik* was heading east, when ‘we saw two enemy cruisers 25–30 cables [2½-3 miles] away southwards.’ Paletskiy immediately sent a wireless alarm, ordered a turn away to the north-northeast and raised steam for *Novik*’s full speed of 36 knots. No more signals could be sent, as a mistake was made adjusting the wireless apparatus, putting it temporarily out of action. Evidently, *Novik* had reported contact before the Germans identified her.

At 6:45am next morning, *Novik* repaired her wireless. Paletskiy reported sighting two cruisers and a destroyer. The fleet soon came into sight, off the Gulf of Finland. Paletskiy explained that his speedy withdrawal was ‘due to the momentary nature of the meeting and the indistinct outlines of the ships, I could not be sure in time that these ships were enemy.’ Essen sent *Novik* to round up 4th Divizion, which had failed to answer the recall signal. The fleet returned to Nargen around midday.

To add to Essen’s despondency, as they arrived *Ryurik* hit an uncharted bank, causing a gash in the outer skin and flooding four compartments outside the inner hull. *Ryurik* took on 400t of water, but was not in danger. Signals warned the battleships astern to reverse course. Nevertheless, *Imperator Pavel I* touched ground, but escaped with a small dent. Essen could not afford for *Ryurik* to be out of action. He refused permission to dock. Divers confirmed a 60cm gash in the plating. The compartments were caulked, and sealed with cement.

The fleet coaled and the battleships returned to Helsingfors. Essen reported to Fan-der-Flit that he was, ‘leaving the cruisers in Revel’’, and allowed the destroyers and cruisers to begin overhauling machinery and cleaning boilers, as, ‘since July 27 these ships have worked almost without rest, carrying out guard and screening duty’.

Night encounters call for quick reactions to exploit fleeting opportunities to inflict significant damage at close range, with crews and weapons at the ready to exploit them. Essen made clear his ‘displeasure for poor reporting and missing the opportunity to attack enemy cruisers’ to Paletskiy. He was justified in ensuring that he had not caught sight of his destroyers by making recognition signals, but soon identified cruisers, which could not have been Russian in this position. Crews on both sides had neither the mindset, nor the right training to seize these opportunities. Paletskiy simply moved off as quickly as possible. Mischke’s orders precluded close night action, but given the raw state of his crews, this was probably sensible. He explained his withdrawal and came up with a new plan: ‘It could be assumed that an enemy outpost line had been positioned on the Dagerort–Gotska Sandön line. Since the Gulf of Riga … was behind [us], lacking certainty about the intentions and presence of enemy destroyers and possibly other forces, the advance further north could

Magdeburg, August 1914. Armed with 5x10.5cm guns, a deck torpedo tube for trial work and an underwater 50cm torpedo tube on each side. Hull protected by 5cm armour, speed 24 knots. (Public domain)

not continue.' Mischke headed back northwards at daybreak, getting a position fix off Fårö. Daylight would favour his cruisers in an action with destroyers, so he then turned, 'towards the supposed enemy outpost line in order to roll it up.' This detour meant that the destroyers now had insufficient fuel to continue. They detached to refuel at Danzig, then to guard the coast off Memel, awaiting the cruisers' return.

Magdeburg and *Augsburg* advanced in good visibility, but found nothing on the supposed reconnaissance line. The Baltiyskiy Flot was retiring far ahead of them. Mist shrouded the coast of Dago, so Mischke continued to his next intended target, the lighthouse on the rocky outcrop of Bengtskär, off the Finnish coast, at the entrance to the Gulf of Finland. At mid-day, the lighthouse came in sight. The cruisers went to battle stations. They closed and bombarded the lighthouse and attached residence from a range of 2½ miles for 15 minutes. *Magdeburg* fired 86 shells, *Augsburg* 75. There was no military presence on Bengtskär. Like all other Russian lighthouses in the area, it had been extinguished when war broke out. However, the lighthouse-keeper and his young son were still there. They assumed that the approaching warships were Russian and set sail to meet them in a boat from the far side of the island. They therefore escaped the bombardment and took shelter in the lee of the island. Around 30 shells hit the structures. The keeper's house sustained significant damage, but the stout lighthouse was largely unaffected by the small shells. Mischke then retired to the Swedish coast, arriving south of Stockholm at 6:30pm. The cruisers then steamed down the coastline outside territorial waters, encountering only two neutral sailing vessels.

That night, Mischke headed back towards his original target, at Nizhniy Dagerort. Next morning, *Magdeburg* was detached to bombard the lighthouse, whilst *Augsburg* covered to the northwest. Habenicht fired 54 shells, then fired another 22 at the nearby naval signal station. The cast-iron lighthouse largely escaped damage. The signal station was unaffected, but shelling damaged the observation tower. The watchers reported the approach and bombardment, and the departure of the cruisers to the northeast. Essen concluded that they were the same cruisers encountered by *Novik*, but had no vessels near enough to intervene. Mischke retired again to the Swedish coast. He encountered only two neutral steamers. The cruisers returned to Memel past the west coast of Gotland, arriving at 11am on the 13th.

The Memel military and civil administration informed Mischke that the German border was poorly defended. As a result, Russian troops had been making increasingly frequent border incursions. They asked him to deter these by bombarding the Russian guard stations and barracks on the border. Both cruisers steamed to the border that afternoon, where *Augsburg* delivered a short bombardment of four buildings pointed out by a local official, firing 48 shells. The *Vestnik Libavy* reported that a fragment wounded a soldier in the thigh inside the customs post. He seems to have been the only casualty during the entire operation. Mischke went back to Danzig to coal, rest and make his report.

Whilst Mischke had done better than Fischer on the last operation, Heinrich had concerns about his performance, especially the early withdrawal of his covering destroyers, which had not been fully fuelled, but accepted his explanation for losing contact with the enemy destroyer, as it had been, 'over in a moment' and had, 'disappeared in funnel smoke.' The lack of enemy shipping indicated little scope for commerce warfare. The encounter with a single destroyer and absence of a daylight patrol led to the erroneous conclusion that the Russians had largely retreated behind defences in the Gulf of Finland. The entire Russian fleet had simply been retiring after the cancelled advance. The conclusion led to a bolder plan for the next German operation.

News of the attack on Bengtskär only reached Revel' on the 16th, but the Dagerort bombardment had the immediate psychological impact that the Germans were seeking. Confusing signals from jumpy observation posts followed. The Dago Border Guard reported smoke from 22 vessels later that morning. Bogskär observation post reported 'three large enemy ships … heading west'. That night the post at Verkhnego Dagerort reported 12 enemy vessels heading towards the Gulf of Finland. Powerful enemy wireless traffic was detected.

At 1am on the 13th, Essen ordered all vessels to prepare for sea. He sent 3rd and 5th Divizions to reconnoitre Dagerort and had the submarines take up their defence positions. At dawn, all stations reported an empty sea in high visibility. Air reconnaissance revealed nothing. The fleet stood down, but sightings of German forces on the coast from the German border up to Libava continued through the day. Then news of the bombardment at the border arrived. It was feared that the Germans had laid mines off Dago, Ezel', Moon Sound and within the Gulf of Riga. On 15 and 16 August, Essen sent destroyers with mine sweeps, supported by cruisers, to all these areas as far south as Irben Strait. They found nothing.[1]

1 BA:RM92 *Magdeburg*, *Augsburg* KTB, RM60-II KTB; Firle, *Ostsee*, pp.52–60; Козлов, 'Винтера', pp.107–118; Эмме, 'походов', pp.154–156; РГАВМФ:Фонд 716, Опись 2, Дело 21, pp.272–273; Денис Ю. Козлов, '"Новик" против "Magdeburg", август 1914 года', *Гангут № 104*,

Freya's demise

Freya, an old protected cruiser, launched in 1897, was the only vessel in Heinrich's forces with a medium calibre gun armament. She arrived in Kiel on 9 August from Danzig. Considerable work was required to prepare her for action.

On 12 August, *Freya* was in Kiel Bay, moored for combat drills. The crew of the underwater torpedo flat were exercising rapid reloading drill at the starboard tube. After simulating the firing of a torpedo, the crewman responsible for retracting the bar that supported the torpedo as it left the tube made a mistake. He failed to fully retract the bar. When the outer door of the tube closed, it caught on the bar and failed to lock. The crewman at this position failed to recognise this and reported the door closed. The rear door was unlatched and the sea burst through the empty tube. The door slammed open, trapping the leg of Torpedo-Oberheizer Mendritzki. Desperate attempts to free him failed. The compartment filled in only 30 seconds. His shipmates had to abandon him and seal the compartment. Many more compartments forward flooded before the crew closed watertight doors. Water continued to spread, through leaky bulkheads in coal bunkers and other compartments, affecting the forward boiler room and as far aft as the starboard engine room. The pumps could not keep up. Flooding reached critical levels. Tugs pushed *Freya* onto a bank to stop her sinking. Divers plugged the open tube. Pumps drained the water, and *Freya* docked to survey the repairs required. On the 14th, the initial estimate was for over two weeks. The ship obviously had serious issues with watertight integrity. Heinrich obtained agreement to replace her with the armoured cruiser, *Friedrich Carl*, currently lying idle in reserve. Although old, she was newer and more powerful. On 28th August, *Freya* decommissioned and her crew transferred to *Friedrich Carl*. However, it would be many weeks before the ship was ready for service. The accident illustrates the challenges, both with ageing vessels and inexperienced reservists that Heinrich would have to overcome to create an effective fighting force.[2]

The first clash; Mischke's advance on the Gulf of Finland

On the 15th, encouraged by Mischke's report, Heinrich decided, 'to launch an offensive mine operation against the Gulf of Finland in order to continue to hold the Russians there, inflict losses on them and forestall any planned offensive on their part.' The Admiralstab had intelligence that a minefield blocked the Gulf, with a gap for passage south of Nargen. Mischke received strict orders about where to lay mines in order to foul the approach to this gap. The barrier was to be laid northwards, from a position off the Russian coast, between ten to fifteen miles west of Nargen. The auxiliary minelayer *Deutschland* was to lay 200 mines, unobserved, at night. Nevertheless, Mischke was to expect a destroyer screen at the entrance to the Gulf.

A converted train ferry, with a maximum speed of just 16½ knots, was to advance to the doorstep of the Russian defensive position, on a short summer night. *Magdeburg* and *Augsburg*

(2018), pp.23–46; Сергей Евгеньевич Виноградов, *Броненосный крейсер "Рюрик". Флагман Балтийского флота* (Москва: Эксмо, 2010), p.100.

2 BA:RM92 *Freya, Friedrich Carl* KTB; Firle, *Ostsee*, p.75

Deutschland, a railway ferry on the Trelleborg to Sassnitz route, post-war. Wartime appearance virtually identical, with the addition of 8x8.8cm and 2x5cm guns. Rails for 420 mines, speed 16½ knots. (Public domain)

had much higher speed and could carry more than 200 mines themselves. Using the slow steamer reduced the chance of success and put all of the vessels taking part at risk. If spotted, *Deutschland* had no chance of escaping pursuit.

Essen had revised the watch at the entrance to the Gulf of Finland. His cruisers needed maintenance time to keep their machinery in order. Each Brigada now took turns mounting four-day patrols. One pair of cruisers patrolled towards Dagerort and between Hangö, Odenskhol'm and Cape Takkhona. The second pair was at high readiness to support them. The cruisers withdrew to Revel' each night and were replaced by a destroyer Divizion of 2nd Minnaya Diviziya.

On the 16th, Mischke's force left port, the cruisers and *V.186* from Memel, *V.25* and *V.26* from Danzig and *Deutschland*, commanded by Kapitänleutnant Franz Claassen, from Kiel. They rendezvoused at sea, east of Gotland, at 5am next morning. Mischke reviewed the orders with his commanders on *Augsburg*. The cruisers would precede *Deutschland* one mile to either side, one destroyer behind each ship, at the maximum sustainable speed, 16 knots. Mischke's misgivings about the plan resulted in additional verbal orders to Claassen: 'in the event of excessive enemy resistance that could delay the advance of the cruisers. In this case, laying the barrier before reaching the intended target is essential. [I will] Signal S.E.' He planned to reach the target area at 8pm, using the cruisers to push back any destroyers. This was just before sunset, allowing him to get a position fix, then lay the mines in the dusk and retire under cover of darkness. Laying the barrier too early in daylight could result in discovery, but navigating out of sight of land would make positions uncertain.

The force set off under clear skies and high visibility at 6am. They soon encountered and stopped two westbound neutral steamers. Their skippers confirmed that they were required to pass south of Nargen with a pilot and that they had seen several Russian cruisers off Odenskhol'm.

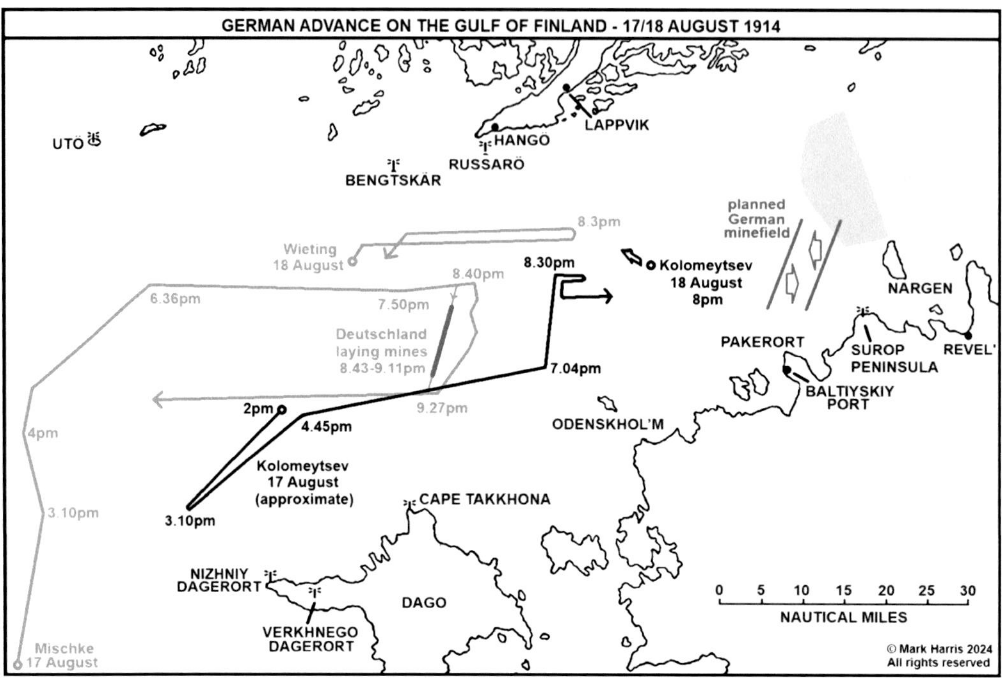

That afternoon, sustained full speed had resulted in *Deutschland*'s boilers clogging with ash. Claassen had started banking some boilers to clear the grates, temporarily limiting speed to 12 knots. The timing could not have been worse. At 3:05pm, Mischke's fears were realised: 'Two heavy clouds of smoke on the starboard beam.' Within minutes, 'Two ships were clearly visible, one with four funnels … smoke obviously coming from Russian warships.' Korvettenkapitän Franz Wieting, the senior destroyer officer, commanding *V.25*, identified two large destroyers. Mischke ordered the ships to clear for action. He turned away to break contact. Heavy Russian wireless traffic broke out. To his relief, the smoke receded, and the ships, 'steered at high speed into the Gulf of Finland.' Mischke stood down the combat alert and gave Claassen new orders. If the force encountered resistance, *Deutschland* was to lay the mines at the entrance to the Gulf between Russarö and Odenskhol'm lighthouses. Occasional smoke persisted to the east and became heavier as the ships headed into the Gulf, but no ships approached. By 7:50pm, Mischke was passing south of Bengtskär: 'The enemy forces are getting very close.' There was still almost three hours to the destination. Mischke ordered *Magdeburg* to fall in astern. As the sun set in the west, the enemy closed. Mischke ordered, 'Signal: "Clear for action!" Two Russian cruisers are clearly visible; to the northeast and southeast, heavy clouds of smoke are visible from several other warships, whose masts were clearly identified by the crow's nest [lookouts].' At 8:30pm, Mischke decided that it was impractical to continue. He ordered *Deutschland* to stop, to open up a gap and keep the minelayer concealed. *Augsburg* soon slowed to 10 knots. With battle apparently imminent, Mischke signalled, 'Destroyers assemble.' They formed battle formation to port. He wirelessed Claassen to head southwards and begin laying mines immediately on a line estimated to be directly between Hangö and Cape Takkhona, 40 miles short of Heinrich's orders. Mischke waited for the Russian response: 'The Russian ships are at a distance

Gromoboy, seen in 1911. Armed with 2x20.3cm and 11x15.2 cm guns in armoured casemates and an underwater 45cm torpedo tube on each side. Hull armour 15cm, speed only 18 knots. (Public domain)

of 16hm [8½ miles]. They approached quickly and turned north, then south. ... The minelayer moves off on the course ordered. *Augsburg* and *Magdeburg* turn 8 points [90°] to starboard to accept action.' This kept them between the Russians and *Deutschland*, which began laying mines, three miles to the west.

At 8:47pm, with dusk rapidly deepening: 'The head of the enemy line turned towards *Augsburg*. Closing fast.' *Magdeburg* identified a *Rossiya* and a *Bayan* class armoured cruiser. Their 20.3cm guns could open fire at any moment. Another vessel, resembling *Novik*, was in sight to the northeast and a large unidentified vessel on the horizon eastwards. The German 10.5cm guns would be ineffective against the armour on the armoured cruisers. At closer range, the Russians could also bring their numerous 15.2cm guns into action. Wieting described the scene: 'Behind us in the west the blood-red sun setting, in the east the stately enemy fleet, proudly flying its large war ensigns with the St. Andrew's cross at their tops, then our ships also with top ensigns, sailing in line... Breathless silence, not a shot fired.' Mischke edged away to starboard to open the range. The crisis passed. The Russian vessels turned away. Mischke turned west to rejoin *Deutschland* as soon as the last mine was laid. The growing darkness to the east swallowed up the Russian ships, which were last seen heading towards Revel'. Wieting could not believe their luck, assuming the enemy had, 'thought the minelayer with the high superstructure was a particularly powerful armoured cruiser.'

Mischke set course for the Swedish island of Gotska Sandön. The destroyers took station astern as insurance against any Russian vessels that might follow. Mischke wirelessed Heinrich, 'On the advance eastward, enemy encountered ... four ships and torpedo boats, distance [15,000m]. Therefore, mines were laid at square 94, 95, 96 delta ... Unnoticed by the enemy.' Mischke recorded that, 'After the formation had advanced so far into the Gulf of Finland, the minelayer ought not to return without having accomplished its objective. The position and the water depths ... were not unfavourable.'

Mischke had twice run into Kolomeytsev's flagship, *Gromoboy*, patrolling with *Admiral Makarov*. The Verkhnego Dagerort observation post had made an unusual report that morning: '33 smoke plumes visible on the horizon to the west, course northeast.' This could be a large fleet approaching the Gulf. At 9:28am, Essen ordered Kolomeytsev to head towards Nizhniy Dagerort, 'to investigate the meteorological observations.' *Bayan* and *Pallada* were ordered to break off coaling at Revel' and steam at full speed to a support position off Cape Takkhona, leaving around 2:15pm. A loose bearing on the port propeller shaft soon forced *Pallada* to return to harbour on one engine.

At 3:15pm, Kolomeytsev reached the position. Although the report had nothing to do with Mischke's force, in an incredible stroke of luck, it led him directly to them. Lookouts sighted the smoke and silhouettes of ships. Rather than close to make an identification, inexplicably, Kolomeytsev deemed his task completed. He ordered *Admiral Makarov* to open out to form a screen to the south, and then returned at a leisurely 10 knots towards the normal patrol line at the entrance to the Gulf of Finland. *Admiral Makarov* later rejoined astern. At 6:03pm, fleet command received his delayed sighting report, 'With certainty, two cruisers were in company during the day around Square 79.'

At 7pm, Kolomeytsev approached Odenskhol'm, and then turned north, intending to remain on the patrol line throughout the night. An hour later, lookouts spotted smoke, ahead to port. It approached. The silhouettes of German armoured cruisers came into view. Apparently outnumbered and outgunned, Kolomeytsev increased speed to 18 knots and turned away at 8:30pm. As the Germans did not pursue, he turned back to shadow them. At 8:52pm, his wireless reports of enemy in sight off Hangö, reached Fleet Headquarters. The delay was possibly due to jamming. As darkness closed in, he broke off and headed east. *Gromoboy* reported 'enemy cruisers in square 40 and 39 [south of Hangö] and several enemy destroyers [in] 40. Class *Roon*, *Prinz Heinrich* and four armoured reconnaissance cruisers.' The setting sun in lookout's eyes perhaps complicated identification. *Deutschland* had a similar profile to the armoured cruiser *Prinz Heinrich*. However, three ships and three destroyers had been mistaken for six ships and attendant destroyers. Closer inspection would have revealed the mistake. After confirming that the Germans had departed, once darkness fell, Kolomeytsev wirelessed that he was returning to Revel': 'due to the presence of [enemy] destroyers at sea.'

The contact reports had arrived too late to mount a response. *Bayan* had arrived off Odenskhol'm earlier. She may have been the ship seen by *Magdeburg* in this direction. The night defence destroyers were already coming out. Essen ordered all cruisers to be ready for sea next morning.

Mischke halted in the small hours of the 18th, southeast of Gotska Sandön, to hold a council of war with his commanders to decide on next steps. Meanwhile, *V.25* transferred some oil to *V.186* to extend her range. Mischke decided to attempt to draw the Russians across the new minefield, using his destroyers as bait. *Deutschland* was despatched to Danzig. At 8:30am, Mischke headed towards Bengtskär in blue skies and high visibility. At 1:15pm, he detached Wieting's three destroyers to bombard the lighthouse and observation post at Nizhniy Dagerort, aiming to provoke a response. Wieting writes, 'It was certainly not a heroic act! However, on the other hand, the morale effect on the enemy should not be underestimated, especially in the early days of the war … The Russians certainly would not have enjoyed the bombardment. I also used it as target practice for our gun commanders, who did their job brilliantly.' The destroyers fired 75 rounds each from around a mile offshore. Wieting rejoined the cruisers at 5pm, reporting rather optimistically that: 'The border guard station, wireless telegraph building and signal tower have been completely destroyed; the lighthouse has been destroyed.' Both *V.26* and *V.186* recorded that the lighthouse was intact. By 7pm, the force was six miles south of Bengtskär. It

V.186 class, in black paintwork used until mid-war. Armed with 8.8cm guns at bow and stern, 4x50cm deck torpedo tubes, two firing directly ahead and two on the centreline, speed 33½ knots. Note torpedo out of tube. The similar *V.25*'s were longer, with another 8.8cm gun amidships and twin centreline tubes, speed 36 knots. (Public domain)

was time to bait the trap. Mischke ordered Wieting to, 'Advance eastward in close order at high speed. Choose a course north of the [mine] barrier and, if possible, contact enemy ships. Do not allow yourself to be fired upon. Retire on the same course. Turn back by 9pm at the latest.' The destroyers headed east at 23 knots.

Magdeburg had stopped and questioned two neutral steamers just before arriving at Bengtskär. At 7:45pm, Habenicht got around to transmitting a summary of information obtained to *Augsburg*: 'Lappvik, 15-20 destroyers, coaling station and a two-funnel ship. Entrance to Lappvik mined. Outside there is apparently a [mine] barrier from Russarö lighthouse to a point [12 miles southeast]. Approximate line Pakerort-Lappvik today at 11am three armoured cruisers sighted.' The minefield news alarmed Mischke, as his destroyers were heading towards it. He immediately issued a recall and warned them. The cruisers set off at their best speed of 24 knots to meet them.

Wieting had sighted smoke 30 minutes after commencing his advance. He pushed on to a point between Lappvik and Odenskhol'm. The sun was close to setting:

> [I sighted] Two formations, each of three ships in line, steaming abreast, direction East by South. Ships of the northern formation each had four funnels, definitely identified as *Rossiya* type. The first ship in the southern formation had four funnels, two or three funnels on the other two, not identified with certainty. Two separate clouds of smoke in the direction of Lappvik. Between Pakerort and Odenskhol'm, five to six clouds of smoke, apparently destroyers. The northern squadron steered on a roughly northwest course at 7:55pm. [My own] Boats made an about turn to an opposite course. Southern squadron continued on a course roughly westward. In order to identify the ships of the southern squadron, we turned again to course North-Northeast. Northern squadron opened fire at 8:03pm at about 100hm [5½miles]

Wieting later recalled with irony that:

> … our 'brave enemy of yesterday' turned into line ahead, and, God only knows, we had surely overestimated the distance, as the two foremost ships suddenly opened a heavy fire on the three boats from every pore. The first shot hit 100 meters behind the stern of *V.25*, throwing up a high column of water. The other shots were not too far away. Since a single hit from the 20.3cm guns could destroy a boat, we now chose to retreat courageously, hidden behind a massive cloud of smoke of our own making.

His report left irony aside, stating that shells landed, 'about 400 to 800 meters behind the boat. Well adjusted for line. Steamed westward at utmost power. Made as much smoke as possible to obscure targeting.' His two newest destroyers were entirely oil fuelled and could rapidly generate a thick black smoke screen from their funnels, which the wind carried towards the Russian cruisers. *V.26* and *V.186* reported only 6–8 shell splashes. The mine warning arrived after the retreat was underway. Wieting met Mischke at 9pm.

Kolomeytsev's contact report had triggered a deluge of further reports on the previous evening and overnight. Searchlights were seen off Dago, Ezel' and the coast down to Libava. Powerful wireless signals were reported. The result was confusion and information overload, with Germans seemingly everywhere. Kolomeytsev steamed out with three cruisers to patrol in the morning, leaving *Pallada* in Revel'. In mid-afternoon, a series of signals arrived reporting German ships northwest of Dago. At 3.45pm: 'Nizh[niy] Dagerort, Ver[khnego] Dagerort report two enemy cruisers of the *Kolberg* [*Augsburg*] type continue to move northeast, distance 20 miles, three enemy destroyers approached Nizh[niy] Dagerort, distance four miles, and opened fire on the lighthouse.' The 8.8cm shells had no appreciable effect on the lighthouse, but they wrecked one building in the observation post and destroyed navigation markers. There were no casualties. After 15 minutes, they left. The observation post used the intact wireless to report them rejoining the cruisers before going out of sight.

Essen ordered Kolomeytsev to proceed at his own discretion with the available cruisers and destroyers. He ordered Kontr-Admiral Pëtr Leskov, with the three fastest cruisers of 2nd Brigada, *Rossiya*, *Bogatyr'* and *Oleg*, out of Revel' to reinforce him. The standby destroyers of 5th Divizion, Kapitan 1st Ranga Nikolay Tyrkov, were to proceed along the coast. The Germans were reported from Hangö moving east, off Bengtskär. Kolomeytsev ordered Leskov and Tyrkov to close his position and waited for them.

At 7:30pm, the smoke from Wieting's destroyers was in sight. Kolomeytsev turned to close and requested the despatch of another destroyer Divizion to support the attack. Leskov and Tyrkov were now nearby. Kolomeytsev detached Tyrkov to attempt to work round behind the Germans by advancing along the coast to the south.

At 8:03pm, Kolomeytsev turned north to bring his full broadside to bear and opened a deliberate fire with the 20.3cm guns of *Gromoboy* and *Admiral Makarov*. This was kept up for the next 30 minutes until Wieting went out of sight, at ranges estimated at 7–8½ miles, a very long range for such small targets moving at high speed. Kapitan 1st Ranga Aleksandr Veys, the commander of *Bayan*, the third in line, writes that:

> The shells fell short, and the enemy did not respond, therefore, since *Bayan* was last in line, I did not allow shooting, so as not to hurl our shells in vain, which I considered pointless and criminal. Later, I learned that this order of mine caused discontent among the crew, who apparently did not understand the purpose of my prohibition and considered me almost

> a traitor, spreading a rumour that my relative was on the *Augsburg*, which was among the enemy ships at the time, but they soon became convinced of the opposite.[3]

The armoured cruisers' broadside was only two guns each. This was problematic at long range, but had been unimportant with the short ranges prevalent when the ships were designed. A four-gun salvo was required to give a good chance of a straddle, with shells falling both short and over the target. This was essential for effective fire control. The Russian shooting was reasonably good at the brief target. Hits on small, fast moving destroyers were unlikely at long range. They were beyond the range of their own 8.8cm guns. Veys sums up his own frustration: 'Without making any attempt to get closer to the enemy, after shooting aimlessly for some time, the admiral turned back, signalling the destroyers present to attack the enemy… in my opinion, this attack was pointless and impossible during the day.'

The cruisers returned to Revel'. Tyrkov pressed on along the coast of Dago and on past Ezel'. Kolomeytsev wirelessed Tyrkov, 'Act independently. I have left the position and exchanged fire with enemy destroyers.' By 10pm, Tyrkov was off the west coast of Ezel' and reported, '5th Divizion at Fil'zand; I see an enemy cruiser in square 77.' Tyrkov possibly had Wieting in sight, but darkness ended the pursuit.

Mischke's plan was poor. The bombardment had wasted time. Given the late hour and the danger of torpedo attack in the darkness, Russian heavy units were hardly likely to pursue destroyers. Ironically, Kolomeytsev suspected that the destroyers could have laid mines before retiring. He requested sweeping south of Hangö as a precaution. The mines reported by the steamers restricted the immediate approaches to Hangö and Lappvik, posing no danger to Wieting, but it suited the Russians for steamer captains to believe a more extensive minefield was in place.

Kolomeytsev had thrown away two ideal opportunities to engage a greatly inferior force on the 17th. The low speed of *Deutschland* would have forced Mischke to either accept battle on unequal terms to protect her, or abandon her to her fate. Losses would have been inevitable. Kolomeytsev had been slow to respond on the 18th. An early, vigorous deployment of his force might have enabled him to cut Wieting off, although the difference in speed made this difficult. Kolomeytsev's suspicion of mines was well founded. Tyrkov did his best, but a blocking force needed to have already been in place to cut Wieting off.

Kolomeytsev had gained fame as commander of the destroyer *Buynyy*, rescuing the Russian Commander in Chief from his sinking flagship at the Battle of Tsushima in 1905. However, he was a controversial, socially awkward character. He had been at the centre of a serious breakdown in the relationship with his officers commanding *Slava* a few years earlier. After meeting with Kolomeytsev, Essen confided a damning criticism to his diary: '[He] created a bad impression. Before the war, he was always considered a selflessly brave man, but here I saw a man who had fallen into a state of mental decline. You cannot go into battle with such thinking.' However, Kolomeytsev retained his command.

Meanwhile, Mischke had detached his destroyers soon after leaving the area of Bengtskär, as they were short of fuel after the extended high-speed run. Mischke ordered Wieting to bombard the lighthouse at Bakgofen on the way back to Danzig. The destroyers stopped for *V.25* to top

3 Veys records *Pallada* as also being present firing ahead of him. He was writing some time later from memory and this appears to be an error.

up the oil tanks of *V.186* again during the night. She was partly coal fired and could not match the range of the other destroyers at speed. At 8am on the 19th, Wieting formed line ahead and headed directly inshore to the target. The destroyers approached to about a mile offshore. Mischke ordered each destroyer to fire, 'about 20 shells', but they took their turns firing 30 to 40 as they passed. *V.26* was last: '37 rounds were fired, from forward and aft guns only. The tower fell with the last shot.' The shelling demolished the upper part of the lighthouse tower, with severe damage to surrounding buildings. The only casualties were some horses in the stables. The border guards opened fire with their rifles, believing that the Germans were attempting a landing, but this went un-noticed. Wieting arrived in Danzig that evening. *V.186* was almost completely out of fuel, with only 1t of oil and 1t of coal left.

Mischke returned to Gotska Sandön for the night. Next morning, the cruisers headed back to Bengtskär, gathering intelligence on the way from two neutral steamers about the passage south of Nargen and Russian patrols. At 6pm, they reached Bengtskär and headed for the southern end of the new minefield. Mischke had plans to return and extend it southwards. He wanted to check that it was not too deep for mine moorings. The cruisers steamed at a leisurely 10 knots to Cape Takkhona taking frequent depth soundings. There was no sign of patrols, apart from some smoke to the northeast. With coal running low, Mischke departed at 8:10pm for Danzig, arriving 24 hours later.

Essen had ordered 2nd Divizion to sweep the area off Hangö that morning for mines. *Bogatyr'* was on the patrol line. Once sweeping completed, she advanced to investigate a false report of German warships off Bengtskär. Finding nothing, *Bogatyr'* returned to the patrol line. From 2pm, real sightings of *Magdeburg* and *Augsburg* from aerial reconnaissance and shore posts started to come in. A combination of the earlier false alarm, delayed transmission and German wireless interference seems to have delayed any response. Wieting's bombardment and a sighting off Steynort suggested that the Germans were withdrawing southwards. At 8pm, Cape Takkhona reported the two cruisers just two miles offshore. At dusk, destroyers of the Poludivizion and 1st Divizion finally arrived to investigate, just in time to see Mischke disappearing in the distance. Another chance for action had been lost.

Essen was frustrated with trying to divine a picture from the deluge of wireless reports. He ordered all cruisers to coal by 8am next morning. He would steam out and attack any German force at the entrance to the Gulf with his entire cruiser force. The cruisers of both Brigada (except the slow *Avrora*) left Revel' at mid-day with the destroyers of Kontr-Admiral Ivan Shtorre's 1st Minnaya Diviziya. Essen placed him in overall command, sidelining Kolomeytsev, and left Helsingfors in *Ryurik* to offer support, accompanied by *Avrora*. However, Mischke was long gone. After patrolling all day, Essen anchored his force off Baltiyskiy Port for the night, then returned to Revel' next day. Wireless reports continued to pour in over the next few days from coastal observers. By day, there were distant formations of ships and transports. By night, there were mysterious searchlights and aircraft. Aerial reconnaissance spotted nothing.

There were significant movements of real warships reported from the western Baltic. They were old battleships of 4th, 5th and 6th Geschwader and armoured cruisers, all activated from the reserves, working up in Kiel Bay prior to joining the fleet in the North Sea. Their destination was unknown, so they posed a distant threat. Essen was relieved that *Andrey Pervozvannyy* completed repairs and rejoined on the 19th.

The Russians had organised a system of escorting merchantmen through their waters past the Central Position. On the late afternoon of the 19th, a convoy of 13 steamers completed the passage from Sankt Peterburg. The pilot boat that had led them through released them. The vessels headed west independently. The Dutch steamer *Alice H.* was first through. It grew dark. Most of the crew were off watch, sleeping. Seaman Heeres was at the helm. At 1am, there was an explosion, shattering the forepart and blowing the hatch off the forward hold. Captain Jan Smit leapt up from his sleep in the chartroom; his bewildered wife Jansje emerged on deck barefoot, in her nightgown. He ordered all engines stopped. The crew swung the two lifeboats out and prepared them for launch. Half an hour later, there was another explosion, possibly two. The crew abandoned ship. The port lifeboat launched and got clear. Seaman Heeres watched the ship rear up and plunge to the bottom, pulling down the starboard lifeboat in the suction. Two survivors managed to cling to flotsam until the other lifeboat reached them. They searched in vain for two hours. The thirteen survivors set sail for the northern coast of Dago. Ten crew in the sunken boat, including the captain and his wife, had perished. *Deutschland*'s mines had struck. Shortly afterwards the Dutch steamer *Houtdijk* hit three mines and sank, with the loss of 14 crew. A lifeboat got away with 11 survivors. The first to lose their lives at sea in the Baltic had been Dutch civilians.[4]

Like Kolomeytsev, Nepenin had suspicions about potential minelaying. He had ordered the communications posts at the mouth of the Gulf of Finland to monitor the sea that night as the steamers passed. They had observed the explosions. Cross plots of the bearings indicated the position. After eight hours, the survivors of *Alice H.* reached shore. They confirmed the position. This was where the German ships had been manoeuvring on the 17th. The mine type was soon confirmed when one washed up on Moon Island. Minesweepers recovered intact samples for examination. This indicated that they were inferior to Russian designs, especially the inadequate mooring arrangements, which caused an ongoing navigational hazard.

Mischke's operation was heavily criticised by Heinrich: 'The barrier … is approximately 40–50 nautical miles further west than intended. Some of the mines are lying at very great depths (96m); the task was not executed in accordance with the instructions … [It] was intended to bar access to the passage south of Nargen and keep the Gulf of Finland clear for our forces …. right up to the Russian minefield.' Mischke came in for further criticism: 'The report … is incomplete. Times are missing. Also the reason why destroyers were not sent forward to attack the four ships is absent.' Later he added, 'it is clear that as early as 7:55pm … the enemy cruisers were moving eastward and were losing sight of him. Nevertheless, the laying continues instead of maintaining contact with the enemy and carrying the remaining mines as far east as possible.' However, Heinrich was responsible himself for a plan with fundamental flaws in its conception.

Mischke had achieved widespread alarm. Frustrated by the froth of misleading reports from border guards that resulted, Essen pushed for better management. However, the minefield blocked the entrance to the Gulf, convincing Essen that the Germans did not intend to attack the Central Position, the opposite of Heinrich's intention. In a report to the High Command on the 22nd, he sought permission to move to offensive activity, including minelaying off the German coast. He stressed that activity was necessary to maintain morale, which languished whilst passively waiting for the enemy. Leytenant Vasiliy Merkushov, the commander of submarine *Okun'*, provides an example. His comrades lobbied their commander, Kontr-Admiral Pavel Levitskiy, with options for more imaginative offensive use of their boats, as 'the brigade personnel are languishing in forced inaction.' He eventually agreed to put the ideas to Essen. He returned with

4 *Alice H.* (1912, 3,052 GRT), *Houtdijk* (1902 2,336 GRT).

agreement to move the patrol line and base west to Lappvik, and allow the best boat, *Akula*, to begin patrols off the favoured German target of Dagerort.

German activity against the coast of Dago and north of Libava had given Essen concerns about German designs on the Gulf of Riga. The islands were undefended, but vital for observation of the approaches to the Gulf. On his own initiative, he ordered 1st Minnaya Diviziya to construct batteries to defend the approaches to Moon Sound and pressed for troops to be sent to Dago and Ezel', to resist a landing attempt. He had similar concerns about Hangö and made arrangements with the local corps commander for troops to defend the port itself and the naval base at Lappvik. However, Essen received no agreement to offensive action outside the Gulf. The army were still fearful that risking the fleet could result in leaving the Gulf defenceless. The initiative remained with Heinrich.[5]

Ehler Behring. (Public domain)

Behring advances into the Gulf of Finland

Heinrich had already requested a second flag officer to support operations in the Baltic. Mischke had disappointed, but it was also impossible to command defence of the Western Baltic and offensive operations in the east at the same time. On 21 August, Kontreadmiral Ehler Behring was appointed with the rather odd title of 'Detachierter Admiral in der Ostsee', an admiral without portfolio. He would not have administrative command of any vessel, but would command those ships assigned to him by Heinrich on a strictly operational basis. Mischke would continue to command the Küstenschutzdivision. Behring had returned to duty after illness to serve in the war. His reputation was as a man of great courage, seamanship and experience. This had been

5 BA:RM60-II KTB, RM92 *Magdeburg*, RM99 Hilfskriegsschiffe der Kaiserlichen Marine, *Deutschland* KTB, RM93 *V.25*, *V.26*, *V.186* KTB; Firle, *Ostsee*, pp.61–76; РГАВМФ:Фонд 716, Опись 1, Дело 13, pp.3, 5, and Дело 15, p.25, Опись 2, Дело 18, pp.26, 63, Дело 22 pp.74–89; Киреев, *Траление*, pp.13–17, Рис.1; Эмме, 'походов', pp.154–162; Рафаил М. Мельников, *Броненосные крейсера типа «Адмирал Макаров» (1906-1925)* (Санкт-Петербург: М.А. Леонов, 2006), Дополнения; Р. Фирле, (Translated П.В. Гельмерсен and А.В. Тимонова, ed. Ю. Ралль,), *Война На Балтийском Море, Том I* (Москва: Государственное Военное Издательство Наркомата Обороны Союза Сср, 1937), p.107; Stichting Maritiem-Historische Databank <https://www.marhisdata.nl/>, accessed 19 August 2024; Василий Александрович Меркушов, (ed. В.В. Лобыцын,), *Записки подводника 1905–1915* (Москва: Согласие, 2004), pp.209–213; Franz Wieting, *Der Ostsee Krieg 1914–1918* (Berlin: Gustav Braunbeck G.m.b.H., 1918), pp.16–21; А.К. Вейс, 'На крейсере «Баян» в годы Первой мировой войны', *Гангут № 44* (2007), pp.34–55.

consistently demonstrated commanding destroyers, individually, then as half-flotilla and flotilla commander. He was a leader who could connect with all ranks and inspire their trust. He had a thirst for action and had little time for theory. Heinrich complemented his leadership abilities by assigning his own principal staff officer, Kapitänleutnant Hermann Gercke, to be Behring's Stabsoffizier. Gercke had a good reputation as a naval staff officer and had extensive knowledge of the Russian Navy and the peculiarities of the Baltic. *Augsburg* headed to Kiel for the handover.

The reserve cruisers and destroyers that made up Mischke's force were finally all available by 24 August. Heinrich directed that they should take turns working under Behring: 'So that the spirit of the crews does not wane in the long drawn out exclusively defensive work guarding and protecting the western and central Baltic Sea.' Heinrich was also keen to sustain activity in the eastern Baltic. On the evening of the 21st, *Amazone*, Korvettenkapitän Johannes Horn, with destroyer *S.94*, left Kiel, with orders to destroy the Libava coastal radio station at daybreak on the 23rd. They would then patrol between Gotland and the Russian coast. Despite searching at the reported position a few miles south of Libava for 1½ hours, from as little as 1,500m offshore, there was no trace of a radio station. It was destroyed in the mayhem on the first day of the war. Nepenin had been furious. A replacement was installed in the abandoned power plant of the naval port, with the wireless mast ingeniously concealed from the sea by the chimney. The observation post correctly identified and reported the German ships, assumed to be taking soundings for a subsequent landing.

Augsburg left Kiel with Behring on the evening of 23rd August. Heinrich had given him a verbal briefing rather than written orders for the next operation. He had the freedom to operate within quite broad written operational guidelines. Heinrich no doubt also trusted to Gercke to be his representative on the spot. The guidelines reiterated that until the crews received adequate training, cruisers were to avoid action with a superior enemy. Behring was to engage torpedo boats, destroyers and minelayers. However, for now there would be no more minelaying, due to a shortage of mines. Behring was allocated the five vessels in recent operations, plus *Amazone* and *U.3*. Heinrich wanted to test the potential for the use of submarines, but *U.3* had limited endurance, so *Panther* would act as a towing tender.

Behring ordered all ships under his command to rendezvous at sea off the southern point of Gotland at 8:15am on the 25th. *Panther*, towing *U.3*, would arrive later, at mid-day. At a council of war aboard *Augsburg*, Behring told his commanders that he was resolved to press forward for a fast moving attack with his fastest vessels. This would involve taking risk, since 'if we take no risks we can win no successes.' He issued the orders:

1. Reports of probable enemy destroyer outpost on the line Bengtskär–Takkhona. Probable cruiser support units in their rear. Enemy battleships anchor at night off Sveaborg (Helsingfors) or west of Nargen.
2. I intend to approach Bogskär during the afternoon of 25 August, eluding observation by the enemy as far as possible, and to advance from there into the Gulf of Finland during the night of 25–26 August.
3. The advance will commence at 7pm. Speed 15 knots. No smoke to be made after 10pm. I shall break through the northern wing of the Russian outpost line, if possible unobserved, to the north of our minefield.
4. Cruisers and destroyers are to attack with torpedoes on sighting enemy ships.

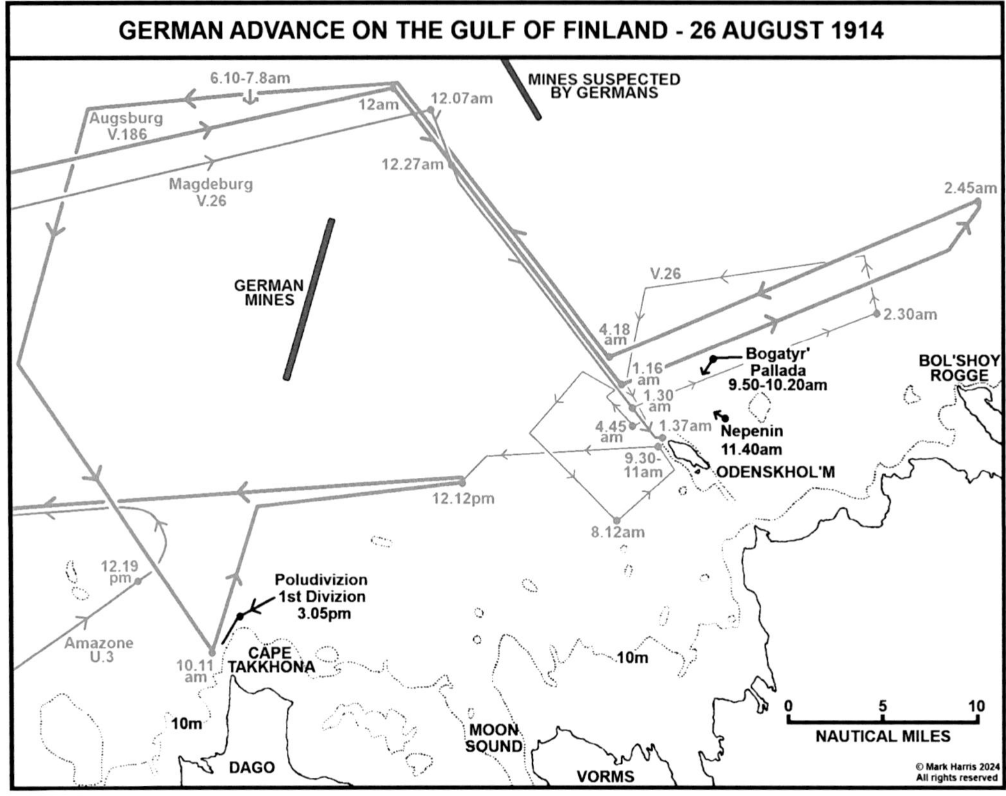

5. I shall turn back at about 2:45 a.m. on 26 August, and return at 18 knots. Ships will split up at 3:30am, or on signal. When returning: *Magdeburg* to the south, *Augsburg* to the north of our minefield.
6, During the retirement: Enemy destroyers sighted at or after dawn are to be chased and destroyed. Enemy destroyer outpost line to be rolled up.

The orders specified a regroup point northwest of Dagerort. In the event of bad weather or fog, operations would continue unless cancelled by wireless. The slower *Amazone* would remain off Gotland to pick up the tow of *U.3* from *Panther* and take her to the regroup point. The plan was to draw Russian forces into a submarine ambush there in the next phase. *Panther* would retire to Memel. Behring summoned the collier *Oberpräsident Delbrück* to Gotland, to enable continuous action by coaling at sea. *S.94* would stay to act as a wireless link to the collier. *V.25* would join them, having been delayed by dockyard maintenance at Danzig.

At 9:30am, Behring set off at 20 knots. *Augsburg* led with *V.186* astern, then *Magdeburg* with *V.26* astern. That afternoon, an astronomical sight coincided with the estimated position of *Augsburg*. As a result, Behring skipped the planned position fix at Bogskär, unknowingly avoiding observation from its clandestine occupants. It was still and misty approaching the Gulf of Finland. As night fell, patches of fog appeared. It would be easier to pass the destroyer outpost line. However, it just kept getting thicker. At 9:10pm, *Magdeburg* lost sight of *Augsburg*.

Kapitänleutnant Erich Dolberg, the First Officer, was on the bridge: 'The fog was so thick that the officer on lookout at the forecastle was occasionally invisible, even with binoculars.' Habenicht increased speed and altered course slightly to close a plume of smoke spotted from the crow's nest, but failed to regain touch. *Augsburg* continued to signal course changes. The force passed the German minefield. By midnight they were south of Russarö. *Augsburg* signalled the planned course change, towards Odenskhol'm. The Russian cruisers had frequently been seen by steamers between Odenskhol'm and Pakerort. *Magdeburg*'s navigator was constantly correcting his plot for variations in speed and course. He had to allow for *Augsburg* turning seven minutes before her message reached the bridge. The recent removal of the troubled centre turbine made his task even more difficult. The revised speed/engine revolution conversion tables contained approximations.

Magdeburg was sounding depth every 15 minutes approaching Odenskhol'm. When 34m was sounded, Habenicht concluded that unless a signal was received, he needed to turn eastwards at 1:30am to ensure that he cleared the island. At 1:30am, the wireless sprang to life. Habenicht waited for the signal to be decoded. Four minutes later it confirmed that *Augsburg* had turned east at 1:16am. Habenicht immediately ordered a matching course. Three minutes later, the helmsman reported *Magdeburg* steady on the new course. There was a thump forward. The ship then bumped five or six times and came to a grinding halt. Habenicht ordered full astern power. It had no effect. *Magdeburg* was aground on the enemy coast. Damage reports came in. Some of the double bottom compartments were flooded amidships. The ship had been pushed upwards 1.5m forward, with a slight list to port.

Habenicht raised the alarm with a wireless message and requested assistance. Behring ordered him to destroy the signal station on the island, to delay any report of the grounding, if necessary with a landing party. *Magdeburg* reports makes no mention of any attempt to do so, or of the order itself. A boat crew did go round the ship to sound the water depth.[6] The stern had not grounded. A tow cable was prepared. The crew worked feverishly to lighten the ship forward and shift weight aft. They jettisoned the forward anchors and moved ammunition boxes aft from the forward magazines. Washing and drinking water was pumped overboard. Coal was blown out with ash ejectors and thrown off the bow in bags. For each increasingly desperate attempt to go astern, all hands went aft. The ship refused to move.

At 2:30am, the crew heard rifle fire from the island, off the starboard bow. *Magdeburg* had been located. They returned fire with one of the ship's machine guns into the fog. After 10 minutes the shooting stopped. It would not be long before Russian ships arrived and the fog lifted. The situation called for desperate measures. The crew laboured through the night. All of the ammunition except for 10 ready rounds per gun and 60 rounds in the aft magazine went over the side. Any removable metal followed it; steel cabling, the coal rig, mine rails, armoured doors and bulkhead doors. A boat pulled the stern anchor aft and let it go. Three times the engines went full astern, as the capstan hauled on the anchor cable. *Magdeburg* would not move.

As the light grew, the rocky bottom was visible all around. More double bottom compartments had flooded. It was obvious that the ship had hit hard on the rocks on her port side. At 8:30am, a siren sounded to port. *Magdeburg* flashed her call sign, 'MB', into the fog. Nothing happened. Suddenly, an hour later, a searchlight stabbed through the fog. Shouts in German followed. To the intense relief of everyone, the bow of *V.26* loomed out of the murk, just 50m astern.

6 This is not in German reports. It is in Russian notes on the interrogation of *Magdeburg* prisoners.

Kapitänleutnant Diether, Baron Röder von Diersburg, the captain of *V.26*, had clung tenaciously to *Magdeburg* as the force advanced. At times, the fog was so thick that he could not see the bow from the bridge, just 20m away, let alone the ship ahead. He kept a close eye on the plot. At 1:23am, *Magdeburg* vanished again. Röder checked the chart. *V.26* was getting close to Odenskhol'm. Seven minutes later, he altered course to port to head east, along the pre-planned route of advance, concluding that *Magdeburg* must have already turned. Before the wireless operator could send a confirmation message, *Magdeburg* reported herself aground. Röder continued with the mission, advancing into the Gulf as per his orders until 2:45am. Another message from *Magdeburg* had confirmed her position, at the northern tip of Odenskhol'm. Röder headed back to his 1:30am position, and then advanced toward Odenskhol'm, swinging the searchlight and making recognition calls with the steam whistle and siren. At 3:40am, he received a wireless message: 'You were seen here five minutes ago.' Röder sounded. He was in deep water and concluded that he must be somewhere east of Odenskhol'm. He steered two long sounding lines looping round to the northwest, then southwest. Comparing the various depths to the chart he deduced that he was west of the middle of Odenskhol'm. He headed eastwards until he sounded 10m, and then followed this line north. Visibility was still only 200m, with occasional glimpses of land. The sound of activity carried through the air. *V.26* headed towards it and *Magdeburg* appeared. His effort won an accolade from Heinrich on his copy of Röder's report: 'First-class navigational performance!'

Röder took the towline from *Magdeburg*. The crew mustered aft. *Magdeburg* went full power astern and *V.26* took up the slack. Röder saw the result: 'When the destroyer went up to high speed, both bollards on [*Magdeburg*] gave way slightly and the shank bolt on *V.26* broke.' As the crews prepared to make a second attempt, the fog began to clear. The Russian signal station and lighthouse appeared, just 350m off to starboard. Habenicht ordered the starboard guns to open fire with the ready ammunition on deck, 120 rounds. Dolberg reported that 'the signal house set on fire and the lighthouse [was] riddled with holes from top to bottom.' The firing destroyed some wooden buildings, but the lighthouse suffered only minor damage and the wireless station was unharmed. Meanwhile, Röder recorded an increasingly desperate situation: 'During the second towing attempt, the current coming from the east pushed [*V.26*] so far around that it was dragged abeam, but the ship did not move. At this time, numerous strong Russian signals were reported from various senders by the wireless room and these must have been in close proximity.' *Magdeburg* had delayed action explosive scuttling charges forward and aft. Dolberg continues: 'In order to ensure that the ship did not fall into enemy hands, evacuation and demolition work was commenced. I had agreed with the T[orpedo] O[fficer] [Kapitänleutnant Waldemar von Münch] that after the ship had been evacuated, the explosive cartridges attached to the powerful [war]heads in the torpedo room would be lit, the man would run on board the boat and the boat would be cast off.' The signal books went into the boiler fires, except for two copies and the signal encryption cypher still in use. It was 10:25am. Habenicht abandoned a third towing attempt, ordering 'Engineering personnel to go to the boat [*V.26*].' Röder was signalled to drop the towline and come alongside.

The Russians had not been idle. Dense fog had plagued the Gulf for three days, although considerable German wireless activity continued to be detected. The frequent use made of the wireless in all of the German operations had been noticeable and appeared to be attempts to jam Russian wavelengths. The fog had delayed plans to send minesweepers to explore the position of the German minefield. It was too thick for patrolling to be of use. The duty cruisers, *Pallada* and

Bogatyr', armed with twin 15.2cm turrets fore and aft, plus 4x15.2cm, 6x7.5cm guns and an underwater 38.1cm torpedo tube on each side. Armour limited to main gun positions and lower deck. Speed 23 knots, the fastest Russian cruiser. (Public domain)

Pallada, July 1912. The two turrets have a single 20.3cm gun, with 4x15.2cm and 10x7.5cm guns, plus an underwater 45cm torpedo tube on each side. 17.5cm hull armour, speed 21 knots. *Bayan* was almost identical. (Public domain)

Bogatyr', were anchored off Baltiyskiy Port. The 1st Divizion of destroyers had gone out that night, but dropped anchor off Lappvik in the fog. As soon as *Magdeburg* slammed noisily into the island, the observation post at Odenskhol'm reported that a German ship was aground two cables (370m) away. Conversations in German carried through the fog, as well as the engines. The post sent regular updates. A second vessel had approached, then: 'The enemy has lowered boats, probably for sounding, and is disembarking troops from the destroyer'. Nepenin, who commanded all of the communications posts, spoke to the post commander and ordered him to fire on the boats.

Starshiy Leytenant Count Mikhail Gamil'ton was First Officer of *Leytenant Burakov,* one of the destroyers under Nepenin's command, kept at readiness for urgent communications. He writes that, '[Nepenin] called … and related that the post on Odenskhol'm reported … German speech and believed that some ship had run aground on the island. [Nepenin] added that he reported this to the Fleet Commander's Headquarters, but that they were sceptical … [He] ordered us to raise steam and be ready to go to sea.' Nepenin arrived an hour or two later on another of his boats, the smaller *R'yanyy*: '[He] said that since Headquarters was not doing anything, he decided to go to Odenskhol'm himself to find out what was going on.' At 4:20am, *Leytenant Burakov* and *R'yanyy* left Revel' through thick fog. Gamil'ton writes that Nepenin had been told that no Russian ships were at sea, but 1st Divizion had been ordered to the scene. At 3:50am, Essen also ordered *Bogatyr'* and *Pallada*, 'as soon as the fog allows, to proceed immediately to Odenskhol'm, where an enemy ship has run aground.' At 4:30am, *Pallada* intercepted a report from 1st Divizion that they had reached Odenskhol'm.

At 7:15am, the fog began to clear at Baltiyskiy Port. *Bogatyr'*, Kapitan 1st Ranga Evgeniy Krinitskiy, the senior officer, got underway, followed by Kapitan 1st Ranga Sergey Magnus with *Pallada*. The cruisers crept forward at just 7 knots. At 8:25am, *Bogatyr'* confirmed her position

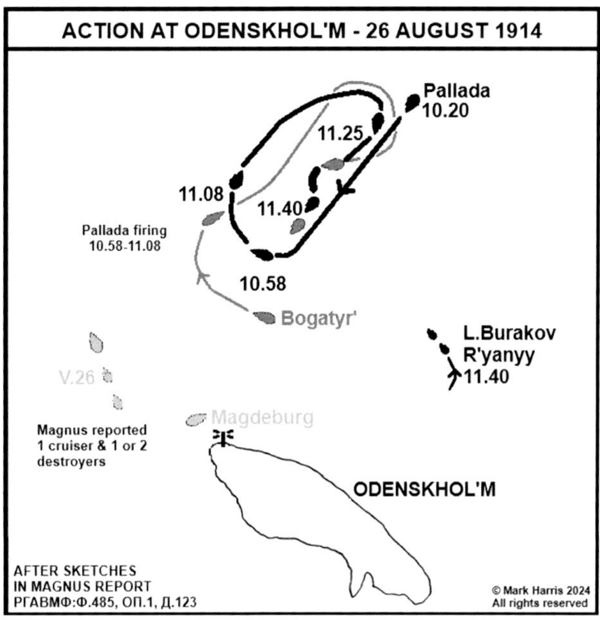

by spotting the flashes of the Pakerort lighthouse and was able to set course for Odenskhol'm, increasing to 14 knots. A message soon came in: 'enemy 4-funnel cruiser and destroyers aground near Odenskhol'm Island.' As they neared the island, Krinitskiy ordered Magnus to take station to starboard. *Pallada* lost sight of *Bogatyr'* in thick fog. Magnus tried to keep his distance by shadowing her wake, but soon heard her blowing off steam and concluded that she had stopped. He followed suit. Krinitskiy did not wish to approach Odenskhol'm in the thick fog, fearing that 1st Divizion were nearby and might attack his cruisers, so he anchored five miles northeast of the island.

At 10:20am, frequent gun salvos suddenly broke out in the direction of the island. Krinitskiy assumed that 1st Divizion had engaged and moved forward to support, wirelessing *Pallada* to follow. Magnus tried to keep station to starboard to avoid crossing into the path of *Bogatyr'*. He sounded constantly, wary of the 6.7m draught of his ship. Both cruisers used their sirens to sound out their call signs as they advanced. *Pallada* intercepted a wireless message for 1st Divizion: 'assemble at Bol'shoy Rogge Island.' This was to the east, off Baltiyskiy Port. A distant siren sounded eastwards, with the call sign of *Emir Bukharskiy* of 1st Divizion. Magnus concluded that 1st Divizion was retreating. The firing ahead ceased.

At 10.58am, as the fog began to thin, Odenskhol'm appeared ahead. A large destroyer was attempting to pull a cruiser off the shore. Krinitskiy turned to starboard to bring his broadside of 8x15.2cm and 6x7.5cm guns to bear. Both batteries opened fire at an estimated range of 14 cables (2,500m), concentrating on the larger of the two targets, but quickly switching to *V.26* as she pulled away. The Germans replied with rapid salvos, but the shells fell widely, both long and short. A few burst close, causing fragments to strike the ship, but they caused no significant damage or casualties.

Shortly afterwards, *Pallada* came into sight and turned up ahead of *Bogatyr'*. Magnus ordered full speed ahead. It was impossible to make out the target type or numbers clearly from the bridge or get a range from the rangefinders. The fog was thicker at superstructure level. The conning tower took over fire control. The officers on the lower decks later reported a cruiser and either one or two destroyers pulling away from the stranded cruiser. *Pallada* opened fire at an estimated range of 20 cables (3,700m) with her broadside of 2x20.3cm, 4x15.2cm and 10x7.5cm, although the latter fired only a few shells.

The cordite hung heavily in the damp air. At times, targets disappeared completely. The gunlayers on both ships often found it impossible to see anything through their sights and simply fired as best they could. It was almost impossible to spot the fall of shot. A few enemy shells fell short of *Pallada*, but none hit. Magnus told his torpedo officer to fire if he got a chance. Six minutes after opening fire Leytenant Izmaylov had a solution on the torpedo director. He ordered the port 45cm underwater tube to fire.

Bogatyr' now spotted two torpedoes in the water. Krinitskiy ordered a turn to starboard to avoid them, inevitably opening the range and interrupting fire. A third was then sighted and *Bogatyr'* turned again. The enemy disappeared in the fog a few minutes later. *Bogatyr'* and *Pallada* ceased fire. The action had lasted ten to fifteen minutes. When last seen from *Pallada*, the lead enemy vessel had been ploughing through the water at speed with a high bow wave, with flames visible at the stern.

The approach of the two Russian cruisers ended the orderly evacuation of *Magdeburg*. Just three minutes after the order, *V.26* was 25–30m away, creeping forward to come alongside. Münch approached Dolberg and informed him that Habenicht, who was 'nowhere to be seen', had already ordered the fuzes on the charges in the torpedo room to be set off. Presumably, the sirens sounding the imminent arrival of the Russian ships was responsible. There were scant minutes remaining before the ship exploded. Dolberg immediately ordered, 'All hands aft.' He called for three cheers for the ship and another three for the Kaiser, then, '"All hands abandon ship; launch both cutters"... The men jumped overboard with hammocks and both empty and unopened wooden cordite boxes [to help them stay afloat]'. Röder witnessed the result:

> Just as I intended to dock alongside *Magdeburg*, a large part of the crew lined up at the ship's bulwark jumped overboard and tried to reach *V.26* by swimming [100–150 men]. This prevented me from coming alongside. I then had the people swimming rescued and had life jackets, rescue buoys and other floating objects thrown to them. I also had the cutter and dinghy launched. From the *Magdeburg*, on which there were probably still 150 crew, I was hailed: 'Go back, the ship is about to blow up.' This call immediately prompted me to place the bow alongside to rescue the crew still on board, regardless of the 30–40 people still in the water. At that moment, the explosive charge in the forecastle detonated. The entire forecastle up to about the second funnel was completely torn apart ...

Magdeburg's Doctor was still aboard:

> ... then suddenly, without anyone being aware of what was going on, there is a huge explosion – our forecastle flies into the air. The debris kills many people. I jump overboard with my sick and men in full uniform. Everyone else that can swim follows. We make a detour to get out of the crowd. All of my staff and my sick are rescued aboard the destroyer. Two boats are launched, one capsizes! Many drown. Insane tumult.

The three top-secret signal documents were still in use. The men responsible for them were to take them to *V.26* when the order came to evacuate. A subsequent investigation documented the chaotic result. Funken-Telegraphie (F-T)-Obermaat Wilhelm Neuhaus grabbed the signal book from the wireless room and F-T-Maat Kiehnert grabbed the cypher key tables. Panicking crew pushed Kiehnert into the water. When he came to the surface, he realized that he had lost the cypher tables. Neuhaus was last seen in the water. F-T-Maat Szillat took the signal book on the bridge. He was in the crowd on the aft deck when he heard the order to abandon ship. He hurled the book towards the stern, reporting that it fell about 5m from the ship and sank immediately. Other important documents were left to chance. Steuermann Wilhelm Jeske took some of the secret charts from the map table drawers, but drowned after jumping overboard. Signalmaat Wilhelm Steinthal grabbed another handful, but lost them in the water when another man jumped on top of him. Some charts had almost certainly been left in the charthouse. The bag containing the War Diary was last seen on deck, waiting to be thrown overboard.

Despite being warned that the stern was now also about to explode, Röder pushed right up to *Magdeburg* to allow those still on deck to drop directly onto the destroyer. Habenicht had appeared, Dolberg, 'heard the commander ask the Torpedomaschinisten if there was any damage aft, to which he replied "no".' This implies that Habenicht had expected the aft charges to explode, which would have resulted in complete carnage. Dolberg now had all of the gun breeches and sights thrown overboard, along with *Magdeburg*'s two rangefinders, once they had been smashed. Having confirmed that the valves below had been opened to flood the hull, he reported to Habenicht, '"All hands have left the ship, would you please go to the boat, Captain?" The answer I received was: "One moment!".' The cutter in question began pulling away, so Dolberg swung down into it on a rope hanging from one of the guns. Röder pulled *V.26* back to pick up some men still in the water. His boats were still at work pulling men from the water. Dolberg had boarded. As he was asking Röder to send his dinghy back for Habenicht and some men clinging to the propeller guards of *Magdeburg*, Röder spotted a three-funnel cruiser emerging from the fog about 2,000m away. Perhaps it was *Augsburg*. Nevertheless, Röder ordered the three 8.8cm guns to prepare for action. This was extremely difficult with decks crowded with men from *Magdeburg*. It was impossible to bring the torpedo tubes into action. When a larger, four-funnelled cruiser also loomed out of the fog, any hope that they were not Russian vanished. Röder ordered the guns to open rapid, independent fire. Crewmen from *Magdeburg* began helping, but, 'the people on deck prevented the guns from being turned, the gun crews could not get to the guns, and the people who initially tried to turn them mostly did not know anything about the guns.' Röder now saw another smaller three-funnel cruiser away to port. The Russians opened fire. *V.26* was in a desperate position. Röder had to make a slow tight turn to allow the boat to head west into deeper water. This made *V.26* a sitting duck: 'One cruiser seems to have got into its stride very quickly, because its salvos covered the boat.' Almost immediately, a shell smashed the wireless aerials aloft. As the boat swung round, Röder ordered, '"clear guns" "fire torpedoes".' As *V.26* completed the turn, he accelerated to 30 knots. Röder had to leave his boats behind. A shell passed close over the stern and took eight men with it. *Magdeburg*'s Doctor had a lucky escape: 'A splinter … hits my left leg; I slip and fall overboard, but luckily I catch the propeller guard and hold on for about a quarter of an hour, most of the time the waves go over my head.' As *V.26* sped away, shells continued to crash round. Röder continues:

> Suddenly I saw a thick cloud of steam coming out of the rear (port) turbine room and realized that [it] had been hit. The crew abandoned the turbine, the port turbine stopped – the escaping steam made it impossible to stay at the rear twin-[torpedo] tube, so that the

> turning outboard of the twin-tube, which had begun in the meantime, had to be stopped. The front twin-tube could not turn either.
>
> As *V 26* was travelling at a speed of about 23 knots with the starboard turbine, the distance to the cruisers was increasing. I therefore decided to give up the intended torpedo shot, especially as I did not know how long I could continue to run at high speed with the great loss of steam, and headed away on a westerly course. The enemy cruisers continued to follow, and could still be seen indistinctly for a long time after the fog cleared. The firing stopped on both sides at a distance of about 3,500–4,000m. The duration of the battle is uncertain. I estimate that it lasted about 15 minutes.

Fragments identified the hit as a 15.2cm shell. It came through the starboard side just above the waterline and exploded. It destroyed two cabins, the officer's mess amidships and damaged cabins on the far side of the boat. Fragments holed the deck above and the bulkhead to the aft engine room, piercing the exhaust steam pipes, which put the turbine out of action. The damage interrupted the ammunition supply from the aft magazine, forcing the centre and aft guns to cease fire temporarily. The officer's mess was being used to treat seriously injured men from *Magdeburg*. The explosion killed *V.26*'s medical officer, along with seven *Magdeburg* crewmen, including her Navigating Officer. One of the aft torpedoes was damaged. After the action, there was concern that these would explode because of heat from the escaping steam. Both were fired to jettison them. Splinters from near misses and at least one 7.5cm round hit. A *Magdeburg* crewman found it unexploded and threw it overboard.

In the circumstances, fire control had been impossible. Both sides apparently saw phantom ships in the drifting smoke and fog. *V.26* fired 106 rounds. Röder reported several hits and an ammunition fire. Despite the short range to the big Russian cruisers, these claims were mistaken. *Pallada* fired 16x20.3cm, 53x15.2cm and 18x7.5cm shells. *Bogatyr'* fired 167x15.2cm and an unknown number of 7.5cm. *V.26* was a small target, but the extensive damage from one 15.2cm shell explosion demonstrated how vulnerable destroyers were to medium calibre shells. She had survived largely thanks to her high speed, helped by the cloud of escaping steam. Even on one turbine, *V.26* was at least as fast as *Bogatyr'* and faster than *Pallada*. Even so, it had been a narrow escape. Whether *Bogatyr'* had spotted *Pallada*'s torpedo or imagined the tracks is unclear. Whilst her turn away had opened the range, *V.26* was already going out of sight.

With the action over, *Pallada* joined astern of *Bogatyr'*. The cruisers turned back towards Odenskhol'm. At 11:40am, two shapes began appearing out of the fog to the east, about 3,000m away. They were destroyers. They turned side on. The leading destroyer fired two torpedoes. The cruisers opened fire and immediately turned away to starboard. They ceased fire after four salvos. The destroyers were Russian. It was *Leytenant Burakov* and *R'yanyy.* Nepenin had arrived in the area and been drawn by the sound of gunfire. The destroyer reports claimed that the cruisers opened fire first, resulting in torpedoes being fired by *Leytenant Burakov*, before the cruisers were recognised to be Russian. One shell from *Pallada* burst just a few metres from *Burakov.*

With the mystery vessels identities clarified, Krinitskiy approached *Magdeburg* and the cruisers began firing as she came into sight at 11:50am. There was no reply, so fire ceased after two salvos. Gamil'ton takes up the story:

> Finally, we approached *Bogatyr'*... After a series of unprintable greetings and reproaches between the commander of *Bogatyr'* and [Nepenin], he reported that *Magdeburg* had just

ceased fire and ordered [Nepenin] to approach *Magdeburg* as close as possible, and if it began to fire, to move aside and he would open fire again ... We approached two cable lengths [400m], and stopped. There was no one on deck, which, however, was not surprising, since all the guns of *Magdeburg* were behind shields and people could be behind them. Our torpedo tubes were aimed at *Magdeburg*.

Seeing that there was no movement ... [Nepenin] ... sent me to the cruiser. The whaler was lowered, and four rowers with rifles got aboard. I decided to take the command revolver, put the cord around my neck and stuck the revolver in my trousers. We took a signalman with signal flags and the St. Andrew's flag [the Russian naval ensign] just in case... As I approached *Magdeburg*, I saw a storm ladder hanging from the stern and went up to it... When my head was level with the deck, I saw Germans running towards me – about 6 or 7 men. I decided to pick up my revolver, but while I was climbing the storm ladder, it fell out of my trousers and dangled on a long cord between my legs. I yanked the cord, took the revolver in my hand and climbed up onto the deck.

The Germans surrounded me, but they were all unarmed. Not knowing German well enough ... I asked if anyone spoke English or French. The quartermaster answered me [in French], explaining that he was an Alsatian. He told me what happened to them ... Only the sailors who surrounded me remained on *Magdeburg*, as the rest jumped into the water and headed for Odenskhol'm. ... I told him that I would now go and lower the German flag and that we would raise the Russian one, to which he replied: 'This is war, Mr. Lieutenant.'... We cut the halyards, rolled up the German flag and raised the St. Andrew's flag. The crews of our destroyers ... shouted "Ura"... I told the quartermaster that ... we would all go to the *Burakov* ... [he] reported to me that they still had a captain who was sitting in his cabin. I ordered him to go and announce me to him, whilst I myself stood on the deck, poking various objects with my feet, and suddenly under a package with shirts, I noticed a signal code book. Not wanting to attract the attention of the Germans, I began to push it with my feet to the side, and when our whaler was under us, I threw it into the whaler...

I entered the cabin and introduced myself to the captain, who handed me his sword. I asked him to put it on, since he was still on his ship and that he should give it to my superiors on the destroyer. He was very touched by this gesture and shook my hand again. I noticed that what I said to him in English or French, he barely understood, and my German was very weak. After thinking, I finally uttered a phrase that, despite the tragic moment, made him smile. I said, 'Wollen sie nach Torpedo gehen?'[7] This prospect (of riding on a torpedo) did not appeal to him, of course, but he only asked me if he could take some personal belongings with him... He looked around the cabin, opened his American bureau, then slammed it shut, waved his hand and said he was ready.

The men who had reached Odenskhol'm had been rounded up at gunpoint by the eight staff of the observation post, who were unscathed despite everything fired in their direction. The destroyers' boats collected them. The prisoners included one officer and two men from *V.26*'s boat. There were 57 from *Magdeburg*: Habenicht, his adjutant and 55 men. Habenicht had demonstrated an erratic approach to command, leaving an impression of being out of his depth and overwhelmed by events. The most important consequence was the seizure of the top-secret

7 Crudely, 'Will you go to the torpedo?' He meant torpedoboot.

signal book, which had gone unnoticed. Essen ordered *Leytenant Burakov* and *R'yanyy* to take the prisoners back to Baltiyskiy Port to hand them over to the army.

There were 335 survivors crammed aboard *V.26*, including seven severely wounded and 10 with lesser injuries. *Magdeburg* had 16 dead, and at the final count 17 missing, presumed dead. Another crewman died in hospital a few weeks later. *V.26* had two dead and one wounded. After steaming westward for an hour, around mid-day the shape of a cruiser emerged from the fog off the port bow.

Behring had been able to do nothing for *Magdeburg* during the night. He proceeded as planned, heading east to a position off Baltiyskiy Port at 1:45am. He then turned back towards Odenskhol'm. Dense fog concealed everything. On arrival near Odenskhol'm the fog was thicker than ever. *Augsburg*'s position was uncertain. Behring notified *Magdeburg*, 'Will wait for [weather] to clear up west of our minefield, then provide assistance.'

Augsburg headed to a position off Bengtskär, on the supposed Russian patrol line, but found nothing to attack. The fog persisted, so he anchored. He decided to call up *Amazone* and *U.3* from Dagerort to join him, then move in and assist *Magdeburg*. There was now more bad news. A turbine on *V.186* broke down. *Augsburg* had to transfer water to her boilers to avoid a complete breakdown. She was given permission to return to Danzig. By 7am, Behring tired of waiting. He headed south to locate the cliffs at Cape Takkhona. They proved elusive, but by sounding, and comparing to Mischke's records, *Augsburg* confirmed her position near the cliffs, then set course for Odenskhol'm. At 10:30am, gunfire broke out ahead. *Augsburg* cleared for action. She passed through a thunderstorm and heavy rain. On emerging, the fog began to clear. *Augsburg* accelerated to full speed. *V.26* appeared out of the murk ahead, with her decks crowded with men.

Behring halted at 11:45am. Röder, 'went alongside and delivered the crew and the wounded of S.M.S. *Magdeburg*.' Behring received the news of her destruction. Meanwhile, the sun broke through. The skies cleared from the west. *Augsburg*'s lookouts were alert: 'The sighting of three destroyers is reported. *V.26* casts off. *Augsburg* heads toward a cloud of smoke, which disappears again.' Röder was alarmed that, 'the Russian cruisers were sighted on the horizon.' *Augsburg* was in no condition to fight with decks crowded with survivors and a severely damaged destroyer in company. Behring turned round and headed at full speed to meet *Amazone*, at a rendezvous well out to sea to the west, with *V.26* following. Loss of steam quickly forced *Augsburg* to stop and take her in tow. *Amazone*, with *U.3* in company, soon came in sight. *V.25* arrived that afternoon. *V.186* had stuck with *Augsburg* and managed to fix the turbine problem.

Behring was full of fight: 'Consideration given to whether it seems possible and right to continue operations … despite the failure of the 25th and this question is decided in the affirmative. A message to that effect sent to [Heinrich]. [He] announces that 4th Geschwader, *Roon*, *Prinz Adalbert*, going to sea today to cover [my operations.] … thus receiving the support they so desperately need.' *V.186* received oil from *V.26*, then coal from *Augsburg*, which took *U.3* in tow for the night. Wieting later recalled his first words at the briefing for the next day's mission: 'We have lost *Magdeburg*, but that should not prevent us from looking confidently into the future.' The rescued crew transferred to the slower *Amazone*, which was detached back to Danzig at 6:30pm with the badly damaged *V.26*. The destroyer then headed to Stettin for repair.

Meanwhile, Essen had been mobilising reinforcements. At 9:30am, he despatched *Rossiya* and *Oleg* from Revel', then followed in *Ryurik* an hour later, screened by Shtorre, with the destroyers of the Poludivizion and 2nd Divizion. As they approached Baltiyskiy Port, Shtorre encountered 1st

Divizion. They had failed to find Odenskhol'm, and got lost in the fog. After realising where they were, they were regrouping. They fell in with Shtorre. As the force approached Odenskhol'm at mid-day the fog finally began to lift, although patches persisted. Cape Takkhona had already sighted *Augsburg*, but the report arrived too late. A report was received from Dagerort that a German cruiser had been sighted heading northeast that morning. This was *Amazone*. Essen ordered Shtorre to attack the enemy with the Poludivizion and 1st Divizion, advancing to Cape Takkhona, then Dagerort. *Augsburg* glimpsed his destroyers, but their tracks then diverged. Shtorre did not sight Behring. He reached Dagerort at 5pm, but the observation post reported seeing nothing more.

If *Bogatyr'* and *Pallada* had attempted to keep in touch with *V.26*, there is a possibility that they would have caught up with her whilst she was transferring crew to *Augsburg*, as the German Official History suggests. However, this is an exercise in hindsight. Röder assumed they were pursuing, having probably seen the steam they were blowing off, after stopping near *Magdeburg*. Once Behring headed out to sea at full speed, there was no chance of a further encounter. At 2pm Essen's cruisers arrived at Odenskhol'm. *Bogatyr'*, *Pallada* and *Oleg* were despatched to establish a patrol line to the north, whilst *Rossiya* guarded *Magdeburg*. The staff from *Ryurik* inspected the prize. They arranged for a thorough search of the ship next day, and for divers to search the water around it and assess the scope for salvage. That night, Essen reinforced the watch, with 6th Divizion on the outpost line and 4th Divizion guarding Odenskhol'm. The Poludivizion remained off Cape Takkhona. The cruisers returned to Revel'.

Heinrich received the news that *Magdeburg* was stranded on Odenskhol'm at 5:20am. He wrote that, '... there seems little prospect of preserving *Magdeburg* unless the ship is towed off quickly. Regardless, the appearance of a larger force off the Gulf of Finland should make it clear to the Russians that we are not abandoning our operations because of the loss of a light cruiser.' Heinrich summoned Vice-Admiral Ehrhard Schmidt, commanding the seven old battleships of 4th Geschwader, and Kontreadmiral Hubert von Rebeur-Paschwitz, commanding the armoured cruisers *Roon* and *Prinz Adalbert* of 3rd Aufklärungsgruppe, to a meeting at the castle to formulate a response. These Hochseeflotte units were working up at Kiel. Only then did he contact their commander, Ingenohl, who agreed that they, 'be made available until the *Magdeburg* matter was resolved.' Schmidt thought that his force was too vulnerable. He approached Ingenohl for light cruisers and destroyers to screen it. Pohl was with the Kaiser at General Headquarters, and now chipped in to back the request. He ordered Ingenohl to send two light cruisers and a destroyer flotilla through the Kaiser Wilhelm Canal to support Schmidt.

Heinrich considered the reinforcement unnecessary. He ordered Schmidt's force, 'to hasten to the Gulf of Finland, show itself on the Russian coast and ... hold the Russians behind the Nargen–Porkala-Udd barrier.' Schmidt's understanding was that: 'The primary object of our advance was to protect the *Magdeburg* whilst being towed off.' Heinrich assigned the light cruiser *Gazelle, S.91*, *S.93* and *S.94* to act under his orders. *Gazelle* left Swinemünde to rendezvous at sea to scout for the armoured cruisers. The destroyers needed to coal at Sassnitz before joining 4th Geschwader. 3rd Aufklärungsgruppe headed out as soon as it was ready at 11am. The battleships needed to coal and followed at 2:15pm. They would not arrive in the Gulf until the afternoon of the 28th. With his forces heading east, Heinrich was concerned about the defence of Kiel Bay. The Hochseeflotte's four old training cruisers of 5th Aufklärungsgruppe, (*Hansa*, *Hertha*, *Vineta* and *Victoria Louise*) were working up at Kiel. Heinrich cut across the chain of command and requested their commander, Kontreadmiral Gisbert Jasper, to patrol the Fehmarn Belt whilst the operation was underway. Jasper complied with the Grossadmiral's 'request'.

At 4pm, the message arrived from Behring that *Magdeburg* had been abandoned. Ingenohl's reinforcements had not yet entered the Kaiser Wilhelm Canal. He asked Heinrich's permission to return them, to which he agreed, as, 'it is possible to carry out the task at hand with the forces available.' Heinrich then wirelessed Schmidt: 'Consider demonstration against Russians to be even more essential in the new situation.' Schmidt was concerned that the Russians would now mine the approach and requested minesweeping support. Heinrich had none to offer and responded, 'Operations restricted to showing the flag and disturbing the coast near Vindava and Dagerort Lighthouse should suffice.' When Pohl realised what was going on, he was alarmed at the despatch of an inadequately screened squadron to such an advanced position, with no clear objective. He had no direct authority over Heinrich. He requested an audience with the Kaiser. He then wirelessed, 'His Majesty commands that Hochsee forces sent to help *Magdeburg* are to be recalled if the safety of *Augsburg*, *Amazone*, etc., permits.' Heinrich disagreed. He discussed objecting with his staff, but concluded that the, 'categorical wording', left him no choice. He recalled Schmidt at 1:40am. The armoured cruisers were south of the Swedish island of Öland and the battleships were west of Bornholm. Heinrich's plan was an exercise in flag waving hubris, which would have put a squadron of largely unescorted, slow, second-class vessels with raw crews on the doorstep of the entire Russian fleet, hundreds of miles from support.

That evening Nepenin presented the ensign taken from *Magdeburg* to Essen. Gamil'ton says, 'he was received very coldly, since everyone at Headquarters was outraged that it was we who took *Magdeburg* and not the favourites from the 1st Minnaya Diviziya [Essen's old command].' Whilst the navy was not immune to such rivalries, it is more likely that Essen was unhappy with his rash actions. If Nepenin was crestfallen, the Russians had a success to celebrate, even if it was largely an own goal by their enemies. Essen ensured that the prompt signal work, initiative and steadiness under fire of the Odenskhol'm observation post was rewarded. Signal'nyy Konduktor Kivalkin and Mashinnyy Unter-Ofitser 1st Stat'i Kurskiy were awarded St. George's Crosses 4th class, and their six men received St. George's Medals 4th class. Their work had led to the panic that the appearance of *Bogatyr'* and *Pallada* had caused. Nepenin's impulsiveness had resulted in the seizure of the signal book before anyone had noticed it still lying on the deck. The cascade of consequences would have a fundamental impact on the outcome of the entire war.[8]

8 BA:RM49 Befehlshaber im Flottenbereich der Kaiserlichen Marine, Detachierten Admirals KTB, RM28 KTB, RM92 *Magdeburg*, *Augsburg*, *Elsass*, *Wittelsbach* KTB; Эмме, 'походов', pp.164–169; Firle, *Ostsee*, pp.73–92, 98; Эмме, В., (Винтер, Е.Ф.), 'Балтийский флот в начале Первой мировой войны', *Гангут № 102*, (2017), pp.50–52; Контръ-адмиралъ Б. П. Дудоровъ, 'Вице-адмиралъ А. И. Непенинъ', *Морскія Записки, Vol. XVIII, № 51* (1960), pp.45, 49–61; М.А. Партала, 'Рифы и мифы острова Оденсхольм. К истории захвата секретных документов германского флота на крейсере «Магдебург» в августе 1914 г.', *Защита информации. Инсайд. № 13*, pp.84–90, *№ 14* pp.80–86 (2007); М.А. Партала, Д.Н. Симонов, 'Радиоразведка Русского императорского флота на Балтийском море: история создания', *Защита информации. Инсайд. № 1* (2005), pp.90–96; Anon., *Verlustliste No.2*, pp.3–8, *4*, p.24, *9*, p.13, *20*, p.14; РГАВМФ:Фонд 716, Опись 2, Дело 6, pp.152–153, Дело 22, p.115, Фонд 418, Опись 1, Дело 3661, p.6; Hugo von Pohl, *Aus Aufzeichnungen und Briefen während der Kriegszeit* (Berlin: Karl Siegismund, 1920), p.30; Сергей Евгеньевич Виноградов and А.Д. Федечкин, *Крейсера «Адмирал Макаров», «Паллада», «Баян»* (Санкт-Петербург: Галея Принт, 2006), pp.107, 110; Меркушов, *Записки*, p.218; Wieting, *Ostsee*, p.23.

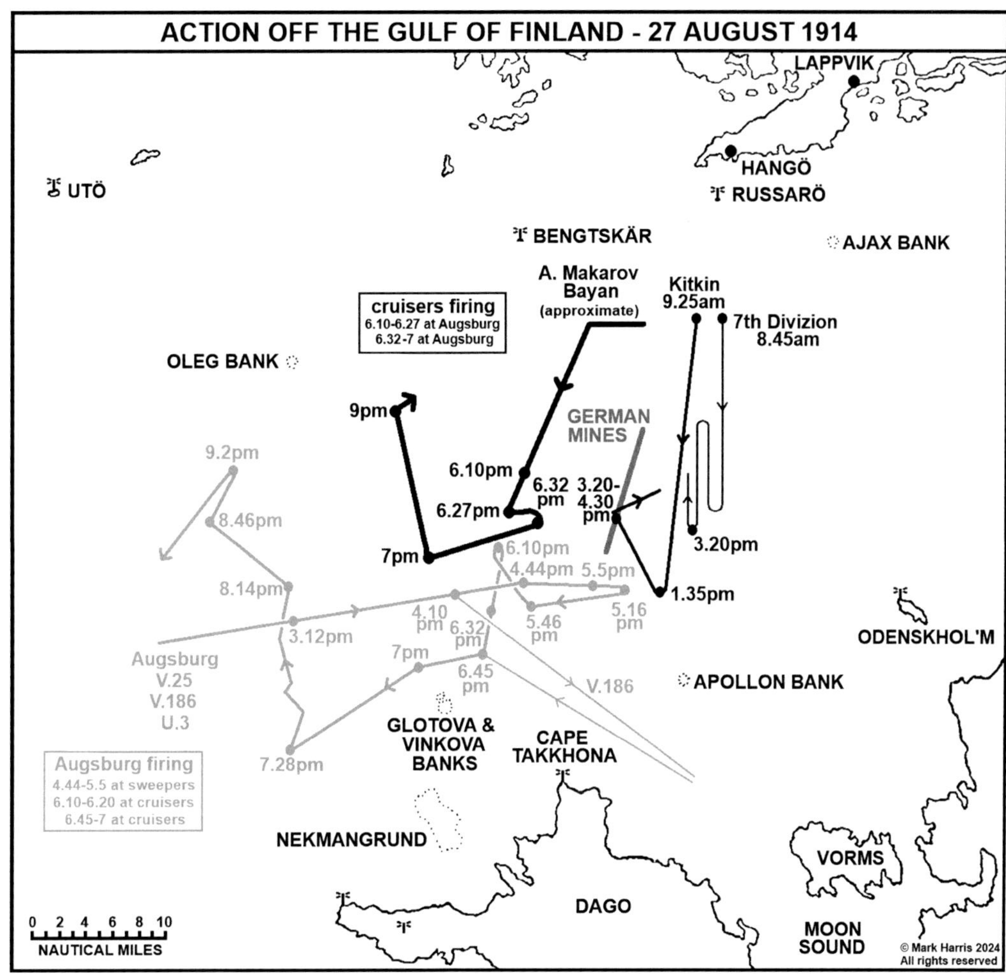

Behring baits a trap

On 23 August, Essen had issued orders to confirm the position of the German minefield. On the morning of the 27th, the fog was finally gone. The Morskaya Partiya Traleniya (Minesweeping Group), Kapitan 2nd Ranga Pëtr Kitkin, was ready to begin work, apart from *Fugas* and two torpedo boats absent for maintenance (see Appendix I for organisation). The main task was assigned to the 2nd and 3rd Otdeleniya (Sections). The deeper-draught torpedo boats of 1st Otdeleniya (7th Divizion), which were less experienced, would shadow the work to the east of the suspected location of the minefield. This was the '39th Square', with mines on a north–south line. The sweepers would start north of the area, zigzagging east and west until they located the northern end. They would repeat this to locate the southern end. Patrolling cruisers had standing orders to keep minesweepers in sight at all times. Patrols were on alert after the events of the previous day, and destroyers had remained out during daylight. Destroyers were assigned to cover the minesweepers, west of the usual patrol line. *Admiral Makarov* and *Bayan*

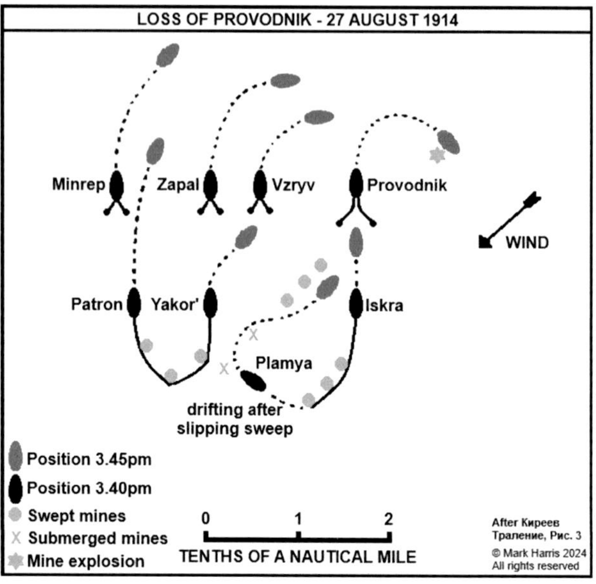

were the duty cruisers. Essen gave specific orders to stay within sight of the minesweepers and protect them from attack from the west. They were to manoeuver in the area between Hangö and the suspected minefield, keeping east of it. If they needed to advance west, they were to pass the dangerous area well to the north with two minesweepers sweeping ahead. In an emergency, they could dispense with this precaution.

At 6am, Kitkin's force left Lappvik. The two cruisers spotted the minesweepers off Hangö. Kapitan 1st Ranga Konstantin Stepanov of *Admiral Makarov* was senior officer. He decided to halt, and wirelessed Kitkin to send back a pair of minesweepers before proceeding further. Kitkin never received the message.

Meanwhile, Kitkin began sweeping at 9:25am. The four shallow draught minesweepers, *Provodnik*, *Zapal*, *Vzryv* and *Minrep*, advanced in line abreast with 'Snake type' trawls, designed to sever mine cables. About 400m directly behind were *Iskra*, *Plamya*, *Patron* and *Yakor'* with standard 'Schultz type' trawls, which caught the mine cables on a line between two sweepers. In theory, the trawls ahead would clear their path and they would catch any mines in between. The torpedo boat *Prochnyy* took station to starboard, acting as wireless link for the force. The 7th Divizion began work to the east. The front sweepers could only make three knots, despite all but one having light boat trawls. The wind was pushing them westwards. At 3pm, destroyer *Voyskovoy* of 2nd Divizion approached. The commander of the outpost line was aboard. He asked for a progress report and enquired where the cruiser escort was. This prompted Kitkin to wireless via *Prochnyy* for them, 'to come closer.'

The sweepers finally reached the minefield 20 minutes later. *Provodnik*'s trawl struck three mines almost simultaneously. Many mines rapidly caught in the sweeps of the second line, bringing *Iskra* and *Plamya* to a standstill and snapping the trawl cable. Mines were all around, just below the surface. The wind pushed *Plamya* towards them. She carefully manoeuvred to get clear. *Deutschland* had reduced the mine interval to just 70m, laying the field as quickly as possible, dropping alternately from each side of the ship. This resulted in a confusingly dense zigzag line. Kitkin, on *Iskra* in the second line, incorrectly deduced that the mines lay in a line from northwest to southeast. In fact, they were northeast to southwest. He ordered a turn to starboard to get clear. This took the front line of sweepers back into the mine line that they had broken through. Kitkin ordered *Provodnik* to double back, through what he thought was clear water, to hook the mines out of *Iskra*'s sweep. As she turned to starboard, *Provodnik* hit a mine abreast the boiler room. It blew a huge hole in the hull, destroyed the funnel and mainmast, and smashed the bridge, killing the commander of the Otdeleniya, Leytenant Valerian Knyazev.

The senior petty officer, Starshiy Botsman Fedor Nikitin, kept his head, loaded a boat with all the wounded he could reach and managed to get it away. Fifteen minutes after the explosion, the wrecked vessel broke in half and sank, leaving the other survivors in the water. The First Officer, Podporuchik Sharl' El'zenger, had a head injury and had lost an arm in the explosion. His orderly refused to leave him and tried to support him in the water. It proved a hopeless struggle. His last words were, 'We can't swim out together, save yourself and goodbye, brother Proshka.' The commander of *Zapal*, Poruchik Vitolin, moved in to rescue the survivors, despite the obvious mine danger. *Minrep*, *Yakor'* and *Prochnyy* all lowered boats to help. From a crew of 30, 11 were dead and seven wounded.

Vidnyy, the leader of 6th Divizion, was screening west of the danger area. She soon approached at high speed, flying a signal. At 4:20pm, Kitkin made it out: 'Enemy in sight to the west.' *Vidnyy* closed and semaphored. Three *Kolberg* class cruisers were pursuing her. The news was relayed by wireless to the cruisers, which were still nowhere in sight.

Behring had intended to head east, towing *U.3* overnight, then, 'penetrate into the Gulf of Finland, passing to the north of our minefield... *U.3* will be detached to attack enemy ships. When passing Bengtskär and Hangö, *U.3* must be kept out of sight of land, if possible.' This time, he planned to abort the operation in the event of poor weather. Events intervened, as Wieting relates, 'It was a nasty night. Thick, thick fog – the towline broke a few times, and how often the outline of the submarine suddenly appeared ghostlike in front of me on board *V.25*. Only "hard rudder" and "full power astern" avoided a serious accident. It was really not easy for our destroyers to follow a tow moving at seven knots.' At 11:40pm, a more serious problem arose. The tow shackle broke and the submarine began to disappear astern. *Augsburg* stopped for *U.3* to come alongside. Valentiner reported that the steering engine was out of action. His crew were also exhausted. *U.3* was a small, virtually obsolete submarine, with limited facilities and had been at sea for over 72 hours. The crew of *Augsburg* worked through the night to make repairs and re-forge the shackle, whilst *U.3*'s crew rested. There was more bad news, when Heinrich notified Schmidt's recall.

Next morning, Wieting was pleased to see that, 'it cleared up. A beautiful day dawned.' At 8:30am, the repairs completed. *Augsburg* took *U.3* in tow and got underway. With so much time lost, Behring headed east from his position south of Bogskär, intending to pass south of the minefield to Odenskhol'm. At the end of the advance, *U.3* was to make her presence obvious. He hoped that reports of a German submarine in the area would deter Russian advances.

The wind picked up, setting up a heavy swell. *Augsburg* had to stop again for *U.3* to repair the engine starter. Valentiner recalled that, 'Admiral Behring called over the megaphone: ... "I will try to draw the action towards *U.3*. Watch my searchlight; short flashes mean you're to surface, long flashes mean you're to dive."' Valentiner started the engines and followed astern, with *V.25* scouting to port and *V.186* close to starboard. At 3:15pm, the lookouts sighted two enemy destroyers. *Prytkiy* was patrolling with *Vidnyy*. They fell back. Numerous columns of smoke came into sight beyond them. At 4pm, a distant mine explosion was spotted, apparently beyond the German minefield. Behring ordered, 'clear for action', and increased speed to 17 knots, leaving the slow *U.3* behind. *V.25* took station astern. As they closed, *Augsburg* observed, 'nine small grey vessels with funnel rings next to the explosion cloud, presumably minesweepers or minelayers. Next to them are the two destroyers.'

Behring detached *V.186* to the exit from Moon Sound. She would give warning if Russian forces tried to cut off his retreat from here. He had to advance to starboard of the enemy, to avoid

Augsburg underway. (NH:64245). *U.3* in harbour. Armed with two 45cm torpedo tubes at the bow and two at the stern. Surface speed 11½ knots, using the paraffin engines and tall exhaust aft. It took several minutes to rig for diving. Endurance underwater was limited. (LC:ggbain.18519). *U.3*'s commander, Max Valentiner, one of the highest scoring submarine aces. His attacks attracted great controversy. (Public domain)

the minefield lying between them. This made it impossible to close quickly. There were red marker buoys around the enemy vessels. Behring deduced that they were laying mines, east of the German minefield. By 4:44pm, the rangefinders on *Augsburg* registered 11km to the enemy. It was long range, but the port battery opened fire. Twenty minutes later, *Augsburg* was passing the southern end of the minefield. The enemy had made off at high speed to the northeast after rounding a marker buoy. They were now out of range. *Augsburg* ceased fire, with no definite hits observed. Behring pressed on. After passing the mines, he could turn north and quickly close. However, at 5:16pm, smoke from two big ships appeared at the northern end of the minefield, forcing a response: 'Turned around because ships were sighted abeam to the north, threatening to cut us off.' Valentiner had seen them too. He was now far astern, and decided to stop the engines. Their thick white smoke drew too much attention. The enemy approached. They were two *Bayan* class cruisers.

At 4:30pm, Kitkin had realised that he faced imminent attack. He ordered the minesweepers to cut their sweeps and retire. Six minesweepers, *Vidnyy* and *Prochnyy* safely crossed the minefield, close to the marker buoy at the site of *Provodnik*'s sinking. *Yakor'* was unable to move, as several mines were snared in her trawl. *Augsburg* opened fire. *Vidnyy* and *Prochnyy* turned back. It seemed inevitable that the minesweeper would be sunk and the crew would need rescuing. Shells began exploding around *Yakor'*. Finally, one hit. It smashed through the whaleboat, pierced the upper deck and exploded in the coal bunker. Fortunately, there was little damage. At last, the crew cut the trawl away and she was able to follow her consorts. Essen later picked out two crewmen in a general order: 'the senior boatswain of the minesweeper *Zapal*, Grigoriy Bindas, showed particular resourcefulness, lowering and raising boats under enemy fire, thanks to which it was possible to save the captain of the minesweeper *Provodnik* [Leytenant Lamanov] and six lower ranks. The boatswain ... of *Yakor'*, Tikhon Solodyankin ... inspired the crew with his example and resourcefulness.' The torpedo boats working to the east had been largely oblivious to events. Kitkin encountered them on the way back. They took in their trawls and the whole force returned to Lappvik.

Stepanov received Kitkin's plan of action from *Prochnyy* at mid-day, but his cruisers stayed put at low speed, 10–15 miles southeast of Hangö. When the minesweepers headed out of sight, Veys, commanding *Bayan*, had signalled Stepanov, reminding him of their order to stay in sight. He was ordered to stand by. When German wireless became active, he tried again, with the same result. Veys continues:

> Around 4:45, the minesweepers reported by wireless that smoke from an enemy ship was visible on the horizon, but they themselves had virtually disappeared over the horizon and were about 15 miles from us. For the third time, I told *Makarov*'s captain [pointedly, Veys never uses his name] that we needed to go to the minesweepers, and for the third time I received the answer that we would go in due course: at this point, without entering into further discussion, I ordered full speed ahead and set course for the minesweepers. On *Makarov*, they raised a signal demanding that I stop, but I did not obey it, ordering the response to be half raised [meaning the message was not understood].
>
> Soon the minesweepers wirelessed that an enemy cruiser was pursuing them, and then that the enemy had opened fire on them, but we had already seen the enemy and were rapidly approaching him. It turned out to be *Augsburg*, and since she was weaker than we were, she had to abandon the pursuit of the minesweepers. We set a WSW course in order to cut off *Augsburg*'s exit from the Gulf of Finland; *Makarov* also set off and followed me, hoisting a signal to join her astern, and then, seeing that I was not obeying it, began to repeat this signal with a searchlight. In the end, we had to obey his order in view of his seniority and join astern.

As they closed, *Bayan* identified a cruiser and two destroyers. Behring was still heading east when sighted. Stepanov assumed that the Germans were trying to entice him to follow them across their minefield. He maintained course to cut them off, intending to sacrifice the

Admiral Makarov, 1912. Differed from her sisters in having an additional 7.5cm gun on each side near the bow. (Public domain)

minesweepers if necessary. It was actually the most effective way to help them, forcing Behring to break off.

As Behring fell back, *Augsburg* increased to full speed, over 26 knots. He flashed the order, 'Follow', by searchlight to the distant *U.3*. Unfortunately, Valentiner read this as the pre-arranged signal, 'Dive.', and did so. Behring repeatedly made the pre-arranged signal, 'Surface'. Valentiner eventually saw it and complied, 'although this seemed questionable because of the nearby armoured cruisers.' He had wasted a lot of his limited battery power running his motors to dive, then surface the boat. *Augsburg* closed *U.3* and then turned toward the approaching Russian cruisers. Behring ordered Valentiner to follow. The range quickly dropped to 18km. Behring ordered Valentiner to dive. It would take several minutes. Behring pressed on, with the rangefinder operators reporting the rapidly falling range. At 6:10pm, it reached 13km. Behring ordered a turn hard to starboard and reversed course. As *Augsburg* steadied on the new course, she opened fire at virtually maximum range. *V.25*, still following, turned in her wake and opened fire. Behring was aiming to draw the Russian cruisers into the path of *U.3*.

Stepanov advanced cautiously. The cruisers returned fire with their bow 20.3cm guns. However, whenever the 10.5cm salvos came close, Stepanov slowed or turned away, to keep outside *Augsburg*'s range, whilst also trying to bring his broadside to bear. Essen later commented:

> *Admiral Makarov* made indecisive movements, frequent turns interfered with accurate shooting, and besides, the commander kept reducing speed and even stopped the engines. Instead of sending the nearby *Bayan* ahead to intercept the retreating enemy, for some reason he kept demanding that *Bayan* follow in his wake; he himself held a course to open the range, but was only able to use the bow gun, and *Bayan* could hardly shoot [as she had been ordered to take position behind].

In contrast with Stepanov's excruciating caution, Oberleutnant Werner Grassmann, *Augsburg*'s Gunnery Officer, saw Behring in his element: 'a born leader, alert, daring, charismatic; ...

he walked up and down the command bridge with calm, decisive steps, and when the first heavy shell landed close to our bow, he greeted it with a cheerful wave of his cap.' Despite the long range and only one gun firing consistently, the Russian shells continued to pitch around *Augsburg* and *V.25*. Wieting recalled that: 'A column of water about 20m high rose about 30m beside *V 25* … Laudon, later my brave war comrade in so many operations, makes a particularly deep bow, despite having previously mocked this "novice's disease". One of the Russians' big 20.3 cm shells had hit right next to *V 25*, so that the fragments whizzed past our heads.' Wieting dropped back to 300m astern. *V.25* had quickly ceased fire after her shells fell short. Fragments from near misses littered the deck of *Augsburg*. A shell hit on the machinery of either vessel could have been disastrous. Behring also ceased fire, as he was concerned his shells would endanger *U.3*. Stepanov's tactics were causing them to fall short anyway.

Suddenly, at 6:27pm the Russian cruisers ceased fire, turned hard to port and headed east. The range increased rapidly. Behring hoped that *U.3* was responsible. To guarantee an opportunity to attack, he struck on a ruse. He ordered, 'Hard a starboard! Blow off steam! I am pretending to have a steering failure.' *Augsburg* reversed course, enveloped in clouds of white steam. Apparently, he also sent un-coded wireless messages implying rudder damage. Essen mentions them in his report. The Russian cruisers appeared to take the bait and turned back to engage. They re-opened fire at 6:35pm. After completing a full circle, *Augsburg* worked back up to speed, deliberately steering erratically. The shallow water of Glotova Bank was ahead. Behring turned west. The Russian cruisers had passed the probable position of *U.3*. *Augsburg* began returning fire. Stepanov turned parallel, but again kept out of *Augsburg*'s range. A running fight developed at steadily increasing range, but finally allowed the Russian cruisers to bring their stern guns consistently into action. At maximum elevation, *Augsburg*'s guns could reach 12.7km. The shells fell short, and there were no hits, but they would have distracted the Russian fire control to some extent. Nevertheless, Behring reported that, 'Russian salvos are very good despite the great distance (not less than 130hm). Straddling +/- 150m.' Despite good shooting, the two-gun salvo of the Russian cruisers continued to handicap the volume and effectiveness of their fire at longer ranges. Essen sums up the fundamental error: 'The enemy salvos fell very close, but the distance was about 70 cables [13km], and they fell short. *Admiral Makarov* did not close in to bring its 6-inch [15.2cm] guns into action, and as soon as the enemy shells fell closer, it slowed down and thus allowed *Augsburg* to escape… One good hit from a 6-inch salvo, and the cruiser would have been sunk.'

At 7pm, Behring turned away and ran out of range. There was no point prolonging the action. Both sides ceased fire. The Russian cruisers lingered, and then retired slowly to the north. They had no damage. Stepanov reported three definite hits, possibly five. Several shells had come very close, but none hit. The observers on *Augsburg* had counted about 40 large calibre shell splashes during the action.

By 7:28pm, the sun had set, although dusk persisted. Behring turned to a northerly course to keep in touch. He shadowed the Russian cruisers from a distance, intending to order a torpedo attack with his destroyers that night. *V.186* had returned from Moon Sound, but her fuel supplies were critical. Behring detached her to Danzig. At 9pm, the Russian cruisers withdrew to the east. Behring abandoned an attack with *V.25* only, as chasing on a clear night with nearby mines made success risky and unlikely. He headed for the pre-arranged rendezvous with *U.3*, well out at sea, west of Dago. As he did so, the Russians picked up a message sent in un-coded German: 'Danzig – armoured cruisers and a flotilla of destroyers will approach the Russians and pursue them.' Whether it was a deliberate ruse or a garbled interception, it added to an illusion of powerful German forces over the horizon.

Stepanov took his cruisers back through the night destroyer screen to Revel', rather than waiting until the morning. He made a general wireless signal, warning that he was going to do so. This would have been dangerous normally, but with destroyers on alert, it was foolhardy. Veys describes the result:

> … patrol destroyers, not warned of our passage as they would expect, mistook us for the enemy … the night was very dark, and so they wirelessed that enemy ships were breaking through the screen line. We started making identification signals, but it did not help, the destroyers opened fire from their guns and launched torpedoes, which, fortunately, missed… At the same time, *Makarov* opened fire on the destroyers, and my artillery officer also approached me with a request to open fire, but I did not allow it, since I knew that these were our destroyers. Shells from the destroyers flew over the cruiser, but none hit. I ordered our call signs signalled with a masthead lamp, after which the shooting from the destroyers stopped. Thus, we safely got out of this mess.
>
> When we returned to Revel', I prepared a report on everything that had happened and was going to go with the report to Admiral N. O. Essen, but … the captain of *Makarov* signalled that he would report everything himself and that I should not go. After waiting for some time, estimating that it was enough for the commander of *Makarov* to report everything, I boarded a whaleboat and went to the *Ryurik*, where the admiral received me immediately. Approaching his cabin, I heard his irritated and unhappy voice; in the cabin were Admiral N. O. Essen, his Chief of Staff, Kontr-Admiral L[yudvig] B. Kerber and the captain of *Makarov*. Admiral Essen addressed me sharply … 'what have you done here?' I did not answer and handed him my report. He read it and handed it to the Chief of Staff, saying that the picture here was completely different, but then he asked in a disgruntled tone, 'Why did you fire at our destroyers?' I was very surprised by this question and answered that *Bayan* had not fired a single shot at our destroyers. Then Admiral N. O. Essen said that *Makarov*'s commander claimed that *Bayan* had fired the first salvo from her 6-inch guns. This outraged me and, already embittered against *Makarov*'s captain for all his antics, I said that if they did not believe me, then let them conduct an investigation into this matter immediately.

Stepanov's actions had serious and permanent repercussions for his career, as Essen relates:

> *Admiral Makarov* and *Bayan*, contrary to orders, went deep into the Gulf at night, passing the screen of 5th Divizion at about 11pm… *Dostoynyy* attacked the cruisers, launching a torpedo and firing her guns. Fortunately, the torpedo missed, and Michman Yavlenskiy fell overboard from *Dostoynyy* and drowned. I consider it necessary to appoint a thorough investigation into this matter…
>
> Stepanov came to me to justify his actions during the protection of the minesweeping party and the exchange of fire with the cruiser *Augsburg*. He realized his tactical mistakes, essentially that having the opportunity to cut off the cruiser's retreat from the Gulf, he did not do so … I told the captain that by his behaviour he had shown that he lacked any initiative, did not know how to use his armament, and had lost my trust and the trust of

> his subordinate personnel. He was not fit to be a cruiser captain, and it would be better for him to leave, giving this position to another, more enterprising and capable officer. In the evening ... Stepanov submitted a report, asking me to give him another assignment.

On 2 September, the findings of the investigation were published in a general order. It cleared Kapitan 2nd Ranga Nikolay Zheltukhin of *Dostoynyy* of any blame, as he was carrying out his orders in attempting to stop warships breaching the screen. It also cleared Veys of any criticism. However, it listed a catalogue of faults by Stepanov: he had 'misunderstood' his orders to protect the minesweepers, had committed basic tactical errors in engaging *Augsburg* and had 'acted incorrectly' by passing the screen at night. Rengarten, who was serving on the flagship, summed up the mood: 'completely ridiculous actions'. It was a publicly damning verdict. Stepanov was assigned command of the hospital ship *Nikolayev* in Kronshtadt, out of harm's way. Kapitan 1st Ranga Pavel Plen replaced him. Rengarten commented that, 'this one will not ruin things'. Stepanov had thrown away the opportunity that Behring's impetuosity had given him. Whilst serving under him, Leytenant Garal'd Graf had found Stepanov, 'a narrow-minded formalist, a pedant, and a very closed-minded person ... the letter of the regulations was everything.' Officers who thrived in peacetime bureaucracy could be ill suited for war.

At 5am next morning, Valentiner arrived at the rendezvous with Behring: 'The Admiral was very angry. He had lost *Magdeburg*. ... my attack had failed miserably. But I believe he appreciated my explanation for the attack's failure.' His war diary describes the events:

> Whilst the boat was still carrying out the dive [which took about five minutes to complete], the enemy opened fire. The impacts in the water could be heard nearby, as *U.3* was steering in the firing lee of *Au[gsburg]* at the time. I went ahead at full power and turned across the stern of *Au[gsburg]* towards the enemy. During this manoeuver, *U.3* was almost rammed by one of its own destroyers [*V.25*]. I avoided the danger by diving underneath her. The screws of the destroyer could be heard clearly above the submarine. The boat had taken on a lot of water [ballast], resulting from the rapid dive to 16m. It took quite a while until this was pumped out, the boat trimmed, and brought back to 10m [periscope depth].

The hydroplanes on *U.3*, which controlled depth, had no power assistance. This made them unresponsive and exhausting to work. *U.3* continually broke the surface in the heavy swell. However, the low Russian speed meant good attack prospects:

> When it was possible to look out again [through the periscope], the enemy was in a very favourable position for a passing attack. He then changed course to starboard, so I decided to make a bow approach and headed towards him at full power. He was travelling very slowly, I calculated the deflection angle [for the torpedo] based on [an enemy speed of] 6 knots. The depth control was badly affected by the sea, so that the boat broke the surface completely several times and then plunged back to a depth of 23m. I shouted: 'The shot must be fired in half a minute'; a joyful excitement went through the boat. At a distance of 1,600m the boat broke the surface completely again, but I did not fire yet because I considered the distance as too great and wanted to be certain of a hit. I had the boat dive. When it came up again, the enemy had turned and was heading east at high speed, with its stern to me. I stopped and lay there to wait and see what the enemy would do...

Valentiner later wrote that: '[I] was furious: The whole thing had been thoroughly botched and had got off to a terrible start. Admiral Behring had most gallantly exposed his *Augsburg* to the fire of two armoured cruisers for an hour just to lead me into an attack, and *U.3* had failed so badly.' His report continues:

> My power consumption was so high due to the full power running in heavy seas and the two dives that the L[eitender] I[ngenieur, the senior engineering officer] reported to me that we only had enough power for about three hours at low speed … So I could only cover 6 nautical miles [underwater]. Whilst I was discussing what to do with my officers, the enemy had set course out of the Gulf again and [with the action over] had stopped 4,000m away from me. I now decided to make a second attack at low speed. While I was doing this and had prepared the torpedo tubes, the enemy turned away again, so that after five minutes I finally gave up the attempt because the depth controller [Obermaat Hanke] was also completely exhausted.

Valentiner crept away at low power. Two hours later, he surfaced in the darkness, despite the vague outline of a ship nearby. He could not dive again. The engines started to charge the battery. *U.3* then left for the rendezvous. Despite Behring's hopes, none of the Russian signals or reports mention a submarine.[9] Valentiner's report advised that *U.3* be restricted to defensive work in calm coastal waters. The old boat had many design flaws, too many defects and no wireless. Despite Hanke's herculean effort, the water pressure from the deep plunges resulted in the gyro compartments of all four torpedoes in the open tubes flooding, which would have resulted in misruns if fired. Behring sent *U.3* back to Kiel, for essential maintenance only possible there. Experience showed that mixing ships and submarines in the battle space did not create attack opportunities, with enemy ships constantly making unpredictable changes of course and speed during an action. As Valentiner had found, friendly ships were also a source of danger. However, Stepanov made himself an easy torpedo target. The result could have been different with a modern boat. Indeed, Behring was convinced that two modern submarines, each working with a fast cruiser to north and south of the minefield, would have better luck and recommended this to Heinrich.

The events of the last two days convinced Behring that no vessel with a sustainable speed under 20 knots should enter the Gulf, lest they fall prey to Russian patrols. The antiquated *Gazelle* was on her way to join his force off Gotland. Behring ordered her to coal from *Oberpräsident Delbrück*, and then occupy a patrol line between Östergarn and Vindava, well away from the Gulf. She was to show herself off the Russian coast and destroy the lighthouse at Steynort, if possible. Behring now returned to Danzig for essential maintenance and resupply. He was anxious to launch another raid as soon as possible, and ordered *Amazone* back out to patrol between the southern tip of Gotland and Öland from the evening of the 29th.

Behring had lived up to his reputation, but had ultimately failed and lost a valuable cruiser. His advance on the 26th in such a dense fog was a poor balance of risk and reward. There had been no chance of engaging any enemy vessels. It would have been more prudent to have turned back and tried again the next day. The gamble led directly to the loss of *Magdeburg*. His gamble

9 There is a suggestion by Гельмерсен and Тимонова in their notes that a lookout sighted *U.3* from the bridge of *Admiral Makarov*. This is not in any other source.

on the 27th also bordered on recklessness. Pohl had a polar opposite attitude to risk. He wrote on Behring's report, '… our ships were repeatedly in very dangerous situations in the Gulf of Finland. The O.d.O. [Heinrich] must be aware of this, and he ought not to expose his ships in this way.' A prudent approach lay between these extremes, since Behring was right that if nothing is risked, nothing is gained. Heinrich forwarded his own conclusions, championing Behring's idea:

> The forces that can be allocated to me in view of the military situation will always be inferior to those of the Russians. It is therefore necessary to keep up the deception as to the actual situation, and whenever possible, endeavour to gain a success against the Russians with our meagre resources. I am convinced that much might be done with submarines, and I therefore request that two modern submarines for offensive work may be detached to me.

When Valentiner reached Kiel, his reception by Heinrich reflected his mood after the recent setbacks:

> He didn't listen to my arguments at all, but shouted and pounded his fist on the table so heavily that the ink-bottles danced. 'Of all people, I would have expected you to destroy at least two Russians.' I was incensed by the treatment and replied rather sharply: 'Your Royal Highness, *U.3* is an old horse; you can give it as much sugar as you like, but it just won't gallop anymore.' The Prince looked at me with hostile eyes, seeming even more displeased by the answer. He didn't say a word. He pointed to the door with a tiny, imperious movement of his long, slender fingers…

Pending reinforcements, Heinrich could not risk further losses. He ordered Behring, 'to restrict himself for now to keeping watch on the Russian forces in suitable positions, and not to undertake any offensive operations in the Gulf of Finland.'[10]

10 Киреев, *Траление*, pp.16–23, Рис.2; РГАВМФ:Фонд 716, Опись 1, Дело 11, p.31, Фонд 716, Опись 2, Дело 21, pp.351–352, and Дело 8, pp.55–56, 113, 127; Фирле, *Война*, p.133, 135; Мельников, *Макаров*, Глава 18, Дополнения; BA:RM97 Unterseeboote der Kaiserlichen Marine, *U.3* KTB, RM49 Detachierten Admirals KTB, RM92 *Augsburg* KTB, RM93 *V.25* KTB; Franz Wieting, 'Torpedobootsfahrten in der Ostsee', in Eberhard von Mantey (ed.), *Auf See unbesiegt, Erlebnisse in Seekrieg erzählt von Mitkampfern, Band 1* (München: J.F. Lehmans, 1922), pp.64–68, Werner Grassmann, 'Die brave alte "Augsburg"', in *unbesiegt, Band 2,* p.197; Firle, *Ostsee*, pp.92–100, Karte 7; Меркушов, *Записки*, pp.220–224; Valentiner, *Schrecken*, pp.44–58; Г. К. Граф, (ed. А.Ю. Емелин), *Императорский Балтийский флот между двумя войнами. 1906–1914* (Санкт Петербург: «БЛИЦ», 2006) p.219, 248; Вейс, «Баян», pp.37–38; *Вести Лисьего Носа*, Выпуск № 16 (352) 30 августа 2023 года, p.7.

Salvage underway on the still smoking wreck of *Magdeburg* at Odenskhol'm. The nearby lighthouse has little apparent damage. (EM:SA AMN5650_041)

4

Fleet operations: September 1914

The *Magdeburg* windfall and British relations

Whilst the action unfolded on the 27th, a thorough search of *Magdeburg* had netted further valuable documents. The ship had suffered only minor damage to the superstructure from shell-fire. Next day, the depot ship of Nepenin's Sluzhba Svyazi, *Silach*, arrived. They were to remove anything valuable and evaluate the scope for salvage. Next day, a team of divers began recovering all of the fittings thrown overboard, as well as ten bodies. In the hands of one was apparently clasped another copy of the signal book. The dramatic story of this find by an ordinary sailor overshadowed that of Gamil'ton. In the post-revolution narrative, it dominates. Gamil'ton was a Tsarist officer and left Russia after the revolution. More material was found all over the hastily abandoned ship, including a complete set of manuals and tables for *Magdeburg*'s guns and machinery. However, the real prize was the documents with intelligence value, much of which came from the charthouse, which survived the explosion. A Naval Ministry report listed the most important:

1. Signal Book of the German Fleet with rules for making signals by all methods.
2. Peacetime cyphers for encryption of signals.
3. Approved draft of manoeuvring rules for the fleet.
4. Charts of squares [A list of various charts covering the entire Baltic and North Sea. These square co-ordinates identified the position of German ships in signals].
5. Secret instructions for navigation [through the minefields] in the Little Belt with a map.
6. Map of observational posts in the North Sea.
7. Wireless logs.
8. Diaries and letters of personnel.

The wartime cypher key tables were missing. This was inconvenient, but they changed regularly anyway. The signal book itself was far more valuable. It was the most secret of the three naval code systems, used for the most important operations. It contained 34,304 three-digit code groups, each equating to words or phrases used to build a complete message. This would normally then be encrypted, using the cypher table, prior to transmission. Without the signal book, an unencrypted message was a string of meaningless letters and numbers. Now that the Russians had it, they would be able to read the meaning of the messages, if they could decrypt them. Cracking the key would take time, but the Ministry report identified some early benefits:

> … some [documents] have already been partially analysed, for example: the Naval General Staff has published a Russian translation of the draft manoeuvring rules, made at the Headquarters of the Fleet Commander; from the wireless log, it was possible to determine in sufficient detail the geographical position of the minefield placed by the Germans in the Gulf of Finland; from the diaries, the composition of the forces operating against us in the Baltic Sea was determined; the signal book has been photographed and partially translated.

Nepenin had issued orders for the retention of every German signal intercepted since war broke out. He tasked a unit headed by Kapitan 1st Ranga M.P. Davydov with breaking the cypher. In parallel, a team led by Rengarten, with a staff on *Ryurik*, went to work. The Black Sea Fleet received copies of the material.

A decision was also made to share the find with Russia's allies. Britain had already been in contact about naval co-operation in the Baltic. On 19 August, the First Lord of the Admiralty, Winston Churchill, the cabinet minister responsible for the navy, invited the Naval Attaché, Volkov, for discussions at the Admiralty, then telegraphed Grand Duke Nikolay. He sought his views on a scheme that his fertile mind had been considering to leverage British naval power: 'The operation of sending a British Fleet through the Bælts to enter the Baltic is feasible, and, if the main strategic situation [a decisive victory in the North Sea] were satisfactory, c[oul]d be achieved. Transports to carry a large invading army c[oul]d be supplied at any time from England.' Churchill listed three options to land a Russian Army on the German Baltic coast: near Danzig, north of Berlin and at Kiel. Nikolay's response on the 24th was guardedly positive:

> We appreciate in the highest degree the First Lord's offer to co-operate with us in the execution by our land forces of a landing operation on the North German Coast, should the British Fleet gain command of the Baltic Sea. … We therefore gratefully accept in principle the First Lord's offer, but we add that we could avail ourselves thereof only should the general military situation lend itself to its application.

On 15 September, the proposal resulted in Kapitan 1st Ranga Mikhail Kedrov and Kapitan 2nd Ranga Mikhail Smirnov setting out on a mission to, 'establish cooperation between the British fleet and the Russian fleet in the Baltic Sea.' They would also 'study the combat experience of the British fleet.' However, there was a secret component to the mission. On 6 September, Churchill had received a visit from Volkov, revealing news of the captured documents. He requested a warship to pick up Russian officers from Aleksandrovsk, in the Russian Arctic, to bring them to Britain. On 2 September, the cruiser *Theseus* had left Scapa Flow in the Orkneys on a covert mission to pick up a shipment of Russian gold from the nearby port of Arkhangel'sk. She received orders to call in at Aleksandrovsk to pick up the officers on the way back. After a two-week delay, waiting at Arkhangel'sk for gold that never arrived, *Theseus* picked up Kedrov and Smirnov. Also on-board were six trunks of clothes destined for Princess Victoria, the wife of Admiral Battenberg. Her sister was married to the Tsar. *Theseus* reached Scapa Flow on 10 October. Smirnov and Kedrov took the train to London, presumably with the trunks. Perhaps these concealed the documents, which could have attracted attention. On the 14th, Volkov accompanied the officers to the Admiralty. Here Churchill writes that, 'late on an October afternoon Prince Louis [Battenberg] and I received from the hands of our loyal allies these sea-stained priceless documents.' Smirnov's report makes no mention of transporting or delivering the documents, but Kedrov provided the fleet commander, Admiral John Jellicoe, with a list of those handed over a few weeks later. Churchill was enamoured of the story of their recovery from the deep and featured it in his history of the war.[1]

Russian records confirm that 'one copy of [the signal book], as well as the quadrant maps, map of observation posts and draft manoeuvring rules have been sent to the British fleet. The latter has also been sent to France.' The British naval code-breaking unit, soon to be named 'Room 40', set to work. By the beginning of November, Fleet Paymaster Charles Rotter deduced the cypher key. The Battle of Dogger Bank in January 1915 was one action that occurred as a direct result of decoding the orders for the operation, almost as soon as they were transmitted. It was a serious defeat for the Hochseeflotte.

It is not clear whether the British or Russians broke the cypher first. Rengarten may have achieved a partial decryption of a signal in September. However, a report by Al'tfater to a colleague at STAVKA strongly implies that the British shared the cypher key with their allies soon after breaking it. He refers to a discussion with Essen in early November. He had been forbidden to discuss an, '... encrypted German wireless intercept, which was deciphered using the signal book from *Magdeburg* and certain information from Britain.' One of Nepenin's subordinates, Kapitan 2nd Ranga Boris Dudorov, relates that whichever team broke a new cypher first would share it with their ally. In contrast, Kedrov and Smirnov struggled to get a discussion going on operational co-operation. The decisive action in the North Sea that Churchill envisaged as a pre-requisite for British entry into the Baltic had not materialised. He was now focussed on other schemes.

By mid-November, the Russian teams had keys for the original cypher and the replacement introduced in October. Rengarten began compiling fortnightly intelligence summaries based on signal intercepts, attributed to Agentura (Agency) B, a device used to misdirect the Germans as to the source of the information, should they obtain it. It implied a mysterious, pervasive spy network operating behind German lines.

As early as 29 August, Heinrich had warned that, 'Whereabouts of the ship's signal books not yet fully clarified' and suggested issuing a new key immediately. On 3 September, he added: '[Behring] has orders that in communications with his forces and with the K.F.S. Danzig he must encrypt all wireless messages [derived] from the signal book.' Some messages had previously been transmitted without encryption, trusting to their obscured meaning. The report on the loss of *Magdeburg* by Marine-Hilfs-Kriegsgerichtsrat (Naval Assistant War Court Counsel) Tolki, issued on 17 September 1914, included an important finding: 'Since the depth in the area around the ship was only shallow, the possibility of the [signal] books and one cypher being fished out cannot be dismissed.' Even so, it took a further month to issue a new cypher. The response to both Heinrich and the report was complacent. The Admiralstab offered the opinion that: 'No fears of dangerous consequences are entertained here through

1 The signal book, copy number 151, has no water damage, implying it is the copy found by Gamil'ton. Held by The National Archives (TNA):ADM137/4156. Copies 145 and 974 were also on *Magdeburg*.

the possible loss of the signal book.' Heinrich continued to press for a thorough revision of the cypher system and a new signal book, but both the Admiralstab and Hochseeflotte rejected this repeatedly. The cypher key changed only seven times during 1915. However, the German habit of repeating common instructions at similar times, coupled with transmissions of the same message with both the new and old cypher, undermined the changes. The cypher system used was also far too simple. It took just two days for the Russians to break the cypher after a change in March 1915. As the campaign unfolded, the intelligence advantage for the Russians would begin to tell.

The compromising of their top-secret signals was already disastrous for the German fleet. Another development promised to reveal where they were coming from. On the same day that the divers began their work, the new radio direction station at Kil'kond began tests. Progress was rapid. By 8 September, the station was providing the bearing of signal intercepts. By the end of 1914 additional stations were in place at Hangö and Verkhnego Dagerort, allowing cross plots to establish the position from which signals emanated. More stations were under construction, to become operational in early 1915.

It proved impossible to salvage *Magdeburg*, so everything useful was stripped out, including guns, turbines and fire control equipment. The Russians copied the German fall of shot indicator system, issuing it from 1916. However, it was the captured signal books, and the Russian decision to share them, that had fundamental impacts on the course of the entire conflict.[2]

Essen emboldened

German minelaying had convinced Essen that the Germans had no intention to attack the Central Position. The material recovered from *Magdeburg* included diaries and logs confirming how weak the German forces that had been raiding the Gulf of Finland had been, and that only second line warships were in the Baltic. They revealed the position of the German mine barriers. Essen decided to leave the German minefield in the Gulf in place as an advanced defence. However, it was vital to confirm that no additional mines had been laid later to extend it. Over the next few days minesweepers used the information to confirm and mark the exact position of the northern end of the German minefield, then ensure that there were no other mines north of this.

With the completion of the new battleship *Sevastopol'* imminent, Essen was determined to engage the German fleet with his own, should he encounter it. Kolchak issued regulations for conducting a fleet action on 29 August, based on the recent intelligence about German forces, indicating that the 4th and 5th Geschwader were in the Baltic. The instructions therefore assumed the presence of 12 of the older German battleships, 10 armed with medium calibre

2 Эмме, 'походов', p.173; Винтер, 'походов', p.192; BA:RM92 *Magdeburg*, *Blücher* KTB, RM28 KTB; Patrick Beesly, *Room 40, British Naval Intelligence 1914–1918*, (London: Hamish Hamilton, 1982), pp.5–6, 14–15, 22–24, 42; РГАВМФ:Фонд 716, Опись1, Дело 15, pp.6–7, 40, Фонд 418, Опись1, Дело 3356, pp.2–3 and Дело 389, pp.4–5; Дудоровъ, 'Непенинъ', *Записки, № 52*, pp.17–23; Партала, 'Рифы', № 13, pp.84–90, № 14 pp.80–86; Партала, Симонов, 'Радиоразведка', pp.90–96; Winston S. Churchill, *The World Crisis 1911–1918* (London: Odhams Press Limited, 1939), pp.414–415; Martin Gilbert, *Winston S. Churchill: Volume III Companion Part 1, Documents July 1914–April 1915* (London: Heinemann, 1972), pp.46, 53.

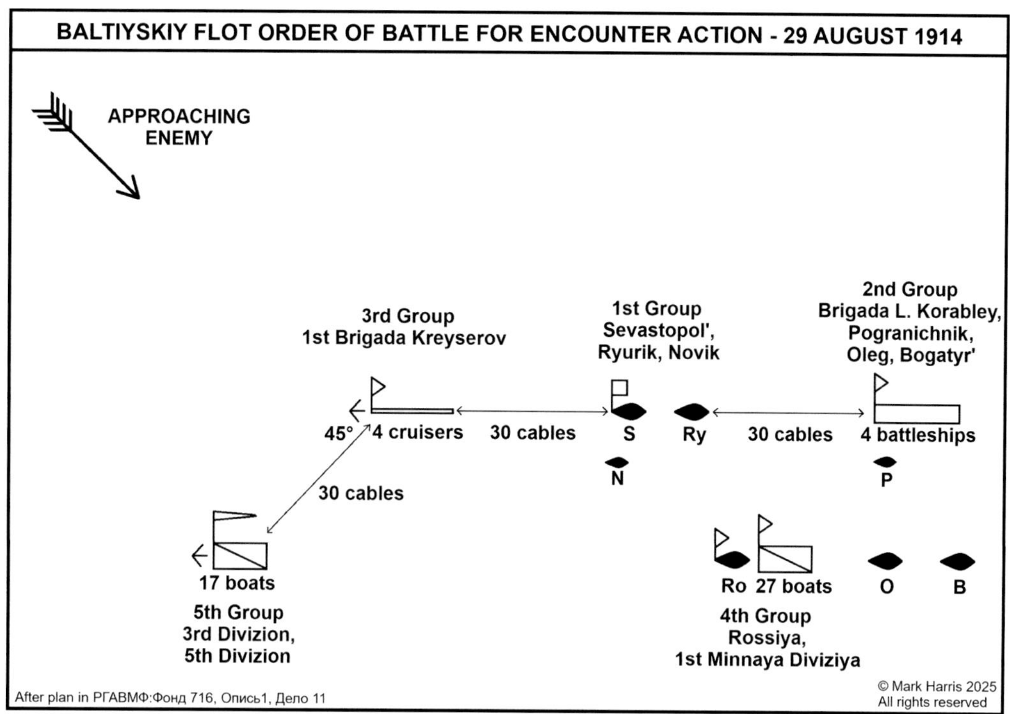

24cm guns, two with 28cm guns. It envisaged support by four armoured cruisers, eight light cruisers and several flotillas of destroyers. Essen would still engage, even if the German force included one or two dreadnought battleships or battle cruisers armed with 28cm guns. The plan divided the fleet into five manoeuvre groups (see diagram). The most powerful vessels of 1st Group, with *Sevastopol'* as fleet flagship, would engage any dreadnoughts or battle cruisers as a priority, otherwise seeking the best position to support the 2nd Group against the enemy main body. The 3rd Group, the best cruisers, would attack the enemy cruisers. The 4th and 5th Groups would launch torpedo attacks on the orders of the Brigades that they were shadowing, and counter any enemy advances for torpedo attack. General instructions were to keep at least 45 cables (4½ miles) from the enemy battle line. Whilst the German battleships had a weak main armament, they mounted very large numbers of 15cm guns, which gave them an advantage at shorter ranges. Where possible, the Russian heavy ships were to concentrate in pairs on the leading enemy vessels to disable enemy command control.

On 30 August, Essen also revised his defence arrangements. He explained the changes to Fan-der-Flit: 'The participation of the British fleet in the war has radically changed the balance of forces, and in the waters of the Baltic Sea we now have only secondary forces of the German fleet. Therefore, having fully provided the Central Position with minefields and equipped it as far as possible with coastal batteries… I have begun to defend Moon Sound with batteries at Vorms and Verder [the northern and southern exits]. Now 75mm coastal batteries are ready and work on installing 6-inch [15.2cm] guns [4 of each type of gun at each point] is being completed.' Much of the credit for the rapid progress went to Nepenin, who was now responsible for naval fortifications, as well as communications. Merkushov writes that:

> ... Nepenin, appointed to the post of Chief of the Primorsky Front and simultaneously promoted to Kontr-Admiral, developed the maximum of his characteristic energy.
>
> Under his unflagging supervision, the work of building batteries and arming them with guns is carried out with remarkable speed. The admiral's loud voice, his ability to motivate and make all his subordinates work well, his persistence in his demands, together with his general inspiration, work wonders.
>
> As if by magic, batteries are springing up from the ground, armed with long-range naval artillery from 8 inches to 75 mm inclusive, covering minefields and providing the fleet with all-round support in its fight against a powerful enemy.

Moon Sound had narrow, shallow, winding, easily defended exits to north and south, with a significant anchorage in the middle. The entrances were too shallow for cruiser passage. From the 31st, the gunboat *Khrabryy* was based there to defend it and act as a depot for two submarines. During the day, these would patrol off Cape Takkhona, attacking any enemy vessels attempting to pass south of the German minefield, modifying a plan already agreed with Levitskiy. *Magdeburg* was to be guarded around the clock pending salvage, with two destroyers of 4th Divizion assigned each night. 1st Minnaya Diviziya moved their forward base of operations to Moon Sound. As a result of these changes: 'it is now possible to control the Gulf of Riga and develop the operations of minelayers and submarines, both in the Gulf of Riga and in the northern part of the Baltic Sea, through the Irben Strait, as well as in the sea area off the entrance to the Gulf of Finland.' Essen was thinking ahead to using minelayers offensively during the long nights in the coming months.

The recent attacks and lessons learned prompted further changes. New cruiser anchorages were created on the northern coast at Örö Island, Hangö and Lappvik. The forward base of 2nd Minnaya Diviziya advanced to Örö. On the 28th, 2nd Brigada received a useful reinforcement. *Diana*, the sister ship of *Avrora*, had been reactivated and re-armed to assist with patrol work. From the 30th onwards, Essen moved the daytime cruiser patrol line west of the German minefield, on a line running north from Dagerort. Two cruisers would patrol for two days at a time. They were to:

> ... cruise at the entrance to the Gulf of Finland, not moving east of the meridian of Verkhnego Dagerort, and with the onset of darkness, stay in the open sea or, if desired, anchor in this area, in no circumstances approaching at night within 10 miles of the screening line of destroyers from Odenskhol'm–Ajax [Bank]... The task of patrol cruisers is to prevent enemy ships from entering the Gulf of Finland and from laying new minefields. Any vessel passing the screen at night will be attacked.

Essen's biggest concern remained 'unprotected Hangö', which was exposed to enemy landings. He pressed Fan-der-Flit to begin building batteries there, if necessary at the expense of fortresses in the Pacific. However, expanding the defences was not enough. The fleet had spent the first month of the war in a morale-sapping wait for an overwhelming German assault that never came. Essen's own general order on the day war broke out had reflected the expectation of a potentially unwinnable battle against hopeless odds: 'The fleet cannot leave the battlefield I have designated – there is no other in our waters, and we must defend it, no matter what the cost.' With the weakness of the enemy fleet laid bare, Essen was now determined to shatter the inertia and take the fight to the enemy.[3]

3 РГАВМФ:Фонд 716, Опись1, Дело 11, pp.37–42; Фонд 716, Опись1, Дело 17; Фонд 716, Опись2, Дело 10, pp.54–57, Фонд 719, Штаб Начальника 2-Й Бригады Крейсеров Балтийского Моря (1914-1918), Опись 1; Меркушов, *Записки*, pp.195, 226–227, 244.

Amazone underway pre-war. Armed with 5x10.5cm guns and an underwater 45cm torpedo tube on each side. Armour on the deck only. Speeds for this class, which included *Gazelle*, *Thetis* and *Undine*, varied from barely 20 to just over 21 knots. (Public domain)

Essen's raid on the German outpost line

Fregattenkapitän Ernst Mysing of *Gazelle* certainly made his presence known off the Russian coast after receiving his orders on 28 August. He headed straight to Steynort, arriving at 5.10am next morning. With a remarkable contempt for submarine attack, Mysing anchored 1.7 miles off the coast. He opened fire with the 10.5cm battery. Over the next 45 minutes, *Gazelle* fired 108 shells, reducing the lighthouse, which was near the shoreline, to rubble. The nearby keeper's house and border guard outpost also received damage. The antiquated cruiser's wireless failed to get through to Danzig as he headed out to sea afterwards. On the 30th, observation posts correctly identified and reported his aged cruiser, just a few miles offshore, moving at low speed from Vindava southwards. Mysing had collected information from every passing neutral steamer. On the morning of the 31st, Behring returned with *Augsburg* to take up the eastern end of the outpost line off the Russian coast. *Gazelle* moved to cover the eastern coast of Gotland. Behring also ensured that he could be clearly seen from the shore. He had been uneasy about leaving two old, weak cruisers on the patrol line, as *Amazone* was still west of Gotland.

The reports received allowed Essen to conclude that a German reconnaissance screen lay between the Russian coast and Gotland. On the evening of the 31st, he decided to lead a cruiser raid against it. The plan was unlikely to meet with the approval of his risk-averse superiors, but Essen was increasingly concerned about the corrosive effect on morale of passive inaction. At 8am next morning, a meeting of the senior officers involved was convened on *Ryurik* to brief them.

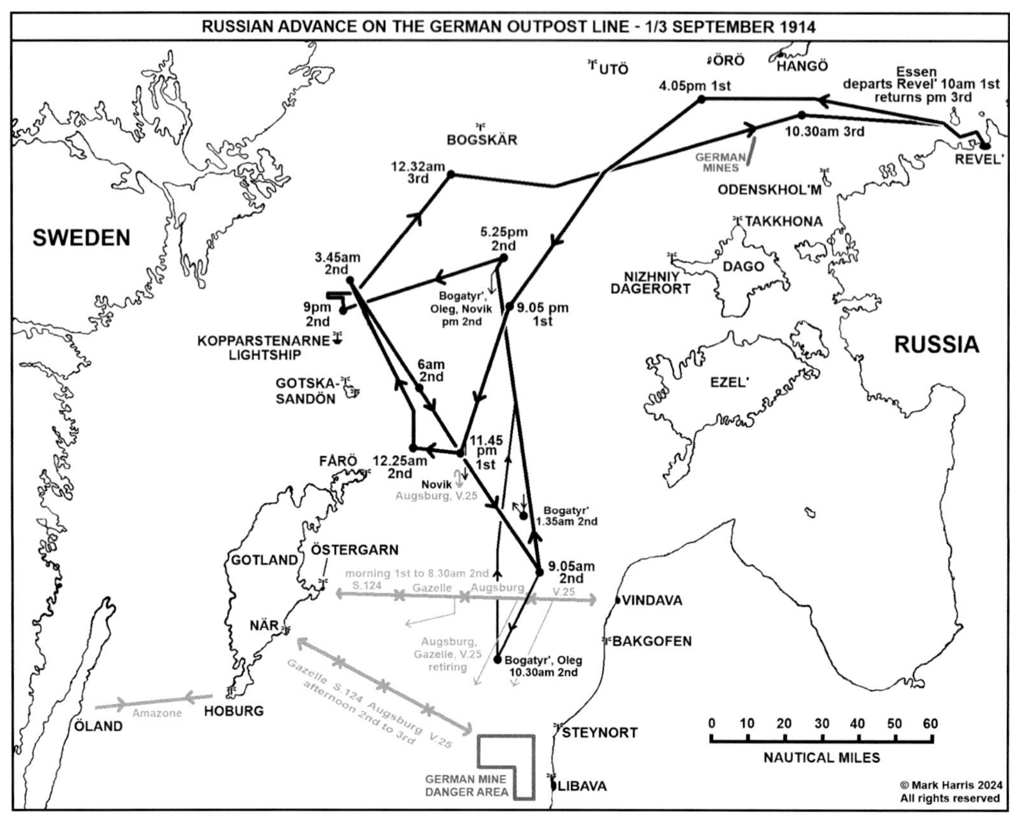

Two hours later, Leskov, flying his flag on *Rossiya*, led *Bogatyr'* and *Oleg* of his 2nd Brigada Kreyserov out of harbour. *Ryurik*, with Essen aboard, followed. Six destroyers of 2nd Divizion preceded the cruisers out of harbour. *Novik* took station to port and the four destroyers of the Poludivizion took station to starboard. The force headed out, north of the German minefield, with 2nd Divizion sweeping ahead. German mines breaking adrift were causing a navigational hazard. Once danger passed, *Ryurik* steamed to the head of the line, and 2nd Divizion went in to Lappvik, to await the force's return.

The weather was blustery. In the open sea, the breakers prevented the four smaller destroyers from keeping up with the formation. Essen sent them to shelter at Utö and then headed for the eastern shore of Gotland, expecting to reach the southern point by dawn. If no German vessels were encountered, he would send *Bogatyr'* and *Oleg* to shell the German coastal observation stations at Brüsterort and Rixhöft, whilst *Novik* carried out a reconnaissance of Danzig Bay. *Ryurik* would remain off Gotland in support, with *Rossiya*.

At 9 p.m., *Bogatyr'* suffered a breakdown of her port engine. She was given permission to return to Revel', but stopped to make repairs. An hour later, the engineers had fixed the problem. *Bogatyr'* got back underway, aiming to rendezvous with the main body in the morning. Essen pressed on through the night. *Novik* took station astern to keep in touch. As the detachment neared Gotland, Essen was on the bridge of *Ryurik*:

At 11:30pm, smoke was seen aft of the detachment, on the port side, rapidly gaining on us – obviously an enemy light cruiser. Soon, off the port bow, below the moon, another smoke trail was sighted; apparently, it was an enemy cruiser, with a destroyer in company. We went to action stations. The cruiser first turned to cross our course, then – towards us or away from us – it was hard to make out, although later we realised it had turned away. I ordered *Novik* to proceed to attack. It was not possible for us to shoot. It was impossible to determine the distance, and I personally could not make out the silhouette of the cruiser in binoculars, so aiming would have been problematic … I therefore did not want to reveal ourselves, which would have been certain if we had opened fire; this would have been difficult to stop at night, and naturally, given our inability to shoot at night, would have been haphazard and, due to the impossibility of determining the distance, unproductive …. Fearing an attack, I turned first 8, and then 16 points, [completing a turn to head in the opposite direction] deciding that I would receive the attack at a distance …

The enemy vessels were soon out of sight. Leytenant Graf, recently appointed Second Torpedo Officer of *Novik*, was asleep:

The enemy ships, having discovered our forces, turned and began to quickly retreat to the south.

… we immediately left the line and quickly began to increase speed. However, we had difficulty catching up with the retreating enemy; only when we increased the speed to 32 knots, did the distance start to decrease quickly.

During the pursuit, we sounded the battle alarm … I was sleeping and, quickly jumping up, ran to my place on the quarterdeck … in a few minutes everything was ready, and everyone was in position.

… The full moon illuminated the gently swaying sea, and the *Novik*, with everything shuddering, rushed forward, clad in silver and foam … Our mood was tense, but overall everyone was calm. The enemy had not yet opened fire, despite the fact that we were already close … a silhouette appeared; it was a three-funnelled cruiser of the *Augsburg* type, and behind it was a destroyer. … It was clear that the cruiser was going full speed, obviously trying to get as far away from our forces as possible. Probably, it did not open fire precisely in order not to reveal its position.

Novik had now apparently arrived at the required range [after a 40-minute chase] … The prearranged bell rang from the bridge. … Immediately four bright flashes flared, and the torpedoes, whirring, fell heavily into the water.

At the same moment, the cruiser turned sharply towards us and with this manoeuver avoided the torpedoes. We mirrored the manoeuver. For a few minutes, she followed us, and then again turned sharply to the south; we did the same. Soon, in the darkness, we lost sight of her.

At that moment, we noticed something resembling the silhouette of a ship to port, and almost all the officers on the bridge thought that it was also an enemy, and advised the commander to attack it. However, the commander did not dare to do this, since the *Bogatyr'* could be in that direction…

For the remainder of the night, following the Admiral's orders, we set course for Dagerort.

On 1 September, destroyers *V.25* and *S.124* had joined Behring east of Gotland. *V.186* was refitting, and earmarked to replace a destroyer lost in the North Sea. *S.124* had been mobilised from reserve, replacing *S.102*, which needed a major refit. *Gazelle* and *S.124* were poor replacements for *Magdeburg* and *V.186*. Behring patrolled the outpost line during the day. That night, he decided to carry out a reconnaissance with *Augsburg* and *V.25* up to the Gotska Sandön–Dagerort line. At 11:10pm, they sighted columns of smoke ahead. It was a clear moonlit night, with very good visibility. However, a heavy sea was running, with a stiff breeze from the north, causing the waves to break over them. Three cruisers were soon sighted on a southwesterly course.

Behring turned around to keep in touch ahead of the presumed enemy. Another vessel then came into sight eastward of the main force, and gained rapidly. A vessel this fast could only be *Novik*. At 12:04am, at a range of about 5,000m, there was the distinctive flash of torpedo tube firing charges, but no tracks approached.[4] The destroyer was about 45 degrees aft of the beam. *Augsburg* turned on her searchlight, but it did not make the attacker any clearer. Wieting's officer of the watch also had his attention fixed astern: 'On the port side, about 4,000 meters away, there's an enemy destroyer!' Wieting then saw, 'two flashes and then two more! … the fellow fires four torpedoes at this distance and at a terrible angle at a single ship, *Augsburg*. He must have very many torpedoes to spare or he wants to make a name for himself at home with an attack!' Behring now turned to close. The enemy turned away and *Augsburg* began to pursue. Her high speed steaming into the heavy seas shipped so much water forward that it was impossible to fire the guns.

The destroyer went out of sight. *Novik*'s attack had ensured that none of Essen's cruisers had been seen clearly enough to identify them. *Augsburg* gave up the hopeless chase and turned southward. Shortly afterwards another vessel, making a lot of smoke, was sighted. *Augsburg* turned to close after it was identified as a destroyer. The Russian destroyer also turned. The pursuit ended in the same outcome. By 2:10am, the enemy was out of sight. Paletskiy had possibly missed the chance to deliver a second attack on *Augsburg*, but he may have been correct that it was *Bogatyr'*. Recognition in a heavy sea at night is not straightforward. His torpedo attack had never had much hope of success, despite the large salvo fired. Attacks from astern require short range, as the torpedo will otherwise run out of fuel before reaching the target. The angle of attack was also unfavourable. Torpedoes are much easier to avoid if spotted when fired.

Meanwhile, Essen retired north of Gotska Sandön. Once the moon set, reducing visibility, he turned back round. *Bogatyr'* had been advancing separately and was probably the vessel sighted by Essen immediately before Behring. Later, 'having learned from the wireless about the encounter with the enemy', she altered course to rendezvous with Essen. At 6am on the 2nd, *Bogatyr'* rejoined astern of *Oleg* in the early morning light. The encounter that night had foiled the plan to pass the German patrol line unseen, cutting off their retreat. Nevertheless, Essen pressed on, aiming to strike the eastern end of the patrol line. He would have to make do with a daylight attack now that surprise had been lost.

4 Behring reports 8,000m, repeated by Firle, but *Augsburg*'s log records about 5,000m.

Oleg underway, shortly before the war. The same class as *Bogatyr'*, but speed only about 21 knots. (LC:ggbain.16924)

At 9am, the smoke of three ships came into sight to starboard. Essen immediately detached *Bogatyr'* and *Oleg* to attack. Despite *Oleg* pushing her speed to 21 knots, after 90 minutes pursuing the closest cruiser, they could not reduce the range. They turned back to rejoin Essen. The enemy had sent numerous wireless messages. Their call signs were those of *Augsburg*, *Amazone* and *Gazelle*, all presumably confirmed using call sign tables captured from *Magdeburg*.

Behring had returned to his outpost line before dawn. When faced with the advance of the two Russian cruisers he had to retire. *Augsburg* was no match for any Russian cruiser, let alone two, but had a considerable speed advantage. Behring matched speed to keep in touch out of range, about 14km ahead. They were identified in the excellent visibility as *Bogatyr'* class. His destroyers were at the eastern and western end of the patrol line. With rough seas and excellent visibility, attempting a torpedo attack was pointless. *V.25* also fell back. Behring's concern grew when the much slower *Gazelle* came into sight to the west. Behring ordered Mysing to retire, but *Gazelle* could only sustain 17 knots, logging, 'enemy armoured cruisers following, coming slowly closer.' Behring wirelessed: 'Enter Swedish territorial waters at your discretion.' There was relief when the Russian cruisers turned back.

Later, the weather calmed considerably. Essen ordered the Poludivizion to rejoin from Utö and *Novik* from Dagerort. Around 5pm he rendezvoused with the destroyers, *Bogatyr'* and *Oleg* well to the west of Dagerort. His plan was to neutralise the German speed advantage. An officer was summoned to the flagship from *Novik*. Paletskiy sent Graf:

> When I climbed aboard the *Ryurik*, they ordered that I go to the aft bridge to see the admiral. When I got there, I saw Admiral Essen himself, who quickly grabbed me by the sleeve and dragged me into the wheelhouse, where he began asking me about the details of our night attack. Perhaps the admiral remembered … when he … dashingly led

> his cruiser, the former *Novik*, to approach the Japanese squadron. It seemed as if some invisible thread had stretched between us and connected a similar situation separated by a ten-year gap …
>
> After my report, the Admiral and Kapitan 1st Ranga Kolchak began to explain to me the upcoming operation, which consisted of the *Ryurik*, *Rossiya* and the Poludivizion separating from the rest of the detachment and heading south between Gotland and the Swedish coast. Having bypassed Gotland, they would turn and advance to the north. *Bogatyr'*, *Oleg* and *Novik*, after setting up a screen, would go straight to the south in the darkness, on the other side of Gotland and then turn north. The task of this detachment was to prevent enemy scouts from getting through the screen; if this succeeded, then by morning the enemy would be between our two detachments.
>
> When I had returned to *Novik* and the boat was hoisted in, we immediately turned to the south and with *Bogatyr'* and *Oleg* set up a screen [reaching a line between Östergarn and Bakgofen], but prior to darkness we saw nothing on the horizon and, according to the orders, turned to the north. During the night, on the *Novik* we were twice confused by the smoke from *Bogatyr'* and *Oleg* and even tried to chase them, but fortunately we recognized the mistake in time and everything turned out well. Of course, our inexperience was to blame for this, but it is quite understandable and excusable, since the war had only just begun.
>
> We did not see the enemy all night.

Essen had set off for the west coast of Gotland. At 8:30pm, he encountered a steamer north of Gotska Sandön running without lights in the moonlight. *Pogranichnik* inspected the vessel. She was Swedish, in ballast. The steamer's documents were in order, so she was released, but would doubtless report his presence. Essen now decided to abandon the operation. The night was very bright again. With the element of surprise gone, he believed that the plan had no realistic chance of success. Perhaps he also reflected how far he had already exceeded the scope of his standing orders. Essen recalled his forces. On the morning of the 3rd, they entered the Gulf of Finland, and in the afternoon dropped anchor at Revel'. Essen's report makes no mention of plans to bombard the German coast, nor of intending to sweep round Gotland to envelop the German patrol line. The purpose of the sortie is described as being 'to conduct reconnaissance in [the Steynort–Vindava] direction and try to attack the enemy cruisers.'

If Essen had chosen to steer further west, he would have directly encountered *Gazelle*, which would not have been able to escape. Behring raised this with Heinrich: 'Had a favourable opportunity today for submarine use. In pursuit, *Gazelle* was endangered because it was too slow.' Behring pulled back to a shorter line between the lighthouse at När on Gotland and the minefield off Libava after the pursuit by *Bogatyr'* and *Oleg*. *Gazelle* was repositioned close off Swedish waters, allowing escape if the Russians approached again.

Essen had confirmed his assumptions about the weak German patrol line. He returned to news that the army was concerned about a possible landing by the Germans on the Russian coast north of Memel, aimed at outflanking the Russian First Army fighting in Ostpreussen. He responded that in order to defeat such a landing, he would need to take the entire fleet to break through the German fleet and attack the troop transports. He therefore required an assurance freeing him from the need to protect the Gulf of Finland, as the fleet could be lost in the attempt. The response was prompt: 'The task of the Baltiyskiy Flot remains the protection of the capital from the sea. It is necessary to preserve the fleet for this purpose.' Therefore, the landing would be unopposed. Essen issued orders to reinforce and expand the number of observation posts on the threatened coastline.[5]

Heinrich's first fleet sortie

Behring had reported his initial contact with *Novik* to Heinrich. This was what he needed to revive his arguments for a major advance. He saw it as evidence that the Russians had been emboldened by the loss of *Magdeburg*. Heinrich immediately asked Pohl for 3rd Aufklärungsgruppe and 4th Geschwader, both still at Kiel, to reinstate the previously aborted operation. The ever-cautious Pohl responded: 'Ships of 4th Geschwader which are ready for action will sail if the Russians make a further advance. However, no further east than Memel. The 4th Geschwader must remain in instant readiness to proceed to the North Sea. ... *Prinz Adalbert* and *Roon* cannot be spared from the North Sea.' He was under pressure to do more: 'Tirpitz absolutely insists that a large cruiser is sent to the Baltic to improve the situation there. I would gladly offer it up, but this would greatly weaken the North Sea Fleet.' When Heinrich relayed Behring's report of the Russian advance on the afternoon of the 2nd, Pohl shifted his stance:

> The continued advance of the Russians, reported as far as Gotland, requires an additional despatch of vessels to the Baltic. A fight in the Baltic Sea, a bombardment of coastal areas – Kolberg – must be avoided, the Baltic must be kept free. This can only happen if warfare in the North Sea is abandoned. The deployment of 4th Geschwader to the East also requires protection by cruisers and destroyers.
>
> A discussion with [Tirpitz], in the presence of Admiral [Georg] von Müller [head of the Marinekabinett], demonstrated that the former has abandoned his previous view that all our forces must be concentrated in the North Sea in order to be able to confront the British fleet. ... He therefore wants to give up warfare in the North Sea and even advocates sending the 3rd Geschwader [the best battleships] to the Baltic Sea, as the ships have better resistance to flooding.
>
> ... I cannot agree to sending 3rd Geschwader because it is absolutely necessary to protect the German Bight, there is no protection against destroyer attacks in the eastern Baltic Sea, and these valuable ships cannot be exposed to losses. I declare myself ready to divert *Blücher* [a powerful armoured cruiser] a fast light cruiser and two Torpedobootsflottille ... from the North Sea forces and use them to keep the Baltic clear for our use.

At 3:40am on the 3rd, the Admiralstab informed Heinrich of the decision, with a caveat, 'His Majesty orders that ships are to take no risks. Slow, old light cruisers must not be pushed forward as far as has been the case, without support.' Heinrich ordered Schmidt to proceed immediately

5 BA:RM92 *Gazelle*, *Augsburg* KTB, RM49 Detachierten Admirals KTB, RM28 KTB; Эмме, 'походов', pp.172–177; Firle, *Ostsee*, pp.102–104; Фирле, *Война*, p.146–147; Г. Графъ, *На „Новикъ", (балтiйскiй флотъ въ войну и революцiю)* (Мюнхенъ: Р. Ольденбургъ, 1922), pp.15–17; РГАВМФ:Фонд 716, Опись 2, Дело 10, pp.54–55, Фонд 716, Опись 1, Дело 15, p.23; Wieting, *Ostsee*, pp.29–30.

with 4th Geschwader, to rendezvous with Behring south of Gotland. *T.94* left Sassnitz to act as Schmidt's despatch vessel.[6] *Undine* soon left Kiel to join him.

Next day, the forces despatched by Ingenohl began arriving in Kiel, via the Kaiser Wilhelm Canal. As soon as they had topped up with coal and provisions, they headed off independently to the rendezvous. Heinrich received his instructions: 'As soon as you have concentrated all available forces, the operational restriction excluding the area east of Memel is cancelled. A short demonstration is to be carried out in the limited time available, and withdraw as soon as possible.' Heinrich would command the force: 'After leaving the harbour and out of sight of land, in order to avoid attracting attention, I raised my own flag on S.M.S. *Blücher'*. She was the most powerful of the German armoured cruisers. *Blücher* was faster than any Russian cruiser and better armed, with the exception of *Ryurik*. The modern light cruiser *Strassburg*, and 22 destroyers of 2nd and 6th Torpedobootsflottille completed his force. Three more colliers left Swinemünde to join *Oberpräsident Delbrück*. Heinrich had, '... entrusted ... Kontreadmiral Mischke, with day-to-day business and the protection of the Belts.' He had only *Lübeck*, *Thetis*, *Panther* and a handful of minor vessels to hand. Whilst he awaited Heinrich's arrival, Behring maintained the new patrol line and began coaling his vessels in turn off Gotland.

As Heinrich headed east, a powerful northeasterly gale blew up that night. At General Headquarters a storm of another sort had blown up, as those around the Kaiser competed for the adoption of their preferred strategy. The Kaiser was experiencing a bout of caution, resulting from the loss of three light cruisers in a British raid on the Heligoland Bight on the 28th. He was now insisting that Ingenohl seek his permission, prior to any engagement with the British. On the evening of the 3rd, Tirpitz dined with the Kaiser. He raised the topic of the use of the battle fleet, using the Kaiser's caution about action with the British to promote his own scheme. Pohl's ally, Müller, informed him that Tirpitz had briefed against Pohl for sending the old battleships of 4th Geschwader to Gotland, as they were too vulnerable. He proposed that the bulk of the modern battleships should go to the Baltic, for a decisive action there instead. He had also sent a memorandum to Pohl to that effect.

For their part, Müller and Pohl were increasingly critical of Tirpitz's decision to continue arming German light cruisers and destroyers with small calibre guns, in the interest of numbers over quality. The actions against both the British and Russians had already demonstrated that these classes of German vessels were at a major disadvantage.

Tirpitz's airing of reservations about the use of 4th Geschwader only triggered a further dose of caution aimed at Heinrich. On the evening of the 4th, he received a wireless message: 'His Majesty once more recommends Your Royal Highness to observe the greatest caution during operations. Action against superior forces and entry into waters suspected of being mined are to be avoided.'

As a result, Heinrich sent back three barrage breakers that had left Kiel to operate with his fleet. These were old merchant ships loaded with buoyant material. He had planned to use these to literally barge through dangerous waters. The gale resulted in four of his destroyers having their forward boiler rooms flooded. They failed to turn up at the rendezvous with 4th Geschwader at mid-day on the 5th. The weather also caused problems for the larger *V.25*, which was rejoining Behring after refuelling with oil in Danzig:

6 Previously *S.94*. All boats with numbers less than 114 renamed on 4 September 1914, freeing their designations for new destroyers.

Blücher, 1913, after fitting an experimental gun director on a tripod mast. Armed with 12x21cm guns in twin turrets, giving an eight-gun broadside. 4x15cm and 8x8.8cm guns on each side, 4x45cm underwater torpedo tubes. Hull protected by 18cm armour, speed 25 knots. (Public domain)

> I soon had to slow down to 19 knots. The sea was raging ever more violently. Solid waves roll over the boat, covering everything in white spray. The glass panes on the command bridge shatter with a clatter, a violent sea smashes the large iron fan head on the foredeck… The First Officer reports 'The last few waves have filled all the store and crew spaces in the foreship with water.' Now I have to report by wireless, 'Cannot reach the assembly point until 9pm due to heavy seas.'

The weather forced Heinrich to postpone a meeting to discuss his plans. The fleet had to move into calmer waters in the lee of Gotland, risking detection. Behring arrived in *Augsburg* from the outpost line.

At 4pm, the senior officers finally convened aboard *Blücher*. Heinrich outlined his plan. The aim was to check growing Russian confidence and drive them back to a defensive posture. His orders were:

a) To lure Russian forces out of the Gulf of Finland, to draw them south and cut them off.
b) To use the flotillas [to attack] as the opportunity arises.
c) To bombard lighthouses and signal stations.
d) Through demonstrations by the forces currently at my disposal, to make a lasting impression on the Russians at as many points on the Russian coast as possible, in order to facilitate [Behring's] task in the Baltic after the return of those formations to … the Hochsee forces.

Heinrich detailed his orders for the first day. The available vessels were to split into two groups and advance out of sight of land that night. Heinrich commanded the first, which included the two fastest battleships of 4th Geschwader, with their 28cm guns. He would advance west of Gotland to a point 70 miles west of Dagerort. Schmidt commanded the second, with the remaining battleships, with Behring scouting ahead. He would advance east of Gotland to a point east of Gotska Sandön. Behring would bait a trap by bombarding Dagerort and showing a light cruiser off Vindava at dawn, then advance to the Gulf of Finland's entrance. He would entice any Russian response towards Schmidt. Heinrich could then advance towards Bengtskär and trap the Russian forces between his two groups. After his recent experiences, Heinrich found Behring unusually cautious:

> He believes he can conclude from the behaviour of the cruisers that they are expecting German ships to advance towards the Gulf of Finland and will attempt to block the German ships' escape route. He assumes that Russian cruisers are somewhere near Bogskär … [and that] they will advance to the southeast to cut them off. The bombardment of Dagerort by *Augsburg* and *V.25* … is abandoned based on [his] assumptions.

There were also concerns that the Russians had mined the approaches to *Magdeburg*. Consequently, all points east of a line from Bengtskär to Cape Takkhona were to be regarded as potentially mined. The orders stressed the 'express and oft repeated order of His Majesty the Emperor to avoid engaging superior forces and channels suspected of being mined.' No doubt all left with the Kaiser's words firmly lodged in their minds. There were some last minute changes to the force. The stray destroyers came in that night, but *Amazone* and *S.124* returned to Danzig, as they had not been able to coal at sea during the gale. The two groups were as follows (see Appendices IV and V for warship details):

Grossadmiral Prinz Heinrich
- *Blücher* (flagship)
- 4th Geschwader detachment: (Kontreadmiral Hermann Alberts) *Braunschweig* (flagship of 2nd Admiral), *Elsass*
- *Strassburg* (Kapitän zur See Heinrich Retzmann)
- 2nd Torpedobootsflottille: (Korvettenkapitän Heinrich Schuur) *S.149* (leader boat), 3rd Halbflottille; *S.138*, *S.139*, *S.141*, *S.140*, *S.142*, 4th Halbflottille; *S.144*, *S.145*, *S.147*, *S.146*, *S.148*

Vizeadmiral Schmidt
- 4th Geschwader: *Wittelsbach* (flagship), *Wettin, Mecklenburg*, *Schwaben*, *Zähringen*,[7] *T.94* attached
- 6th Torpedobootsflottille: (Korvettenkapitän Max Schultz) *V.150* (leader boat), 11th Halbflottille; *V.151, V.153, V.154, V.152, V.155,* 12th Halbflottille; *V.156*, *V.157*, *V.159*, *V.158*, *V.160*
- Ostseestreitkräfte: (Kontreadmiral Behring) *Augsburg* (flagship), *Undine*, *Gazelle*, *V.25*

As the advance began, the wind dropped and the sea calmed. The destroyers were able to keep up without difficulty. Heinrich remembered that, 'A wonderful, clear moonlit night was followed by one of those overwhelmingly beautiful days that tend to occur at this time of year in the high latitudes before the autumn storms set in; it was as if the air was washed clean, visibility was very good.' The advance went off without a hitch. Behring formed a scouting line, 30 miles

7 The first four battleships formed 7th Division; *Zähringen* was normally part of Alberts's 8th Division.

Mecklenburg underway, pre-1908. Five battleships of this class had 4x24cm in twin turrets, with 9x15cm and 6x8.8cm guns on each side. 6x45cm underwater torpedo tubes. Hull protected by 22.5cm armour, speed around 17 knots. The five old Kaiser class were similar. (NH:46823)

wide, 10 miles ahead of Schmidt with his light cruisers, *V.25* and 6th Flottille. At dawn, Behring sent 6th Flottille back to coal off Gotland. *Undine*, on the right of the scouting line, steamed past Vindava, just three miles offshore. By 8am, both Heinrich and Schmidt's forces were in position. Heinrich spent the next two hours halted, transferring bagged coal from *Blücher* and the battleships to top up the bunkers of 2nd Flottille, with *Strassburg* keeping watch to the east. The limited endurance of the German destroyers imposed significant operational complications this far from German bases. It was a perfect target for submarine attack, but Wieting summed up the prevailing view: 'Enemy submarines had not been sighted yet anywhere [in the Baltic]. Russian mine warfare had actually not yet begun, so that apart from the very real possibility of encountering superior enemy surface forces, there was rarely anything to fear'.

At 10am, there was no enemy in sight. *Augsburg* and *V.25* advanced towards the Gulf of Finland, keeping in touch by signal light. Heinrich completed coaling and commenced his advance on Bengtskär. Two hours later, he was 25 miles south of Bogskär, which was clearly visible in the crisp air. There was no news from *Augsburg*. Heinrich halted. He was, 'Influenced by several orders I received from the Naval Command about the need for caution, I did not push further east at first, but decided to wait for reports from the reconnaissance squadron. This gave me the opportunity to examine the Bogskär lighthouse'. On approaching the lighthouse, *Blücher*'s rangefinder operators identified four masts, which proved to be a large wireless aerial frame. It was obviously a Russian signal outpost. Heinrich ordered Schuur to 'destroy it with a Halbflottille' Schuur led 3rd Halbflottille off to attack:

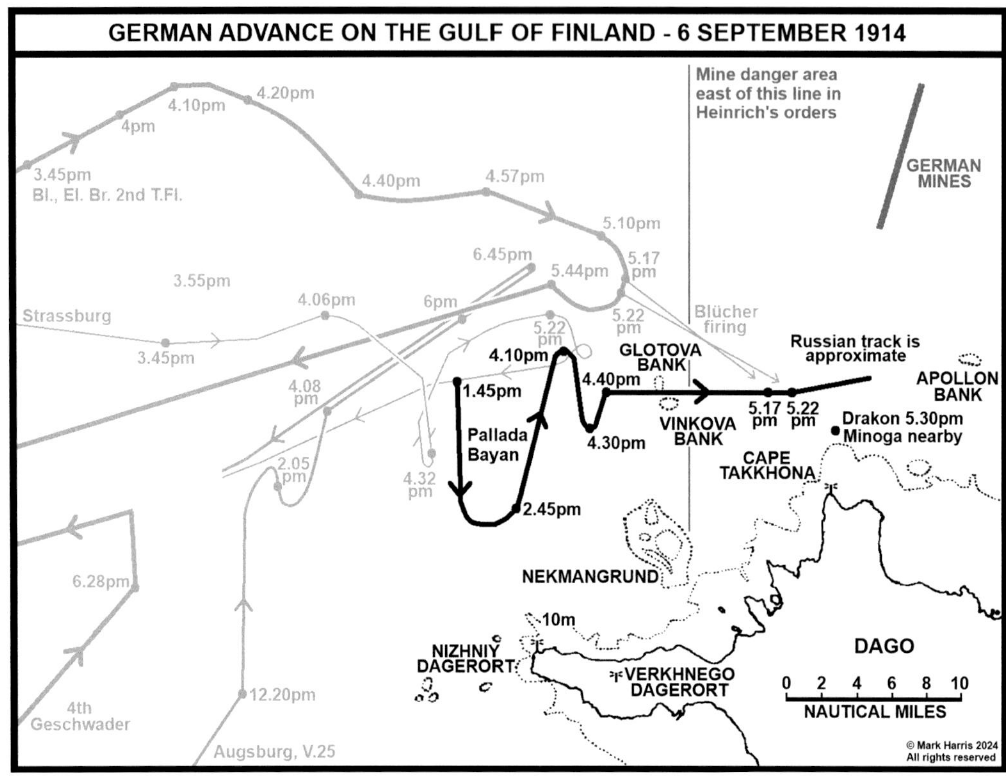

> … the Halbflottille commander, Kapitänleutnant [Heinrich] Boest, began the operation at high speed, opening a fierce and well-aimed fire on the lighthouse, which in a very short time developed a huge black plume of smoke, which was in stark contrast to the otherwise sunny, quiet day; the oil and petroleum supplies had probably been set on fire.. [three] destroyers sent out landing parties, which succeeded in capturing the Russian lighthouse crew, who had meanwhile taken cover on the island, without encountering any resistance; there was 1 deck officer, 3 sailors and 1 radio operator, who were brought on board *Blücher*. The interrogation of these people revealed that they had not seen any Russian ships since the outbreak of war, but had dutifully reported the approach of our ships to Helsingfors.

The fire gutted the inside of the lighthouse and the landing party had not been able to enter. Schuur had noticed smoke before opening fire. The occupants had burnt everything to avoid capture.

At 1:56pm, Heinrich finally received a report from Behring: 'Two large enemy cruisers in sight about 22 miles WNW½W from Cape Takkhona.' This was 40 miles to the east. It gave Heinrich, 'the impression that the Russian fleet was actually advancing. I briefly informed the crew of my suspicions and the contents of the report, urged them to do their duty and concluded with three cheers for our Supreme Commander; these cheers came from enthusiastic hearts and throats, they spread like a storm throughout the entire ship as the crews hurried to their battle stations.' Heinrich set course at 16 knots, the maximum sustainable speed of his battleships, to cut the Russian cruisers off from retreat north of the German minefield. Retzmann was ordered ahead to get in visual contact with *Strassburg*. Behring soon confirmed that the Russian cruisers were steering south after him. Despite their best efforts, the battleships were only able to reach 16½ knots. Kapitän zur See Hugo Langemak, commanding *Elsass*, complained that his stokers had to use rotten coal, left in the bunkers after their long stay in reserve. This clogged the boilers. Heinrich decided to forge ahead. *Blücher*'s stokers worked furiously to feed the boilers as she worked up to 24½ knots, with thick black smoke pouring from her funnels. Schmidt also picked up Behring's reports and headed towards him, but Heinrich was 70 miles ahead. His stokers managed to push the speed of his five older battleships towards 16 knots, creating a huge smoke plume in the clear air. At 2:40pm, there was unwelcome news from Behring. The enemy had turned north. *Strassburg* soon sighted enemy smoke 35 miles away. Retzmann increased speed and closed. He and Behring kept up regular reports on the enemy speed and course to Heinrich, as they shadowed, just out of range from the Russian cruisers, trying to entice them west. *Blücher* steadily closed, with 2nd Flottille in company. Retzmann confirmed two *Bayan* class armoured cruisers. *Blücher*'s main armament was more than a match for both of these vessels combined. When the enemy came in sight, Heinrich signalled *Strassburg* and *Augsburg* to close in and take station on the flagship. He was on the bridge:

> Apart from these two cruisers, no other enemy forces were visible. Despite the fact that the 4th Geschwader was still far behind at this time, I decided to engage both Russians.
>
> The Russians, for their part, must have recognized this intention, because it was soon observed that the smoke was increasing, and that they too were speeding up, steering widely varying courses from north to east, southeast and south, thereby giving the impression that they were first trying to bypass the [German mine] barrier to the north, then, recognizing this attempt as hopeless, to aim for the southern gap.

Blücher closed inexorably. By 5:17pm, the rangefinders gave a range of 14.7km. The mine danger line in Heinrich's orders was fast approaching: 'I ordered the commander, Fregattenkapitän [Alexander] Erdmann, to turn *Blücher* broadside on, reduce the speed of the ship and open fire; therefore *Blücher* put the rudder hard to starboard, turned to a southerly course, set the engine telegraphs to "low speed" and opened fire with the [eight] 21cm turret guns on the port side.' About 20 seconds later, the fall of shot bells sounded and the lookouts focussed their attention for the splash of the exploding shells. The salvo fell short. More followed: 'Five salvos, which were very good for direction, but too short due to the rapidly increasing distance, were despatched after the cruisers, which were heading east at their highest speed'. After five minutes, the estimated range was 17.8km. The Russian cruisers would quickly be beyond the 19.1km maximum range of the guns, if they were not already. The firing had gone, 'unanswered by the enemy, although the rangefinder [operator] could clearly see that their guns were aimed at *Blücher*, at their maximum elevation.'

Blücher ceased fire. Retzmann signalled by light that the behaviour of the Russian cruisers indicated that they had been attempting to make him follow in the direction of Glotova Bank, suggesting the presence of mines there. Heinrich also needed no reminder of the Kaiser's warnings: '... evening was approaching, the Russians' behaviour suggested that the "*Deutschland* barrier" we had put in place was being expanded, which I had neither the time nor the means to investigate; in addition, I had to reckon with the probability of night attacks by Russian destroyers...'. Heinrich withdrew to the west. Schmidt altered course to join him.

Drakon, one of four *Kayman* class. Armed with twin internal 45cm torpedo tubes at the bow and stern, and two external deck frames, but limited range, speed and seakeeping abilities. (Public domain)

Behring had seen distant smoke as early as 11:50am, but made a wide approach 'because of the danger of mines off Dagerort'. Perhaps he also hoped that Russian ships would approach to investigate his smoke, before giving himself away by wireless. However, an earlier report would not have changed the outcome. The visibility was so high that there was no opportunity to outflank and cut off a Russian warship unless it could first be enticed much further west.

Pallada and *Bayan* were on patrol duty that day. They had left Örö at 5.45am, under the command of Magnus. Submarines *Drakon* and *Minoga* were at the ambush position off Cape Takkhona. *Avrora* was moored off Odenskhol'm, guarding the depot ships *Afrika* and *Silach*, which were supporting salvage work on *Magdeburg*.

The first sighting that morning was *Undine* off Vindava, but it seemed routine. From 10am onwards, further reports began to arrive with increasing frequency as Behring's cruisers advanced past Ezel'. The first was by aerial reconnaissance out of Kil'kond. Later an armoured cruiser of the *Prinz Adalbert* class was reported to have fired two shells near Fil'zand Lighthouse. The cruiser was *Undine*, but the supposed shelling was a fantasy. At 2:20pm, the last report from Bogskär reached fleet headquarters. It reported five battleships of the *Wittelsbach* class, screened by light cruisers, 15 miles south of the lighthouse. Essen repeated it to ships at sea and issued a warning by wireless for ships in harbour to raise steam for departure.

Meanwhile, at 1pm, the patrol cruisers had sighted smoke to the southwest. Magnus went south to investigate and identified a *Bremen* class light cruiser, which kept just out of range to the west. It was *Augsburg*. A large smoke cloud soon appeared to the northwest. By 2.45pm, Magnus was approaching the shallows north of Dago and turned back north along his patrol line. *Strassburg* and *V.25* joined Behring, with the former mistaken for the armoured cruiser,

Roon. Since both had four funnels, this was understandable at a distance. The enemy seemed to be baiting him into pursuing. Ironically, each side was suspecting the other of trying to lure them in their direction. The smoke to the northwest was closing off the Russian cruisers route north of the minefield. Magnus turned back south. *Pallada* kept up a steady stream of reports.

By 4:20pm, 14 separate smoke plumes were closing from the northwest. With an overwhelmingly large force approaching, Magnus needed to retire on support. To get to the gap south of the minefield, he needed to head northeast to pass round the shallow Glotova Bank. This allowed the northern group to close rapidly. Magnus made an early turn to the east, although this meant sailing dangerously close to the shallows. Fortunately, the *Bayan* class had a lesser draught than typical armoured cruisers by design. In theory, they had a couple of metres clearance, based on the chart. Magnus had been steaming at low speed, but increased to 15 knots. The enemy continued to gain rapidly. Magnus increased to 19 knots. The leading enemy ship, surrounded by destroyers, had a tripod mast. It was identified as the battle cruiser *Moltke*, with ten 28cm guns and a speed of over 28 knots. The observers in the spotting top on *Bayan*, bringing up the rear, identified the similar *Von der Tann* or *Blücher*. Veys writes:

> … the rangefinder operator then called out a distance of 84 cables [15.6km], *Blücher* quickly turned broadside on and fired a salvo. Then the agonizing wait for where the shells would land – it turned out to be short, then salvo after salvo, thus he fired 4–5 salvos, and all of them landed short quite close astern. Then we breathed a sigh of relief, the tense state passed, since the distance was quickly increasing…

The Russian cruisers could not reply, as they were out of range. *Blücher* had underestimated the range when she opened fire and had not adjusted quickly enough to straddle. Magnus noted that the shell splashes were smaller than expected from 28cm shells.

Cape Takkhona signal station kept *Drakon* and *Minoga* informed of developments. By 4:40pm, it was obvious that the Germans were pursuing *Pallada* and *Bayan* towards the southern gap in the minefield that they were guarding. The submarines set off on the surface to intercept. When *Blücher* opened fire, Starshiy Leytenant Nikolay Gudim of *Drakon* had closed to within six miles of *Pallada*. The Russian cruisers swept past three miles to the north, 15 minutes later, spotting *Drakon* as they did so.[8] If *Blücher* had pursued them, the submarines might have been able to attack her as she went past. The Germans had not sighted them.

However, Heinrich gave up the chase and retired to the west. Magnus rendezvoused with Kolomeytsev at Odenskhol'm. He had stopped there after leaving Revel' at 1:25pm with *Gromoboy* and *Admiral Makarov*, as the latter was apparently limited to 12 knots by engine problems. Veys was unimpressed with the lack of support and suspected deliberate delay by Kolomeytsev. All available submarines had taken up a patrol line west of Revel'. Heinrich's concern about destroyer attack were also well founded. These advanced west in the dusk, to scope the possibility for a night torpedo attack. At 7:55pm, *Sil'nyy* of 5th Divizion was the last ship to report sighting the Germans: 'Enemy armoured cruiser in sight in Square 72 [35 miles northwest of Dagerort], course north.' 1st Divizion advanced south of the minefield. However, Heinrich continued to fall back far to the west. The destroyers had to retire when contact was

8 Emme incorrectly identifies the submarine as *Akula*, which Gudim later commanded.

lost as darkness fell. The cruisers and submarines returned to port for the night, leaving the defence to 5th and 1st Divizions, which both remained on the outpost line.[9]

Behring raids the Gulf of Bothnia, *Akula*'s first patrol and the Baltiyskiy Flot advances

The Russians quickly realised that the attacking cruiser had been *Blücher*, as it was the only German warship with a tripod. Based on reports from Magnus, Dagerort, Takkhona and Utö, Essen concluded that the enemy fleet had been made up of, 'five *Wittelsbach* class battleships, armoured cruiser *Blücher*, one *Yorck* class cruiser, two *Friedrich Carl* class cruisers, a *Prince Heinrich* class cruiser, a *Bremen* class cruiser, a *Gazelle* class cruiser, and a flotilla of 11 destroyers.' The enemy actions indicated a reconnaissance rather than a serious attack. Nevertheless, he ordered his fleet to be ready to proceed to sea for 4am on the 7th.

At dawn, the submarines reinforced the defence line. Essen ordered 2nd Brigada Kreyserov to reconnoitre off Dago, whilst 1st Brigada took up position west of the minefield in support. Leskov saw only one possible warship, in the distance, in Square 55, about 10 miles south of Örö. There were two steamships with it, which he suspected of minelaying. Otherwise, the enemy had vanished.

Essen's cruisers were too slow to risk unsupported further west, so he sent his best submarine, *Akula*, Kapitan 2nd Ranga Sergey Vlas'yev, to reconnoitre 15 miles west of Dagerort. Once there he was to use his discretion as to further action. *Akula* reached the position at 7pm. There was nothing in sight. The sea was very choppy with wind from the southwest, a slight haze and a full moon. Vlas'yev decided to head west to get in the lee of the Swedish coast, recharge his batteries, then return. Suddenly, at 12.20am a cruiser was spotted crossing *Akula*'s path, 700-1,000m ahead. It would take three minutes to dive. Vlas'yev ordered the diesel engines stopped immediately, and bought himself some time by turning parallel to the cruiser to delay a collision. As soon as the clutches allowed, he ordered full speed ahead on the electric motor, allowing diving to commence. A gun boomed out from the cruiser as *Akula* slid below. Due to the speed of the emergency dive, she rapidly drove down to 25m. The beat of the cruiser's propellers closed inexorably. There was relief as they passed overhead, just behind the wheelhouse.

The deep dive had started a leak on the central propeller shaft, but the pumps were able to keep the water down as she steered clear of the area. About an hour later, *Akula* surfaced and headed west, charging the batteries. At 4:05am, two destroyers came into sight just 200-400m ahead to starboard. As *Akula* once more began an emergency dive the destroyers doubled back, one coming up aft and the other approaching from port. As the boat dived, Vlas'yev fired a torpedo from the stern tubes at 200-400m. It had little chance of hitting, but apparently caused the destroyers to turn away. Once dived, *Akula* was unable to escape the destroyers, which

9 Винтер, 'походов', pp.179–187; Pohl, *Aufzeichnungen*, pp.43–50; BA:RM28 KTB, RM92 *Blücher*, *Elsass*, *Strassburg*, *Undine*, *Wittelsbach*, *Zähringen* KTB, RM56 Torpedobootsverbände der Kaiserlichen Marine, 2.Torpedobootsflottille KTB; Firle, *Ostsee*, pp.104–118; Albert Stoelzel (ed.), *Ehrenrangliste der Kaiserlich Deutschen Marine, 1914-1918* (Berlin: Thormann & Goetsch, 1930), p.14, 120; Меркушов, *Записки*, pp.231–234; Prinz Heinrich von Preussen, 'Der Vorstoss S.M.S. "Blücher"', in *unbesiegt 1*, pp.32–38; Wieting, *Ostsee*, p.29–33; РГАВМФ:Фонд 716, Опись 2, Дело 23, p.5, Опись 1, Дело 392, p.3; Вейс, «Баян», p.40.

Akula, with *Kayman* class in background. Armed with twin internal 45cm torpedo tubes at the bow and stern, and four external deck frames. Unloaded starboard frames are visible. These swung out to fire. (Public domain)

appeared to be following her movements for the next two hours. They finally seemed to have gone, but when *Akula* surfaced, were about a mile away. They fired as she headed straight back down. The weather had calmed. Vlas'yev realised that *Akula* was trailing oil waste, which was being pumped out with the bilge water. He ordered the pumps turned off, although this meant risking the leaking water reaching the motor and shorting it out. Finally, at 11.10am the destroyers were gone. The battery was almost completely exhausted. *Akula* surfaced, started the diesels and remained stationary to build up some charge quickly. She then headed northeast. When a *Gazelle* class cruiser was spotted in the distance, Vlas'yev dived briefly once more that afternoon, but it passed too far off to attack. *Akula* reached Oleg Bank as darkness fell and spent the night there.

Whilst falling back from the encounter with the Russian cruisers, Heinrich had issued orders for a display of force off Vindava next day. Pohl's deputy, Behncke, was just completing an operational review of 'Targets of attack for decisive action against the Russian coast.' He considered that there was scope to disrupt trade in the Gulf of Bothnia. Heinrich therefore received a wireless message from the Admiralstab that changed his plans: 'Promise of great effect from disrupting daily Finnish steamer traffic Raumo–Gävle.' Behring and his captains boarded *Blücher* to be briefed by Heinrich and a pilot familiar with the Gulf of Bothnia. At 2am, *Augsburg*, *Strassburg*, *Gazelle* and *V.25* left for the Gulf of Bothnia. The main body kept underway off the Swedish coast for the rest of the night, rendezvousing off Huvudskär Island next morning.

On the 7th, Heinrich remained off the Swedish coast. 2nd Flottille had to coal again from *Blücher* and the battleships, resulting in significant periods stopped, but *S.147* had to return to Kiel with overheated shaft bearings. Whilst coaling, 6th Flottille arrived from Hoburg, less *V.154*, which returned to Kiel with storm damage. Heinrich had concluded that it had been a mistake not to eliminate Russian wireless outposts in the area. After coaling, he ordered 2nd Flottille to reconnoitre the Åland Islands, destroy the wireless station assumed to be on Lågskär and capture any Russian personnel found. The lighthouse would be unharmed, as it was an important navigation mark for Swedish and German vessels. *Blücher* remained stopped to coal *T.94*, whilst Schmidt exercised formation manoeuvres with 4th Geschwader. Heinrich had clearly discounted the possibility of submarine attack.

Schuur sent ashore 30 men at Lågskär, using one boat from each of his ten destroyers. They found the island completely deserted, with no traces of military activity or a wireless. Schuur then reconnoitred off Mariehamn, the principal port on the largest of the Åland Islands, but found nothing suspicious. The Flottille returned to the main body that evening. Heinrich sent it back to Kiel.

Behring had better luck in the Gulf of Bothnia. Commerce warfare was to adhere to international law and prize regulations, but any prizes taken were to be sunk, as it was too far to take them to Germany. Behring left *Strassburg* and *Gazelle* patrolling the trade route between Raumo and the Swedish coast. *Augsburg* and *V.25* headed for Räfsö Island, off Mäntyluoto, the outer harbour of the port of Björneborg. Behring intended to bombard kerosene storage tanks that the pilot had mentioned, but they were too close to civilian buildings and a church. He therefore abandoned the bombardment. On the way back, Behring sent *V.25* to search a Swedish passenger steamer, *Gauthiod*. Wieting found 34 British passport holders of military age. He thought they were, 'young sailors from the British [merchant] steamers in Finland.' Wieting had them politely rounded up, and then took them to *Augsburg*. *V.25* was soon approaching another small passenger steamer, flying the Russian merchant flag:

> The sun had already set in the magnificent evening light and we had to get close to see the national flag! The whole deck was full of people! Enthusiastic waving of handkerchiefs and shouts greeted the 'Russian' destroyer. ... Only a small group of people stood sadly to the side. Then suddenly the picture changed. The 'enthusiastic' group became 'dismayed', the sad group, 'Germans', cheered loudly...
>
> I gave them a quarter of an hour to pack their suitcases and climb over... 'Cast off.' 'Open fire at 200 meters.' One shot hits the waterline, a second a little higher, the next ones all on the waterline. However, *Uleåborg* refuses to sink. Then a shot hits the beautiful salon aft. In an instant, the whole ship is in flames, a splendid picture in the dark night! And soon there is nothing left to see of *Uleåborg*.[10]

The 46 crew and passengers from *Uleåborg* were transferred to *Augsburg*. Behring withdrew his ships from the Gulf as planned, to rendezvous with Heinrich next morning. His other cruisers had only intercepted neutral shipping, with no contraband.

Heinrich spent the night of the 7/8th steaming up and down off the Swedish coast with *Blücher* and 4th Geschwader. The ten destroyers of 6th Flottille dispersed to the east on a defensive screen from Almagrundet Lightship to Gotska Sandön, with *Undine* at the southern end. *Amazone* had returned from Danzig that afternoon and covered the gap from Gotska Sandön

10 Built in 1876, 548 GRT.

to Fårö with *T.94*. The aim was to prevent a night attack by Russian destroyers. *Akula* had encountered *Undine*,[11] then the 6th Flottille destroyer screen. Vlas'yev had remained close to the 7:30am rendezvous point for Heinrich's fleet, which had resulted in constantly sighting patrolling destroyers just to the west of *Akula*'s position. The vessel sighted in the distance at 4pm was not a German warship. There are no indications that any of the German vessels suspected the presence of a submarine at any time. The manoeuvres observed were simply routine turns on their patrol positions. Patrolling destroyers were very difficult to attack and virtually impossible at night. The German screen, whilst intended to intercept destroyer attack, also ensured that *Akula* remained submerged, away from the fleet.

For a submarine, getting a clear picture of events on the surface at night, especially during an emergency dive, was challenging. Contemporary periscope optics made it even harder once dived. Adrenalin transforms bangs and light flashes to shellfire. Vlas'yev was making his first offensive patrol. Night encounters are disorientating. The discrepancies between actual events and his experience of them is unsurprising. On inspection, the detonators on the torpedoes exposed to the sea were found to be have been damaged by the deep dive. They would have failed to detonate if fired. It was an inevitable drawback of externally mounted torpedoes.

Late on the 7th, Baltiyskiy Flot headquarters received messages that German forces were active in the Gulf of Bothnia. Essen had the fleet concentrate at Revel'. He called a meeting of his senior flag officers that evening and announced his intention to advance west. Essen responded to doubts that some expressed about the advisability and risk of doing so: 'tomorrow we will go out, and if we meet the enemy, we will engage him in battle.' Leskov's report of possible minelaying in Square 55 gave him the necessary pretext. The German advance had interrupted sweeping work. The declared objective was to, 'cover the work of the minesweeping party with a fleet sortie.' Essen warned the fleet: 'It is assumed that the enemy has placed a minefield north of the first one – at Oleg Bank.'

At 4am on the 8th, *Ryurik* led out the four battleships, *Pallada* and *Bayan*, escorted by *Novik* and the Poludivizion. 2nd and 7th Divisions preceded them with their sweeps out. The other two minesweeping Otdeleniya joined them off Lappvik. The force passed north of the German minefield and rendezvoused with Leskov, who was still on the patrol line with *Rossiya* and *Oleg*. The four cruisers then proceeded with all three minesweeping Otdeleniya to cover their work in Square 55, whilst Essen remained with the battleships and the destroyers in a supporting position. *Novik* was despatched to reconnoitre, as Graf relates:

> The weather was fine; there were almost no waves, and our destroyers rolled only slightly in the subsiding swell. The speed was from eight to 10 knots.
>
> The enemy was still nowhere to be seen, and reports that his ships seem to have penetrated the Gulf of Bothnia were only from civilian sources. Therefore, about 3pm, the Fleet Commander ordered us to go to the Åland Sea and conduct reconnaissance and, if we discovered the enemy, immediately report this, and try to attack him ourselves.
>
> We increased to 26 knots and by 6pm were already in sight of the Swedish coast. Suddenly smoke appeared on the horizon; then masts, a funnel and a hull began to appear.

11 Emme assumes *Akula* encountered *Augsburg*, as did Russian reports. Behring was still in the Gulf of Bothnia. Tomashevich suggests *Amazone*. However, *Undine*'s charted track converges with *Akula*. *Amazone*'s does not.

> Undoubtedly, it was a warship, but, alas, not a German one, but a Swedish one – a coast defence battleship of the *Oden* class, and with it a destroyer of the *Magne* class. The commander, having instructions not to disturb the Swedes, did not want to come too close to them, and therefore we turned south. Having gone on this course long enough for the Swedish ships to disappear from view, we turned back to the Åland Sea, examined it and, when it got dark, went back to the Gulf of Finland. In order to avoid meeting our ships in the dark, we cruised all night near Oleg Bank; only at about 8am did we join the main body.

During the afternoon, Essen received news that the German fleet had been off Vindava, later passing Libava. Apparently, they were retiring. There were sporadic reports of enemy light forces, from Utö and the southern Gulf of Bothnia. Mariehamn reported six battleships in sight. However, *Novik*'s wireless report led him to conclude correctly that these forces were Swedish. Essen decided to anchor for the night off Hangö and investigate further next morning.

Essen raised anchor at dawn and headed west with *Ryurik* and the battleships, screened by 5th Divizion, with 2nd Divizion sweeping ahead. The minesweepers were despatched with the four cruisers to complete the work on Square 55. Essen was concerned that nothing more had been heard from Bogskär. He sent three destroyers of the Poludivizion to investigate. *Akula* spotted the fleet as it approached. Vlas'yev surfaced to make his report that the enemy had vacated the area to the west and then returned to Moon Sound.

The enemy had vanished. Essen looped round west of the sweeping force and headed back east, passing the German minefield to the south, with 2nd Divizion again sweeping ahead. This was the first time this area had been swept since the German minefield was laid. The destroyers disposed of three floating German mines. Essen stopped off to carry out an inspection of the salvage work on *Magdeburg*. He was unimpressed with damage to equipment on the ship and took action to ensure the organisation of the work was improved. The Poludivizion reported that evening that Bogskär was deserted. The post was not replaced, as the rocky outcrop was isolated and impossible to defend. A search began for the missing. It was some time before the Germans confirmed that they were prisoners.

Despite the lack of contact, the cruise had helped to lift spirits and shake off the gloom of awaiting attack: 'The sight of the sunken enemy ship [*Magdeburg*] made a powerful impression on the crews.' The Russian submariners had also demonstrated that they could do something other than mount a defensive guard. Essen made a point in his report of highlighting the consequences of the restrictions he was working under. Since he could not use the fleet, if the Germans returned to the Gulf of Bothnia, all he would be able to do was to mine the entrance in the Åland Sea, cutting it off from navigation.

As Essen suspected, on the 8th, Heinrich had reverted to his plan for a 'show the flag' cruise down the Russian coast prior to a return to base. The strain that the old vessels in his force was under showed itself when *Undine*'s starboard engine broke down. Heinrich sent her directly back to Danzig. The force made its demonstration by steaming down the coast 8 miles off Vindava and then withdrew to the southwest. That evening they split up, with Heinrich heading for Kiel to coal and re-provision, whilst Behring returned to Danzig with *Augsburg*, *Gazelle*, *Amazone* and *V.25*.

The British prisoners were detained. They were crews of four British merchant ships stranded in the Baltic, returning home, as Wieting suspected. However, the Admiralstab ordered their release on 18 September, as Prize Law only authorised the capture of persons, 'serving with an enemy Power.' It was just as well, as the British Admiralty had spotted that, 'This forms an excellent pretext for the removal of German subjects from neutral vessels.'

Like Essen, Langemak saw benefits from active operations on the crew of *Elsass*: 'the six-day voyage in enemy waters was of great value for the training of the entire crew. The efficiency of the engineering personnel, especially the stokers in the stokeholds, has increased considerably. The entire crew is more accustomed to a wartime mentality than it was during the training period in the western Baltic Sea.' Langemak also highlighted the complete lack of any minesweeping capability for the German force. The contrast with the very thorough arrangements in place for the Russian fleet is stark. However, both sides were still ignoring the possibility of submarine attack. The fact that there had so far been no confirmed sightings of enemy submarines had created a dangerous complacency.

Ingenohl contacted Pohl to, 'request the early return of the forces detached to the Baltic Sea, as there are signs that the British are planning an advance into the German Bight.' Pohl was unimpressed by the results: 'Prinz Heinrich has been in the Gulf of Finland and the Gulf of Bothnia, but without much success.' On the evening of the 8th, he wirelessed Heinrich: 'All forces detached to the Baltic from the Hochseeflotte are to hasten their return to the North Sea.' Next day, Pohl saw the Kaiser to confirm his decision. He was alarmed that, 'The Baltic will then be defenceless against a breakthrough via the Belts.' Pohl had to make a concession: 'in order to avoid the withdrawal of North Sea forces, I request permission to relocate three older submarines to the Baltic Sea. He agrees.' Heinrich would get the submarines that he had requested after Behring's last sortie, but the Hochseeflotte warships went through the Kaiser Wilhelm Canal to the North Sea as soon as they arrived at Kiel.

Ultimately, Pohl was right that Heinrich's advance had little impact. The Russian Sixth Army command was already firmly rooted in its defensive posture, whilst Essen saw no reason to change his assessment of the current German force as posing no serious threat to his defences. On the 9th, the Brigada Podvodnykh Lodok moved its main base to Moon Sound. Merkushov wrote that, 'the submarines will be sent out on duty to the Nizhniy Dagerort or Takkhona lighthouse in turn and, on receiving information from the post about the enemy's movements, will go out to meet him.' More boats in forward ambush positions increased the chances of a successful attack if the Germans returned, but Merkushov worried that mooring in the open anchorage would affect the efficiency of the small submarines. As autumn weather loomed, 'a stay in Moon Sound, in the absence of a coastal base there, will differ little from being at sea and will in no way facilitate any rest for the personnel.'

The constraints under which both Essen and Heinrich were operating had virtually guaranteed an indecisive result to any encounter. Something would have to change to break the deadlock, but in the meantime, Essen's expanding defence area was gradually narrowing the scope for German attacks and laying a foundation for offensive actions.[12]

12 BA:RM92 *Elsass*, *Strassburg*, *Undine*, *Zähringen*, *Augsburg* KTB, RM28 KTB; Firle, *Ostsee*, pp.119–128; Графъ, *Новикъ*, pp.17–19; Киреев, *Траление*, pp.26–27; Винтер, 'походов', pp.187–194; Pohl, *Aufzeichnungen*, pp.53–54; Меркушов, *Записки*, pp.235–241; РГАВМФ:Фонд 716, Опись2, Дело 10, pp.54–57; Wieting, *Ostsee*, pp.33–35; Виноградов and Федечкин, *Макаров*, p.111; TNA:ADM137/271 Baltic Sea Operations, Docketed papers, 1914, 1915, pp.236–242.

An operational pause

On 10 September, Behncke completed his review of offensive options in the Baltic. There would be no shift of strategy and no 'decisive action':

> For none of the targets of attack [in the Gulf of Finland] are the expected losses even remotely commensurate with the probable success. Only a large-scale landing operation by the army can lead to a decisive success. The navy would have to accept heavy losses for its achievement.
>
> … strong security of the western Baltic Sea would be necessary to prevent British forces from breaking through the Danish waterways. As a result, the North Sea would be greatly depleted of vessels.
>
> Outside the Gulf of Finland, the occupation of the Åland Islands as a base could be considered in the event of a prolonged blockade [of the Gulf of Finland]. Repeating advances into the Gulf of Bothnia from time to time appears advantageous and feasible …

However, with Heinrich's depleted force, all of this was academic. Behring's cruisers were in need of repairs and boiler maintenance after six weeks of continuous service at sea. *Gazelle* needed a new wireless. Heinrich ordered an operational pause, trusting that the fleet sortie had deterred further Russian advances for the time being. Operations off the Russian coast were suspended. On the 13th Heinrich reorganised his forces. Advances would only resume once Behring was reinforced, as *Augsburg* and *Amazone* were the only cruisers he retained. Even then, Heinrich ruled the Gulf of Bothnia out of bounds, due to the danger of his small force being cut-off by superior Russian forces.

V.186, *V.25* and *V.26* were joining the Hochseeflotte. The ageing *T.91*, *T.93* and *T.94* transferred to a North Sea harbour defence flotilla. In return, Heinrich received eight destroyers, largely from reserves, with raw crews, which needed time to prepare for operational use. It was a small increase in quantity, but overall, a less capable force. Heinrich re-organised them into two Halbflottille. Behring would receive the newest boats, but all were of limited capabilities:

19th Halbflottille (Kapitänleutnant Ralph Graf von der Recke-Volmerstein) under Mischke: *S.120*, *S.123*, *S.125*, *G.134*, *S.124*, *S.127*, *T.97*, *Carmen*
20th Halbflottille (Kapitänleutnant Hermann Ehrhardt) under Behring: *G.133*, *G.132*, *G.135*, *G.136*

Behring would also receive Pohl's reluctant allocation of three relatively modern diesel powered submarines. *U.23* and *U.25* arrived at Kiel on the 11th. These boats were still working up and training their crews. *U.26* had recently been mobilised after completing extensive maintenance repairs at Kiel. They had shorter range than the latest boats, with temperamental early pattern diesels, but were a huge improvement on the *U.3* class. Pohl had requested even older, paraffin-fuelled submarines, but their use in the Baltic was impractical, as the unusually fresh water made them difficult to control underwater. Kapitänleutnant Hans Adam, with destroyer *D.10* as leader, would command them as 5th Unterseebootshalbflottille, based at Danzig.

Heinrich made training a priority for Behring: '… the [destroyers and submarines] are not trained to work with cruisers, and torpedo and gunnery training is not yet adequate. These gaps must be addressed. This was the main reason for requesting Halbflottille commanders ... The completion of this work, which ensures success, competes for time with offensive activities ... This must be accepted.'

U.1, *U.3* and *U.4* returned to training duties, under the Marinestation der Ostsee. Two additional auxiliary minelayers, *Hertha* and *Odin*, also entered service, the latter replacing *Prinz Waldemar*, which returned to civilian use. The provision of reconnaissance aircraft was improving slowly. A small non-rigid airship, *P.L.6*, had joined on 1 September. On the 17th, the somewhat larger *P.L.19* arrived. It had been constructed for a British order, and was deemed unsuitable for North Sea operations. There were still only 20 seaplanes. They were mostly concentrated around Kiel.

During the operational pause, the Russian offensive into Ostpreussen collapsed. The army was concerned that the Russians might fall back via Memel, which was almost undefended. On the 12th, his opposite number in the army, General Helmuth von Moltke, approached Pohl. He wanted the navy to cut off the Russian retreat by destroying their pontoon bridges over the Memel River to the south of the city. Pohl was baffled: 'how is a boat supposed to get in there in the shallow water? And on the river itself, it will be shot up by the fleeing armies before it can get to the bridges.' However, he was reluctant to refuse, and contacted Heinrich: 'Extremely important, disrupt the Russian retreat via Memel and the [neighbouring] Kurischem Lagoon and support the army by destroying pontoon bridges across the Memel River beyond Tilsit [25 miles inland]. With the boats and aircraft there, Putzig should support the transfer of troops from Danzig to Memel.' When Behring received the orders from Heinrich, he was unable to find anyone with whom he could set up an effective liaison. No aircraft were available at Putzig. *Amazone* and *S.124* were despatched to Memel. Horn, the senior officer, agreed with the local army commander that attempting to attack the pontoon bridges with steamers was futile. A naval landing party remained on standby to assist the army, but German cavalry soon arrived to secure the area, also making troop transport unnecessary. The Russians retreated to the south. After a few days, the navy stood down. The incident demonstrated how little thought had gone into the practicalities and procedures for co-operation between the army and navy.

With the crisis over, ships moved to their stations in the new organisation. Behring began a programme of intensive drills and exercises with his two cruisers, *D.10*, *U.23* and *U.25*. The eleven auxiliary armed trawlers based at Neufahrwasser helped keep watch off the Bay of Danzig.

The Baltiyskiy Flot also took advantage of the lull to catch up on maintenance and carry out exercises and practice shoots. Reports suggested that the Germans had withdrawn, with only occasional sightings of German warships off Memel. The directional wireless station picked up nothing further north. The fleet had been consuming around 10,000t of coal every week. Fortunately, a 40,000t emergency reserve had been stockpiled in anticipation of an intense period of activity when war broke out, avoiding a crisis. The pause allowed the depleted stockpiles of coal to be replenished. Imports of high quality Welsh coal were needed to supplement domestic supplies, but this could now only be delivered via the Arctic. A steady stream of colliers began arriving via the port of Arkhangel'sk. This tenuous route became a vital lifeline for the Russian war effort and coal supply remained an ongoing concern for Essen.

The minesweeping force expanded, by forming the 2nd Morskaya Partiya Traleniya under Kapitan 2nd Ranga Sergey Kovalevskiy. This had 10–12 small requisitioned commercial steamers, including German vessels interned in Russian ports. The work to define the limits of the German minefield and sweep the channels used by the fleet continued on a daily basis. It was vital to ensure that the fleet had freedom of manoeuvre, but it was highly risky work.

On the 22nd four of the newly equipped vessels, *No.5*, *No.6*, *No.7* and *No.8*,[13] with relatively inexperienced crews, headed out of Lappvik to sweep off the eastern side of the barrier. Recent strong westerly winds could have dragged mines to the east and these needed clearing. At 8:35am, they set their sweeps and advanced south in line abreast, with the destroyer *Prochnyy* at the eastern end, once again serving as a wireless link. At 10:06am, the sweepers reached a point three miles east of the position of the northern end of the barrier. They were working in pairs, with the sweep line running between each pair. Suddenly, a mine detonated on the line of the easternmost pair, *No.5* and *No.6*. They stopped to drop a marker buoy. As they did so, another mine exploded at the bow of *No.7*. The small steamer was shattered and sank in under two minutes. The officer on watch, Michman Nikolayev, was dead. Many men were struggling in the water. The commander of *Prochnyy*, Kapitan 2nd Ranga Konstantin Mertvago, took a considerable risk by moving in immediately to pick them up. *No.8* stopped her engine to lower lifeboats. Her stern drifted onto another mine, which exploded. The commander, Leytenant Boris Mant'ev was mortally wounded. *No.8* was sinking fast. Mant'ev sent Mashinist 1st Stat'i Andrey Zimin down at great risk to the engine room to blow off the steam, as the boilers were in danger of adding to the mayhem by exploding. Ignal'shchik (signalman) Zakhariy Savchuk tried his best to save Mant'ev, risking his own life to stay with him until the ship went under. Fearing that the entire unit was now surrounded by mines and could all be sunk, *Prochnyy* sent an SOS in clear language: 'Two minesweepers exploded.' *No.5* and *No.6* lowered their boats to assist with rescuing the survivors. They searched for two hours, until all hope of any further rescues was gone. Of the 71 crew, eight from *No.7* and four from *No.8* had been lost and 14 of the survivors were wounded, two of them seriously. The surviving vessels headed east to clear the area. Four destroyers of 2nd Divizion responded to *Prochnyy*'s signals. They provided some much needed medical assistance to the wounded, as neither *Prochnyy*, nor the minesweepers, had any medical personnel on-board. The force then returned to port.

Since the sweepers had clearly entered the minefield itself, the associated danger area was extended 10 miles east. More experienced crews would have reduced the risk by operating in a staggered formation, with the rear pair partially covered by the forward pair. *Prochnyy* was also unnecessarily at risk in not following astern. Essen praised the steadiness of the crews during the incident in a general order, but they were gaining their sweeping skills at a high cost.[14]

13 *No.5* ex-*Ryurik*, (1900), 509 GRT, *No.6* ex-German *Stella*, (1889), 469 GRT, *No.7* ex-*Triton*, (1890), 659 GRT, *No.8* ex-*Moon* (1880), 632 GRT.

14 BA:RM5/831 Admiralstab der Marine / Seekriegsleitung der Kaiserlichen Marine, RM28 KTB; Firle, *Ostsee*, pp.128–135; Pohl, *Aufzeichnungen*, pp.56–57; Киреев, *Траление*, pp.28–29, 355; Винтер, 'походов', pp.194–198; Форум Журнал Кортик, <https://kortic.borda.ru/?1-10-0-00000192-000-0-0-1715354985>, retrieved 17 September 2024; Меркушов, *Записки*, pp.247–248; РГАВМФ:Фонд 716, Опись 2, Дело 10, p.176.

Heinrich's second fleet sortie

The German Army had triumphed in Ostpreussen, but the Austro-Hungarian Army was retreating in Galizien and had requested help. General Erich von Falkenhayn had stepped in to replace the ailing Moltke. On 19 September, he approached Pohl for help:

> [He] asked … whether the fleet could not carry out a demonstration off the Russian coast, with the aim of simulating a landing operation, in order to prevent the Russians from moving the troops stationed in northern Poland to Galizien. – A detailed examination reveals that the transport ships, which are to be made available in Stettin, other Baltic ports and Hamburg, need at least 14 days to be fitted out. The promised brigade [of infantry] therefore cannot board until then.
>
> At 6pm I make a report to His Majesty, who is very enthusiastic about the expedition and approves that the 4th and 5th Geschwader, *Blücher*, two modern light cruisers, two Torpedobootsflottille and a Minensuchdivision from the Hochsee forces, under Prinz Heinrich, can be used for this purpose. The 3rd Geschwader can also be used … when the heavy cruisers return [from an operation planned in the North Sea].

Ingenohl had already asked for the new battleships of 3rd Geschwader go to the Baltic to work up, as the North Sea was now considered too dangerous for training, due to ongoing British submarine attacks. Pohl had ruled out a fleet advance in the North Sea at this time. He was therefore happy to seize on Falkenhayn's idea to appear useful to the army.

Vindava was selected as the target, solely because it was easy to approach for a token attack. Behncke considered the Gulf of Riga preferable for a serious landing, but this would require a more substantial covering force. Late that evening Heinrich received his orders: 'Go to Vindava with the forces mentioned and available Baltic forces. Prepare for a conspicuous landing of a large number of troops. Embark the brigade as soon as possible in Neufahrwasser'. Pohl had asked the army to have the troops ready for transport at Neufahrwasser by the 25th, but as he quickly discovered, this was wildly optimistic. He communicated a revised plan to Heinrich on the 20th:

> Since the initially intended landing of a brigade in Vindava cannot be scheduled in time … the operation will have to be limited to a demonstration with the available naval forces. Through conspicuous measures such as minesweeping, reconnaissance and, if necessary, small landing operations, an attempt will be made to create the impression that a large troop landing is planned and being prepared at Vindava.

A deliberately ostentatious preparation of a transport fleet capable of moving an entire division of troops also commenced. A weary Ingenohl commented: 'Always just demonstrations.' He also highlighted that the need to remove coal from his newer battleships for passage through the Kaiser Wilhelm Canal would mean a significant delay. Heinrich went ahead without them as, '4th and 5th Geschwader are sufficient.' To support the watch on the western Baltic for the duration of the operation, 5th Aufklärungsgruppe was again made available.

Heinrich's plan used the oldest battleships of 5th Geschwader to transport the landing force. They took in additional boats, small arms and ammunition. Each of the seven ships would accommodate around 100 troops and their equipment, greatly reducing their ability to engage in combat. The armoured cruiser *Yorck*, which was working up in the Baltic, substituted for *Blücher,* which required work on her turret electrical systems. It took time to concentrate and coal all of the ships. Heinrich delayed departure until the morning of the 22nd, to allow sweeping of the Fehmarn Belt. Mines had broken free and drifted there in high winds. However, he was under pressure, receiving a telegram the previous evening: 'His Majesty orders that a demonstration on the Russian coast should take place as soon as possible.' Since the troops were not ready, Heinrich decided to head straight to Vindava next morning, hoisting his flag on the battleship *Braunschweig.*

Hochseeflotte light cruisers and destroyers had already reinforced Behring at Danzig. Heinrich ordered him to take up an outpost line for the morning of the 23rd from Fårö to the western exit of the Gulf of Riga. Behring left behind his submarines to continue their exercises, considering them still inadequately trained.

This was the largest force yet deployed in the Baltic. By mid-morning on the 23rd, all vessels were in position to begin the demonstration (see Appendices IV and V for details of vessels, flotillas organised as above):

Main outpost line under Behring:
Light cruisers: *Augsburg* (flagship), *Graudenz* (pennant of Kapitän zur See Karl von Restorff, 2nd Führer der Torpedobootsstreitkräfte), *Stralsund*; 6th Torpedobootsflottille – 11 destroyers

Demonstration force, approaching Vindava:
2nd Torpedobootsflottille – 9 destroyers

Main body under Heinrich in support position mid-way between Gotland and Steynort:
Cruisers: *Yorck, Amazone, Gazelle*
Braunschweig (fleet flagship), 4th Geschwader: (Schmidt), 7th Division, *Wittelsbach* (flagship), *Wettin*, *Mecklenburg*, 8th Division (Alberts), *Schwaben* (2nd flagship) *Elsass*, *Zähringen*
5th Geschwader: (Vizeadmiral Max von Grapow), 9th Division, *Kaiser Wilhelm II* (flagship), *Kaiser Barbarossa*, *Kaiser Wilhelm der Grosse*, *Kaiser Karl der Grosse*, 10th Division (acting 2nd Admiral Kapitän zur See Alfred Begas), *Kaiser Friedrich III* (2nd flagship), *Wörth*, *Brandenburg*
Attached to Geschwader as despatch vessels: *S.139*, *S.141* (from 2nd Flottille)
2nd Minensuchdivision: (Kapitänleutnant Hermann Schoemann), *D.6* (leader boat), *T.30*, *T.39*, *T.49*, *T.50*, *T.51*, *T.52*, *T.53*, *T.54*, *T.55*, *T.57*
Fleet auxiliaries: Three sperrbrecher (mine barrier breakers), colliers *Hedwig Heidmann*, *Lissabon*, *Edmund Hugo Stinnes 4*, *Hornburg.* Four old merchant ships assigned for use in the Baltic as blockships would join them shortly.

Outpost line between northern tip of Öland and Gotland:
20th Torpedobootshalbflottille – 4 destroyers

S.145, battleships of 2nd Geschwader in distance. The 12 boats of this class were armed with 3x45cm torpedo tubes firing to either side, one 8.8cm gun aft and 3x5.2cm guns; one amidships, one each side of the bridge. Speed 30 knots. (Public domain)

That morning, Behring's screen only spotted smoke, which disappeared into the Gulf of Riga. This was assumed to be Russian outpost destroyers. At 3:50pm, 2nd Flottille arrived off Vindava. Schuur split his destroyers up into four pairs and sent them to scout close in to the coast as far south as Bakgofen. They were to launch boats and look like they were looking for a suitable spot to land, by taking soundings. The leader boat of 4th Halbflottille, *S.144*, led the southernmost group, with *S.145*, Kapitänleutnant Heinrich Schickhardt. The two destroyers sounded in to about 1,500m off the partially destroyed Bakgofen lighthouse, which initially appeared deserted. They stopped and lowered their dinghies. These closed the shore, taking soundings. *S.145*'s dingy, with a crew of three, was closest to the lighthouse. It had just signalled a depth of 6m from about 500m offshore. Suddenly, rifle and machine-gun fire broke out.

Signal'nyy Konduktor Ivan Kotel'nikov, the senior petty officer commanding the observation post, had observed them approach. He was concerned that the Germans intended to land and sabotage the post's communications:

> [He] took the entire crew, consisting of six men with rifles; keeping out of sight, they ran through the forest from the post, closer to the enemy's anchorage and, having taken a convenient position, opened fire with volleys at the boat heading for the shore.
>
> The second volley killed an officer on the boat and he fell overboard, both sailors jumped into the water, but were also killed. The destroyers responded with fire from artillery and

> machine guns, but the post crew continued to engage, shifting their fire to the bridge of the nearest destroyer.
>
> Despite the enemy's intense fire, the shooting of the lower ranks of the Bakgofen post was so accurate that it was visible how several people fell killed or wounded on the bridge of the destroyer. The destroyers raised their boats and, continuing to shell the shore, retreated to the west.
>
> The enemy fire slightly wounded Signal'nyy Botsmanmat Stepan Karev in the head, destroyed the telephone line and damaged the lighthouse.

The Germans mistook the accurate volley fire for a machine-gun. *S.145* had a draught of 3m. Nevertheless, Schickhardt risked the shallow water and advanced to rescue his crew:

> *S.145* returned fire with 5.2cm guns and machine guns [from the bridge] and turned towards the dinghy. The dinghy crew had meanwhile jumped into the water, except for the seriously wounded Torpedoobermatrose [Karl] Rusch, and were swimming to the destroyer. *S.145* itself now came under fire. [Two crewmen on the destroyer] … were seriously wounded. Whilst the two swimmers and the dinghy with the injured man … were being picked up, shelling … continued. An 8.8cm hit silenced the machine gun apparently mounted near the lighthouse. The remaining positions replied with isolated shots, but the fire soon ceased completely.

The nearby *S.144* had also engaged with her entire armament. Once the dinghies were secured, the destroyers retired. One of the other dingy crew had been shot in the hand. Two of the four wounded quickly died of their injuries. The disparity in accounts and the disproportionate German casualties demonstrate the difficulty of effectively engaging positions on land from the sea, even with a massive advantage in firepower. For initiative and courage in defending the post in the face of such odds, Kotel'nikov received the St. George's Cross 4th class and promotion to the junior officer rank of Podporuchik. Four of his men received St. George's Medals 4th class, including Karev. By the next morning, the telephone line was restored and the outpost resumed watch. Kotel'nikov requested more ammunition.

Schuur himself, with *S.149*, *S.140* and *S.142*, had approached the piers at the entrance to Vindava harbour, to determine if any Russian warships were present. In the outer harbour, there were only a few merchant vessels. The inner harbour entrance was blocked by three sunken steamers, which had been there since war broke out. There was no resistance. The local commander ordered the wireless station to close and fled to Riga with most of the small force of military and communications personnel, after sending the alarming telegram, 'Ceasing operation, border guard retreating, approaching enemy destroyers landing troops in Vindava.' Only a handful of observers remained. An outraged command ordered them to return next morning.

On the 22nd, Russian spies had spotted Heinrich's fleet passing the Fehmarn Belt. Essen quickly received the report. *Gromoboy* and *Admiral Makarov* were on the patrol line. Next morning, Essen left Revel' with *Ryurik*, *Bayan*, *Pallada* and *Novik* to reinforce them and take command. Reports of German warships concentrated west of Vindava arrived in a steady stream. *Bogatyr'* and *Oleg* were sent to investigate reports of smoke from Utö. Four destroyers of 4th Divizion reconnoitred the northern Gulf of Riga. Levitskiy scouted northwest of Dago with *Molodetskiy* and *Drakon*. They returned to Nizhniy Dagerort, joining *Alligator*, *Kayman* and *Minoga* there. *Krokodil* and *Akula* took position off Takkhona with *Khrabryy*.

That afternoon, news of the attack at Bakgofen arrived. Requests for clarification revealed that the alarming landing at Vindava was a false alarm. Essen now had a significant force in place to defend the entrance to the Gulf of Finland, but could not intervene to the south with the fleet. Nevertheless, that evening he ordered his two best submarines, *Akula* and *Drakon*, to advance to Vindava and attack. However, *Akula* suffered a breakdown and had to retire. Gudim's *Drakon* proceeded alone. He was able to make little headway against a powerful swell. Eventually Gudim had to close the hatch and steer using the vision blocks in the conning tower. Realising that it would be impossible to reach the target area before darkness the next day, *Drakon* took shelter off Fil'zand lighthouse to obtain fresh intelligence. The Russian submariners were willing, but were constrained by the capabilities and temperamental engines of their boats.

Meanwhile, at 7:00pm, the German destroyers withdrew from the coast and reassembled at a rendezvous 15 miles offshore with *Yorck*. Schickhardt transferred his fallen and wounded. The medical staff on *Yorck* were unable to save Rusch. He had lost three men. The destroyers spread out for the night from Bakgofen to Östergarn, backing up Behring to the North. Heinrich had spent the day exercising his battle squadrons off När. He planned a demonstration off Vindava by the fleet for next morning. At 8pm, a signal came in from the High Command: 'Great importance is attached to demonstrations. To simulate larger troop landings, the army will provide several companies in field-grey uniforms. Ships should determine the number of troops and their embarkation … in agreement with the Danzig Command, troop transport must take place from there.' Heinrich despatched 5th Geschwader to collect the troops.

A report also came in from Jasper. On the evening of the 23rd, *Vineta* had spotted the periscope of a submerged submarine on his screen, southeast of the Danish island of Møn. Jasper reported that he had concentrated his old cruisers at the narrows to the west, off Gedser 'to intercept it there.' Langemak noted in *Elsass*' war diary, 'The danger of enemy submarines entering the Baltic Sea … is always present … it is hardly possible to defend against this with ships. Therefore, I do not know whether it was advisable to send *Hansa*, *Hertha* and *Vineta* to Gedser Reef. … the ships in the narrow area near Gedser will only fall victim to the submarines even more easily. In my opinion, the greatest danger to submarines are still destroyers.' The contrast between one who understood the danger of submarine attack and how to combat it and one who imagined a cruiser could somehow 'intercept' a submarine was stark. This was despite both German and British submarines graphically demonstrating the vulnerability of unescorted patrolling cruisers, by sinking them in the North Sea. However, the next morning, Jasper signalled that it had been a false alarm.

Heinrich went ahead with the planned demonstration on the 24th, whilst he waited for 5th Geschwader. That morning, 2nd Minensuchdivision arrived off Vindava with *Amazone*, to sweep and buoy a channel up to and past the port. *Yorck* and *S.145* slowly steamed backwards and forwards near the marker buoy marking the entrance to the channel, acting as a guide for the approaching fleet. The other eight boats of 2nd Flottille formed a submarine defence screen around six miles to the north. Mid-morning, *D.6* captured and sank a small local fishing vessel, taking the crew of four prisoner. After questioning on *Braunschweig* about Vindava harbour, they were released.

The sweepers finished at 1pm. Heinrich approached with the battleships, *Gazelle* and 10 of the auxiliary steamers. The latter made a lot of smoke offshore, behind the screen of 2nd Flottille, whilst the battleships and *Yorck* slowly paraded down the swept channel to within 5,000m of Vindava, then turned and withdrew. Heinrich used the advance to assess potential spots for a landing.

Heinrich had sent *Amazone* to Bakgofen with *S.145* to bombard the area from which it had come under fire. Just after 3pm, *Amazone* opened fire with her 10.5cm battery. After 30 minutes, the already battered lighthouse had been thoroughly smashed and the telephone line destroyed in several places. Nearby village buildings were also shelled. Kotel'nikov had to move his observation post a couple of miles up the coast and relay reports with mounted couriers.

At 4:30pm, with the demonstration over, Heinrich halted the battleships and *Yorck* for over an hour, whilst the destroyers of 2nd Flottille took in bagged coal from their decks. The force made a perfect target for submarine attack, only 10 miles from the enemy shoreline. At 5:45pm, Heinrich ordered the fleet to get underway. *Amazone*, *S.139* and *S.145* remained on guard at Vindava to prevent minelaying in the swept channel, with *Yorck* stopped at the entrance buoy. The other vessels took the same positions as the previous night. Meanwhile, having coaled at Danzig, Grapow took aboard 750 men of the Reserve Battalion of 128th Infantry Regiment. To support them, the ship's crews formed a machine gun platoon with 14 machine guns and an engineer platoon. Grapow left at 4pm, aiming to rendezvous with Heinrich off Vindava at 7am next morning. His plan was to land the troops immediately.

However, from 11pm onwards, a series of wireless signals gave Heinrich deep concerns about the situation in the western Baltic. The first was from Mischke: 'German consul from Malmö (the Sound) reports: "Received information that British submarines intend to pass through Kattegat tonight."' Half an hour later, an alarming message arrived from the Admiralstab: 'Military Attaché Stockholm telegraphed to the Army Generalstab: – "I have just been informed, trusted source in Malmö (the Sound) reported by telegraph at 5:30pm: 'British fleet has entered the Great Belt after mine barriers were removed by old ships.'"' Whilst he was digesting the implications, another signal arrived just after midnight: 'Attaché Stockholm reported on 24 September at 9am submarines resembling British E class near Vinga Island [in the Kattegat] on a southwesterly course, 8 miles.' Perhaps Jasper's message was not a false alarm.

The information was forwarded without instructions or context. Heinrich felt compelled to act, as his threadbare forces around Kiel could offer little resistance to a serious British attack. First, he ordered Mischke to lay mines to reinforce the German minefield blocking the exit from the Great Belt, off Langeland. He was in danger of being cut-off from Kiel: 'Based on the message from the Admiralstab … it was decided to abort the operation against Vindava and to return with all forces.' Vessels were to rendezvous at 7am, at the point to which Grapow was heading, 20 miles west of Bakgofen. Adam received orders to bring his submarines to Swinemünde.

Kapitän zur See Viktor Harder's *Stralsund* was the easternmost cruiser on Behring's outpost line. At 2.30am, he received the orders to retire. He records a reaction that was widely felt in the fleet: 'The landing attempt was therefore abandoned, which in my opinion would have been a failure due to the small number of troops – 700 men – the prevailing weather – SW strength 4-5 – and the resulting surf on the coast.' He could have added that the two days of demonstrations off the coast would have resulted in a defence now being on high alert to repel any landing. At 5:50am, *Stralsund* was approaching the rendezvous, as the first glimmers of light appeared in the eastern sky, after a moonless, cloudy night. A signal came in from *S.145*, still covering the channel off Vindava with *S.139*: 'Being chased by enemy destroyer, 075β top right [fifteen miles to the east]. [Enemy to] W[est] by N[orth]. We will immediately head east at full speed.' Schickhardt spotted four large destroyers. His course would draw them away from the fleet. Harder altered course towards *S.145*, which was only seven miles from the rendezvous position of the fleet. Heinrich picked up the message and immediately turned south to open the distance. Fifteen minutes later another message followed: ‘Vessel steaming away to the northeast, type not identified.’ By 6:30am, the sun was up. Harder had reached the area. He signalled the nearby *Amazone*, which had also carried out a search and only discovered four stray boats of 2nd Minensuchdivision. The nearby *S.139* had seen nothing. The reports were ascribed to a false alarm. All vessels headed for the rendezvous. Heinrich formed his fleet and headed west.

Essen had been receiving reports as the German demonstration unfolded. Grigorovich sent him an order to remain with the fleet in the Gulf of Finland, even if German troops landed at Vindava. Essen moved his cruisers as far forward as he could, to Örö, leaving *Oleg* and *Bogatyr'* on the outpost line with the submarines. However, the increasing swell prevented the submarines at Dagerort from getting to sea. Gudim’s *Drakon* received a steady stream of reports in his shelter at Fil’zand, including a seaplane that stopped to update him. He could only hope that the sea calmed. Unable to use the fleet or his submarines, Essen did what he could with his destroyers. He instructed Shtorre to, ‘Make a reconnaissance tonight past Cape Domesnes, Lyuzerort lighthouse, examining the coast off Vindava.’ The destroyers of 1st Minnaya Diviziya sighted two German destroyers, six miles south of Vindava, at the limit of their reconnaissance, which fled into the gloom. As dawn approached, the Russian destroyers retired to Moon Sound. They lost the chance to attack the German vessels off Vindava in the half-light. It was another opportunity that slipped by, for lack of initiative from the commander on the spot.

Next morning, the coastal outposts reported the few remaining German vessels off Vindava departing. By mid-day, Kotel’nikov’s team repaired communications at Bakgofen. They saw some distant ships in the haze that afternoon, but Heinrich was long gone. Essen had been planning to send *Novik* to lay mines off Vindava that night. Instead, he headed out beyond Dagerort with *Ryurik*, 1st Brigada Kreyserov, *Novik* and 5th Divizion, to make sure that the Germans had not come north, leaving Kolomeytsev alone with *Gromoboy* on the patrol line. That evening, he was informed that the German fleet had been seen heading west off Bornholm: ‘... the German squadron, consisting of 5 *Deutschland*, 5 *Wettin*, 5 *Barbarossa*, 1 *Yorck*, 2 *Prinz Heinrich*, 1 *Strassburg* and 18 destroyers, passed the meridian of Warnemünde.’ It was a reasonably accurate identification of Heinrich’s force.

As Heinrich steamed west, messages continued to arrive, casting doubt on the reports about the British. By 3.30pm, aerial reconnaissance and information from Danish sources confirmed that there were no British warships, other than submarines, near Danish waters. At 6:07pm, he received the Kaiser’s agreement to his decision to cancel the operation from General Headquarters, almost 18 hours after informing them. Behring’s forces headed for Swinemünde with orders to resume training off Danzig. Heinrich continued west with the rest of the force to Kiel, where the troops disembarked. On the 28th, he wrote a lengthy communiqué to General Headquarters. He advised against a repeat of the operation, as ‘carrying out a landing in Vindava seems inadvisable to me.’ Any landing on the narrow piers was exposed to fire from the town and surrounding forest: ‘As the bombardment by ... *S.145*, shows, guards with machine guns are posted along the Russian coast, most likely also in Vindava, so that even in the event of a surprise landing, a defence, albeit numerically weak, must be expected. In my opinion, the companies would be quickly wiped out during the landing, despite the strong protection of a battleship squadron, by a few cleverly positioned machine guns.’ The open sea off Vindava would be problematic in difficult weather. Even a moderate swell would cut the troops on land off, making embarkation and disembarkation impossible.

The plucky opposition at Bakgofen had a disproportionate impact on Heinrich's assessment of Russian coastal defence. A landing at Vindava on the 24th would have been completely unopposed. There was almost no military force on this stretch of the coastline beyond the naval observation teams and small detachments of border guards. However, Heinrich was right that getting out would have been a lot harder than getting in, especially if the weather deteriorated, as was likely at this time of the year. Kapitän zur See Ernst-Oldwig von Natzmer of *Kaiser Barbarossa* was under no illusions about the force he was transporting: 'the landing detachment provided by the army, consisting of 700 young reserves with six weeks of training, was not sufficient for the operation. The reinforcements of around 200 men from 5th Geschwader suffered from a lack of equipment and training, reservists without shooting practice and also without infantry training.' His view was widely shared. In one message that sums up the lack of thought behind the operation, Headquarters had suggested that: 'To secure the landing troops at Vindava, it seems advisable to destroy the railway as far inland as possible.' Exactly how this was to be accomplished with the resources provided was moot. The railway would certainly have allowed the Russians to move troops rapidly forward to counterattack.

Heinrich, like Behncke, suggested that the Gulf of Riga offered better prospects for a successful landing. The Gulf was sheltered from heavy weather. For anything more than a demonstration, the need to maintain transports offshore for logistical support would require a larger naval force. Heinrich proposed a blocking force with a dreadnought battleship Geschwader, to prevent the Russians coming out of the Gulf of Finland, with 4th Geschwader guarding the landing zone. These would need a reconnaissance force of two armoured cruisers, four new and four old light cruisers. Screening and minesweeping would require at least four flotillas of destroyers and two sweeping divisions, due to the need to take turns coaling so far from friendly bases. In other words, a major part of the Hochseeflotte. What Heinrich did not say, was that events had laid bare the fact that the army and navy were completely unprepared to mount an amphibious assault. The Admiralstab quietly ignored the suggestion.

The operation did not have the intended impact on Russian troop deployments. Indeed, the absence of a landing reinforced Essen's belief that the Germans were intent only on periodic demonstrations and raids. The ostentatious display simply confirmed the force levels that Russian intelligence had identified in the Baltic. With autumn looming, both Essen and his British allies began to formulate new plans.[15]

15 BA:RM92 *Stralsund*, *Elsass*, *Wettin*, *Yorck*, *Wittelsbach* KTB, RM5/831, RM56 2.Torpedobootsflottille, 4.Torpedobootshalbflottille KTB, RM8/943 Kriegswissenschaftliche Abteilung der Marine (Marinearchiv), Operationen der Flottenstreitkräfte in der Ostsee; Firle, *Ostsee*, pp.135–159; Pohl, *Aufzeichnungen*, pp.68–69; Винтер, 'походов', pp.198–204; РГАВМФ:Фонд 716, Опись2, Дело 23, pp.46–57, Фонд 479, Опись 2, Дело 508, pp.108ff transcribed in В. Эмме, (Е.Ф. Винтер), 'Балтийский флот в начале Первой мировой войны', *Гангут № 105*, (2018), p.63; Anon., *Verlustliste No.9*, pp.2–3; Меркушов, *Записки*, pp.249, 253; Графъ, *Новикъ*, p.21.

5

Submarines ascendant: September to October 1914

Britain causes a panic

The alarming signals that Heinrich received on the night of the 24/25 September had resulted from a new British initiative. On the 14th, the British Admiralty had notified the fleet commander, Admiral Jellicoe, that, 'A considerable portion of the German Fleet being actively occupied in the Baltic. It is a good time to rest the battle fleet for engine-room defects.' On the 16th, during this lull in operations, a conference was convened at Loch Ewe, the fleet's base on the west coast of Scotland, attended by senior commanders, the Naval War Staff and Churchill. The latter wanted action to increase pressure on the German fleet. After options in the North Sea were rejected, the discussion turned to the Baltic. Jellicoe insisted that a superior force must be maintained in the North Sea, so a Baltic attack would require the French battle fleet to come north from the Mediterranean. Vice-Admiral Lewis Bayly, commanding 1st Battle Squadron, therefore proposed an attack on Kiel by light cruisers and destroyer flotillas. Commodore Reginald Tyrwhitt, who commanded the flotillas, disposed of the idea, later writing to his wife that, 'I was not going to agree to murdering half my command.' Commodore Roger Keyes was responsible for the Submarine Service. He was always looking for opportunities. He saw an opening to propose a Baltic expedition by submarines, as it would, '... provide a wider and more profitable field for submarine activity than the Heligoland Bight.' Jellicoe offered his support. Keyes was delighted: '[It was] decided that enquiries would be made, as to the feasibility of basing a few of our "Oversea" submarines on Russian naval ports. In the meantime I proposed to send two submarines to reconnoitre and cruise in the approaches to the Belts.' This was not new strategy, just a tactical expedient.

Submarines *E.1* and *E.5* arrived in the Kattegat on the 24th. They were the first British warships to do so since the war began, and made no secret of their presence. They cruised extensively over the next two days, being seen repeatedly by steamers and from the shore. Lieutenant-Commander Noel Laurence of *E.1* even had to ask a fishing vessel to take a crewman ashore to Denmark for treatment, after an accident in the engine room.

Real submarine sightings snowballed in a remarkable way. They sparked a rumour that the British fleet was penetrating the Great Belt. The embassy in Sweden passed it on as serious intelligence. A subsequent investigation revealed the farcical origin:

> The news about the forcing of the Great Belt comes from the confidant of the [Swedish] General Staff in Malmö and, according to the investigation now concluded, has the following origin: A Landstorm man [local militiaman] who was stationed between Malmö and Falsterbo telephoned Trelleborg that he had observed foreign warships. The news was passed on from Trelleborg to the confidant, who then asked a business friend who confirmed the 'common' rumour. When the bell ringer of a church east of Trelleborg reported that he had seen two or three apparently British vessels heading towards Bornholm, the confidant felt compelled to report to the intelligence officer of the military attaché in Stockholm. The investigation was unable to identify anyone who made the claim of recognising two or three vessels of the British fleet in the Sound or the Great Belt.

It seems that nobody had asked how someone in Sweden could possibly see what was going on 65 miles away on the other side of Denmark before passing on this 'intelligence'.

However, the response showed just how sensitive the German naval staff was to the possibility of British attack, as well as the force that they would have encountered. Pohl received the Embassy's message at 11pm on the 24th. Within twenty minutes, he ordered Ingenohl to, 'immediately send as many cruisers, destroyers and submarines as possible to the Baltic Sea and to arrange for measures to speed up the passage of 2nd Geschwader through the Canal.' Orders followed for the two dreadnought battleship squadrons to prepare for passage, but this would take four to five days, as they had to offload coal and ammunition first.

Meanwhile, Mischke had ordered the laying of the additional minefield off Langeland as soon as he received the news, without waiting for Heinrich's orders. It was in place by 2am. He then requisitioned every seaworthy warship in Kiel, regardless of command affiliation. Mischke raised his flag on *Friedrich Carl* and headed out with his force to patrol south of the new mine barrier. It was a rag-tag collection of ships, with many under trial or with raw crews: the new battle cruiser *Derfflinger*, armoured cruiser *Prinz Heinrich*, *Hertha*, *Vineta*, the obsolete training cruiser *Kaiserin Augusta*, light cruisers *Berlin* and *Thetis*, *S.121*, *S.123*, *S.125*, the five Kiel torpedo boats, *U.1*, *U.A*, *U.3*, *U.4*, *U.26*, *U.27*, *U.29*, *U.30*, and their destroyer leaders, *D.5* and *T.101*. *Lübeck* and *Panther* went to the Little Belt, with the minelayer *Hertha*, to lay an additional minefield if the enemy approached. Jasper took *Hansa* and *Victoria Louise* to block the southern exit of the Sound. *Carmen* and *T.97* pushed forward to observe the Flintrinne, just outside Swedish territorial waters. Minelayers *Deutschland* and *Rügen* took position in the Fehmarn Belt, ready to block it. Ironically, the focus was on surface ships, whilst the measures would have little effect on submarines coming through the Flintrinne, which were the only vessels definitely spotted.

By mid-morning, it was obvious that the Great Belt report had been false. Two seaplanes and Hochseeflotte Zeppelin *L.3* found nothing. Reports from Denmark and steamer arrivals confirmed that there were no British surface ships in the Kattegat. The nearest British cruisers were in the Skagerrak. Around midday, after an audience with the Kaiser, Pohl issued an order standing down the transfer of the battleships: 'News of breakthrough of British fleet into Baltic probably false. Advance of British submarines into Baltic is possible.' Mischke released the requisitioned cruisers. A large number of warships were already heading through the Kaiser Wilhelm Canal. As a precaution, they were to remain until Heinrich returned to Kiel. Rebeur-Paschwitz, with the two armoured cruisers of 3rd Aufklärungsgruppe, took overall command of the Hochsee forces: light cruiser *Hamburg*, nine submarines, 1st and 3rd Torpedobootsflottille.

These arrived from 4pm onwards. Rebeur-Paschwitz anchored in the Fehmarn Belt, complaining that 'he had not received any orders up to that point and did not want to get in the way of the ships of the coastal protection division, whose tasks were unknown to me.' Next morning, the 25th, he patrolled with *Roon* and *Prinz Adalbert* off the Great Belt. These vessels from the North Sea had become wary of submarine attack and zigzagged whilst underway. The lookouts were jumpy. Twice *Roon*'s lookouts sighted phantom periscopes close to the ship. Submarine reports from the Kattegat continued to come in and Heinrich was particularly concerned about them coming through the Flintrinne. *V.25* and *V.27* left dock to reinforce the guard there. On the morning of the 26th, 3rd Torpedobootsflottille replaced them. Heinrich was unimpressed with the command muddle, which left the two formations unaware of each other's actions: 'It appears that [Mischke] relied on Admiral von Rebeur, and Rebeur relied on Admiral Mischke.'

The British submarines returned to port with the unremarkable news that they had seen no German forces in the Kattegat. This was hardly a revelation. Local coastal intelligence could have confirmed this. The clumsy reconnaissance potentially compromised the element of surprise for any subsequent attempt to pass through the Flintrinne into the Baltic. The Germans assumed that the submarines had failed to pass the Sound for an unknown reason. Despite the potential for submarine attack in the Baltic, Behncke pointed out that, 'In my opinion, the Flintrinne must remain open if we do not want to unduly impede or even cut off trade between [German ports in] the Baltic Sea with København and other neutral ports.' However, Sweden was requested to restrict navigation in the Flintrinne, remove navigation aids and extinguish lights. The Swedish government did not want British warships in the Baltic, but trade was paramount. The rejection of the request was unequivocal: 'Sweden alone, as a sovereign state, has to decide when its neutrality and its trade is endangered by the penetration of British warships into the Sound and the Baltic Sea and when measures have to be taken against it.'

On the 27th, Heinrich's fleet returned. Most of the Hochsee forces returned to the North Sea. In view of the increased submarine threat, Heinrich was temporarily allocated Jasper's four cruisers and 2nd Torpedobootsflottille. The cruisers were worthless for defence against submarines, but conventional wisdom dictated that light forces needed cruiser support. Heinrich gave Jasper command of the Sound guard, with 2nd Flottille and 19th Halbflottille, operating from Warnemünde and Sassnitz. A cruiser patrolled east of Møn, with typically half of 2nd Flottille south of the Sound, outside neutral waters, within 6 to 7 miles of the southern exit of the Flintrinne, day and night. Another cruiser and two destroyers of 19th Halbflottille patrolled between Trelleborg and Sassnitz by day and between Møn and Rügen at night. The remaining cruisers and destroyers would be coaling and resting on a two-day rotation. During the day, it was unlikely that submarines would break through unnoticed, as it was difficult to avoid surfacing to pass the Flintrinne. The guard was unlikely to spot a surface breakthrough on dark nights. After recent events, Pohl mused that, 'One cannot help fearing that enemy submarines may penetrate through the Belts into the Baltic.' Jasper's force watched and waited.[1]

1 Mark Harris, *Harwich Submarines in the Great War: The first submarine campaign of the Royal Navy in 1914* (Warwick: Helion & Co., 2021), pp.140–145; Keyes, Roger J. B., *The Naval Memoirs of Admiral of the Fleet Sir Roger Keyes – The Narrow Seas to the Dardanelles 1910–1915* (London: Thornton Butterworth, 1934), p.105; TNA:ADM186/620: Naval Staff Monographs Volume XI: Home Waters – Part II September and October 1914, p.159; BA:RM92 *Roon* KTB, RM5/831, RM51 Geschwader und Gruppen der Kaiserlichen Marine, 5.Aukklärungsgruppe KTB; Firle, *Ostsee*, pp.152, 160–184; Pohl, *Aufzeichnungen*, p.74.

Left: Lyudvig Berngardovich Kerber, Right: Aleksandr Vasil'yevich Kolchak. (Public domain)

A new plan and a storm

Essen convened a meeting on 26 September to review the draft of a new plan of operations by Kapitan 2nd Ranga Knyaz' (Prince) Mikhail Cherkasskiy, the most senior officer on Kolchak's Operations Staff. Essen's Chief of Staff, Kerber, as well as Kolchak were present.

Timirëv describes the relationships behind the working of Essen's staff: 'For all his virtues, Admiral Essen was first and foremost a man of "the moment" in his actions and did not tolerate office work and bureaucracy. He somewhat mistakenly identified any staff work with bureaucracy, which is why he tolerated it only as an unavoidable evil. … As a result, the work of the Staff … was unsystematic, frenetic, and uncoordinated. In addition the Staff was too small.' His Chief of Staff, Kerber, was: 'an educated and capable naval officer, who developed plans for operations superbly and carried these out … with his characteristic daring and courage, but was too highly strung and hot-tempered to coordinate and direct the work of the entire Staff.' Kolchak was Kerber's Head of Operations: 'He had an amazing ability to draw up the most unexpected, always ingenious, and sometimes brilliant, plans for operations'. However he: '… did not recognize any superior except Essen, to whom he always reported directly. On this basis, Kolchak and Kerber always had conflicts, and Essen, who respected and valued them perhaps equally, quite unexpectedly found himself in the role of conciliator of both of his hot-headed and unyielding assistants.' Cherkasskiy played an important part in bringing the inputs of these disparate characters together into a detailed plan: 'This outstanding and highly educated naval officer (he graduated from the Naval Academy of the General Staff) to some extent compensated for Kolchak's shortcoming – his dislike of sedentary work: Cherkasskiy was an excellent office worker and diligent systematiser.'

The 'Change to the Basic Operational Plan of the Baltic Sea Naval Forces' was a major departure from the defensive posture of the 1912 Operational Plan. It proposed a succession of operations off the German coast, designed to disrupt naval operations and seagoing commerce. Evidence indicated that outside of their sporadic advances, the Germans were withdrawing to the area around Danzig. Before submitting the plan for approval, Essen wanted to confirm this with a cruiser advance, whenever the next spell of bad weather threatened. Reconnaissance was the stated aim, but Essen was also hoping to attack outpost vessels under the cover of bad weather. With the barometer dropping fast, he seized the opportunity.

Ryurik left Lappvik next morning, the 27th, with Essen on-board, into rain, gale force winds and a heavy sea, apparently intending to carry out the reconnaissance alone. For Rengarten, Essen's actions were too impulsive:

> This decision was condemned at Headquarters: the catchphrase 'spasmodic operations' was in circulation, and this advance was classified as such.
>
> Without even touching on the question of the advisability of an advance in stormy weather, the main and obvious drawback of this operation was that it did not contain a specific, clear plan and was not in any way connected with the plans or the activities of the fleet either before or after this advance. Furthermore, it seemed completely unacceptable for the admiral to personally participate in this advance, breaking away from his fleet for the sake of a completely personal aim, certainly secondary and, moreover, of highly dubious importance.
>
> This whole matter was made worse by the fact that the admiral decided to leave with only *Ryurik* – a risk that was not justified in any way.

Essen was undoubtedly frustrated by inaction. After a number of bungled opportunities by subordinates, he had already been taking direct control of cruiser operations. However, going out on reconnaissance alone was taking this to another level. His staff evidently prevailed on him not to do so. *Ryurik* rendezvoused with the cruiser patrol. Magnus fell into line behind *Ryurik* with *Pallada*, leaving *Bayan* to patrol.

Essen headed down the west coast of Gotland. That night the weather moderated somewhat. *Ryurik* picked up wireless transmissions with the call signs of *Augsburg* and the coastal battleship *Hildebrand*. Perhaps there would be contact. By 5am on the 28th, the cruisers had reached a point southeast of Öland. This was the farthest any Russian vessel had advanced since the war had begun. The cruisers turned east. Any German outpost line north of Danzig Bay, would be struck from behind. The wind picked up again. Hopes of contact faded. The only vessel sighted was a sailing vessel heading west. That afternoon, the barometer plummeted. In the evening, the wind shifted northeast and began to blow hard, gusting to force 11 – a violent storm of almost hurricane force. This was Baltic weather at its unpredictable worst. It precluded any chance of a gun action. Both cruisers turned for the return leg up the east side of Gotland. They pushed onwards into the pitch-black night. The big cruisers were tossed around and deluged by the waves. By 7am next morning, the smaller *Pallada* had fallen far behind, out of sight. Wireless contact was lost. *Ryurik* slowed to 6 knots to allow her to catch up, but was barely able to maintain headway against the sea. *Pallada* reappeared a few hours later. The ferocious winds had damaged her wireless net. The cruisers finally arrived at the sheltered waters of Örö anchorage on the evening of the 29th. Essen had confirmed the absence of German screening forces, but this was unsurprising in the atrocious weather.

On the morning of the 27th, Behring was returning to Danzig, along the coast from Swinemünde. He ran into the heavy weather, passing the small torpedo boats of 2nd Minensuchdivision, returning to Kiel in the opposite direction. That night, they found themselves heading into winds from the west that quickly whipped up mountainous seas, with waves over 15m high. At 6am, the Minensuchdivision had to turn back. A wave inundated *T.39*, extinguishing her boiler fires. She fired distress flares. Despite the appalling conditions, *T.53* took her in tow. The same thing happened to *T.50*. *D.6* got a towing line across. Around 2pm, the waves finally overwhelmed *T.50*'s crew and pumps. *D.6* came alongside and took off the crew. *T.50* foundered. The boats straggled back to Danzig.

Whilst Essen had been at sea, the Russian submarines had retired from their patrol billets to ride out the storm in Moon Sound. Merkushov's concerns about the anchorage were borne out. Both *Makrel'* and *Minoga* suffered severe damage to their hydroplanes and were out of action. *Drakon* was still stuck at Fil'zand and also took a beating, but managed to avoid serious damage by taking refuge inside a sheltered bay. The storm marooned over 100 men working on *Magdeburg* for days. They were cold, wet and without food. The waves dislodged and further damaged the hull. Essen stopped off on the way back to Revel' to help co-ordinate relief efforts. On the night of the 30th, the sea finally calmed. The men on *Magdeburg* were evacuated. Behring resumed exercising in Danzig Bay, pending the availability of additional cruiser reinforcements.[2]

Essen pushes for an offensive

Essen returned to Revel' on 1 October. That evening, Cherkasskiy went to Petrograd to present the revised plan to Fan-der-Flit and the staff of Sixth Army, then the staff at STAVKA. Essen summarised the rationale in a covering note:

> The participation of Britain in the present war, during almost two months in which the German fleet has not undertaken any active operations against our fleet, have completely changed the strategic situation in the Baltic Sea theatre, giving us the opportunity to expand the operational zone of our fleet, extending it beyond the Gulf of Finland, and, having strengthened Moon Sound, to develop operations in the Gulf of Riga.
>
> The commissioning of the battleships *Sevastopol'* and *Gangut* in the near future, and subsequently of *Poltava* and *Petropavlovsk*, increases our forces so significantly that I find it timely to request a change in the main plan of operations of the Baltiyskiy Flot as follows:
>
> Whilst continuing to ... ensure the security of the capital to seaward, the execution of operational missions should be approved – laying minefields on the transit routes of enemy combat vessels, having our fleet appear on the communication routes of Germany and Sweden in order to destroy enemy commercial vessels, destruction of observation posts on his coast, etc.

2 Винтер, 'походов', pp.204–209; РГАВМФ:Фонд 716, Опись2, Дело 10, pp.176–177; Тимиревъ, *Воспоминанія*, pp.11–12; Меркушов, *Записки*, pp.251–254; BA:RM62: Minensuchverbände und Räumverbände der Kaiserlichen Marine, 2.Minensuchdivision KTB; Firle, Ostsee, pp.187–188.

> The fulfilment of these missions requires the commitment of the main body, or at least a part thereof, into the Baltic Sea, to support the work of our cruisers and minelayers … however, … I accept the guiding principle – being able to retreat to the Gulf of Finland without engaging in a decisive battle…
>
> As winter approaches, the threat to the capital via the Gulf of Finland completely disappears, and the enemy will have to abandon the operational zones – Gulf of Finland and Gulf of Riga.
>
> Meanwhile, a favourable situation is created for our forces in terms of developing active actions against the shores and communications of the enemy in the Baltic Sea, which will force him to conduct an extremely difficult winter campaign and compel his forces in the Baltic Sea to maintain a high state of readiness.

The short days at the end of the year were critical to the argument that the German fleet no longer threatened a landing in the Gulf of Finland. Maintaining German forces in the Gulf would be suicidal during the long dark nights, making them easy prey for torpedo attack. The Russian fleet could also operate further forward, knowing that the long nights veiled any retreat over a great distance. Cherkasskiy's plan was ambitious:

> … [whilst] having the main task of ensuring the security of the capital from the sea, [the fleet] must keep the southern part of the Baltic Sea under surveillance up to the Danzig–Karlskrona line … [this] will allow us to extract greater benefit from the fleet, ensuring the security of the right flank of our army from landings … and creating great concern on the part of the enemy to protect their sea communication routes.

Cherkasskiy made detailed calculations, demonstrating that the Russian fleet could use the darkness to evade unwanted contact with the German Fleet. Three key assumptions underpinned this:

1. The operation should be carried out only when intelligence and reconnaissance establish a favourable disposition of enemy forces [German battle fleet forces at their base in Kiel] …
2. The surprise of the first operation and irregularity of repetition inherently create a favourable security situation.
3. The transfer of forces from Kiel to Danzig takes 22 hours at 15 knots and 16½ hours at 20 knots. Thus, even if the movement of our fleet is detected by ships of the enemy screen on the Steynort–Hoburg line, the fleet will still have enough time to carry out the planned operation and withdraw north in a timely manner.

The operations would involve:

> Main task. … the laying of a minefield near the enemy coast on the routes of movement of the enemy navy.
>
> Supplementary tasks. … the fleet appears on the communication routes of Germany and Sweden, destroying enemy commercial vessels, and destroys observation posts on the enemy coast.
>
> If significant or overwhelming enemy forces appear, the fleet, without entering into battle, withdraws to the Gulf of Finland, and if it encounters weak forces, it destroys them.

The operations would involve the entire fleet, including the powerful new dreadnought battleship, *Sevastopol'*. A lower risk variant of the plan left the slower 1st Brigada Lineynykh Korabley on stand-by at Revel'.

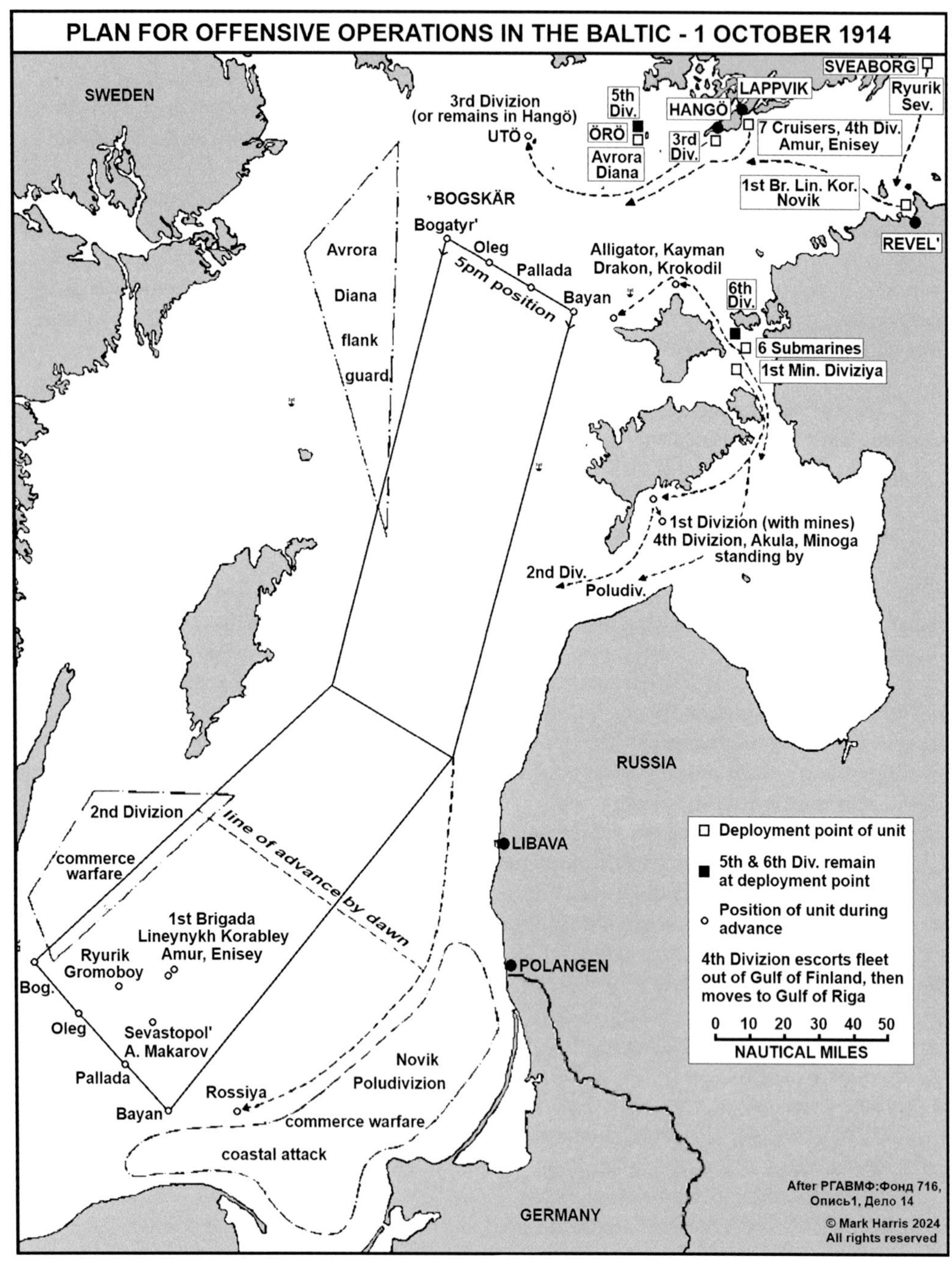

On the day of the operation, the battleships and minelayers would form up with their scouting cruisers on a start line running roughly northwest from Dagerort. *Avrora* and *Diana* would take a flank guard position to interdict any minelayers approaching up the west coast of Gotland. Covering destroyers and submarines not advancing with the fleet would take position in the Gulf of Riga and the approaches to the Gulf of Finland, to support the fleet in the event that it was engaged in a fighting withdrawal.

At 5pm, the fleet would begin the advance south, timed to arrive off the operational zone at dawn. It would drive back or destroy any German screening forces. Advancing destroyers would join from the Gulf of Riga and move to the flanks to conduct commerce warfare and attack German coastal observation points, whilst the minelayers, *Amur* and *Enisey*, detached to lay their mines unobserved, under cover of the fleet. As soon as the minelaying was complete, the fleet would retire. It would be at the safe distance from Kiel before darkness, avoiding any possibility of encountering a German fleet from there.

On the 3rd, the plan met with a complete rejection by General-Leytenant Nikolay Yanushkevich, the Chief of Staff at STAVKA:

> … given the current general situation, active actions by the Baltiyskiy Flot, outside the limits of its main task – securing the capital from the sea – are premature for the time being for the following reasons:
>
> 1. Active actions by the fleet in the Baltic Sea area, outside the operational zone provided for by the main plan of operations, are associated with a decision to engage in battle under the most unfavourable conditions, since the German fleet is quickly able to concentrate significantly larger forces without weakening its fortified position in the [North] Sea.
> 2. The possibility of avoiding combat during the active operations proposed by the fleet commander is based on the timely receipt of intelligence information about the appearance of a strong enemy in the Baltic Sea – this can hardly be considered assured.
> 3. The goal of the proposed operations does not seem important enough to send the main forces of the fleet for its achievement, risking weakening the defence of the Gulf of Finland and the capital.
> 4. Admitting the possibility of carrying out these operations for the first time with minimal risk, taking advantage of the enemy's surprise, I believe that their repetition will undoubtedly provoke active actions by the enemy, i.e. a battle with a stronger fleet.

The reasons for the rejection betrayed a misunderstanding of naval operations from an unremarkable General, with no experience of either leading combat operations or staff work. He owed his position to being a court favourite. It ignored the fact that significant German forces were known to be absent from the eastern Baltic. Cherkasskiy had carefully planned to make it almost impossible for a force at Kiel to interfere with the operations. Commander Harold Grenfell, the British Naval Attaché at the Petrograd Embassy, visited Essen at the end of October. He recorded his observations about Essen's situation and the long shadow of caution that the painful defeat by Japan still cast over naval operations:

> Admiral von Essen himself, who is a vigorous, daring, and capable commander, took his Flagship … about a month ago for a reconnaissance of Danzig, but I fancy has since received an intimation that this sort of excursion is not to be repeated. … [The Russian Baltic Fleet] is hampered executively and administratively to an extraordinary degree by the strange views of the supreme authorities, who understand no other way to regard it than as primarily an immediate defence of the capital, and in other respects as solely an extension of the right wing of the main armies. [Essen's] purely naval dispositions … are occasionally interfered with by a military hand acting under the influence of a military psychology. One of Admiral Essen's closest relations [one of his three daughters] is my authority for the following incident. At the time the general mobilisation order was issued, her father was received by the Emperor … the latter at the close of the audience said 'We do not want a second Tsushima'.

The plan could be criticised for having no destroyers to screen the heavy ships in the advanced position. This did leave them open to submarine attack, although this could be mitigated by maintaining high speed and zigzagging. The 1st Divizion had similar endurance to the 2nd and could have advanced with the fleet. The plan is also notable for using *Sevastopol'* almost as a battle cruiser, leveraging her unusually high speed for a dreadnought battleship. Her firepower would have enabled her to destroy any German cruiser based in the Baltic and she was faster than many of them.

Yanushkevich set two conditions for expanding operations. The first was the completion of all four dreadnoughts, ruling out operations in 1914. There would also need to be either a decisive success by the British fleet in the North Sea, or a decisive defeat of the German army on a scale that precluded any possibility of a landing by German troops. Worse was to follow. On 8 October, Essen received a final decision after further discussion with the Supreme Commander, Nikolay:

> By command of his Sovereign Highness: the Baltiyskiy Flot shall take decisive action only upon receipt of His Majesty's personal permission to do so and permission to commit the brigade of battleships of the *Sevastopol'* class into battle. Expansion of the operational zone in the Gulf of Finland to the Dagerort meridian with the inclusion of Moon Sound is permitted.

The battleships on which Essen had placed his hopes of seizing the operational initiative were to be placed out of harm's way. Maintaining the morale and efficiency of the crews condemned to such inaction was going to be a major challenge. The supposed 'expansion' simply approved arrangements already in place since the beginning of September. However, Essen was not going to let this setback stop him. He needed another approach.[3]

3 РГАВМФ:Фонд 716, Опись1, Дело 14, pp.18–45; Винтер, 'походов', pp.209–226; TNA:ADM137/271, pp.272–275.

No reports of the enemy

The cruiser watch in the Gulf of Finland resumed after the storm. On 30 September, Essen received intelligence: 'Four [German] submarines left Danzig for the north.' He issued new orders for the patrol: 'I warned the commanders of 1st and 2nd Brigada Kreyserov, and 1st and 2nd Minnaya Diviziya about this and ordered the cruisers to patrol at high speed and on variable courses, and in addition, I assigned a destroyer to each cruiser on patrol to screen against submarines.'

When the weather moderated on the 5th, *Akula* was despatched to Vindava, in case the Germans returned. Vlas'yev then patrolled for two days off Dago, but found only empty sea. Nothing had come of the German submarine threat. Essen reported, 'From 2 to 8 October, there were no reports of the enemy'.

As he was unable to advance with the fleet, Essen turned to his submariners, telling Fan-der-Flit that he 'wished to expand the area of operations of our submarines and move it closer to the enemy coast'. The deployment of one of the oldest, Leytenant Gavriil Dikht's *Beluga*, had been agreed as early as 15 September, in response to the German raid on the Gulf of Bothnia. On 5 October, she arrived at the sheltered anchorage of Munkholmen, near Mariehamn on Åland, with the transport *Oland* to act as a depot. As well as defending the port, *Beluga* would be able to attack any German ships entering the Gulf of Bothnia, as they would have to pass close by to do so. Two destroyers of 2nd Minnaya Diviziya also arrived, to inspect commercial traffic and carry out a survey of the channel between Åland and Sweden. The move had the potential to cause difficulties with Sweden, as under the terms of the Åland Convention of 1856, Russia agreed that, 'the Åland Islands shall not be fortified, and that no military or naval establishments whatsoever shall be maintained or created there.' However, the convention did not strictly rule out the presence of warships. On the 8th, Headquarters received reports of a fleet off Mariehamn and vessels heading down the Swedish coast that night. A sortie by *Beluga* discovered nothing.

Meanwhile, Leytenant Yakov Podgornyy had suggested that his boat, *Krokodil*, move to Libava to carry out offensive patrols in Danzig Bay. Essen had initially rejected the idea 'due to the unreliability of the *Krokodil* petrol engines, the enterprise had very little chance of success, especially in the autumn.' He now changed his mind. *Krokodil* arrived on the 8th, once support for the submarine was in place. Podgornyy sortied next evening, the 9th, to carry out the first patrol in Danzig Bay. The wind picked up overnight. At 7am next morning, gale force winds and a heavy swell forced Podgornyy to turn back off Polangen, having seen nothing. A particularly large wave damaged the distance log, causing him to overshoot Libava. *Krokodil* straggled back in to port that evening. It was an inauspicious start.

On the same day, Essen took action to ensure that any further German appearances off Vindava would encounter Russian mines. The Poludivizion laid 100 mines in two fields offshore, where the German Fleet had loitered in the recent operation.[4]

4 РГАВМФ:Фонд 716, Опись 2, Дело 10, pp.238–239; Томашевич, *операциях*, pp.37–38; Винтер, 'походов', pp.209, 227–228; Меркушов, *Записки*, pp.293–294.

Behring's first submarine offensive: *U.26* strikes

Behring had been waiting for reinforcements and good weather before carrying out his next operation. By 7 October, both *U.26* (Kapitänleutnant Egewolf Freiherr von Berckheim) and the light cruiser *Lübeck* arrived at Danzig, having completed crew training.

The plan was to feint a landing, in order to draw Russian ships into a submarine ambush. At 5am on the 10th, *Amazone* (now commanded by Korvettenkapitän Max Lutter) and *D.10*, with colliers *Oberpräsident Delbrück* and *Ursula Fischer*, would rendezvous between Gotland and the Russian coast. They would approach Vindava to make a landing demonstration. Behring had suggested that at Lutter's 'discretion' a parley go ashore at Bakgofen, threatening bombardment if there was resistance to a landing. When Heinrich read this in his copy of the orders, he wirelessed a veto of this rather theatrical ruse. The seven trawlers of the Neufahrwasser Hilfsminensuchdivision, commanded by Kapitänleutnant Franz Weidgen, with colliers *Hedwig Heidmann*, *Hornburg*, *Annie Hugo Stinnes* and *Lissabon*, would steam past Libava at around 7am. Both forces would make as much smoke as possible, with Weidgen's force kept out of sight of land. *U.23* and *U.25* would already be at billets east of the German minefield in the Gulf of Finland to attack Russian vessels leaving their ports in response. *U.26* would either remain with *Augsburg*, *Lübeck* and 20th Halbflottille west of the Gulf of Finland, or loiter northwest of Cape Takkhona. Berckheim's submarine and his newly formed crew had only arrived ten hours before departure.

On the 8th, Behring left Neufahrwasser, steaming slowly to avoid straining the submarine engines. The prototype diesels of the *U.23* class were temperamental. Next morning, *U.25* broke down. The destroyers used the opportunity to top up with coal, whilst the crew tried and failed to repair the engines alongside *Augsburg*. After two hours, the force got back underway. *G.136* towed *U.25* to the collier rendezvous. If the crew could repair an engine, she would head to the position off Cape Takkhona. Otherwise, *D.10* would tow her back to Danzig.

At 4:30pm, Behring reached his holding position, midway between Bogskär and Dagerort. *U.26* took the billet intended for *U.25*. The submarines departed. They were to patrol for three days. To make the best use of surprise, both were only to make attacks, 'when the prospects are good.' Next morning, the 10th, Behring sent the destroyers to coal and take part in the

U.23 class submarine. Armed with 4x50cm torpedo tubes, two at the bow and two at the stern. Speed over 16 knots on the surface, up to 10 knots submerged. (theFrankes.com Collection)

demonstration off Vindava. He considered them a liability in daylight, as they were poorly armed and slower than *Augsburg* in anything other than calm water. At 8:45am, the wireless room intercepted an un-coded message in Russian. Gercke translated it: 'Urgent. Despatch destroyers. Submarine attack in progress.' Behring considered his response: 'The obvious idea that occurred of advancing into the Gulf of Finland to drive away the Russian destroyers was abandoned, fearing that the submarines would be unable to distinguish German cruisers from Russian. It was also considered that the Russians would be much more likely to calm down if they saw as little as possible of German warships in the Gulf of Finland.' He ordered the wireless room to jam Russian signals to hamper their response.

On the 8th, Mariehamn had reported two warships in the distance. Next morning, as a precaution, Essen despatched four submarines to patrol off Nizhniy Dagerort. There was fog and a heavy swell. *Drakon* and *Kayman* arrived safely, but *Alligator* and *Akula* strayed off course and grounded on Nekmangrund Bank. *Akula* quickly got clear, but *Alligator* stuck firm. Destroyers *Kazanets* and *Turkmenets-Stavropol'skiy* failed to tow her clear. *Khrabryy*, with her shallow draught and more powerful engine, was despatched to make another attempt the next morning. Suspicious ship sightings continued to trickle in. Kolomeytsev was concerned that the salvage operation needed better protection. *Pallada* and *Bayan* were on patrol with the destroyer *Ukrayna*. He received permission to take *Gromoboy* and *Admiral Makarov* to reinforce them next morning.

At 6:30am on the 10th, Kolomeytsev's two cruisers left Lappvik, escorted by destroyer *Deyatel'nyy*. After passing east of Ajax Bank, they headed west to the patrol line. A sailing barque came in sight, about five miles south. It was not on the movement sheet for that day. Kolomeytsev ordered *Admiral Makarov* to approach and send it in for inspection. Her captain, Plen, ordered two blank shots fired across the bow as he approached. The Dutch flagged barque turned into the wind and hove to, drifting slowly. At around 9am, *Admiral Makarov* stopped her engine to pass slowly by and order the barque into Baltiyskiy Port by megaphone. Having received an acknowledgement, Plen ordered half speed and manoeuvred clear. Once *Admiral Makarov* gathered way, he ordered 17 knots and a starboard turn to rejoin *Gromoboy*. A lookout cried out. A torpedo track was steaking towards the ship from port. As *Admiral Makarov* crept round to starboard, away from the track, it passed the bow 200m ahead. A second passed just 50m ahead almost immediately. As *Admiral Makarov* continued to pick up speed, ten to fifteen seconds later, a third passed 100m aft of the stern. Binoculars swept the tracks. They appeared to originate about 500m away, beyond the barque, but there was no sign of the firer. The torpedoes ran at high speed and disappeared to the northwest. Plen immediately sent a wireless message reporting the attack, put his stern to the attack point and ordered full speed ahead. The barque had turned to follow, so he ordered two live 7.5cm rounds fired across her bow, considering her actions suspicious.

On the night of the 9/10th, Berckheim had steered *U.26* through a choppy, moonlit sea, in excellent visibility. He had the westernmost billet, north of Odenskhol'm. *U.23* was to the east. At 5:20am, Berckheim approached Odenskhol'm lighthouse to get a position fix. He remained close by. The sea had gradually become rougher. There was now a strong swell running. This was good submarine weather. The swell would help conceal his periscope once underwater. Berckheim spotted a sailing barque eastwards, with smoke beyond it. He dived and headed north to intercept and, 'After about half an hour, a larger ship and destroyer spotted. [They were] Approaching quickly.' The barque lying between *U.26* and *Admiral Makarov* may have

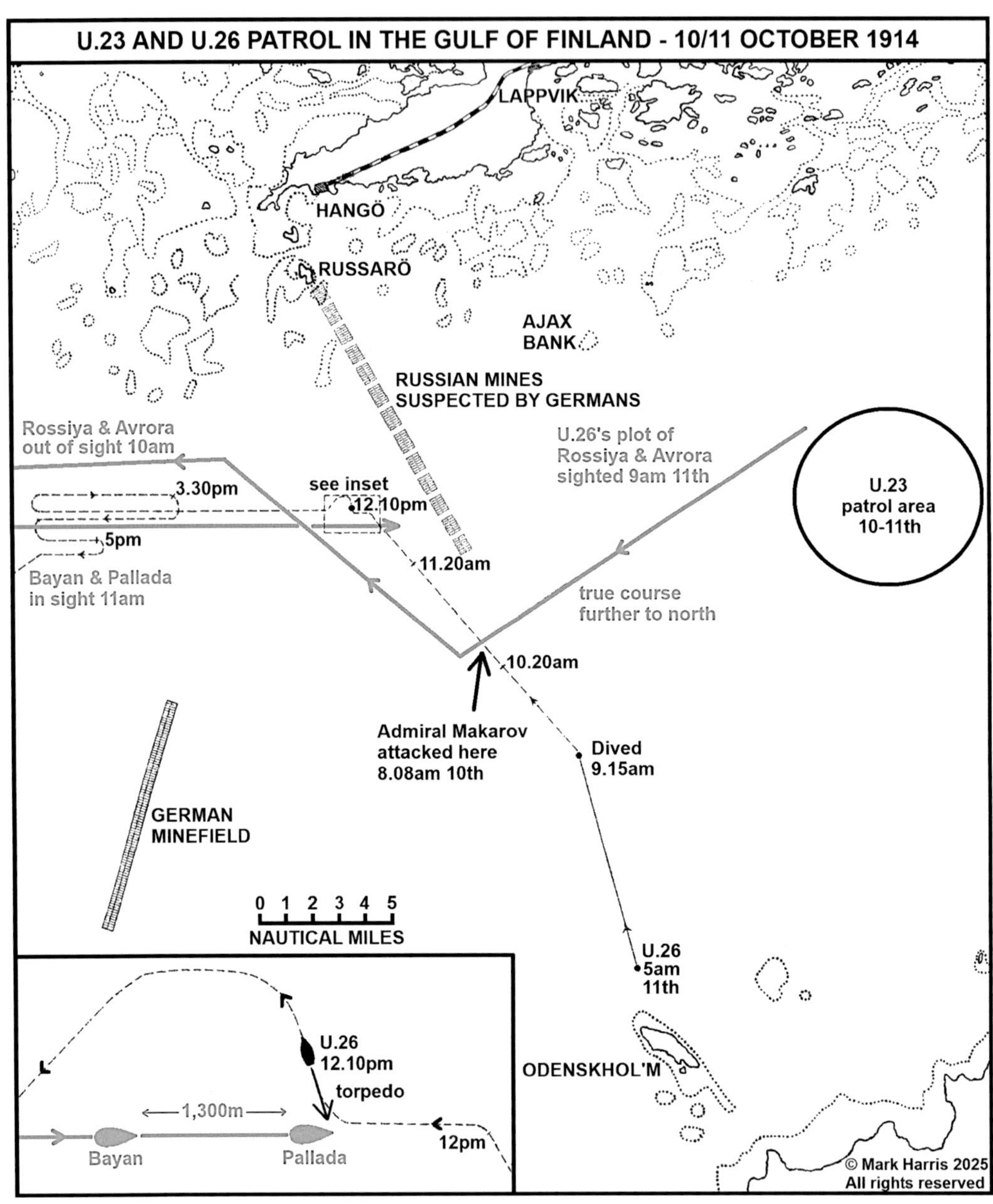

confused or obscured his observations through the periscope in the swell, but his report is scant on details: 'Attacked enemy armoured cruiser with four funnels. Double shot, first shot missed, as ship turns [to] 300° and slows down. Second shot fired whilst turning. Distance approx. 1,200m. Boat appears to have gone unnoticed as ship continues to steer steady course as it leaves.' The attack range was long. Behring reported that the second torpedo was '… probably fired more out of frustration than deliberation… hence my intention of delivering a major strike as the enemy main body left port was probably thwarted.' Berckheim had wrongly concluded that his target's course was looping around a minefield believed to extend south from Russarö. The chance to attack had come as *Admiral Makarov* emerged from behind the barque, which Berckheim does not mention in describing the attack.

The hasty attack at long range and *Admiral Makarov*'s change in course and speed had saved her. Kolomeytsev summoned *Novik* and several divisions of destroyers to hunt for the attacker. He ordered *Deyatel'nyy* to escort the barque in to Baltiyskiy Port for an investigation, authorising her commander to sink her if she did not comply. Once *Khrabryy* signalled that she was towing *Alligator* back to Baltiyskiy Port, he returned with his two cruisers to Lappvik. The destroyers towed two barques in for examination, but this revealed no suggestion of collusion. There was no trace of the submarine. Kolomeytsev spotted an explosion in the German minefield. He optimistically concluded that the destroyers could have driven the submarine to destruction.

After the attack, Berckheim headed south and reloaded his torpedo tubes. At times, he had up to five destroyers in sight, but none came closer than a mile. He turned north again at 2pm. He needed to be away from the patrols, west of the German minefield, to charge overnight. At sunset, the destroyers began to leave. He was able to surface and begin charging.

U.23, commanded by Kapitänleutnant Erwin Weisbach, spent the day patrolling underwater, about 15 miles north of Baltiyskiy Port. At intervals, he saw distant smoke and ships passing the coast to the south. Weisbach chased them backwards and forwards, but accomplished nothing. *U.25* had been unable to get her engine working reliably. *D.10* escorted her back to Danzig.

Behring's demonstrations had no impact on events. During the late afternoon, Vindava reported a cruiser and two transports 15 miles off the coast passing north to Baltiyskiy Flot Headquarters. A cruiser was reported off Bakgofen. The directional signal station got the bearing of Behring's jamming attempts. *Pallada* and *Bayan* had nothing in sight on the patrol line, so the source was obviously well out to sea. *Augsburg*'s wireless room had also attempted to spoof genuine Russian signals.

Behring cancelled the Libava demonstration. The gale force winds and heavy swell proved too much for the small trawlers of the Hilfsminensuchdivision. They were unable to make headway against the seas on the night of the 9/10th and took shelter in Memel. Weidgen sent the four colliers back to Swinemünde. The weather had also turned back *Krokodil*, which might otherwise have been able to attack them.

That night, Magnus's cruisers moored off Örö. *Admiral Makarov*'s luck had provided the Russian fleet with an alarm call about the immediate danger that submarines now posed. Only days before, shocking news arrived of three British armoured cruisers sunk in the North Sea, in an attack by *U.9*. These things were perhaps on Magnus's mind. He came to dine with Veys on *Bayan* that evening: 'when he was leaving, I invited him to stop by again, saying to him: "Come to dine, let's have another drink together", to which he replied: "Who knows, maybe this is the last time", as if he had a premonition.'

During the night, Behring's two cruisers rendezvoused with 20th Halbflottille off Gotska Sandön. *Oberpräsident Delbrück* and *Ursula Fischer* took position east of Gotland. *Amazone* remained off Vindava observing the exit from the Gulf of Riga. Behring assumed that *U.26*'s attack would keep large Russian warships in port. However, '… the Russians may advance with destroyers during the night, to determine whether the submarines have support off the Gulf of Finland and to intercept German submarines that retired overnight. If this occurs, the intention is to attack the Russian destroyers.' At dawn, Behring sent his destroyers to coal and headed east. At 11am, *Lübeck* broke off 20 miles northwest of Dagerort. Her lower speed made it risky to go further. *Augsburg* pressed on. Lookouts sighted three destroyers to the southeast. Then, around noon, they saw an, 'Explosive cloud to east-northeast at a very great distance.' *Lübeck* also saw a, '… sudden, very dense whitish cloud, as from an explosion.' As the cloud grew, the crews knew that something momentous had happened.

Pallada and *Bayan* had left Örö that morning, to resume their routine patrol west of the minefield, with destroyer *Stroynyy* screening ahead. At 9am, *Moshchnyy* joined. The destroyers formed a screen to port and starboard ahead, but no zigzag was employed. Kapitan 1st Ranga Fëdor Vyatkin of 1st Divizion had assumed responsibility for the destroyer watch and had his destroyers and *Novik* on anti-submarine patrol east of the minefield. It was the appointed day for changing the guard squadrons. Leskov led the four cruisers of 2nd Brigada out of Revel', heading for the coast off Lappvik, the standby anchorage. Despite recent events and standing instructions, he neither requested an escort, nor steered in zigzags. *Bogatyr'* and *Oleg* broke away to anchor. *Gromoboy* and *Admiral Makarov* prepared to depart for Revel' and Kolomeytsev summoned *Novik* as escort. *Rossiya* and *Avrora* headed west to relieve *Pallada* and *Bayan*.

Leskov closed Magnus's cruisers, which turned to meet him. Seeing no destroyers, Magnus raised the signal: 'Destroyers to proceed to cruiser *Rossiya*.' *Stroynyy* and *Moshchnyy* complied. *Rossiya* took the patrol line. *Avrora* headed for Örö. Magnus turned east to return to Revel'. He increased speed to 16 knots, but did not order a zigzag, relying solely on speed for protection. It was 11:35am.

On the previous night, after charging his battery, Berckheim headed back to Odenskhol'm for a position fix. As the light grew, he headed north, towards the position of his attack the day before. Around 9am, he dived when he sighted smoke from ships and destroyers to the north-east. Two cruisers appeared, heading west. Berckheim tried to intercept, but they passed well ahead of *U.26* and disappeared. It was *Rossiya* and *Avrora*. Berckheim rationalised that their course matched that of *Admiral Makarov* the day before, swinging south to avoid the supposed Russian minefield, although in doing so, his track trace credits them with an impossibly high speed of over 30 knots. In fact, Leskov had deliberately passed further to the north than usual to vary his route. Berckheim headed northwest towards the gap between the supposed minefield and the German minefield, to await their return. It was a fateful decision, driven by belief in a minefield that did not exist, but sound tactics. *U.26* slipped past nearby patrolling destroyers. At 11:20am:

> I see two columns of smoke moving towards me from the west, I hold my course, moving directly ahead of them and [then] steering towards them. Meanwhile I see a large destroyer to starboard about 2000–3000m away on the same course.
>
> Shortly after noon I turned to [starboard at slow ahead] to line up for a shot from the stern tubes. [Estimated speed of enemy 15 knots].
>
> 12:10pm. The shot is fired at the first cruiser (four funnels, apparently *Makarov* class) at a distance of about 500m. I see a hit amidships, at the same time I notice that I am being shot at; I dive to 20m and steer away at a low speed (westwards).
>
> In the boat at 20m I heard several dull thuds, probably shells from the second cruiser, 3–4 salvos.

Bayan was at her station, 1,300m astern of *Pallada*. At noon, the crews went to lunch, but the combat watch were at their posts. Several 7.5cm guns were manned and ready to fire on each ship. At 12:14pm, Leytenant Vladimir Selyanin was looking towards *Pallada* from the bridge of *Bayan*. Suddenly, 'three flashes appeared from the starboard side of *Pallada*, three flashes almost simultaneously from the port side, and then the entire cruiser immediately disappeared in smoke and fire.' The officer of the watch immediately stopped the engines and sounded the combat alarm. Leytenant Pavel Lemishevskiy was in his cabin, changing after coming off watch: 'I had hardly done this when I heard sounds as if from a pistol shot. Putting on my jacket and binoculars as I left, I rushed out onto the upper deck. In front of me stood a column of brown smoke mixed with steam.' Veys had just finished lunch in the wheelhouse:

> ... I was already leaving to go up to the bridge, when suddenly I heard the signalman cry out, '*Pallada* exploded!' I was on the bridge in less than two seconds, and the following picture presented itself to me: instead of *Pallada*, there was a huge column of smoke with a cap on top and smoke still coming out from below in the form of a roller at the base of the column. We were quickly approaching it. I set the engine telegraph levers to full reverse; the first thought that flashed through my mind was whether *Pallada* had run into a minefield. I almost immediately realised that it was a submarine that had attacked, and at the same time I ordered the boats to be prepared for launching, so that they could be dropped into the water to save people. I myself could not stop, to guarantee that what had happened to three British cruisers not long before would not happen again.[5]
>
> Seconds passed, and I was still waiting for the smoke to clear and for *Pallada* to appear. By inertia, we approached its location to within one cable [200m], the smoke was blown away by the wind, and a smooth, ripple-free surface appeared before our eyes, as after a mine explosion – there were neither people nor debris from *Pallada*. We looked through the binoculars and even without them, everything could be clearly seen; there was nothing. It was pointless and risky to remain in this place any longer, lest I myself should suffer the fate of *Pallada*.

Nine minutes had passed since the explosion. Lemishevskiy then heard that: 'a submarine periscope or its track was spotted on the starboard quarter. Full speed ahead was ordered [by Veys]. Fire was opened on the track from the starboard side from 8-inch [20.3cm], 6-inch [15.2cm] and 75-mm guns. The supposed position of the submarine was brought astern [by altering course to northeast].' Veys continues:

> Then, as everyone came to their senses and saw that there was no one to save, they all began to imagine the periscopes of submarines, and people began to run to me on the bridge with reports that they saw periscopes and tracks of submarines here and there. They opened up disorderly firing from the guns, which I soon stopped, because it was pointless, and I myself saw nothing. Then with a strident word, I sent back a cadet who had run to me with a report about a submarine, ordering him not to report them to me anymore, and that they should not be seen again; this had a calming effect.

5 *Hogue* and *Cressy* had stopped to pick up survivors from the sunken *Aboukir* on 22 September, making easy targets for *U.9*.

> … When we arrived in Revel' and dropped anchor, the officers told me that they were having lunch [below in the Officer's Mess] at the moment of the explosion and felt such a strong jolt that they thought that *Bayan* had exploded, whilst I, being on the bridge, did not hear either the jolt or the sound of the explosion, but only heard the cry of the signalman.
>
> The impression made by the explosion of *Pallada* was very grave; the junior doctor lost his mind, as did two sailors. After this incident, when I had to go on this or that operation, I was in a very difficult state of mind: a certain oppressive resignation…
>
> Those who saw the explosion from afar determined the height of the column to be 3,000 feet (915m). I assume that two torpedoes hit *Pallada* and the magazines exploded as a result of the detonation, as well as the boilers… Some officers had grabbed life jackets, then some rescue collars were sent up; this outraged me, and I started to despise people who do not have enough willpower to hide their fear.

Berckheim had his periscope up when the torpedo hit. At 500m, it would have taken less than a minute for this to reach *Pallada*. Berckheim obviously thought that he was immediately under fire, although he may have mistaken the explosion flash and splashes from debris for gunfire. The explosion was visible all over the western Gulf of Finland, and from Verkhnego Dagerort, 30 miles away. Finnish divers found the wreck of *Pallada* in 2000. The hull lies upside down in two pieces. The forward section is relatively intact as far back as the third boiler room. The torpedo hit the next compartment, in the space between the third and fourth boiler rooms. This housed the ammunition for the casemate 15.2cm and 7.5cm guns. *Pallada* was inadequately protected against the latest torpedo warheads. The 50cm G/6 torpedo fired by *U.26* dated from 1911. The warhead was 160kg of powerful Hexa-TNT explosive. Only a narrow coal bunker separated the explosion site from the cordite magazines. The brown smoke in the explosion indicates that the shock from the torpedo had triggered a rapid chain of cordite propellant explosions in the gun cartridges stored in the magazines. This explosion in confined spaces destroyed bulkheads and opened up the coal-fired boilers to seawater. Secondary boiler explosions released the large quantities of steam seen in the explosion cloud. The massive explosion broke the cruiser in half. There was no chance of survival for anyone within the ship. Those few above decks who found themselves in the water also stood almost no chance of survival. Explosion debris rained down on them and suction would have pulled anything on the surface below as the two pieces of the ship rapidly capsized and plunged to the bottom.

Minutes after the explosion, the wireless rooms of Russian ships began taking in a shocking message: 'Urgent. To Command of Naval Forces, Commander 1st Brigada Kreyserov. From *Bayan*. *Pallada* blown up.' Veys quickly followed up with more detail: 'At latitude 59°36', longitude 22°47', *Pallada* was attacked by a submarine. Before the explosion of *Pallada*, we sighted the submarine. Opened fire. Results unknown.' This is the only mention of *U.26* being sighted before the explosion, but Essen's report also implies it: 'As far as can be judged, the enemy submarine attacked the cruiser from a very short distance, no more than 1½–2 cables [300–400m].' Merkushov heard the news: 'Soon after the lunch break, the terrible news of the destruction of the cruiser *Pallada*, blown up by a German submarine in the Gulf of Finland, spread through the Admiralty Basin, where *Okun'* was moored. This news shocked everyone, and some rushed to the harbour in the hope of learning details from those who had chanced to survive or were wounded when they were brought to the pier, but there were none …'

Some of the lost crew of *Pallada*, Kapitan 1st Ranga Sergey Reyngol'dovich Magnus is top left. (Public domain)

Once Veys cleared the area, he altered course to east. The destroyer *Rezvyy* had been to the west and approached *Bayan*. Veys ordered her to search for survivors. *No.216* and *No.219* had been sweeping near Bengtskär. When they saw the explosion, they lifted their trawls and headed to assist. The three boats searched in vain. Eventually, *Rezvyy* wirelessed the bad news: 'Nobody found at site of explosion. Small fragments on surface.' The entire crew of 25 officers and 572 men had perished. Only one body was recovered. Leytenant L.A. Gavrilov washed ashore, apparently lashed to a piece of timber, ten days later.

Just before the explosion, *Rossiya* had sighted smoke approaching from the west on the patrol line. Lookouts soon identified the armoured cruiser *Prinz Adalbert* on the far horizon. Leskov summoned his other three cruisers for support against this superior opponent and turned to close, spotting more smoke in the distance. *Rossiya* had sighted *Augsburg*, with *Lübeck* beyond. Behring had succeeded in getting more cruisers to come out as targets for his submarines.

Augsburg identified a *Bayan* class armoured cruiser advancing, being joined by the previously sighted destroyers. Facing a superior force, he became concerned about being cut-off. He also realised that his presence was pulling the Russians towards him and might prevent his submarines making further attacks. He retired west to rejoin *Lübeck*. Behring spent the rest of the day patrolling between Bogskär and Dagerort.

Meanwhile, Essen had been quick to react. He ordered all cruisers to return immediately to port. *Novik* reached Kolomeytsev around the time of the explosion. He ordered her to offer assistance. She reached *Bayan* half an hour later. Veys ordered her to screen ahead. All three of Kolomeytsev's cruisers headed to Revel'. The crew of *Bayan* were understandably jumpy and twice opened fire again with 7.5cm guns on the way back, first, at a periscope, then a torpedo track. By the time she reached Revel', *Bayan* had expended 2x20.3cm, 14x15.2cm and 37x7.5cm shells. Leskov abandoned his pursuit of *Augsburg*. *Rossiya* and *Avrora* headed in to Örö. *Bogatyr'* and *Oleg* had only just left Lappvik and turned back. Several Divizions of destroyers came out of both Moon Sound and Lappvik to hunt for submarines.

The firing by *Bayan* had ensured that Berckheim had remained deep for some time. Coming up to periscope depth was risky near a cruiser that was clearly very alert to his presence. As the afternoon wore on, Berckheim felt increasingly hounded and hemmed in by destroyers. His report picks up about half an hour after firing his torpedo:

> I move shallower [to periscope depth] and see several destroyers and a bigger ship at the location [of the attack], which is moving quickly to the east. (I suspect the second cruiser is a three-funnel *Diana* class ship.) There are several destroyers near me; I continue to move westwards.
>
> [About two hours later] I headed back to confirm my position; around 3pm, I see several destroyers coming towards me, which seem to be searching the area ... I turn [back to the west and] set the bow torpedo to 1.6m [shallow enough to hit a destroyer]... I try to go back again. At 5pm, I see 12 destroyers in a staggered line searching the area towards me, behind them several destroyers at the gap in the minefield... I decide to head out west and surface there in order to charge so that I can be at the minefield gap in the morning.
>
> 5:40pm. I change my mind [about returning in the morning] because there are clouds of smoke everywhere to the right, left and ahead.
>
> 6:30pm. I surfaced, saw three destroyers near me, one of which was heading towards me. Decision: to keep going underwater ... during the night.

None of the destroyers spotted *U.26*, but they had succeeded in driving Berckheim off with three unused torpedoes. Nevertheless, he had scored a spectacular triumph on his first war patrol and had shown good instincts in choosing positions. In contrast, Weisbach of *U.23* had always been in the wrong place at the wrong time. He had headed south that morning from his position mid-channel. As a result he only saw Leskov head out from Revel' in the distance. He then returned to his previous position. He began an attack run around mid-day on what he identified as two *Bayan* class cruisers. However, they passed well ahead. A position closer to the exits from Hangö/Lappvik or Revel' would have improved his chances. They were the obvious start and endpoints for activity.

Russian submarines had also been active. Essen started receiving reports from mid-morning. Wireless direction identified signals approaching the Gulf of Finland and Nizhniy Dagerort observed smoke to the northwest. At 1pm, *Kayman* and *Drakon* went out to attack from their guard position there. By 3pm, Gudim had *Lübeck* in sight. However, he could not get any closer than seven miles, before she turned away and disappeared. Starshiy Leytenant Ivan Messer of *Kayman* apparently got within six miles a little later. The low underwater cruising speed of the boats was a major handicap. At 4:30pm, 20th Halbflottille returned from coaling. Behring ordered his force to head west. Whilst returning to base the Russian submarines once again showed their fragility. The swell broke off part of *Kayman*'s forward superstructure and a petrol engine broke down. She limped back on the remaining engine.

Graf writes that *Novik*: 'went at full speed to the site of the disaster. There were only a lot of small wooden pieces, hammocks, and lifebelts floating there. It was significant that all the wooden objects, even the small ones, were smashed into the tiniest pieces, indicating the terrible force of the explosion. Later, an Icon of the Saviour [from *Pallada*] was recovered, which had floated to the surface and was completely undamaged.' The poignant image went to the shrine for lost sailors in the Church of the Saviour on the Waters in Petrograd.[6]

Russian reactions and a triumphant return

Magnus was one of the least likely captains to fall such easy prey to a submarine. Merkushov writes, '[He] was one of the most educated officers of our fleet.' Prior to taking command of *Pallada* in 1913, he had led submarine units for five years. Merkushov recalled that:

> … in June 1914, the cruisers *Pallada* and *Bayan* were assigned to … offer practice to [submarine] captains in firing torpedoes. All attacks on *Pallada* were successful, and she did not escape a single torpedo salvo.
>
> Particularly memorable is the attack of … *Akula* under … Vlas'yev from three cable lengths [550m], a salvo of five torpedoes, three of which hit the cruiser.
>
> This made such a strong impression on S.R. Magnus that he turned terribly pale, became very upset, and apparently, was pre-occupied with a premonition of impending death from a torpedo fired by a submarine …

Pre-war submarine practice attacks were successful because their targets tended to steam in a straight line at a predictable speed. Despite this, Magnus failed to take the steps necessary to make attack more difficult. He embraced a common misconception that vessels moving at more than 15 knots were too hard for a submarine to attack. Berckheim's attack was regarded

6 BA:RM92 *Lübeck* KTB, RM49 Detachierten Admirals KTB, RM97 *U.26* KTB; Firle, *Ostsee*, pp.188–197; Меркушов, *Записки*, pp.255–265; Винтер, 'походов', pp.237–245; РГАВМФ:Фонд 716, Опись 2, Дело 23 pp.149–163 and Дело 10 pp.224–225, Фонд 719, Опись 1, Дело 1 pp.76–78 transcibed in В. Эмме, (Е.Ф. Винтер), 'Балтийский флот в начале Первой мировой войны', *Гангут № 107*, (2018), pp.27–54 ; Мельников, *Макаров*, Глава 18; Киреев, Траление, p.31; Вейс, «Баян», pp.40–42; Графъ, *Новикъ*, pp.23–25; Eberhard Rössler, *Die Torpedos der Deutschen U-Boote* (Herford: Koehler, 1984), pp.42–43; Fog of War, Armoured cruiser Pallada, <https://digimuseo.fi/en/exhibitions/sodan-sumua/>, retrieved 4 December 2024.

by the German submarine manual as the easiest approach, turning off to fire from the stern tube from directly ahead, waiting for the target to pass. As long as the estimate of speed was accurate, speed itself was no protection. For officers of every fleet in war, with notable exceptions, it seems it took a disaster to bring home the danger. This was despite existing, proven countermeasures and officers who understood the need for them. Merkushov continues, 'The effect produced by the loss of *Pallada* was astounding. There was no longer any ironic attitude towards submarines. Everyone was asking – How did this happen? How can we protect ships from submarine attacks? What should we do? These were the constant topics of conversation in the wardrooms.'

Essen's standing orders specified that when patrolling, each pair of cruisers was to have a destroyer screening ahead to port and starboard. Despite this, a single destroyer, which was not an effective screen, was commonplace, or as with Leskov, ignored completely. The rear cruiser was to follow 1,300m behind the leader, avoiding a continuous target. Whilst told to vary their courses, cruisers were not routinely zigzagging at short intervals, the most effective defence against attack. Essen now took fundamental action. He suspended existing patrol arrangements. All battleships and cruisers were to remain in harbour. Destroyer detachments took over the patrol line north of Cape Takkhona. 2nd Minnaya Diviziya covered the northern end and the 1st the southern. Other detachments searched the areas east of the recent attacks. At 8.35am on the 12th, Dagerort reported German cruisers, trying to entice the destroyer patrols out. *Drakon* and *Kayman* quickly set out to attack, but with the same result as on the previous day. The German cruisers were moving too fast and altering course too frequently for the submarines to close.

Behring had headed west for stop and search of steamer trade on the night of the 11/12th, taking advantage of the bright moonlit night. The Admiralstab had notified him that a batch of electric motors was being shipped from Stockholm to Britain. *Augsburg* observed a lively trade down the Swedish coast from the Gulf of Bothnia. As this was moving in Swedish territorial waters, it was off limits. Meanwhile, his destroyers stopped and searched vessels outside Swedish waters, arriving from the Åland Islands. They were neutral, mainly Swedish, vessels carrying timber to Stockholm. Although the cargo would probably end up in Britain, prize regulations ruled out action. However, the Dutch skipper of *Ameland* had important news, which Ehrhardt wirelessed to Behring: 'Informed by eyewitness steamer captain … a Russian armoured cruiser exploded and sank.' Behring then sent Ehrhardt's four destroyers to make a dawn raid on the lighthouse at Lågskär: 'The intention to land was thwarted … the only cutter mounting a machine gun sprang a leak during launching. I did not want to land with an unarmed cutter, as I concluded from the size of the station that a coast guard must be there. I briefly opened fire on the lighthouse. The lantern itself and the interior of the lighthouse tower are probably destroyed, as approximately 20 shells hit the tower. I saw no enemy forces.' Each destroyer fired around 40–50 shells. Heinrich had spared the lighthouse a few weeks earlier. Encouraged by Ehrhardt's news, Behring briefly took *Augsburg* back to the entrance of the Gulf of Finland. News soon arrived that *U.26* had rendezvoused with *Lübeck* further to the west. Behring retired. The weather and the visibility had deteriorated, forcing the colliers and destroyers to shelter west of Gotland.

On the 13th, both weather and visibility deteriorated further. Behring waited for *U.23* at the rendezvous off Fårö. Once she arrived that afternoon, the entire force returned to Neufahrwasser. On the 12th, Weisbach had seen almost nothing at his billet and left overnight. Behring observed that '… the commander appears to have been somewhat too cautious in using the periscope. Nevertheless, he remained unnoticed, which can be an advantage in a new operation.'

The crew of *U.26* after the award of their medals. Berckheim is the middle officer. (WM:39255/3)

Drakon and *Kayman* sortied on the 13th, but heavy seas quickly forced them back. Russian observation posts and destroyers generated a steady stream of bogus submarine sighting reports, apart from a possible sighting of *U.23* off Dagerort by *Drakon*. Merkushov observed that: 'Now everyone, everywhere and anywhere sees submarines – a pure misfortune for fleet headquarters, where all these mostly nonsense reports are flowing.' Most were discounted, turning out to be items as various as seals and floating logs. *Del'nyy* made a highly convincing report of a diving submarine just 200m away on the 16th near Hangö. 5th Divizion thrashed around the area, but found nothing. There was nothing to find. After this, the reports petered out.

Essen hoped that *Bayan*'s gunfire had sunk *Pallada*'s assailant, in addition to the submarine presumed blown up in the minefield the day before. These hopes rested on the apparent lack of response to German wireless messages by two vessels. Essen therefore wanted details of *Pallada*'s loss withheld. There was little information to hand in Berlin, but the sinking of 'an armoured cruiser of the *Bayan* class' was announced on the 13th. The Russian Naval Ministry immediately issued a communiqué, describing both attacks in some detail, naming the ships and confirming that *Pallada* had exploded with the loss of her entire crew. Essen protested this as 'completely unacceptable.' It made front-page news around the world. Next day, based on Essen's report, the Ministry announced the sinking of two German submarines during the attacks.

On the 14th, *U.26* returned to a hero's welcome. One crewman sent a postcard to his grandparents, which the local newspaper printed: 'A greeting from a hero of *U.26*: … "After our shot was fired, we immediately went to a depth of 30 meters because they were shooting at us. Of course, they hit everything except *U.26*. Everyone on board is still safe and sound!"' There was a personal telegram from the Kaiser: 'Am overjoyed at this success of *U.26*, and have awarded the Iron Cross, 2nd Class, to the commanding officer and each of the crew.' Behring highlights the achievement of *U.26*'s new crew in his report: 'Marineingeneur Carl Schröder and the engine room personnel … deserve special mention; owing to their efficiency she covered 600 miles from Kiel to her area of operations, remained at sea, and then covered 400 miles to Danzig without a hitch.' On 16 October, Kronprinzessin Cecilie awarded the medals in Danzig, in the presence of detachments from all ships and craft stationed there.

A few days later Behring also received the award as the operation's commander. His surface forces had not contributed to the success. Having friendly cruisers nearby was a hindrance, not a help in making submarine attacks. There are hints that Adam, their commander, had counselled Behring to leave the submarines to their work, when he had thought of steaming in: '[He] was a great support to me in training, leadership, and placing the boats. I had him embarked on my flagship during the operation … and I will continue to do so in the future.' Nevertheless, Behring and Heinrich deserve credit for promoting submarine operations in the Baltic. They had been the key to breaking the deadlock.

Merkushov writes of, '… the general depressed mood caused by the loss of *Pallada*.' On the 13th, Essen circulated a message from Grigorovich, acknowledging the loss and conveying the Tsar's, 'gratitude for the combat activities of the Fleet … His Majesty believes that God will bless the final triumph of the combat work of Russian sailors for the glory of our dear Motherland.' Essen appended his own postscript: 'We will make every effort to take revenge on the enemy for the loss of *Pallada* and to justify the high trust of His Majesty the Emperor.' With the rejection of his revised plan of operations and the loss of *Pallada*, Essen needed a new approach and some good news to restore the fortunes and morale of his fleet.[7]

7 BA:RM92 *Lübeck* KTB, RM49 Detachierten Admirals KTB, RM56 20.Torpedobootshalbflottille KTB; Firle, *Ostsee*, pp.197–203; Меркушов, *Записки*, pp.258–267; РГАВМФ:Фонд 716, Опись 2, Дело 10 pp.224–225, 238–239; Винтер, 'походов', pp.245–252; Anon., *Amtliche Kriegs-Depeschen nach Berichten des Wolff'schen Telegr.-Bureaus – Band 1* (Berlin: Nationaler Verlag, 1915), p.158; *Die Presse*, Thorn, 28.Oktober 1914.

6

Reacting to developments: October 1914

Essen's new plan

The loss of *Pallada* was an inflection point in the campaign. Essen took stock of his strategy and tactics. He pushed to close the Gulf of Finland to commercial traffic, by publicising extensive Russian mining. The idea was to prevent reporting of Russian warship movements by neutral steamers and create doubt for German submarine captains about Russian mines. On 18 October, authorities announced:

> In view of the appearance of German submarines at the entrance to the Gulf of Finland and the laying of minefields by the enemy near the shores of Russia, the Imperial Government informs everyone that the Naval Authorities are forced to resort in turn to the widespread laying of minefields, which is why the following should be considered dangerous for seafarers: the areas north of parallel 58°50' north and east of meridian 21°0' from Greenwich, as well as the entrance to the Gulf of Riga and the coastal waters of the Åland Archipelago.
>
> In view of the above and out of reluctance to expose persons not taking part in military actions, the entrances to and exits from the Gulf of Finland and the Gulf of Riga shall be considered completely closed to all ships from the moment of publication of this notice.

This left Raumo and other ports in the Gulf of Bothnia as the only route for commercial goods to enter and leave Russia in the Baltic. Essen's thoughts also turned to winter, when the northern Baltic froze, locking the Baltiyskiy Flot in its bases. It was essential to secure key routes in the Finnish skerries west of Hangö in the Åbo-Åland region. When this area thawed, it would present the Swedes with an opportunity to stage a landing, whilst the fleet was still ice bound. Essen had already become concerned that the Russian defensive mines laid in the approaches around Hangö were hindering the fleet's use of the bases here and access to the west, whilst doing nothing useful. During October, these mines were removed. On the 21st, the depot ship *Khabarovsk* towed *Makrel'* and *Minoga* to Lom Island. She anchored at this sheltered, safe anchorage, deep in the skerries, to provide a base for the submarines. These continued on to Utö, reaching it on the 26th. This sheltered anchorage provided a good operational base to extend the scope of submarine patrols. However, it was exposed to attack from the sea. The auxiliary minelayer *Il'men'*, converted from the impounded German steamer *Prinzessin Sophie Charlotte*, was sent to Utö to enable the laying of defensive minefields if required. Essen also ordered a channel to be cleared and marked out to allow even the big ships to navigate in complete safety all the way through the skerries to Utö. On 3 November, *Bogatyr'* and *Oleg* successfully navigated this passage.

The fleet anchorages needed better protection. On 28 October, a new line of mines was begun at the Central Position, closing the channel south of Nargen Island, with a narrow control gate. This completed on 8 November, and was composed of mines armed electrically from the shore. German submarines attempting to attack the main anchorages to the east had to pass through the mines. Work began on the construction of anti-submarine nets and boom gates to defend all anchorages. This work to set up protected anchorages should have started much earlier and would not complete before winter. The submarine menace had simply been underestimated. Essen was frank about the problem in a general order issued on 9 November:

> The last weeks of the war have clearly shown that in some naval theatres, including the Baltic, submarines, minefields and aircraft are of great importance.
>
> All of these factors were not sufficiently studied by us before the war, therefore I draw the attention of all gentlemen officers to the desirability of a serious acquaintance with questions connected with underwater navigation, mine laying and aeronautics, since knowledge of the matter can not only clarify many misconceptions and incorrect ideas, but will also give rise to proposals for various methods of active and passive combat against these elements of naval warfare.

Taking the three areas highlighted in turn, Russian submariners were keen to play their part. The limitations of their submarines constrained their contribution. Engine reliability and performance was a particular problem. *Akula*, the only long-range boat, was currently out of action after running aground. New submarines were severely delayed, as their engines had been coming from Germany. Engines stripped from river monitors were being adapted to replace them as a stopgap.

The naval air service was also still making a minimal contribution. Reconnaissance flights from Ezel' had been useful, but the number and range of the machines available both needed to improve.

Mines were the one area where Essen had effective resources at his disposal. He had always been determined to use the long nights of winter to begin an offensive to lay mines off the German coast. With the fleet barred from taking part in this activity, he turned to a plan to use destroyers in a covert campaign. There was much less scrutiny of destroyer use by his superiors. Only those with the best speed and endurance were suitable; *Novik* and the four boats of the Poludivizion, screened by 2nd Divizion.

They would target the intersections of sea routes in and out of Memel and Danzig. Small minefields laid out in an irregular pattern, with mines at varying depths, would complicate sweeping. A sequence of minefields, beginning in the east and moving west, would reserve the longer journeys for longer nights later in the year. The aim was to work in secrecy, under cover of darkness. This would prevent discovery of the mines until a ship hit them. It would also ensure the safety of the destroyers. The most advanced positions were allocated to *Novik*. Her high speed was insurance in the event of interception. Nevertheless, this was very risky work. Any vessel with live mines on deck was at very high risk of exploding if engaged. Essen received approval for the new plan on the 14th. He quickly ordered the first operation, as Graf relates:

> On 16 October, we were ordered to proceed to Helsingfors and load from the transport *Tverdo* – moored mines, which we did; afterwards we went to the oil pier and filled up with oil. In the morning, on the 17th, we went to Moon Sound and prepared the mines for laying … Everyone was very pleased with the upcoming operation and impatiently waiting for it to start. However, upon arrival in Moon Sound, news was received … that the operation was postponed indefinitely, and we were ordered to go back to Helsingfors.

The postponement was due to completely unexpected news received by Essen:

> On 17 October, I received a special courier from the Naval General Staff notifying me that on 15 October, the British submarines *E.1*, *E.9* and *E.11* had left Britain for Libava, where they were to arrive from 20 October onwards… With the onset of darkness in October, I intended to begin laying minefields … off the German coast. The arrival of British boats forced me to postpone this operation, since I did not know the intentions of the boats and did not consider it prudent to create danger for them from our own mines.[1]

The British enter the Baltic

A hiatus had followed the British submarine reconnaissance in the Kattegat. On 6 October, Admiral Jellicoe contacted Keyes. He wanted suggestions for operations by submarines that were not required for operations in the Heligoland Bight. Keyes responded on the 10th that submarine availability had been tight, but two or three could be available for service elsewhere within a few days. The most obvious way to use them was to attack the German patrol guarding the entrance to the Baltic. A recent intelligence briefing reported the two cruisers patrolling there, supported by eight destroyers.

Jellicoe also raised the subject of submarine operations in the Baltic with the Admiralty Chief of Staff, Vice-Admiral F.C. Doveton Sturdee. He summoned Keyes to the Admiralty for discussions. Keyes proposed a plan on the 12th. To conserve fuel, destroyers would tow two submarines across the North Sea, escorted by two more destroyers. The submarines would proceed independently at nightfall, aiming to arrive off the Sound unseen. They would each follow a neutral merchantman through, and then attack the German Fleet exercising off Kiel. The latest intelligence indicated that it was carrying out gunnery practice there.

On the 13th, Keyes finalised orders for three of his most modern E class submarines to enter the Baltic for an extended patrol of several weeks. When their fuel was running low, they were to enter Libava for further orders where, 'they will be expected'. They were to approach firing red rocket flares with the white ensign and union jack flying. The increase in the scope and

1 Меркушов, *Записки*, p.259,287; РГАВМФ:Фонд 716, Опись 2, Дело 10 pp.319–320, 375–376; Винтер, 'походов', pp.251–252; Графъ, *Новикъ*, p.26; Pavlovich, *Operations*, pp.86–87, Киреев, *Траление*, pp.30–31.

E.1 underway shortly before the war. Armed with four internal 45cm torpedo tubes firing directly ahead, directly astern and directly to each side. *E.9* and *E.11* had an additional tube in the bow. (NH:43131)

length of the patrol was Keyes own idea. Recognition codes were provided for re-entering the Kattegat in November. He selected three submarine captains whom he highly regarded.

Keyes executed the plan immediately. The submarines left their base at Harwich on the east coast at noon. They stopped at Gorleston, to top up with diesel and meet their tows and escorts. Repairs to an engine on Lieutenant-Commander Martin Nasmith's *E.11* delayed departure. Keyes forwarded additional information received by the Admiralty from Copenhagen. This confirmed that Danish mines blocked the Danish Drogden Channel in the Sound. The Flintrinne on the Swedish side was clear, with navigation lights lit at night. It correctly identified German patrols south of the Sound, but incorrectly identified German destroyers and submarines as 'patrolling the Kattegat'.

The senior officer, Lieutenant-Commander Noel Laurence of *E.1*, was to ensure that all three submarines got through the Sound before any of them made any attacks in the Baltic. The engine repair was due to complete by 5am on the 15th. Laurence notified Keyes that he would depart then. The tows and escorts were now set aside. Keyes ordered that the boats depart together, then enter the Sound at two hour intervals, minimising the opportunity for enemy reaction.

At 5am, *E.11*'s repairs were expected to take another four hours. Laurence left anyway, together with Lieutenant-Commander Max Horton's *E.9*, assuming that *E.11* would follow and pass through the Sound four hours after *E.1*. Laurence soon lost touch with *E.9* when he stopped with his own engine problem. The boats were now proceeding independently.

E.1 got underway within an hour. Laurence dived whenever a vessel came in sight, to remain unobserved. He had an uneventful trip, arriving off the northern entrance to the Sound at 2.30pm on the 17th. There was heavy commercial traffic passing in both directions. He waited on the bottom until nightfall. *E.1* then surfaced and navigated straight through the busy, winding channel. He reached the Baltic by 12.30am. Laurence spotted searchlights ahead: 'as I did not wish to find myself at daylight with exhausted batteries, I deemed it inadvisable to dive past them and so went to the bottom.'[2] Next morning it was overcast and raining, but only a little

2 Laurence's report states that *E.1* spent the night off Møns Klint. He was actually further north at Stevns Klint, off the southern entrance to the Sound.

Victoria Louise after 1908 modernisation. Armed with 1x21cm turrets forward and aft, 3x15cm and 7x8.8cm guns on each side, 3x45cm torpedo tubes. Armour on gun positions and deck only, speed 19 knots. (theFrankes.com Collection)

wind. Laurence surfaced, only to spot a German destroyer close by. He submerged and headed south, looking for targets. At 10:10am, he sighted a German cruiser. Laurence closed in over the course of the next hour until he was, '500 yards [450m] on beam of [the old German armoured cruiser] "Fürst Bismarck". Fired two torpedoes at intervals of one minute.'

Since the British appearance in the Kattegat in September, there had been numerous submarine sightings in the Western Baltic. Although Heinrich was sceptical, surface ships and seaplanes investigated them all, supported by the two airships. Heinrich had recently ordered a thorough investigation of all steamers, on the assumption that a submarine operating this far from its base required the support of a parent ship. The reports all turned out to be bogus. Coast watching stations manned by army reserves had proved to be especially over-zealous. However, they disrupted exercises by squadrons of the Hochseeflotte in Kiel Bay, with ships confined to harbour during alerts.

On the 17th, *S.124* had stopped a Norwegian steamer, *Borgila*. She reported that the crew had seen 29 British submarines heading for Hantsholm in the Skagerrak on the 16th. The number of submarines was perhaps a signal error, but Mischke ordered increased lookouts. Next day, 19th Halbflottille was patrolling south of the Sound. At first light, *Victoria Louise*, Fregattenkapitän Hugo Dominik, arrived from Kiel to relieve *Hertha* at the support position between Møn and Falsterbo. *Hertha* joined *Thetis* guarding the gap between Møn and Arkona, replacing *Hansa*, which returned to Kiel to resupply. At 8:15am, *S.120* was off Stevns Klint: 'at a distance of about

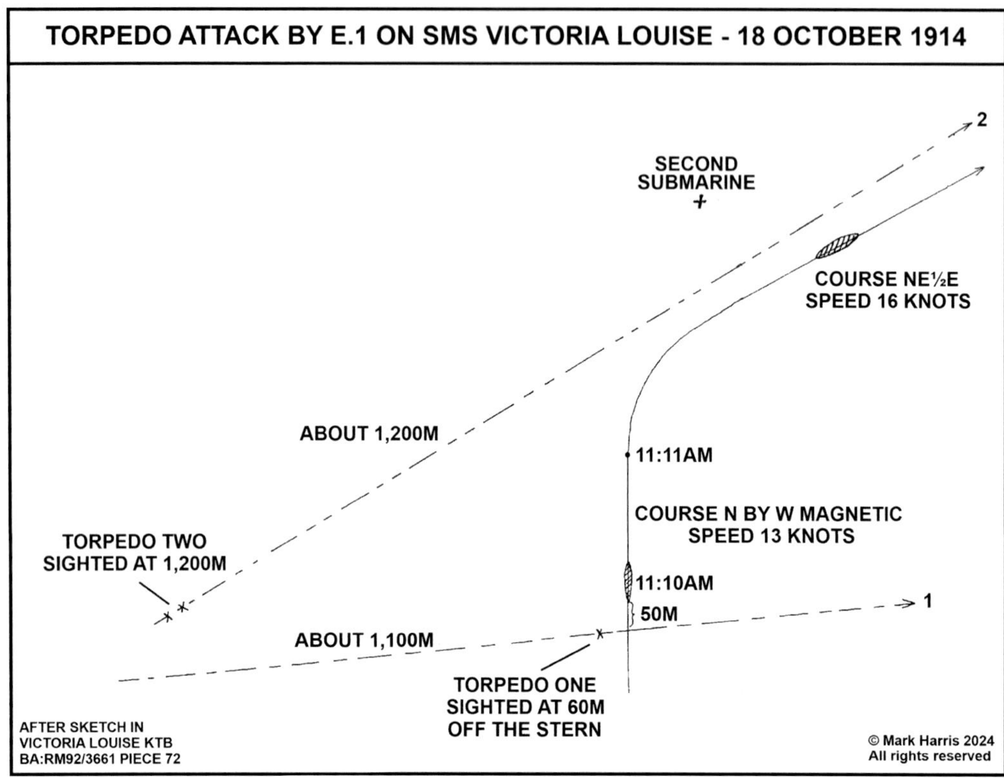

5,000m a semi-submerged submarine was sighted. Northbound, full speed. Submarine pursued at full speed. When the distance was about 2,500m, the boat turned toward *S.120* and dived rapidly. Observed water discharge at the surface. No periscope was visible. No fire was opened, as the effect of a 5.2cm at such long range seemed dubious.' It had been a narrow escape for *E.1*, spotted as she surfaced. *Victoria Louise* picked up the warning sent by *S.120*. Dominik ordered the watch doubled and sent the searchlight crews to reinforce the lookout stations. At 10:45am, despite the warning, Dominik, 'steered at 13 knots on a direct course to Falsterbo Lightship, in order to use searchlight [signals] to find out the distribution of boats off the Sound from the destroyers.' *Victoria Louise* steamed without zigzagging for 25 minutes, making it easy for *E.1* to approach. Suddenly:

> Lookout post on the poop [aft superstructure deck] reports: 'Torpedo track 50m aft of the stern.' About a minute later, the ensigns in the aft crow's nest and on the poop simultaneously report: 'Torpedo track to port astern.' Ship turns away to starboard at all ahead full, maximum speed (16 knots), the second torpedo ran on a parallel course at a speed of about 25 knots along the ship's port side, and sank perhaps 40m from the ship.
>
> About one or two minutes after turning away, a periscope is reported in a direction of 225°, at about 500 m (?).
>
> Firing is impossible, as it immediately disappears and does not reappear, and is also obscured by the ship's smoke [due to the turn away].

The first torpedo passed very close to the stern, as it would be about 50m ahead of the track. *E.1* had only one tube firing in each direction. The first eight E class had a single forward firing tube, unlike British submarines that preceded and followed them. After firing, Laurence needed to turn through 90 degrees and steady *E.1* before firing another tube. The inevitable delay allowed an alerted *Victoria Louise* to take evasive action. Laurence had the periscope up to see the result: 'The first torpedo ran under the ship but did not explode, presumably it ran too deep. The second torpedo missed ahead, the enemy having put his helm hard over to avoid it. Dived to 70 feet [20m] to avoid being rammed.' Dominik's report suggests that Laurence underestimated the range, since neither *E.1* nor the torpedo discharge was observed. The near miss aft was easily confused with an under-run at long range and perhaps made a more palatable explanation in a report. Although Laurence misidentified the target, *Fürst Bismarck* had a similar profile to *Victoria Louise*. The supposed sighting of a second submarine was bogus, but added to the alarm that the attack caused.

Minutes after the attack, *Victoria Louise* began transmitting the news. There was little doubt that British submarines had finally broken into the Baltic. Jasper returned with *Hansa* to lead the search, joined by 4th Halbflottille and Swinemünde Hilfsminensuchdivision. Heinrich ordered these boats to focus off the Sound, preventing the attackers escaping back to the Kattegat. This took them away from *E.1*. As 3rd Halbflottille were cleaning boilers, Heinrich requisitioned the newly formed 17th Halbflottille (*V.25*, *V.26*, *V.27*, *S.31*, *S.32*), and old destroyers of the torpedo school at Kiel to patrol the Fehmarn Belt and nearby coastline. *P.L.19* and the seaplanes carried out an aerial search. *Victoria Louise* stayed east of the position where she was attacked, but Jasper ordered his cruisers to zigzag, combined with regular changes of speed. The aim was to saturate the area until low batteries forced the submarines to the surface. Steamer stop and search was suspended, but Heinrich directed a special lookout for a submarine depot ship identified by intelligence, possibly named *Vitruvia*. All Hochseeflotte battleships in Kiel for exercise remained in harbour. Ingenohl reluctantly agreed to loan 8th Flottille from the North Sea, but only whilst 3rd Halbflottille was unavailable.

Heinrich also requested permission from the High Command to mine international waters directly south of the Sound, citing the attack on *Victoria Louise* and the 'numerous' submarines seen by *Borgila*. That evening, Pohl replied, 'No minefield should be laid off the Sound, as it would be useless against submarines, and commercial traffic must be maintained.' His deputy, Behncke, added, 'there is no objection, under the present circumstances, to advancing our patrol vessels in the Flintrinne right up to the three-mile limit [of neutral territorial waters].' The Foreign Secretary, Gottlieb von Jagow, approached the Swedish government once again: '... to extinguish the lights and remove the navigation marks in the Flintrinne.'

Laurence had come back to periscope depth half an hour after his attack, with nothing in sight. He soon spotted a small cruiser, probably *Thetis*. He could not get close enough to attack. He then sighted a *Hertha* class, probably *Victoria Louise*. After six hours trying to reach an attack position he gave up, foiled by constant changes in speed and course. The frantic German patrol activity focussed in the wrong areas and drew a blank, apart from a bogus periscope sighted by Seaplane 53 in Kiel Bay.

Next day Heinrich concentrated his destroyer patrol on Kiel Bay and blocking the Sound at the edge of neutral waters. Heinrich and his staff were somewhat fixated that a surface tender had to be present this far from a British base. *Hertha* and *Victoria Louise* searched all day for this chimera in the area north of Bornholm. *Hansa* and *Thetis* had to coal in Swinemünde. Their crews were jumpy. Lookouts on *Hertha* and *Thetis* spotted periscopes and the latter a torpedo track. The tender ship concept, and searching with big unaccompanied cruisers, was detached from the reality of modern diesel submarine capabilities. The British E class had a cruising range of 2,600 miles. They could easily transit from Gorleston to Kiel, spend several days on the billet and return without support. The cruisers were only providing potential targets.

Whilst Jasper's cruisers chased phantoms north of Bornholm, Laurence had headed east, south of the island. On the 20th, he headed for Danzig. The timing was bad. Behring's vessels were refitting after their recent operation, with only armed trawlers on patrol. Laurence glimpsed three cruisers, out of reach within the harbour. On the 21st *E.1* headed for Libava. Laurence narrowly missed a chance to attack *Friedrich Carl*, which arrived there on the 16th. The heavy swell had prevented entry to the shallow harbour channel until the 19th, leaving her vulnerable in the roads offshore.

Meanwhile, Horton had been the next boat to attempt the passage. *E.9* had to dive repeatedly to avoid both commercial traffic and a Swedish cruiser in the Kattegat. He was either more cautious to avoid being spotted than Laurence or had chosen a busier route. As a result, *E.9* only reached the northern entrance to the Sound around midnight on the 17th. Horton considered it too late to reach the Baltic before daylight, and assumed the other boats had suffered similar delays. He decided to sit on the bottom and head through on the following night. He twice popped up for a look round and was encouraged to see no warships in sight. Once it was dark, *E.9* surfaced and headed south.

Five and a half hours later, Horton approached the final and most difficult part of the passage, the narrow, twisting Flintrinne. He took the precaution of preparing for a rapid dive: '11pm. Passing Malmo Light trimmed down with the upper deck awash and proceeded through the busy Flint Channel slowly on one engine. Night calm, clear and dark. 11:20pm. Drogden Light Vessel abeam. I kept as far North as possible to avoid enemy's destroyers.'

It was 24 hours since Laurence had reached this point. The patrols were now at the edge of Danish and Swedish territorial waters, off the narrow, shallow, southern exit of the Flintrinne, near the Danish Drogden Lightship. Laurence's recent attack also ensured there were more vessels present, with heightened vigilance: '11:47pm. 2¾ [miles] S.W. of Drogden Light Vessel sighted destroyer 150 yards [140m] on starboard bow. Dived. Submarine was timed under in 15 secs. Hit bottom at 14½ feet [4½m] by gauge. Stopped. Inferred from depth that we were resting on 4½ fathom [8m] patch marked on the Chart. Bottom very stony. Top of periscope standards about 6in. [15cm] above water when resting on bottom.'

Horton's caution had paid off, but with his periscope stand poking out of the water he would make an easy target for ramming. He had to move. Twenty minutes later, he blew some ballast to lift off the bottom. He could make out a destroyer, just 65m to port. The dark night was his only cover. He moved forward at a depth of just 3m in the shallow water. The water depth increased agonisingly slowly. First 4½m. Finally 6m. He was finally safe from ramming by a destroyer.

In the small hours of the 19th, 10 hours after setting off, Horton made out the white cliffs of Stevns Klint ahead. *E.9* was through. Horton took her to the bottom for an hour and a half's rest. When he continued south, there were destroyers all around. Horton pushed on for the next five hours. Finally, the horizon looked clear. *E.9* surfaced, only to spot a destroyer 6 miles away. Horton took *E.9* straight back down, recording in his log: 'Destroyer passed close.'

17th Halbflottille were working on their patrol line. *V.27* spotted a conning tower about 5,000m astern. The stern gun opened fire and the conning tower disappeared. The Halbflottille closed in round the position. *S.31* sighted a periscope and then avoided a torpedo. The outline of the attacker's hull was evident in the water, but escaped by diving rapidly. Danish fishermen saw it again later that afternoon. Aircraft 79 dropped two bombs on a suspected submarine. Heinrich was now convinced that two submarines had broken into the Baltic. He was right, but the reports from the over-zealous crews, seaplane and fishermen were a complete fantasy. Neither submarine was anywhere near the position off Schleimünde, north of Kiel. These reports made it impossible to pick out a real attack from imaginary ones.

Horton was 100 miles away, slipping past the patrols there unseen. It was mid-afternoon before the horizon was clear. The crew had been below almost continuously for over 15 hours. Finally, Horton surfaced, cleared the stale air, and began charging the depleted batteries. *E.9* headed for nearby Møn Bank, which was shallow enough to spend the night resting on the bottom. Horton had covered just 40 miles that day and seen nothing but hunting destroyers.

As with *Pallada* for the Russians, perhaps only a torpedo hit could bring a full realisation of the risks run by unescorted cruisers. These kept up their hunt on the 20th. *Hansa* carried out a sweep of the coast from Kolberg to Swinemünde and back. *Vineta* relieved *Hertha*, which coaled at Swinemünde. *Thetis* replaced *Victoria Louise* north of Bornholm at lunchtime, allowing her to take up a patrol south of the island. As Heinrich groped towards an effective anti-submarine strategy, the Admiralstab passed on advice from Ingenohl. Horton had recently sunk one of his destroyers: 'the use of destroyers against submarines does not promise success, but rather exposes these vessels to great danger. [Ingenohl] considers a larger number of appropriately armed smaller steamers in several successive rows to be promising.' Heinrich had no trawlers to hand, so he requisitioned six harbour steamers, had a machine gun mounted on each and sent them out to relieve 17th Halbflottille and the school boats. Ingenohl's 8th Flottille (*G.174*, *G.175*, *S.176*, *S.177*, *S.179*, *S.131*, *S.139*, *V.180*, *V.183*) arrived to reinforce the hunt off the Sound. The wind picked up, which grounded the airships and fragile seaplanes.

Heinrich's patrols sighted nothing that day. Horton was following Laurence, moving clear of the patrols. He had surfaced to an empty sea that day, headed for Cape Arkona, then turned east. In the early afternoon *E.9* passed well to the south of Bornholm. The cruisers going backwards and forwards to Swinemünde had crossed his track unseen earlier in the day. He only sighted *Victoria Louise* on her new patrol billet, too far away to attack, about ten miles to the north. The seas got rougher as night fell. Eventually Horton had to submerge out of the heavy swell. Soon, there was a problem: 'Starboard Main Motor started burning insulation.' Horton had to surface to stop and examine it. It was a short circuit within the motor, impossible to fix at sea. Horton considered it, 'advisable to give up' the idea of patrolling off Danzig and headed straight for Libava. *E.9* spent the whole of the 21st and the following night ploughing through increasingly heavy seas and head winds. This final twist of fate spared Jasper's cruisers from possible attack. Heinrich had ordered them to Danzig to support Behring's next operation. However, an attack in the prevailing weather would have been difficult.

Nasmith was probably the last of the submariners to attempt the passage. He was a highly experienced submarine captain and had taken command of *E.11* at the builders on the day war broke out. Having only recently completed her trials and working up, this was his first war patrol. The engine had taken much longer to repair than anticipated. *E.11* was therefore the last to arrive at the northern entrance to the Sound, on the afternoon of the 18th. Like Horton, he submerged to wait for darkness, but unlike him, read hostile intent into the movements of steamers on the surface. The Admiralty briefing had not helped by falsely placing German destroyers in the Kattegat. Horton was heading through that same night, reassured that no warships were present. When he began his passage, Nasmith became flustered in the busy channel. He became convinced that destroyers were pursuing *E.11*. What Nasmith encountered is impossible to determine. He did not reach the Flintrinne, let alone any German warships. He gave up the attempt and turned back. He planned to try again. Next morning he headed off underwater, along the Danish coast, to find a quiet spot to charge his battery. He encountered a submarine, which was patrolling slowly on the surface. He identified the German *U.3*. Nasmith fired two torpedoes, one of which probably did not run properly. The other glanced off the bottom of the hull far forward. This was actually lucky. The submarine was the Danish *Havmanden*, which then rapidly left the scene. The tale of woe continued when next morning one of *E.11*'s torpedoes exploded on a nearby beach. The Danes confirmed the British torpedo type and serial number from the remains. It took until January for Keyes to accept the blame for the attack and issue an apology to the Danish government. Nasmith's report goes on to catalogue more encounters with suspicious vessels, suspected torpedo attacks and hostile destroyers in the Kattegat. All were the product of over-wrought imaginations. The parallel with Vlas'yev's first patrol in *Akula* is notable. Patrolling for the first time in hostile waters in a submarine was a unique stressor for a crew. It highlights just how remarkable Berckheim's achievement had been. Nasmith abandoned a second attempt on the Sound and returned to Harwich. After this shaky start, he later went on to become one of the most successful British submarine captains of the war.[3]

The British arrive at Libava

One of the outcomes of the Loch Ewe conference on 16 September had been to identify the feasibility of basing British submarines in Russian ports. However, there had been no follow through. The decision to send the submarines to Libava after attacks off Kiel had only appeared in the evolving plan on 13 October. Next day, Volkov was at the Admiralty with Kedrov and Smirnov. Volkov presumably received a copy of Laurence's orders at or following meeting, as Rear-Admiral Henry Oliver, Churchill's new Naval Secretary, was present. Next day, a surprised Volkov telegraphed Admiral Rusin:

> The British have sent three submarines to the Baltic Sea. They are expected to appear off Libava starting from 7 October, old style [20th]. Approaching Libava, they will raise the British ensign and the British jack, simultaneously firing red flares. The numbers of the boats are *E.1*, *E.9* and *E.11*, but the numbers are painted over. If for any reason Libava should prove unsuitable for their anchorage, and if there were no essential supplies for the boats there, then the Admiralty requests that you assist them by assigning officers to escort them to a more suitable base.

Rusin replied, 'Welcome British intentions. Although Libava entry is possible, nevertheless because of the presence of German mines, it is better, if it is not too late, to send them to

3 Harris, *Submarines*, pp.190–196; BA:RM92 *Victoria Louise*, *Hertha*, *Hansa*, *Thetis* KTB, RM5/831, RM56 19.Torpedobootshalbflottille KTB, RM28 KTB; TNA:ADM137/271, pp.15–22; Firle, Ostsee, pp.203–212.

Tagelakht [Bay] on the island of Ezel'.' Essen acted quickly to manage the situation when he received the news from Rusin on the 17th: 'I sent English speaking officers to both of the indicated points [Libava and Tagelakht Bay] to meet the submarines and facilitate their missions with us, and also prepared supplies for the boats there with everything necessary.'

On the 18th, Rusin received bad news from Volkov: 'The Admiralty informed me of its intentions only after the submarines had left. The instructions that you sent cannot be forwarded to them. The Admiralty now asks us to take all available measures to help the submarines enter Libava, since they will most likely arrive in daylight.' The constantly evolving British plan was a shoddy piece of staff work. The lack of prior liaison with Volkov is baffling. The submarines were unaware that they would be arriving at a mined port. Rudimentary liaison work would have identified the German minefield at Libava. The German official communiqué about the August bombardment even mentioned it. It had been widely quoted in the German press.

Kapitan 1st Ranga Vladimir Forsel' now commanded the naval forces at Libava. He only had a small hired steamer, *Vorms*, plus a few local steam fishing boats and port vessels. Essen now sent the torpedo boat *Porazhayushchiy*, a despatch vessel with Nepenin's force. Only small, shallow draught vessels could access the port, through a gap in the northern exit. The *Magdeburg* documents had revealed the approximate position of the German minefield. *Krokodil* had given it a very wide berth when going in and out. Essen ordered Forsel' to identify its limits: 'Over the course of three days, working day and night, the true location of the enemy's obstruction was determined, measures were taken to facilitate passage through the northern gates, and round the clock duty was arranged for boats and a dispatch vessel [either *Vorms* or *Porazhayushchiy*] at a distance of up to 15 miles from the shore to meet the [British] boats.' This was dangerous work, not only from mines, but exposed to attack from nearby German waters.

E.1 arrived at Libava at 5pm on the 21st. Essen's report says that she was 'met and escorted to the port', but Laurence's report is more alarming: 'An officer from the staff of the C-in-C. Russian Fleet met us, and informed me that the dockyard and plant had been destroyed, and that there were extensive minefields off [Libava] apparently we had come right through one German minefield but fortunately without striking one of the mines.' Next day, Horton arrived: '8am. Sighted tugs off Libau [Libava]. Closed and took aboard Russian Naval Officer who piloted us into harbour.'

Laurence and Horton found *Krokodil* still at Libava. Podgornyy had carried out another patrol before being confined to port, awaiting the arrival of the British boats. He left Libava under cover of darkness on the 15th, headed south down the coast, and arrived off Memel next morning. Merkushov later recorded the details:

> … at 7am being in sight of the Memel lighthouse, we saw smoke rapidly approaching. *Krokodil* submerged and went towards it. After one hour and ten minutes, seeing that the German three-funnel cruiser had changed course and it was impossible to attack her, the boat surfaced and remained in position until midday. Due to the increasing waves, and more importantly, due to the severe carbon monoxide poisoning of the crew whilst cruising submerged, we had to go back. The crew were poisoned by carbon monoxide because considerable exhaust gases broke through into the boat whilst the petrol engines were running, in addition, due to a leak in the petrol line, the air was saturated with petrol vapour; this time there was no time to ventilate the compartment before diving. *Krokodil* remained

> underwater for only one hour, but half the crew and the senior officer were poisoned by carbon monoxide; Ya[kov] I. Podgornyy was unwell himself, and all that remained was to thank God that the German cruiser soon left and it was possible to rise to the surface. That same evening the boat returned to Libava.

It is unclear what ship Podgornyy encountered. The only cruiser at sea in the Bay of Danzig that morning was *Friedrich Carl*, arriving from Kiel. Essen was now concerned about the size of the force in Libava. *Krokodil* had maintained a low profile, going in and out of the port under cover of darkness, but keeping two British boats secret was going to be almost impossible. However, Essen could not issue orders to officers of another navy. Forsel' passed on a message from Essen on Horton's arrival: '... advising us to proceed forthwith to [Lappvik].' Laurence had other ideas: 'As the men needed a rest I decided to wait for *E.11*.'

For the next three days, the British crews concentrated on repairing defects. The biggest problem was *E.9*'s motor. Fortunately, Engineer-Lieutenant Cecil Simpson had accompanied the boats. Starshiy Leytenant Sergey Kukel', an electrical engineering specialist in the submarine force at Revel', also arrived to help. They adjusted the motor to enable operation at low speed, but it needed attention in a functioning dockyard. The two submarines were also beginning to experience problems with their clutches, an issue that had recently been cropping up in the British diesel boats, resulting from intensive use. The British deemed the diesel oil sent to Libava unsuitable. Refuelling would have to wait. The English-speaking officers sent by Essen did allow them to establish an early rapport with their hosts. With no idea about re-supply, the British were pleased to discover that the Russian 1910 model torpedoes used by *Krokodil* could be fired from British tubes. Laurence reported, 'The officers and men have received the greatest kindness from all ranks in the Russian Navy.'

The attempt to keep the presence of the submarines secret was futile. The boats moored without flags. At first, the officers went in to the city in civilian clothes, and the crew stayed in the naval port. However, both officers and crew soon began appearing ashore in uniform. Meanwhile, Essen wanted to get his delayed minelaying offensive underway. The destroyers had advanced to Lyuzerort, assuming that by the 23rd the British boats would all have arrived. Weather conditions were perfect, but Essen ordered them back to Helsingfors. He appealed to Rusin on the 24th to try to get the British to move:

> An extended stay of submarines in Libava is very dangerous, because the enemy will soon know of it and leaving the port is impossible in a combat situation. I request that, if you find it appropriate, to advise them through the Ambassador [George Buchanan] to quickly go north, without waiting for the third submarine.

The British Embassy's response was prompt, but diplomatic. It would be up to Laurence how he responded: 'The amb[assado]r doesn't feel competent to give orders to the boats but he strongly advises the captains, if their orders from Admiralty permit, to act under Admiral Essen directions'. Laurence received the message, 'telling us to go North. As both boats would need to refit on arrival in the Gulf of Finland, I decided to have a try for the cruisers in Dantzig [*sic*] before proceeding there.' He was evidently oblivious as to how this decision might affect Essen's own plans. The command situation was impossible. On the 25th, after another complaint about it from Kerber, Rusin telegraphed Volkov:

> Ask the Admiralty what position the boats should be in relation to Admiral Essen. Desirable is complete subordination, like our cruisers in the Far East [to the British], or at least coordination of actions. Independent actions of the boats interfere with Admiral Essen and hinder the actions of our Fleet. Admiral Essen is preparing a depot base for the boats. It is necessary to send a full set of Whitehead mines [torpedoes] via Arkhangel'sk.

The timing was opportune. Sturdee received a report from Keyes the same day. He concurred with Nasmith that, '… he did not consider it possible to get through the Sound in the face of opposition.' He recommended that, '… it would be advisable to keep "E.1" and "E.9" in the Baltic throughout the Winter. [Libava] is practically an ice-free port, and their presence should be a source of continual annoyance and anxiety to the enemy.' It followed that they should come under Essen's command. Next day, the 26th, Volkov telegraphed Rusin: 'The Admiralty requests that the following message be urgently conveyed to the Commander of the submarine *E.1*: "Place yourself under orders of Admiral Essen for offensive action against German forces in Baltic. Report immediately though him what you have done and what torpedoes you have expended. You are promoted [to Commander] and Horton has [been awarded] D[istinguished] S[ervice] O[order]."'

Keyes was critical of Laurence's failure to ensure that Nasmith passed through the Sound on the same night as the other boats. He did not realise that Nasmith had turned back on the same night as Horton got through. *E.9* had encountered more alert patrols, closer to the Flintrinne exit, but passage was still eminently possible. Nasmith's report gave Keyes a greatly exaggerated impression of the scale of enemy resistance in the Kattegat and the Sound, directly affecting future decisions. Horton and Laurence's reports finally arrived in November. Neither mention any opposition to passing through the Sound itself, as there was none. On reading the reports, Churchill added a file note: 'To send these SM's into the Baltic without telling them of the Libau minefield or what they were to do if they c[oul]d not return, was bad staff work. The Russians also were imperfectly acquainted with this project and possible arrival.' Despite poor planning and significant disruption to the start of Essen's offensive, the operation resulted in a major boost for the Baltiyskiy Flot submarine force.[4]

Responding to the submarine threat in the western Baltic

In the western Baltic, evidence of the British submarine threat continued, both bogus and real. On 20 October, the commander of a torpedo school destroyer reported damaging a supposed submarine. The crew had thrown an improvised explosive charge over the side. He had then seen, '… a large slick of petroleum on the water's surface shortly afterwards.' The press also reported the attack on *Havmanden*. The Danish government issued diplomatic notes to Britain, Germany and Russia. The Danes had already mined their waters, but they now also extinguished navigation lights on their side of the Sound and increased naval readiness, ordering

4 РГАВМФ:Фонд 716, Опись 2, Дело 8, p.117, Дело 10, pp.319–320, 375–376, Фонд 418, Опись 1, Дело 3343, pp.1–69; TNA:ADM137/271, pp.16–24, ADM137/2067 Commodore (S) War Records, Volume I. Reports of proceedings of submarines attached to HMS Maidstone, 1914, pp.355–359; Меркушов, *Записки*, pp.294–295; Anon., *Wolff*, p.12; *Hallesche Zeitung*, 4.August 1914; Графъ, *Новикъ*, pp.27–28; Томашевич, *операциях*, p.47.

their warships to prevent any attempt by belligerent warships to transit Danish waters. The Germans knew that only a British boat could have made the attack on *Havmanden*. More serious for any future British attempt to reinforce their boats was that the Swedes finally took action as well, although this was limited. From the night of the 19th, with a number of important exceptions, lights on the Swedish west and south coast were extinguished.

Heinrich tried two new anti-submarine tactics over the next few days. News arrived that *U.27* had sunk the British submarine *E.3* in a submerged ambush off the Ems. Heinrich decided to try the same tactic, using all four Kiel based submarines, as well as *U.32*, which was doing trials. On the 21st, Heinrich cleared all destroyers, trawlers, steamers and aerial reconnaissance from Kiel Bay. The submarines then began diving patrols, hoping that the empty sea would lure the enemy to the surface. Despite ongoing reports of submarine sightings in the Sound by Swedish merchantmen, a week later the submarines had sighted nothing. Heinrich stood down the submarines, resuming surface patrols.

Heinrich also tried to trap the British submarines reported in Kiel Bay with herring nets at the Fehmarn Belt. Between the 23rd and 27th, 36km of nets were laid in two staggered lines. The 12 armed trawlers of the Kiel Hilfsminensuchdivision patrolled the barrier. The idea was to engage the British submarines when they spotted the nets and surfaced to cross them. However, rope nets were not a real obstacle to an E class submarine. To prevent their passage substantial steel netting was required. On the 29th, a storm swept the entire edifice away. Quite apart from the loss of a vast amount of fishing nets, the wreckage caused a significant navigational hazard in Kiel Bay for some time. The Admiralstab rejected Heinrich's request to replace the barrier with a minefield: 'the necessary moored mines are not available for this purpose. Current mine design against submarines is also not sufficiently effective.'

The coastal defence forces were re-organised at the end of October. The destroyer force was re-designated as 4th Torpedobootsflottille, absorbing 19th Halbflottille (*T.113* leader boat, 7th Halbflottille, *S.120*, *S.124*, *G.134*, *T.97*, 8th Halbflottille, *S.128*, *S.126*, *S.130*, *S.129*, *S.131*). *Carmen*, which now worked with the submarines, and torpedo school boats *S.121*, *S.123* and *S.127* supported the patrols. The latter gradually joined 4th Flottille, replacing losses and transfers. On the 29th, Ingenohl recalled both the 2nd and 8th Flottille to the North Sea. He made the 2nd Minensuchdivision (*D.6*, *T.28*, *T.30*, *T.39*, *T.46*, *T.47*, *T.49*, *T.51*, *T.52*, *T.53*, *T.54*, *T.55*, *T.56*, *T.57*) available in lieu of 2nd Flottille, considering them 'better suited for patrol duties in the Baltic Sea than large destroyers'. Heinrich also received a commercial steamer, *Answald*, converted to act as a carrier for seaplanes.

At the beginning of November, the submarine threat drove a re-organisation of defensive arrangements under Wieting, who now commanded 4th Flottille. Vulnerable cruisers were finally withdrawn from the Sound guard. Instead, *Amazone*, *Undine* or *Gazelle* made daily visits off neutral coasts near the patrol lines to give the impression of close cruiser support. Half of 4th Flottille took turns patrolling south of the Flintrinne and coaling. 2nd Minensuchdivision concentrated on patrolling the approach to Kiel Bay at Fehmarn Belt and the Kadet Rinne, the narrow channel between Gedser on the Danish island of Falster, and the German coast.

Panther and the auxiliary units continued to patrol behind the German minefields in the Belts, supported by the minelayers. The work was not without danger. On 3 November, *Vorpostenboot 3*, Oberleutnant zur See der Seewehr I Wilhelm Witt, was working to remove mines in the Great Belt, displaced by recent storms. She anchored whilst Witt inspected the mines in a boat. Torpeder-Leutnant Kurt Karnath of *Rügen* was aboard:

Vorpostenboot 3, ex-*Augustenburg*. A typical requisitioned trawler of 232 GRT, based in Kiel, built in 1906, armed with a single 5cm gun. (Public domain)

> I advised Oberleutnant Witt to fire at them from the Vorpostenboot [from a distance with the 5cm gun]. Whilst we were raising anchor, a mine exploded forward … Due to the force of the impact and the mass of water crashing down on the steamer, I fell from the bridge, thrown half-conscious to the afterdeck, and when the railing was barely above the water, I jumped overboard and was picked up by the dinghy.
>
> The steamer quickly sank, with only the tops of the masts visible. During the sinking, the boiler exploded. I found the First Officer swimming in a tangle of debris, who called to me to row to the mast to lighten the overcrowded boat. This was accomplished, as floating oil calmed the [choppy] sea. On the way, the First Officer and one man were picked up. After reaching the forward mast, the men who still felt strongest climbed the mast on the orders of the First Officer and held on. I also climbed the mast and was picked up with the rest of the men by a boat from *Rügen*.

Six crew were lost and four of the survivors suffered wounds in the explosion.[5]

Behring's second submarine offensive and new priorities

The new submarine threat also created problems at Danzig. On arrival, *Friedrich Carl* had been stuck for three days in the outer roads at Neufahrwasser, exposed to submarine attack. Behring requested resources from Heinrich for urgent dredging to deepen the harbour channel,

5 Harris, *Submarines*, pp.196–198; BA:RM5/5273, RM92 *Gazelle* KTB, RM28 KTB, RM56 4.Torpedobootsflottille; Firle, *Ostsee*, pp.211–219; Anon., *Verlustliste No.11*, p.17; Erich Gröner, *Die deutschen Kriegsschiffe 1815-1945. Band 8/1* (Koblenz: Bernard & Graefe Verlag, 1993), p.234.

Friedrich Carl leaving port. Armed with 4x21cm guns in turrets fore and aft, 5x15cm and 6x8.8cm guns on each side, 4x45cm torpedo tubes. 10cm hull armour, speed 20 knots. (Public domain)

something that should have been foreseen. This would take six weeks to complete. Behring focussed on following up his last submarine offensive with another, once his vessels completed urgent maintenance. Winter would soon interrupt submarine operations. He was as ebullient as ever: 'The fact that the enemy has assumed the offensive in the Baltic must not cause us to abandon our own offensive.'

On 21 October, a telegram arrived from Pohl: 'Advance of Russian fleet in connection with the appearance of British submarines in the Baltic Sea does not seem unlikely. Recommend taking precautions to counter with the submarines at Danzig. My assumption is that British submarines will make towards the Gulf of Finland.' This message had prompted Heinrich to order Jasper's four cruisers and *Thetis* to reinforce Behring at Danzig.

On the 24th, Behring's force was ready. Following the recent Russian announcement, Behring needed to confirm the extent of new mining in the Gulf of Finland. *Lübeck*, *Augsburg*, *Thetis* and 20th Halbflottille sailed that afternoon, led by Fregattenkapitän Wilhelm Bunnemann, in temporary command of *Lübeck*. On the night of 25/26th, he would occupy an outpost line south-east of Bogskär: 'Do not release detained merchant ships immediately, but rather, under the pretext that a thorough investigation must be conducted, seize them and send them to [my position].' The intention was to discover details of mine free channels from their crews or charts. Behring followed at a sedate 10 knots with *Friedrich Carl*, *Hertha*, *Vineta*, *D.10* and three submarines, to rendezvous with Bunnemann on the morning of the 26th. The cruisers towed the submarines part of the way to spare their engines. Jasper left *Victoria Louise* and *Hansa* behind for machinery repairs. The enterprising Gercke persuaded Behring to embark two seaplanes on *Friedrich Carl*, for hoisting out by her cranes. These were to reconnoitre the Gulf of Finland. Heinrich thought them more useful at Putzig, but had eventually approved.

Bunnemann's outpost line encountered nothing. Behring had been hoping to send his submarines deep into the Gulf. With no details of safe routes, on the 26th, the submarines headed for a position outside the German mined area, just west of a line from Cape Takkhona to Bengtskär. This was inside the Russian exclusion area, but considered likely to remain free of mines. After three days, they would rendezvous with Behring's force. This remained east of Gotska Sandön, whilst his destroyers topped up their coal from the light cruisers.

Once again, Behring planned to offer bait to draw the Russians out for his submarines to attack. On the morning of the 27th, Jasper's two cruisers rendezvoused just east of Gotland with the colliers *Oberpräsident Delbrück*, *Ursula Fischer*, *Edmund Hugo Stinnes 4* and *Lissabon*, with the hospital ship *Schleswig*. Six trawlers of the Hilfsminensuchdivision had escorted them from Danzig.

The force headed for the western entrance to the Gulf of Riga. At 1:30pm, it approached the coast. As a precaution against Russian mining, the trawlers led with their sweeps out, reducing the formation speed to four knots. The wind had dropped and a haze reduced visibility. Smoke approached from the north. Lookouts on *Hertha* spotted several two funnelled warships looming out of the murk, closing rapidly. *Thetis* was the only two-funnelled ship with Behring, so 'it had to be assumed that they were Russian warships.' Jasper ordered: 'Clear ship for action.' However, *Vineta* signalled that she had sighted German destroyers. From *Hertha*, the closing vessels were still indistinct. Recognition signals went unanswered. *Hertha*'s guns were loaded and ready to fire. Finally, the vessels cleared the murk. It was 20th Halbflottille. A cold mirage, typical of the Baltic at the time of year, made the destroyers seem the size of cruisers. Behring had not informed Jasper that he had despatched them to coal from the colliers. A serious friendly fire incident had almost resulted.

Jasper's force resumed its slow progress. At 4pm, lookouts sighted the Russian coast near Lyuzerort. Shortly afterwards, the sweep failed on one of the trawler pairs. Jasper abandoned the operation. The trawlers dropped marker buoys. Jasper retired for the night to the Gotland coast, intending to locate the buoys to resume operations next morning: 'Since … the submarine line had been deployed outside the Gulf of Finland … the prospects for the submarines to fire were relatively slim. It therefore seemed advantageous to postpone the advance into the Gulf of Riga … for a later operation. … I therefore decided … to demonstrate the following day near Vindava.' This would take him into the so far undetected Russian minefields. That evening, *Hansa* left Danzig to join him. However, later that night new orders came in from Heinrich.

In a short space of time during the night of 27/28 October, Heinrich received news that completely altered the focus of his force in the east. At 12:10am, Danzig confirmed the veracity of a report that 'several fishermen' had seen a surfaced submarine just three miles from Neufahrwasser the day before. The British were evidently in the eastern Baltic. Heinrich wirelessed Jasper: 'Enter Swinemünde immediately, preferably not in formation, due to submarine danger in Bay of Danzig.' A formation of these old cruisers exposed to submarine attack now seemed too great a risk.

At 12:45am, Heinrich received a message from Pohl: 'Occupation of Memel by Russia likely. Make all preparations to block the harbour so that it becomes unusable for submarines and torpedo boats.' The Russian army was massing for an offensive in Poland. Whilst the coastal area had so far not seen any fighting, there were reports that troops were gathering around Libava. Heinrich wirelessed Behring: 'Send one light cruiser with 20th Halbflottille to Memel as quickly as possible.' Behring gave the task to Fregattenkapitän Paul Nippe of *Thetis*. He cancelled the demonstration off Vindava, and ordered all cruisers to commence zigzagging. Jasper sent *Oberpräsident Delbrück*, *Ursula Fischer* and *Schleswig* to Behring off Gotland. The other colliers and armed trawlers returned to Neufahrwasser.

Heinrich ordered Nippe to work with the dockyard at Danzig to block the entrances to Memel 'as soon as occupation is imminent.' His force arrived the following afternoon. The army garrison commander, Hauptmann der Landwehr Krause, knew of the rumoured troops at the border, but there had been no signs of anything unusual. He had only 800 men to guard the area. Nippe organised a landing party of 70 men with two machine guns. On the 30th, they took a train to the border, where an incursion by Russian troops had been reported. Six steamers fitted as blockships arrived in Memel from Danzig dockyard, ready to be chained together and sunk, blocking the harbour entrance. Landsrat Cranz, the head of the civilian administration, protested. In winter, ice would back up if the harbour was blocked, flooding the town, with dire economic consequences. Rumours reached fever pitch. Nippe wirelessed that a 'reliable spy' had confirmed enemy troop concentrations on a trip behind Russian lines. Mysterious 'third parties' confirmed that there were 12,000 Russian troops in Libava, although the spy had only seen a troop train and 300 Cossacks themselves. After a day observing unremarkable Russian scout activity across the border, Nippe's landing party returned to *Thetis* on the 31st. The panic subsided. On 4 November, based on Krause's protests and evidence that the Russian troops were heading south to Poland, the High Command cancelled the operation.

Behring had remained in position east of Gotska Sandön on the 28th, hoping to intercept the presumed British submarines if they headed north. Heinrich refused his request for destroyers to provide a screen and anti-submarine patrol. He simply had none to spare. The weather had been too rough on the 27th for the seaplanes. Behring now considered it too dangerous to stop for hoisting out, without a destroyer screen for *Friedrich Carl*. Nevertheless, both *Lübeck* and *D.10* had to stop to coal from the colliers.

That afternoon, Hela observation post reported, 'a submarine has been sighted coming from Danzig Bay and heading north at high speed.' It had been in sight for an hour. A few hours later, the Admiralstab passed Heinrich information from 'a reliable source', namely a spy: 'two British submarines, *E.1* and *E.9*, had arrived in Libava at mid-day on the 21st.' Essen's fears of discovery had proved accurate. Heinrich wanted to strike their base immediately. Late that evening, Behring received two wireless messages: 'British submarines *E.1* and *E.9* at Libava... Abandon operation. Proceed with all forces to Libava. *Thetis* to remain at Memel.' This was soon followed by, 'Libava apparently a submarine base. Request reconnaissance of Libava by aircraft – at your discretion. 20th Halbflottille to join as submarine screen. Only bombard with *Friedrich Carl* if success assured, otherwise permanently blockade with a submarine.' Behring quickly decided that, 'Close surveillance of the harbour by cruisers and torpedo boats during the day would show the British that we are aware of their use of Libava. Based on previous experience, there is little prospect of destroying submarines by day using cruisers and torpedo boats unless the submarines are surprised. Therefore, it is not advisable to position cruisers and torpedo boats within sight of land near Libava.' Observation by his submarines was the only realistic option. He notified Heinrich.

Next morning, the 29th, *D.10* went to recall the three submarines, covered to the west by *Friedrich Carl*. There was no sign of Russian forces, just smoke far to the east. By mid-day, *U.23* and *U.26* were located and sent to billets off Libava, south of the German minefield. *Friedrich Carl* returned to Danzig, picking up 20th Halbflottille as escort on the way. *Augsburg* and *Lübeck* remained at the Gotland rendezvous until *U.25* arrived at the end of her patrol. Apart from *U.26*, they had seen nothing. Berckheim had seen two *Ukrayna* class destroyers patrolling on the 28th, but could only close to 3,000m, too far to attack. Behring's force arrived in Danzig on the 30th. The weather prevented aerial reconnaissance of Libava, as the seas were too rough to hoist out seaplanes. However, they survived the rough weather intact in the superstructure.

Behring's operation made little apparent contact with the enemy, but all was not as it seemed. On 12 October, a second direction finding station had begun operating at Hangö. It was now possible for the Russians to triangulate the approximate position of German wireless signals. On the 28th, there was a lot of activity, located well to the west of the Gulf of Finland. 2nd Minnaya Diviziya was readied for sea should the Germans approach. On the 27th, *Makrel'* and *Minoga* had commenced a day patrol off Bogskär, taking turns to occupy an ambush position south of the outcrop, an obvious position fix for advancing German vessels. However, the German cruisers were out of sight to the south. Essen could not sortie his big ships outside the Gulf, but he ordered both submarines on patrol next day.

As Behring advanced on the 29th, from mid-morning onwards, in the clear air, the observation posts on Dagerort reported *Friedrich Carl* and *D.10*. The outpost destroyers *Finn*, *Dobrovolets* and *Moskvityanin* kept up a steady stream of updates from a distance, confirming the presence of a cruiser. With good visibility, there was no realistic chance of approaching undetected for a torpedo attack.

However, Behring was unaware of the real danger. At 10:30am, three hours after leaving Utö, Leytenant Dmitriy Karaburdzhi of *Makrel'* spotted smoke. He spent hours chasing it on the surface. Changes in target course frustrated his attempts to get closer. Finally, at mid-day, the vessel turned in his direction. Merkushov relates the details: '*Makrel'* submerged and went at full speed (4.5 knots) to close in. At 1:35pm, funnels became visible through the periscope, and on the foremast, apparently, the admiral's flag. The distance was five miles. At this time, the cruiser turned southeast and began to leave. Realising the impossibility of getting any closer, Lieutenant Karaburdzhi ordered low speed, wanting to conserve electrical charge in case the enemy, who was steaming back and forth, returned.' The target briefly reappeared, only to disappear for good. Meanwhile, Leytenant Nikolay Il'inskiy of *Minoga* headed to a position nine miles southeast of Bogskär, five miles west of *Makrel'*. He spotted smoke at 12:30pm and spent the afternoon attempting to close on the surface. He had to limit his speed to avoid making too much smoke. At 4pm, a cruiser came into view as the light began to fail, closing to six miles, only to turn away and disappear.

Makrel' returned to Utö that evening. Il'inskiy decided to heave to off Bogskär overnight, return to the sighting position next morning, then trim down, hoping that the cruiser would return. However, Behring had gone. *Beluga* had also sortied from Mariehamn, but it was another false alarm. She sighted Swedish warships.

Makrel' and *Minoga* were handicapped by their limited speed, but intercepting *Friedrich Carl* whilst frequently changing course across a wide area was largely a matter of luck. That day, the luck was with Behring. However, his approach of combined cruiser and submarine operations meant running increasing risk with his surface force, whilst not actually generating any targets for his own submarines. On the contrary, his presence resulted in Russian patrols being at a high state of alert.

On 4 November, Essen ordered the entire submarine force to shift their base of operations from Moon Sound to Utö. The submariners had never been happy in the exposed anchorage there. The Lom/Utö base provided a better anchorage, with good access to patrol billets in the approaches to the Gulf of Finland, whilst also providing a defence for the area.

The Russian submarine force also received a dubious reinforcement. This resulted from a bizarre piece of procurement. When war broke out, three tiny submarines, *No.1*, *No.2* and *No.3*, originally ordered by the army for local defence of Black Sea ports, were reallocated to the navy. At the beginning of November, they arrived at Revel' by rail, after running trials on Lake Ladoga. The plan was to base them at Kil'kond, but after inspecting them, Essen was so unimpressed by their lack of seaworthiness that he sent them to Baltiyskiy Port as a temporary base.

Meanwhile Jasper's three cruisers arrived at Swinemünde, only for he and Heinrich to receive an order from the Reichs-Marine-Amt on the 29th decommissioning the squadron. The German Navy had formed a division of infantry to support the Army in seizing Belgium's ports and coastline. Tirpitz saw this as a staging area for the navy to take the fight to the British. A second division was now proposed. However, there was an acute shortage of officers. Tirpitz had written to the Kaiser on 25 October: 'Officers and, to some extent guns, can be made available by decommissioning [Jasper's] four training cruisers, which are unsuitable for military use due to inadequate underwater protection.' Pohl raised no objections. Both saw direct support of the Army as a critical priority, demonstrating a tangible impact on the outcome of the war. Müller obtained the Kaiser's agreement, releasing around 2,000 crew for other duties.

Front line use of these cruisers had always been questionable. Apart from their vulnerability to flooding, as demonstrated by *Freya*, their ageing guns and lack of side armour were no match for the Russian armoured cruisers, especially *Ryurik*. Their low speed made escape difficult if engaged. Behring's use of them as bait had been a high stakes gamble.[6]

The first British patrol and withdrawal from Libava

Whilst Behring had been at sea, the submarines at Libava had been busy. Laurence and Podgornyy came up with a plan to carry out a joint patrol of Danzig Bay. *E.1* and *E.9* would make the initial approach, to a position just south of Hela, under cover of darkness. They could make use of their ability to rest on the bottom during the night. *Krokodil*'s hull shape made this impossible. Podgornyy could only approach the coast during the day, heading out to sea overnight. On the first day, he would close Memel, after which he would join the British boats in Danzig Bay. Each day, one submarine would make a submerged approach to Neufahrwasser harbour entrance. At the end of the patrol, the British boats would head for Lappvik, whilst *Krokodil* returned to Libava. The British submarines embarked a Russian officer and telegraphist for liaison.

6 BA:RM28 KTB, RM49 Detachierten Admirals KTB, RM51 5.Aukklärungsgruppe KTB, RM92 *Hertha*, *Thetis* KTB, RM97 *U.26* KTB, RM2 Kaiserliches Marinekabinett, Marinedivision, RM5/5272; Firle, *Ostsee*, pp.219–230; Albert Hopman, (ed. Michael Epkenhans), *Das ereignisreiche Leben eines "Wilhelminers": Tagebücher, Briefe, Aufzeichnungen 1901 bis 1920* (München: de Gruyter, 2004) p.476; Меркушов, *Записки*, pp.287–290; РГАВМФ:Фонд 716, Опись 2, Дело 24 pp.32–35, Дело 10 pp.375–376; Винтер, 'походов', pp.255–256; Томашевич, *операциях*, p.51.

Vorms at the quay in Revel' just before the war. (Public domain)

At 2pm on the 25th, the three boats left Libava together, preceded by two port tugs with mine sweeps deployed. The Germans might have discovered the presence of the submarines, and covertly laid mines. They headed north 11 miles, to clear the known German minefield. The tugs departed. The submarines headed west. The British boats increased speed to make for Danzig, disappearing ahead. Half an hour later, Podgornyy spotted a submarine in the setting sun's afterglow, two or three miles ahead, resembling a British boat. *E.11* was still expected. A signal light was used to attract attention. The submarine seemed to turn towards *Krokodil*, but then dived. Further light signals failed to get a response. Podgornyy decided he should return to notify the port watch of the sighting and position. Fog delayed his return until 11pm.

The vessels in harbour left early, at 4am on the 26th, to attempt contact with the supposed *E.11*. Whilst doing so, *Vorms* apparently spotted a mine at the surface. The crew had been about to destroy it with gunfire when she hit a mine amidships. The explosion killed a crewman. The rest managed to launch a boat before *Vorms* went under. They reached the shore, ten miles to the east, where *Porazhayushchiy* picked them up to take them back to Libava. *Vorms* sank near the northern tip of *Augsburg*'s minefield.[7] Recent heavy seas may have displaced the mines. It was another ill consequence of Nasmith's abandoned patrol. Tragically, the same afternoon, news arrived from London that *E.11* had returned to Britain. *Krokodil* could not have sighted a German submarine, as all three were in company with Behring's cruisers much further out to sea. The most likely explanation is that *Krokodil*'s crew were fooled by a trick of the light, seeing *E.1* or *E.9* silhouetted ahead as the sun set. Ironically, Memel would have made a good hunting ground.

7 *Vorms* ex-*Langfond*, ex-*Sevilla*, (1895), 957 GRT. Divers located the wreck in 2005 at a depth of 43m.

Meanwhile, on the morning of the 26th, Laurence and Horton arrived off Hela in fog. The weather cleared later. The boats patrolled until late evening of the 28th. With Behring's entire force at sea to the north, there was little activity. The boats took turns in an ambush position south of Hela, *E.1* on the 27th and *E.9* on the 26th and 28th. During daylight, *E.1* kept trimmed down, with only the conning tower above water. However, there had been two sightings from the shore to alert the defences. Each day one boat dived to Neufahrwasser roads, *E.9* on the 27th and *E.1* on the 26th and 28th. *Hansa* was the only major warship to come out, but escaped detection under the cover of darkness. Finally, early on the 28th, Laurence sighted a target: 'On the way in [to Neufahrwasser harbour] sighted a German destroyer. She appeared to be a new boat doing trials. Fired one torpedo at her at a range of about 500 yards [450m], but unfortunately missed her.' The attack went unnoticed. Horton had seen her too, around four miles away whilst heading back to Hela, too far away to attack. Laurence's target was probably *S.33*, which was completing her fitting out and engine trials at Pillau.

Laurence and Horton headed for a pre-arranged rendezvous on the morning of the 30th off Bogskär, via the west coast of Gotland. They had information that German cruisers normally used the route. In fact, they usually passed east of Gotland, but *Friedrich Carl* had gone west to return to Danzig, to avoid running into other German forces in the dark. However, Behring passed the British submarines on the night of the 29th, each unaware of the other. At 7am on the 30th, *E.1* arrived off Bogskär to find *E.9* waiting. They headed east together. The Russian destroyer patrol was expecting them. *Gromyashchiy* met them off Bengtskär, to escort them to Lappvik. Here they found *Rynda*, an obsolete, disarmed cruiser, which was to serve as their depot ship. Laurence and Horton headed to Helsingfors next day on a destroyer, to report for duty with Essen. With the command muddle resolved, he was eager to make use of the opportunities that the submarines' long range offered. However, both needed significant machinery repairs, so they were ordered to Revel' to expedite this. Merkushov was there when they arrived with *Rynda* on 2 November. The support from their allies was appreciated: 'They entered the harbour, greeted with shouts of "Ura" from all the ships they passed, as well as from workers and the public who happened to be in the port.'

Essen wanted to get the much delayed minelaying offensive underway immediately. There had also been intelligence that the Germans had mined the northern approaches to Memel, albeit later proved to be bogus. Libava was no longer appropriate as a base for *Krokodil*. *Porazhayushchiy* was not required there anymore. Podgornyy delayed leaving for the Gulf of Finland until 3 November, when the weather moderated. Libava was once again empty of warships. Merkushov summed up *Krokodil*'s time there: 'given the state of the boat's machinery, it cannot be called anything other than a risky adventure, but it once again proves the presence of a vigorous spirit among the personnel of the Russian submariners.'[8]

8 TNA:ADM137/271, pp.17–24; BA:RM97 *U.26* KTB; RM92 *Hansa* KTB; Меркушов, *Записки*, pp.271, 292–298; РГАВМФ:Фонд 716, Опись 2, Дело 24 pp.32–35; Divesport Вспомогательно-потрульное судно SS "Worms" <https://divesport.blogspot.com/2018/10/ss-worms.html>, retrieved 17 January 2025.

7

Essen goes on the offensive: November 1914

Essen's mine offensive begins

On the evening of 29 October, Essen issued orders for the twice-postponed minelaying operation to proceed. With preparations and briefings complete, at 7.30am on the 31st, the force left Moon Sound. The first half of 2nd Divizion left first to screen the advance – *Turkmenets-Stavropol'skiy*, *Kazanets*, *Strashnyy*, *Voyskovoy*. They were eight miles ahead of the destroyers with mines. They were to lead any enemy encountered away from those following, warning them by wireless if necessary. Following behind, with 35 mines each, was the Poludivizion – *General Kondratenko*, *Okhotnik*, *Pogranichnik*. *Sibirskiy Strelok* was absent, under repair. Bringing up the rear was *Novik*, with 50 mines. They headed across the Gulf of Riga to the coast off Lyuzerort. The second half of 2nd Divizion took up a support position behind them off Mikhaylovskiy Lighthouse – *Steregushchiy*, *Donskoy Kazak*, *Zabaykalets*, *Ukrayna*. They waited here, ready to offer support or to cover a retreat. Wireless silence was imposed unless essential.

The strike force increased to 20 knots and headed down the coast. After passing in-shore of the mines off Vindava, they turned west to a point mid-way between Gotland and the coast, then turned south on their final run to the target. This kept them clear of the German minefield off Libava and any laid north of Memel. *General Kondratenko* developed problems with a boiler, reducing the advance to 17 knots, but the force pressed on.

The weather on departure had been good, but had clouded over. After passing Lyuzerort, the wind steadily picked up. At 6pm, in gathering darkness, under a cloudy, moonlit sky, *Novik* accelerated to 24 knots and broke away for the longer journey to lay the mines in barrier 6N. Two hours later, 2nd Divizion reached the latitude of Polangen. There was no sign of the enemy. Their job done, they now doubled back, steered clear of the Poludivizion and returned to Lyuzerort. The wind was whipping up a swell, causing the destroyers to roll from side to side. The Poludivizion pushed on, heading to lay their mines at barrier 1D. The tarpaulins and oilcloths protecting the mines began to come loose. The waves washed over the low decks of the destroyers, potentially dissolving the sugar safety fuses on the mines. Once the fuse dissolved, a mine could arm, with the potential to explode if they took a blow when laid.

At 9 pm, the Poludivizion reached the target area, 15 miles west of Memel. The senior officer, Kapitan 2nd Ranga Klavdiy Shevelev of *General Kondratenko*, had to turn the formation into

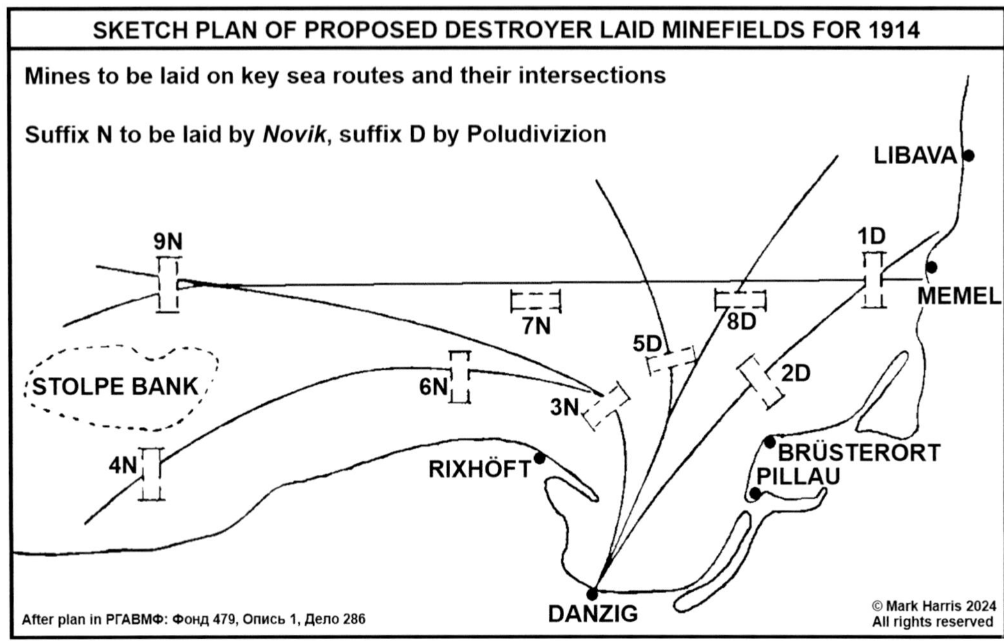

the wind, to steady the roll while laying the mines. The line would therefore be southeast of the start point, not north as planned. He signalled his consorts to begin laying. They spread out in a staggered line and slowed to 12 knots. Every 15 seconds, the crew pushed a mine off the stern rails, leaving a gap of about 90m between each. The depth was set shallow to 3m. In the swell, the mines would lock off at somewhat varying depths. The mines sank to the bottom, then released the buoyant mine. When they reached the set depth, a hydrostatic valve permanently locked the mooring cable. As soon as the last mine was away, Shevelev increased to 17 knots and headed back to the rendezvous at Lyuzerort. Meanwhile, *Novik* was further out to sea, steaming across a heavy swell:

> The wind grew stronger and stronger. At 9pm, due to the heavy seas, the speed had to be reduced to 20 knots, and by 10pm, the wind and waves had increased so much that the question arose whether it would be possible to lay mines… The wind grew stronger; *Novik* creaked and rocked violently. From time to time, the waves covered the entire destroyer and for moments, it was as if she was going under water… By 11pm, the swing from the rolling began to reach 36 degrees, with 14 oscillations per minute. Sometimes it rolled so much that it became unnerving and it seemed that we would capsize. Then the commander himself sent for me to find out whether it was possible to lay mines; I had to admit – it was impossible, and we must turn back.
>
> We turned with difficulty, reducing the speed to 12 knots. The strong pitching began to tear free the mines, and only with great difficulty, thanks to the selfless work of the crew, did we manage to secure them [five mines came off the deck rails and bent them]. All soaking wet, wading with difficulty along the deck as it slipped away beneath our feet, we reached our quarters. However, even there it was hardly possible to warm up and

> dry off: everything was topsy-turvy and, even lying on the bunk, you had to hold on with both hands to avoid being thrown onto the deck. To top it all off, a large jar of honey overturned in the wardroom. This honey mixed with water on the deck and, heated by the steam heaters, gave off an unpleasant smell; a disgusting, sticky mixture spilled from side to side, and the furniture, torn from its places, slid in this liquid, performing some kind of intricate dance. Fortunately, the further we went north, the wind died down more and more, and by 3am, it became quite fine.

Novik had taken a real pounding. In addition to the damage to the mine rails, the mainmast rigging, the head of the bow capstan, railings and stanchions tore loose. The choice of a moonlit night potentially compromised secrecy, although the terrible weather mitigated this. The force was undetected. Shtorre proposed that further operations wait for moonless nights. Visibility had been over three miles under the full moon, despite the weather. Essen disagreed. He wanted all of the key coastal routes off Danzig and Memel interdicted as soon as possible, which required minefields 2D and 6N in place. Further minelaying could then wait until the moonless period starting 8 November.

Before the next operation could set out, outpost destroyers raised the alarm. On 3 November, they sighted German submarines off the Gulf of Finland. Early next day, *Razyashchiy* and *Del'nyy* of 5th Divizion reported two torpedoes passing between them, whilst on patrol off Bengtskär. Previously, German cruisers had evidently taken positions northeast of Gotland to support their submarines. Taking advantage of the long moonlit night, Essen despatched 1st Divizion from Moon Sound to ambush them off Gotska Sandön. On the morning of the 5th, they returned via the Gulf of Riga, having found nothing. It was a false alarm, but Essen had identified an opportunity in Behring's tactics. The German submarines were far away at the time. On 1 November, *U.25* relieved the other two submarines at their billet off the coast, south of Libava. They had seen nothing and returned to Danzig. *U.25* had orders to attack only submarines. Behring's surface ships were cleaning boilers and carrying out repairs at Danzig.

The second minelaying operation used the same operational plan as the first, with one key adjustment. If the sea in the designated position was too rough, destroyers had discretion to mine a suitable sheltered position on the enemy coast. The Poludivizion was back to full strength, under the senior officer, Kapitan 2nd Ranga Georgiy Gadd of *Sibirskiy Strelok*. The second half of 2nd Divizion provided the advanced security detail. Intelligence reported three German warships in Memel.

At 7:30am on 5 November, the force left Moon Sound. Once again, the wind began to blow from the southeast in the Gulf of Riga, causing the predictable roll as the waves hit broadside on. Gadd pressed on to Mikhaylovskiy Lighthouse. On arriving in the lee of the coast there, he conducted a quick survey via megaphone of the other captains. They were unanimously in favour of abandoning the attempt. Gadd ordered the five destroyers to anchor and called their captains on board *Sibirskiy Strelok*.

He proposed a revised plan. Instead of heading straight out to sea, the force would stay in the lee of the coast past Libava. The other commanders pressed to delay until the next day. The barometer was rising, so the weather ought to improve. Avoiding the offshore minefields meant steaming dangerously close to the coast at night. Spies operating in Libava might see them. Despite the concerns, Gadd decided to proceed. He had no authority over Paletskiy, but he decided that *Novik* would follow the Poludivizion. If the open sea became too rough, he would lay his mines inside Danzig Bay, off Pillau.

Destroyer *Okhotnik* after 1910 rearmament. 10.2cm guns fore and aft, one 4.7cm gun each side, three 45cm torpedo tubes firing to either side. Rails for 42 mines, speed 25 knots. (Public domain)

Over an hour had been lost by the time the destroyers got underway. They would have to complete the return in daylight. Gadd broke wireless silence to request the illumination of the Libava lighthouse. This surprising request had to be repeated several times. Eventually Libava acknowledged. The sea proved quite calm in the lee of the land. The force clung as close as they dare to the coast to avoid mines, passing about 400m west of the Libava piers. The city was clearly visible in the bright moonlight.

Once past Libava, the force turned west, heading out to sea for 36 miles. The strong wind whipped up an increasingly heavy swell. At 10pm, the screening destroyers returned to Lyuzerort. *Novik* broke away. Gadd led his four destroyers south to the target area, minefield 2D, off the coast north of Brüsterort. The heavily loaded destroyers were rolling wildly as the sea rolled in from the beam. They struggled to maintain 20 knots. The destroyers were carrying reduced armament to allow them to carry 35 mines each, but the remaining guns and torpedo tubes would be almost impossible to fight anyway. At 11:45pm, the lookouts spotted smoke ahead to port, moving west. Two ship outlines were identified, silhouetted against the moonlit, heavily overcast night sky. Gadd was still 25 miles short of the target area. The enemy vessels were only three miles away, cutting off his advance. Gadd decided to lay the mines immediately. Minefield 8D was to be laid later at his position. He had to get end on to the wind to be able to lay the mines. Heading into the wind was out of the question, as the enemy was this way. Gadd signalled his force to turn to west-northwest, bringing the sea astern. They adopted the staggered line abreast formation for laying. This would be dangerous. The sea would be washing in over the low stern as the mines dropped, but it was his only option. The seas had once again probably washed away the sugar safety fuses. The only thing in their favour was that the moon was behind the German ships, putting his destroyers in relative darkness. They slowed to 12 knots to begin laying. They were extremely vulnerable if the enemy saw them and opened fire. Graf was later told:

> The whole operation took about half an hour and on a slippery deck, heavily pitching in the darkness, it was very difficult and dangerous. There was an expectation that at any moment

Sibirskiy Strelok cutting though a heavy swell. (EM:SA MMF1627_81)

> it was possible that the Poludivizion would be revealed, and therefore this half an hour was even harder. Suddenly, in the midst of the laying, when there were still many mines left, the telltale ringing sound of a blow was heard against the hull of *Sibirskiy Strelok*. All who heard it froze, expecting an explosion, killing everyone. The sound that had rung out was simply the blow against the hull by one of the mines as it dropped and the waves threw it back. A few seconds passed, and everything was quiet; this could only mean that by a lucky chance, the mine had not struck with its horns.

The German ships disappeared in the darkness astern as the laying proceeded. With the last mines away and a profound sense of relief for their apparent escape from detection, the destroyers set course to return to the Gulf of Riga.

On the evening of the 4th, *Thetis* picked up nearby Russian wireless signals on a routine round trip from Memel to make wireless contact with *U.25*. These were assumed to come from a submarine. Next morning, reports of submarine sightings by a steamer and a fishing boat seemed to confirm this. However, seaplane patrols saw nothing. That afternoon, Behring passed on orders to Nippe cancelling the blocking of Memel. All vessels were to, 'Make transit Memel – Danzig in darkness. If enemy submarine comes into sight at night, destroy it. Instruct block-ships to steam back along the coast.' *Thetis* heard loud Russian wireless again that evening. Nippe delayed departure until 9pm, fearing a submarine off the harbour. He then took *Thetis* directly to Danzig across the Bay. At 11:50pm, a large cloud of smoke appeared to starboard. Nippe later reported that:

> … after a short time it quickly split into two clouds of smoke, which became denser and quickly spread out over a great distance. I conclude from this that the vessels were initially heading for S.M.S. *Thetis*, but later turned off to an ENE course.
>
> The first impression was of a large vessel, later of two medium-sized vessels of about the size of S.M.S. *Thetis*, steaming past on an opposite course at a great distance. The number of funnels could not be determined. The vessels soon disappeared from view in our smoke.

Thetis alongside the quay in Memel, with *Lübeck* moored behind. (Public domain)

> The war watch commander – the first officer – had the same impression as I did that they were not destroyers. The vessels were out of range of our searchlights.
>
> *Thetis* turned 4 points [45 degrees away to port] after the ships came into view.
>
> The reasons for this measure were that, on the one hand, it was assumed that *Thetis* was dealing with cruisers and that an aggressive reconnaissance against them did not seem appropriate, since *Thetis*, after continuous boiler usage of over 12 days, only had a maximum speed of 15 knots; on the other hand, firing on them would not have been possible either, because the targets would have remained out of searchlight range and invisible to the gunners. At the time, they could be seen from the chart house deck and the bridge, but not from the gun positions.

Nippe soon resumed his previous course to Danzig. Three hours later, at 2:35am, a darkened vessel loomed out of the blackness ahead. This began turning away at speed, with a white boiling wash astern:

> *Thetis* initially turned slowly to starboard, kept the vessel well ahead and made a recognition signal that was not answered; when the distance had decreased enough for the searchlights to reach the target, I gave the order to illuminate and open fire; a destroyer with three funnels was now spotted. After a few shots, the ship was turned two points [22.5 degrees] to port to bring the full broadside into action… In this position, the ship was rolled so violently by the waves that two [of our own] shells struck close to the ship and it was impossible for the searchlights to hold on to the target. Therefore a turn of two more points to port was made to steady the ship.
>
> A total of 15 shells were fired. The first salvos were much too short, the last were seen to fall 'well'. The salvo orders were for 10, 15, 17hm [1,000m rising to 1,700m].
>
> Three officers and some of the bridge personnel believe they saw a hit.

> The ability to fire ceased when the [enemy] boat entered the smoke of [our own] ship and the searchlights could no longer reach the target; immediately afterwards the boat went out of sight. At this moment, another turn of four points [45 degrees away] was made to avoid the probable direction of a[n enemy] torpedo shot.

Thetis resumed course for Danzig and Nippe sent a wireless message reporting firing on a destroyer. Nippe's report stated that her low speed precluded pursuit and noted fire control problems. The heavy seas caused the aft searchlight to short-circuit. The salvo firing signal gongs had then failed with a blown fuse. Nippe had requested and received confirmation from Behring the previous evening that no German destroyers were at sea in the eastern Baltic. This must have increased his confidence in opening fire as soon as a destroyer was identified.

Thetis had encountered *Novik*. Paletskiy had forged ahead of the Poludivizion at 24 knots, heading for the coast west of Danzig. However, the violent roll from the beam sea steadily increased. Paletskiy altered course to close his alternate target, Pillau, inside the Bay of Danzig. Graf takes up the story:

> ... only half an hour remained; the tension reached the limit. Everyone was feverishly peering into the distance, but there was nothing suspicious. The destroyer continued quietly sweeping forward, with only the turbines humming and the hull trembling slightly... Everyone was already standing in their places – after all, this was our first combat experience, and it was not surprising that we were a little nervous... right under the enemy's nose. However, thank God, some vague outlines began to appear in the darkness, either a shore or a causeway. We were already at the enemy's port itself. At that moment, the long-awaited telephone call from the bridge rang out, and I was given the command: 'Begin laying.' Right, left, right, left... I commanded, and the mines rolled evenly overboard. The crew worked perfectly, so much so that I even had to hold them back. Then the last mine plopped into the water... Everyone sighed happily – as if a weight had been lifted from their shoulders. ... they had been carrying these ridiculous mines for almost a whole month and had not been able to get rid of them. This load was not a very pleasant one, especially in an encounter with the enemy. ...
>
> Having laid the mines, the commander ordered 24 knots, and we set off on a return course.
>
> Suddenly, at about 2:30am, the officer on watch noticed a silhouette to starboard; they had obviously noticed us too, because they began making identification signals to us with a sort of white square lantern. Not wanting to reveal ourselves, we did not respond and increased the speed to 32 knots. Then the enemy immediately illuminated searchlights, and began to shoot. The shells fell in the right direction towards us, but there were large shortfalls and only one shell fell relatively close. We continued to move away, not returning fire. Having fired several volleys, the enemy stopped shooting and only swept the searchlight along the horizon for a few more minutes, but failed to find us. Thus, thanks to our speed, we safely got away from the enemy. In all likelihood, he did not see us clearly, so there was hope that he would not suspect that we could lay mines. Precisely what we encountered was difficult to determine; but regardless, they were two medium-sized vessels. ... The first hostile shots, especially at night, made a rather strong impression on the crew; in particular, the illumination of the searchlights had an effect. When their beams glided over the deck of the destroyer,

> or stopped on it, some of the sailors tried, almost instinctively, to hide behind something; and one sailor, to everyone's delight, even crawled on all fours along the deck, as if the enemy had been able to identify a single person, and only him. Subsequently, our reluctance to engage the enemy gave rise to quite a lot of arguments among our young officers, and many doubted whether we had done the right thing by not returning the enemy's fire. ... from a tactical point of view, it was more advantageous not to open fire, since the enemy was much stronger than us and, besides, there was little chance that *Novik* could cause him serious harm; ... [and] he could still doubt strongly what he had seen...

The sudden, confusing unpredictability of night encounters comes out of these accounts. Choreographed pre-war exercises did not prepare commanders and crews on either side to manage these high stress situations, to exploit the fleeting, but significant opportunities they provided. However, both Gadd and Paletskiy acted correctly. Getting into action would have undermined their mission. Greater alertness might have allowed Paletskiy to fire torpedoes before turning away, but Nippe took evasive action anyway. Later that morning, all five destroyers reached the Gulf of Riga without further incident. They needed a number of minor repairs after their battering by the weather. A few days later, *Novik* discovered damage to the rudder and its supports caused by high speeds in heaving seas, requiring dock repairs in Helsingfors.

Behring was scathing about Nippe's report, correcting erroneous compass directions on his copy:

> [Assumptions] ... The idea that an enemy submarine could be identified by wireless can lead to serious errors. Judging by the signal, heard clearly by *Thetis* on the evening of November 5, this could have been a destroyer [it was almost certainly Gadd signalling to Libava].
>
> [Encounter with Gadd] If the vessels sighted turned away from *Thetis*, they could not have felt superior to a German cruiser sailing alone. The assumption that they were destroyers is therefore obvious.
>
> It was even more necessary to approach them to find out more, as *Thetis* had orders to destroy enemy submarines. They could very well have been enemy destroyers accompanying submarines.
>
> If the enemies were not destroyers, but minelayers, then reconnaissance and the destruction of the ships was absolutely essential.
>
> If they were cruisers, there was an opportunity to identify them in good time in the high visibility of the bright, moonlit night.
>
> It is unproven whether the retreating enemies would have stayed out of reach if they had been pursued, as *Thetis* did not make the attempt.
>
> According to the submitted engine log, the ship maintained revolutions for 17 knots ... *Thetis* has been asked to report the reason why the action report only states 15 knots as the maximum speed. [Nippe's diagrams show *Thetis* steaming at 16 knots]. The omission of a wireless report [on sighting Gadd's destroyers] is incomprehensible.
>
> [Encounter with *Novik*] The manoeuver of S.M.S. *Thetis* was wrong in terms of gunnery, tactics and seamanship. It is not clear why the boat was not pursued. If it had actually been hit, it must have seemed possible, especially in the prevailing strong sea, to catch up with and destroy the boat despite the low speed of S.M.S. *Thetis*.

The lack of offensive spirit against an inferior enemy would have been unfathomable for Behring. If Nippe had chosen to close, things could have turned out very differently. With the heavy seas, gunnery and torpedo fire was obviously challenging, but this gave the bigger cruiser an advantage over the smaller destroyers.

Six days later Heinrich endorsed Behring's report and forwarded it to Pohl: 'I have refrained from pursuing the matter further, as … Nippe, has reported that, due to his poor eyesight, he cannot make his decisions solely on the basis of his own observations, but is dependent on observations and reports from the bridge personnel. For this reason, I have therefore requested his re-assignment.' Nippe had already been effectively relieved of command by Behring on the 10th. He never commanded a ship again.

Behring now ordered that a light cruiser patrol Danzig Bay every night. However, despite all the evidence that destroyers or minelayers had been present, he took no steps to have the Bay swept for mines, despite having an auxiliary Minensuchdivision. Heinrich also had 2nd Minensuchdivision at Kiel. The German Official History offers the feeble excuse that these vessels could not be spared from their duties, or had difficulty working in heavy seas. Not to sweep the area of Nippe's contacts and regularly used channels as a priority over routine patrols was at best complacent. Behring had even pointed out himself that Nippe had not demonstrated that his first contact was not a group of minelayers. The Russians were known to use destroyers for minelaying.

Shtorre's concerns about discovery had proved correct, although it was pure luck that *Thetis* had encountered both groups of Russian destroyers. However, Behring and Heinrich threw away the minelaying clues that this provided. Essen's gamble to get the mines in position as soon as possible had paid off. There were now three undiscovered mine barriers off Behring's bases.[1]

The second bombardment of Libava and discovery of the Russian minefields

On 1 November, Behring wrote to Heinrich, 'I believe my most important task should be the destruction of the British submarines using Libava as a base. In my opinion, these boats are the most dangerous opponents for us in the Baltic Sea, given the relatively unsophisticated behaviour of the Russian Baltic forces to date.' He requested additional submarines for a day blockade of Libava and destroyers for the night. On 3 November, Heinrich communicated a revised operational approach to the Admiralstab, predicated by similar assumptions:

> I expect that the Russians, under British influence, will attempt a westward advance before the beginning of winter, since our weak position in the Sound, which they are aware of, promises success. Furthermore, I expect that Britain may attempt to withdraw the submarines stationed in the Baltic back to the North Sea before the beginning of winter. Support for this attempt by an advance of Russian cruisers is likely. Therefore, whilst maintaining the blockade of Libava, I intend to station submarines off the Gulf of Finland. Cruisers

1 РГАВМФ:Фонд 716, Опись 2, Дело 13, pp.29–30; П. Гельмерсен, 'Заградительные операции Балтийского флота у германского побережья в 1914–1915 г.г.', in *Сборник 1*, pp.4–9; BA:RM92 *Thetis* KTB, RM49 Detachierten Admirals KTB; Firle, *Ostsee*, pp.231–234; Графъ, *Новикъ*, pp.29–37; Pavlovich, *Operations*, pp.90–93.

> are to sail the area between Bornholm and the Russian coast, showing up on Russian and Swedish coasts, making an advance by Russian cruisers to the Sound less likely. I also intend to bombard Libava heavily with several cruisers.

On the 5th, the Admiralstab passed Heinrich information from the Stockholm Embassy that two British submarines had been seen in Helsingfors. Further indications of their presence in the north were received in the following days. However, Heinrich remained focussed on Libava as their presumed forward base. On 6 November, He issued revised instructions to Behring, reflecting the new priorities, with which the Admiralstab concurred. However, they refused his request for three additional submarines and the armoured cruiser *Prinz Heinrich*. The plan had expanded to sealing off Libava:

1. Independent operations by submarines in and off the Gulf of Finland.
2. Heavy bombardment of Libava; blockade by submarines. Closing of harbour entrances by blockships, and if you judge it advisable, by mines. Reconnoitring of Libava by aircraft.
3. Cruiser patrol of the area east of Bornholm and of the Swedish and Russian coasts. Advances into the Gulf of Bothnia at your discretion.

Heinrich emphasised that submarines should operate without cruisers, which: 'will warn rather than entice the Russians.' This ended Behring's attempts to combine their operations. On 7 November, *Amazone* and the coastal submarine, *U.A*, recently requisitioned whilst building for the Norwegian Navy, arrived at Danzig as reinforcements. Four blockships intended for Memel were re-allocated to block Libava. *Amazone* brought 48 mines and rails for laying from destroyers. Heinrich wanted Libava cut off from telegraph communication through its three undersea cables. The Foreign Office agreed, but 'requested that the cutting be carried out unnoticed.' Work began to fit grappling equipment to three of the Danzig armed trawlers.

U.A would work from Memel or Pillau, freeing the longer-range boats from blockading Libava. On the 8th, she relieved *U.25*. To enable bombing and reconnaissance over Libava, seaplanes and their stores were to go to Memel. The interned ex-British steamer, *Glyndwr*, became their depot and began conversion as a carrier. As a stopgap, seaplanes were to re-embark on *Friedrich Carl*. Behring ordered his force to be ready for sea on November 9. The 11th was the provisional date for blocking and bombarding Libava. Scope for mining would be determined later.

Ingenohl's battleship squadrons had been exercising in Kiel Bay, safe from British submarine attack in the North Sea. Scheer's 2nd Geschwader had completed a refit, and exercises were scheduled with *Graudenz*, light cruisers of 4th Aufklärungsgruppe and 3rd Torpedobootsflottille, before returning to the North Sea. A recent bombardment of Yarmouth in England convinced Ingenohl that his squadrons needed to, 'fire [at least] once against enemy targets in order to guarantee fire discipline under combat conditions.' On the 7th, he agreed with Heinrich that Scheer's force would join Behring in bombarding Libava as part of the exercises. Next day, the light cruisers arrived and carried out a security sweep as far as Bornholm. A steamer had reported two destroyers off southern Sweden on the previous night, suspected of being Russian. They found nothing, but *Graudenz* reported an attack by a submarine. Although quickly identified as a probable false alarm, this was ammunition for anyone opposed to the operation. Scheer issued the orders for the bombardment. Behring would come under his command on arrival at Libava.

On the night of the 9/10th, Behring's blocking force left Danzig. *U.A* entered Memel to avoid any potential friendly fire incident. Ehrhardt, with 20th Halbflottille, commanded, with four blockships and four armed trawlers from Neufahrwasser to assist in placing them. The bombardment force of *Friedrich Carl* and the light cruisers would follow that afternoon.

At 7pm on the 10th, the Hochseeflotte units left Kiel. Scheer's eight battleships were screened by six light cruisers, 11 destroyers of 3rd Flottille and 14 boats of 1st Minensuchdivision. This was the most powerful force that had yet set out for the eastern Baltic.

However, things quickly unravelled. Ingenohl had not sought approval for the bombardment, but now notified Pohl. The timing was bad, since Admiral Fisher, known for his offensive mindedness, had recently replaced Battenberg. Kontreadmiral Albert Hopman, of Tirpitz's Reichs-Marine-Amt, on the staff at General Headquarters, was present at lunch that day when the message arrived. The fundamental disagreements, firstly about the priority between the Baltic and the North Sea, and secondly, the appetite for risking battle fleet units, immediately ignited:

> Whilst at the table, dispatch, to the effect that [Ingenohl] has ordered the bombardment of Libava by 2nd Geschwader, now in the Baltic. Incomprehensible. Given the situation, we should aim to have everything in the North Sea. I will set out the case later to the Admiralstab that changes in First Sea Lord and general war policy require concentration of all battleship squadrons in the North Sea. Pohl, who happened to be visited by Müller, went to His Majesty about the Libava operation, who stops it because of the submarine danger.

At 10pm, Ingenohl received the message: 'His Majesty the Kaiser orders the bombardment of Libava by 2nd Geschwader to be abandoned as the risk from submarines is too great. His Majesty has noted that [Ingenohl] was not authorized to issue this order.' Scheer was heading out of Kiel Bay when he received the cancellation. The other exercises went ahead next day west of Bornholm. His force then returned to Kiel. Ingenohl wirelessed Pohl: 'I deeply deplore the cancellation.' He added in his war diary, 'Every opportunity for military action by the German naval forces should be seized, because the fleet absolutely needs action.' The two continued to trade arguments for and against the operation in the following days.

However, the fickle Baltic weather had already put an end to it. A westerly gale sprang up. Ehrhardt reported that blocking was impossible. His force headed into Memel for shelter. *Friedrich Carl* could not exit the shallow channel at Neufahrwasser in the swell. Behring postponed the entire operation until the weather improved.

The blockship *Martha*, Oberleutnant zur See Werner Giebeler, lost touch with Ehrhardt's formation in the storm and failed to arrive at Memel. A search by *G.132* next morning found nothing. Behring ordered *Thetis* and *Amazone* to search that afternoon. Meanwhile, Giebeler was completely lost. In the early afternoon, he approached Libava in the belief that it was Memel. *Martha* got within 1,000m of the southern entrance before the mistake was realised. Giebeler beat a hasty retreat out to sea. Next morning, *Amazone* found *Martha* approaching Memel and escorted her in. The fiasco at least suggested that an approach to Libava from the southwest or along the coast was mine free. Giebeler also reported that 'the southern entrance is clear, the middle entrance is apparently blocked by steamers.' The Libava observation post correctly identified *Martha* as a German flagged merchant steamer. They saw no minelaying, but 'work was observed for some time at the stern on the leeward side.' Watch posts also reported *G.132*. In the absence of another explanation, Essen concluded that the Germans had discovered the new Russian minefields and begun sweeping operations.

On the afternoon of the 15th, the gale finally dropped. Behring ordered *Augsburg* to escort *U.23* and *U.25* to a position west of Dagerort. From here, they would head into the Gulf of Finland, whilst *Augsburg* returned to take part in the bombardment. The good weather held. At 7pm next day, Ehrhardt led his force out of Memel as dusk gathered. He met his escort, *Lübeck*, Fregattenkapitän Franz Halm, and the force headed up the coast to Libava, aiming to arrive at dawn. Behring forwarded some intelligence from the Admiralstab: '... the northern entrance has only a mine barrier, the middle and southern entrances are blocked by steamers, with a gap in the southern entrance.'

The plan had been that *Friedrich Carl*, *Thetis* and *D.10* would leave Danzig on the evening of the 16th. *Amazone* was already patrolling Danzig Bay, and would scout ahead to Libava. However, at the last minute, *Thetis* received orders from Heinrich to dock for a much needed two-week refit. *D.10* was still repairing a leak caused by heavy seas in the previous attempt. *Friedrich Carl* therefore left Danzig alone at 9:15pm, aiming to rendezvous off Libava before dawn. One seaplane was aboard for bombing and spotting. Behring had sent the other to operate from Memel, but it developed engine problems.

The ship steamed through the night. There was only a slight swell and a steady, cold east wind. The war watch was alert. There had been a report of a submarine off Fårö, and *Augsburg* wirelessed news of a submarine off Östergarn, sighted by a Norwegian merchantman that she had examined. It turned into a gloomy night, with limited visibility and rain showers. At 2:46am, her commander, Fregattenkapitän Max Loesch, suddenly felt, '... a violent shaking in the ship, which initially gave the impression on the command bridge that the ship had run over a submarine. The shaking seemed too little for the detonation of a torpedo or a mine. When the ship began to list to starboard, it was assumed that there was a leak forward and speed reduced to slow ahead, to reduce the pressure on the bulkheads... the reports of flooding that soon arrived ... led to the conclusion that a mine or torpedo had exploded.' The situation in the aft boiler room was more terrifying:

> A stoker who was busy trimming coal in the starboard upper bunker was thrown into the air by the detonation. The bunker filled with water in the blink of an eye; a strong smell of gas and a jet of fire were felt. When the detonation occurred, the boiler room immediately went dark and filled with water and steam. The men escaped through the port companionway, which they closed behind them. Nevertheless, after about 1–2 minutes the water was about 2m deep in the companionway. The fire extinguishers were pulled on the port boilers; this was no longer possible on the starboard boilers.

Meanwhile, Behring had come to the bridge: '... on his orders, with the possibility of a torpedo hit on the starboard side, the ship was turned to port at full speed, in order to avoid further attacks from the unseen enemy. ... when the ship had turned [further than intended] to the west due to the failure of the compass lighting, this course was maintained. Maximum speed was only 12 knots due to loss of steam, later only 10.' Attempts to send out a wireless message were frustrated. The explosion had dislodged the spark apparatus and aerials aloft, putting it out of action. News from below was not encouraging: 'Shortly after the report that the Number One

Friedrich Carl underway pre-war. (Author's collection)

Boiler Room [the furthest aft of the four] was full, the report came that the starboard engine was taking on a lot of water through the torn bulkhead [to the boiler room]. Attempts were made to stop water from entering by using leak mats, woollen blankets with benches braced against them, and to seal the popped rivets with plugs. However, this sealing was only partially effective.' Wing compartments on the port side were flooded to reduce the list to starboard.

Eleven minutes after the explosion, *Friedrich Carl* was about 33 miles west of Memel and getting further away every minute. The priority was to head for shallow water and the nearest port. The helm was put over to turn east to Memel: 'During the turn, a second violent detonation occurred port aft, the ship briefly began to right herself, then took a strong list to starboard and settled significantly by the stern. The port engine failed and speed dropped to eight knots. The ship continued to turn to the east. The second detonation occurred as successive explosions, which implied that the aircraft bombs [for the seaplane] stored in the magazine, forward of the stern torpedo room, were also detonated by the hit.' The eight crew in the underwater stern torpedo tube compartment were doomed: 'In the control centre [below decks], water was coming out of the speaking tube of the stern torpedo room. The ship's command was immediately informed that the stern torpedo room was filling up.' The men in the three adjacent engine rooms, which were in separate compartments across the width of the ship, faced a daunting situation, with flooding in compartments ahead and astern of them. Flooding short-circuited the electrical system and blew many fuses. The ship was plunged into darkness:

> … the emergency lighting lamps fell out of their holders and the switches jumped off the boards. Steam came out of the stuffing boxes of the pipes, the floor panels jumped up and the electric lights went out. Large amounts of water from the tunnel entered the aft engine [rooms] through the shaft passages of the three engines. … At the same time, a lot of water entered the engine room from the speaking pipes that were connected to the rear of the ship and Number One Boiler Room. Most of this evaporated on cylinders and steam pipes, so that the engine [rooms] filled with steam. … a jet of fire was noticed coming out of the shaft casing of the port engine, which was immediately followed by water. The port propeller shaft must have broken. The engine was stopped … and the shaft bore was sealed with a leak plug. Driving the plug in against the water pressure was only successful after two attempts with great difficulty.

The men worked feverishly to restore emergency lighting, isolate flooded electrical circuits, replace fuses, stop the leaks with hemp, tallow and wooden plugs and shore up sagging bulkheads and doors with timber. The steam pipes to the two engines still running were heating the water in the flooded boiler room. The hot water poured onto those trying to stop the leaks.

At 3:17am, a lookout spotted a red light on the starboard bow. This could be the flash of a torpedo fired by an attacking destroyer. Loesch ordered *Friedrich Carl* turned hard to starboard, to get end on to the attack point. Behring countermanded this, ordering a turn hard to port to steer away. The steering engine spaces had already been abandoned to flood water. The two extreme rudder movements caused the steering engines to fail. *Friedrich Carl*'s rudder was stuck at hard a port: 'As it was not possible to keep the ship on course with the centre and starboard engines, the ship continued to turn. Stopping did not seem advisable because the turning made an attack by destroyers more difficult.'

Behring's staff officer, Gercke, now showed his worth. Grassmann describes him as, 'outstandingly clever, energetic and … driven by an insatiable thirst for action and enterprising spirit.' He focussed on driving forward the repair work on the wireless, leaving Korvettenkapitän Wilhelm Schleusener, the First Officer, to concentrate on organising the other repair parties. At 3:50am, the aerial net was back in order, and electrical power to the wireless restored. It was an hour since the first explosion. At first, assistance was requested only from Ehrhardt's destroyers. Behring was fearful of drawing his other cruisers into a submarine ambush. As time passed without another attack on the relatively helpless ship, Behring began to suspect mines. A message went repeatedly to all units: 'Square 067ε sequence 9. Torpedo hit. Need immediate assistance.'

There was no reply for some time. The signals were weak and caused confusion. Finally, at 5:14am, there was a message from *Augsburg*: 'Steaming full speed ahead. Arriving 6.30.' *Amazone* also responded, but engine problems restricted speed to 16 knots. She would be even longer. *Friedrich Carl* stabilised for a while with a list of about 10 degrees to starboard. The crew did their best to resist the spread of the water and the list. Small-calibre ammunition from the starboard side went overboard and bigger shells shifted to port where possible. The water continued to spread inexorably, through distorted bulkheads and decks: 'The engine-room personnel, under Stabsingenieur Hans Hoffmann, worked at times in water up to their chins, handling the burning hot valves with asbestos gloves and woollen cloths, and remaining at their posts until the last possible moment. Compartment after compartment had to be abandoned.' By 5am, steam was running low. As the water rose above the floor plates, the starboard engine was stopped. The pumps needed the remaining steam to function. Nevertheless, the central engine had to keep running. Otherwise, the east wind would blow *Friedrich Carl* back to the presumed minefield.

By 6am, the situation was extremely serious. The engineers estimated 2,300t of water in the ship. The list was once again increasing and had reached 14 degrees to starboard. The lack of buoyancy was becoming critical. It was too dangerous to risk further counter-flooding. Loesch ordered the three available boats launched. Their crews carried flare guns. If *Friedrich Carl* suddenly sank, they could use the flares to guide rescuers to the crew in the water. As the agonising wait continued, Behring quipped on the bridge: 'The only certainty we can take with us into the water as a final consolation, my dear Gercke, is that the British torpedoes are good for nothing.'

Half an hour later, there was intense relief when star shells on the northern horizon announced that *Augsburg* was near. *Friedrich Carl* responded in kind to guide her in. As *Augsburg* approached, Grassmann described the desperate scene:

> … the sight was unforgettable: heavy starboard list; the ship's stern deep in the water and already partially submerged; at the main mast there was the wreckage of a collapsed aircraft that was supposed to serve as an artillery observer during the planned bombardment of Libava; between the funnels there were dense clouds of white steam billowing out of torn pipes. The crew crowded around the port railing in deep silence; the admiral, his staff officer and the captain stood high up on the port bridge wing; the barrels of the heavy and port medium guns were swung out to port, the high side, so that we, who were now stopped about 50m alongside *Friedrich Carl* could see into the muzzles.
>
> Now our commander, Korvettenkapitän Horn [previously commanding *Amazone*], showed himself to be a master. He made his decision in a flash! 'Don't lower the cutter! Both engines half astern! Clear to lay alongside to starboard!' his commands rang out and in a brilliant manoeuver, he laid *Augsburg* off the high side of the sinking flagship that night! An outstanding demonstration of seamanship …

At 7:10am, *Augsburg* came to a stop on the port side aft, as the first light began to show in the eastern sky. It took an agonising 15 minutes to transfer the 591 crew. Discipline held to the last. Those fighting the leaks were the last to leave their posts, followed by the officers. The unflagging efforts of the damage control parties had not saved the ship, but had bought the time to save every man aboard, apart from the eight lost in the second explosion. Meanwhile, *Amazone* arrived. Behring ordered her to attempt a tow. It was hopeless. *Friedrich Carl* gradually heeled over to 70 degrees. Suddenly, she capsized and disappeared in a black cloud, possibly resulting from a boiler explosion, 5½ hours after the first explosion and just forty minutes after being abandoned.

Behring ordered *Amazone* to return to Libava. *Augsburg* was overflowing with survivors and unable to use her armament. He ordered Horn to head for Memel to offload and then join the bombardment. Grassmann continues:

> We now headed east at high speed, with the admiral's flag waving merrily in the foretop, once again the flagship. It had become light by now, but visibility was quite limited due to the milky, hazy air. We are very tired – we hadn't slept much during this time – and shivering, standing on the bridge. The rescued people are telling us details about the mine hits, when suddenly a muffled voice comes from the speaking tube leading from the lookout post on the foredeck to the bridge: 'Ahead, just on the port side, three vessels!' … We can already make out the vessels on the bridge, apparently one large one and two small, which are heading directly towards us.
>
> As we see them from directly ahead, we cannot make out any type or other details in the hazy air. … 'Alarm!' Everyone is immediately at battle stations. I stand in the conning tower with my command transmitters and give the preparatory commands to the guns.
>
> … I quickly decide to choose the larger vessel as the opponent, the gunners have it in their sights, ready to fire when the salvo bell sounds, but there is still no order to open fire from the bridge, where the admiral and commander cannot make up their minds about the nature of this 'enemy'…
>
> I run back to the bridge, perhaps there is more to be seen there with the rangefinders and telescopes, and when I look back at the vessels a few seconds later, the larger one, my intended target, is standing vertically in the water, its bow stretched high into the air, and immediately sinks like a stone! We all looked at each other in amazement… However, we promptly drew a conclusion: 'Stop! Full power astern!' Because this instant success could only have been caused by mines …
>
> The two small vessels now turned, and we recognized one as the Memel pilot steamer, the other as a larger motor yacht; both were apparently busy rescuing the survivors of the third vessel.

Kapitänleutnant Karl Overhues, on the Danzig naval staff, had taken in the distress signal from *Friedrich Carl*. He had despatched these three merchant flagged vessels from Memel to offer assistance. The small cargo steamer, *Elbing IX*, struck the mine 15 miles west of Memel, which exploded aft.[2] One stoker was unable to escape from the engine room before she went down. The other two vessels rescued the rest of the crew, about 16.

Luck had saved *Augsburg*, packed with 1,000 men, from a potentially fatal encounter. Behring ordered Horn to retrace his course west. *Augsburg* then turned north to clear the contaminated area, then a long detour to the west before heading to Danzig, where the survivors disembarked.

2 *Elbing IX*, (1913) 886 GRT, operated by the local shipping company, Elbinger Dampfschiffs Reederei.

G.133 underway pre-war. Armed with 4x5.2cm guns, two amidships aft and one on each side of the bridge, plus 3x45cm torpedo tubes firing to either side. *G.135* carried 1x8.8cm instead of 2x5.2cm guns aft. Remainder likewise from November onwards. Speed 27 knots. (Author's collection)

Meanwhile, at 3.30am, Halm gave Ehrhardt's *G.133* the course for the final approach to Libava. At 4am, the destroyers and trawlers arrived off the southern entrance, leaving the blockships a mile behind. *Lübeck* was out of sight in deeper water to the southwest, ready to offer support. Ehrhardt sent *G.132*, *G.136* and two trawlers 'to determine whether there was a gap in the northern entrance and, if necessary, to close it. I went to the southern entrance … and found that only about half of it was blocked.' Whether boldly or rashly, he accepted the possibility of mines: 'I sailed through this gap with a trawler and [*G.133*] and steered along the southern pier to the Winter Harbour. When I had penetrated about 1,000 meters, an alarm sounded in the town. Several steam whistles blew, as well as trumpets and signal flares. As snow started to fall at the same time, reducing visibility, I considered further progress dangerous and turned around.' Ehrhardt left to bring up the blockships. Men landed on the moles to tie off hawsers, holding the ships in position. They were over half a mile from the harbour. *Martha* and *Elfie* were sunk in the gap. However, when the scuttling charges in *Martial* fired, the hawser attached to the other blockships carried away. The current swept her out of position. The trawlers were unable to nudge her back before she sank. A gap of 10–15m remained open.

G.132 confirmed that the middle entrance was completely blocked. Her dingy found two gaps at the northern entrance. The message warning of mines had perhaps engendered more caution. There were no destroyer masts visible in the Naval Harbour. *G.136* brought up *Julia*, which was sunk in the larger gap. Closer inspection revealed that sunken barges and lighters blocked the other. By 8am, the operation was complete. Ehrhardt now made a risky decision:

> As I hadn't been able to determine whether any warships were in the inner area … I entered again through the narrow gap that still existed with [*G.133*], *G.135*, and a trawler … far enough to overlook the Winter Harbour and canal between New and Old Libava. There were no destroyers or submarines in the harbour. Several large steamers and sailing ships

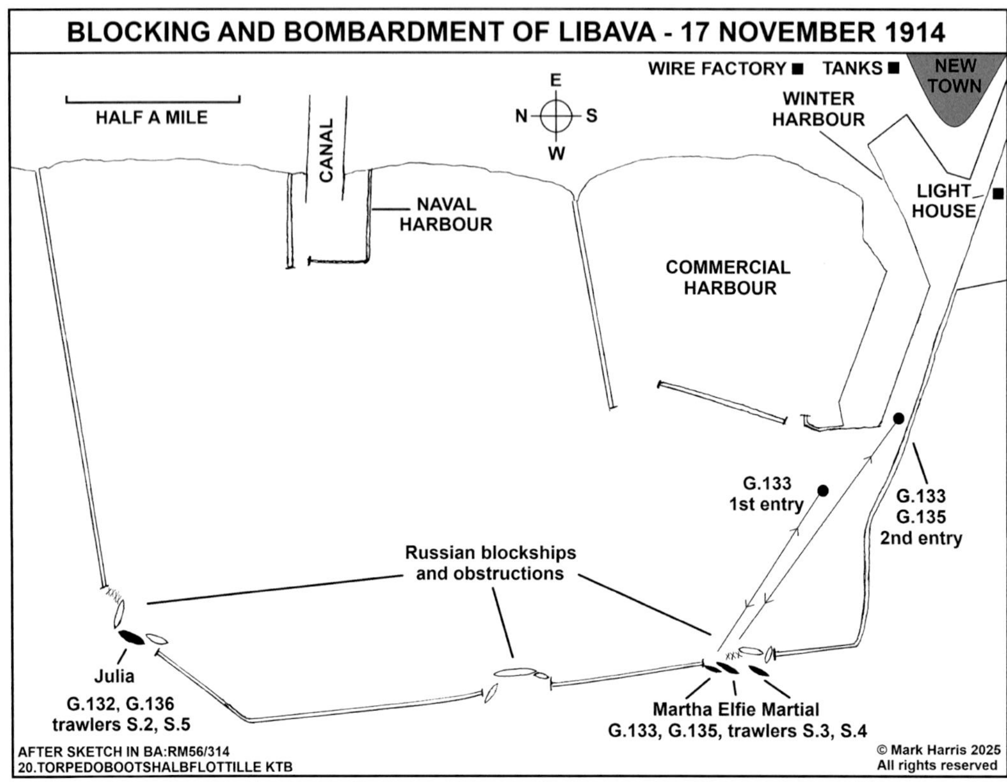

> were in the canal. The sailing ships were flying the Danish flag. The steamers were apparently out of service. I didn't consider it appropriate to fire on them.
>
> When I exited, I got stuck in the gap with [*G.133*], even though I kept close to the sunken steamer *Elfie*. I managed to get free again after a short time. *G.135* also ran aground in the gap.

There had been submerged obstructions, which Ehrhardt had not spotted on entry. Kapitänleutnant Wilhelm Rebensburg's *G.135* was stuck fast. Full speed ahead on the engines accomplished nothing: 'Ammunition, torpedoes, and spare engine parts were then shifted from forward to aft. Attempted to roll off. Towing attempts by trawler *S.3* [*Senator Strandes*] then *G.133* and *S.4* [*Bunte Kuh*].' The forward compartment was holed and full of water, and 1½ hours had passed. At last, *G.135* was, 'Pushed towards the entrance by *S.4* and thus freed.' The two trawlers both ran aground during the work, but got off under their own power without damage. *G.135* was badly damaged, but in no danger of sinking.

Lübeck had received the first assistance call from *Friedrich Carl* and passed it to Ehrhardt. As he was already committed, he decided to continue the operation. Behring later backed this as the right decision. Poor visibility forced *Lübeck* to postpone the planned bombardment. Eventually, the weather improved somewhat. *Lübeck* approached the south mole, and began firing at 10:30am. No gun batteries were identified, so the chimneys of the barbed-wire factory, just under three miles away, were used as the target. It was reputedly the only one of its kind

Lübeck pre-war. Armament and armour as *Amazone*, but turbine engines gave a speed of 23 knots. (Public domain)

in Russia. Later, fire shifted to three oil tanks in the harbour and nearby wood stores, around two miles distant. The tanks were set ablaze. *Lübeck* ceased fire at 12:15pm, after firing 270 10.5cm shells. The destroyers had briefly joined in, firing about 100 5.2cm rounds. *Amazone* now arrived. At 12:55pm, Halm ordered Lutter to take over the bombardment: 'At your own discretion, primarily the wire factory. Only fire at the areas north of the sailing ships, as it is German property south of them.' *Amazone* also fired at the lighthouse and surrounding port installations. At 2.15pm, Lutter ceased fire, after firing 223 10.5cm shells: 'the entire central part of the city … was shrouded in thick smoke.' The force headed back to Danzig. Halm retraced his route exactly, considering this the best way to avoid any mines in his path.

Essen was aware that the Germans were planning an operation against Libava. The British had intercepted the orders cancelling Scheer's participation on the night of the 10/11th. They had recently broken the German cypher and used the *Magdeburg* signal book to de-code the content, although some of the details were obscure. The operation was clearly major, so the Admiralty passed the message via Volkov to Essen. He received it on morning of the 12th: '… the 2nd squadron, several detached cruisers, minesweepers and destroyers were supposed to head for Libava. However, due to circumstances in the west / or western storms … this operation has been postponed.' However, defending Libava had never been part of Russian strategy. The short stay of *Krokodil* in the port did nothing to change Essen's mind. The lack of defences, the proximity to German bases, the shallow water in the approaches and the presence of so many spies all argued against basing submarines or other torpedo craft there. He had already ensured that any action against the port would strike an empty target.

The naval observation station at Libava reported the lights of the German force as it approached. A steady stream of reports followed. There were some troops in the town, but there was no artillery. Resistance was therefore not possible to the events occurring at the pier heads almost a mile offshore. Unlike the first bombardment, the targets were mainly in and around the commercial port and the newer northern extension of the town behind it, housing mainly ethnic

Latvian workers. Halm had been careful to avoid targeting the old town, with its largely more well to do ethnic German residents. Civilian casualties were inevitable. The *Libavskaya Mysl'* carried a number of reports about the consequences over the next few days:

> … the cruiser was sending one shell after another at the unprotected peaceful city, which was later joined by the destroyers, which also fired at our port, the new town, the vocational school and the lighthouse in the old town. For 4 hours and 34 minutes, the gun salvos thundered without ceasing.
>
> … residents … gathered from all the side streets and hurried with crying and sobbing children in their arms, with bags on their shoulders to the city of Grobin. … When the usual morning passenger train departed, the station was crammed with people. At that time, pieces of shrapnel from enemy shells began to rain down, almost completely covering the platform and the track. On Suvrovskaya Street … a woman's leg was torn off and a man was seriously injured, who died on the way to the hospital.
>
> … 110 houses were damaged. Those most damaged were … near the Libava–Romenskoy railway station and the 'Bekkera i Ko' wire factory … where two were killed. … The open-hearth furnace department was badly damaged… By late December, the factory was fully operational again. … Blyumshteyn's lumberyard at the Winter Harbour was almost totally covered with shrapnel fragments … enormous damage was caused to the Oil Factory, where several thousand barrels filled with coconut oil and six tanks of various oils burned … On the same street, in Nobel's kerosene warehouse, both tanks of kerosene were literally riddled with shell fragments, which spilled into the nearby canal. After the squadron left, Nobel's workers scooped kerosene from this ditch and filled hundreds of barrels with it. Thank God, this kerosene did not catch fire from the shells, otherwise many houses would have burned down. Not far from this warehouse, a kerosene warehouse belonging to the Mazut Company was set on fire with shells.
>
> The outer wall of the [Vocational School] was destroyed in several places, and the forge and metalworking shop were destroyed. …. The lighthouse was shelled with a full salvo, but survived, as it was built of iron. During the shelling, a guard was standing at the lighthouse, and by some miracle, he remained unharmed.
>
> The Libava fishermen also suffered a lot from the bombardment … fishing gear and accessories were smashed to pieces; … shell fragments damaged [eight] boats.
>
> … Thus, Libava sacrificed 10 people to the war, including four soldiers, with seven seriously and more than 20 lightly wounded. … At 2:25pm, the squadron broke away … having fired about 700 shells.[3]

The bombardment was harrowing, but the 10.5cm shells were not very destructive; the 5.2cm shells of the destroyers even less so. The civilian casualties, though tragic, were not on a mass scale. The sinking of *Friedrich Carl* spared Libava from bombardment by her bigger guns, as well as those of *Augsburg*. Sea to shore area bombardments without target spotting had negligible military value and a high level of collateral damage was inevitable. Seaplanes might have helped. Targeting the commercial district in this way was questionable, as this was not a defended port. Libava continued to experience panicked exoduses in the following weeks, whenever rumours

3 Essen reported two naval personnel killed and one wounded.

flew round that the Germans were returning. Forsel' was tasked with restoring access to the port past the blockships for small vessels.

Behring considered that the blockships made Libava difficult, but not impossible to access. He was against the use of mines, as this would obstruct further approaches. After deliberation, he recommended a second operation. However, blocking could never close a passage permanently, since blasting could remove any obstruction. He singled out Ehrhardt in his report, whose decisions reflected his own sensibilities: 'In my opinion, the operation was a success; the reconnaissance, especially the penetration into the harbour, was boldly carried out.' The crew of *Friedrich Carl*, Halm and Gercke also received praise for their conduct.

Friedrich Carl had run into the minefield laid by the Poludivizion only 12 days earlier. If it had not been for the encounter with *Thetis*, this would have been farther to the south. *Elbing IX* had run into the minefield laid by the Poludivizion on 31 October. Vessels must have already near-missed both minefields several times. Essen's new offensive had inflicted a serious blow to Behring's forces. The strategic tunnel vision that was resulting from countering British submarines had distracted Heinrich and Behring from the danger signs of recent minelaying. The loss of the 9,000t flagship was a direct result. There was no announcement. Those aware of it were sworn to secrecy.[4]

The submarine patrols in the Gulf of Finland

Behring had been frustrated at the lack of information about Russian minefields on his last mission in the Gulf of Finland. Oberleutnant zur See der Reserve Karl Christiansen was an officer on *Lübeck*, who evidently had an inclination for amateur espionage. On October 25, Behring: 'entrusted me with the special mission of attempting to obtain further information about the location of the enemy minefields in the Gulf of Finland.' His report reads like the pages of a spy novel. Heinrich arranged for the intelligence section of the Admiralstab to issue him a false Dutch passport. He entered Finland via the ferry from Sweden to Raumo. Christiansen befriended the Swedish captain, who allowed him to pass as a watch officer. He then introduced him to his friend, the port commander in Raumo, who helpfully issued him a pass to travel in Russia. Christiansen was able to observe the harbour in Helsingfors and befriended a local Finnish steamer captain. From him, he learnt of a passage that he had used, laying between the skerries and the northern end of the Central Position minefield: '[at] the Kalbådagrund – the barrier itself was passed at a distance estimated by the captain as 1.5 nautical miles outside the outermost shoals.' His recent voyages also indicated that there were no Russian minefields west of Nargen. The information was broadly accurate. On 4 November, Christiansen returned

4 BA:RM28 KTB, RM49 Detachierten Admirals KTB, RM92 *Graudenz*, *Pommern*, *Thetis*, *Augsburg*, *Lübeck*, *Friedrich Carl*, *Amazone* KTB; BA:RM97 *U.A* KTB, RM56 20.Torpedobootshalbflottille KTB; Firle, *Ostsee*, pp.235–246, Karte 10, 11; Hopman, *Leben*, p.493; РГАВМФ:Фонд 716, Опись 2, Дело 24, pp.61–62, 72–75, Дело 13, p.29, 41–62, 82–83, Дело 10, p.406, Опись 1, Дело 15, pp.30, 37–38; Grassmann, 'Augsburg', pp.196–200; Графъ, *Новикъ*, p.39; Holger Buss, Survey Report, Elbing IX, <http://files.mikrokopter.de/Gezeitentaucher/(EN)_ELBING_IX.pdf>, retrieved 4 February 2025; Excerpts from *Libavskaya Mysl'* quoted on Наша Лиепая, <https://nashaliepaja.lv/1914-god.-vtoraya-bombardirovka-libavy.html>, retrieved 7 February 2025.

to Danzig and reported his findings to Behring, who accepted them completely. Heinrich had concerns about whether some of the information provided was still current.

The report shaped Behring's orders for *U.23* and *U.25*. They would first reconnoitre, then attempt to pass through the Central Position using the indicated channel, to patrol directly off the Russian bases. *U.23* would to attempt to pass through on arrival, whilst *U.25* patrolled east of the German minefield. If passage was not possible, Weisbach was to continue patrolling west of Revel'. Two days later, Kapitänleutnant Otto Wünsche would attempt to pass the barrier with *U.25*. The commanders could use discretion to decide when to return.

The submarines headed for their billets after separating from *Augsburg* on the afternoon of the 16th. Next morning *U.23* dived past Bengtskär. Weisbach missed a chance to attack a group of four, four-funnelled cruisers coming from Hangö. He gave an obtuse reason for not steering an interception course: 'I initially assumed that they would soon change course to the south in the direction of Libava, as our ships had started firing at this time.' They maintained course and passed five miles away. They reappeared later, steaming in a loose formation to the west. *U.23* spent several hours manoeuvring, but never got closer than a mile. Weisbach resumed course.

Next morning, *U.23* approached the Kalbådagrund shallows west of Rönnskär, trimmed low on the surface, (see map on page 30). Weisbach submerged: 'We got to within three nautical miles of Kalbådagrund … [to] watch the passage to Helsingfors. I didn't think it was advisable to go any closer to the shallows, as the boat was steering unsteadily in the sea.' It began snowing. As darkness fell, Weisbach retired out to sea to charge.

On the 19th, Weisbach patrolled off Surop Peninsula to observe movements south of Nargen. He approached within 1,000m of a torpedo boat. This met a grey painted steamer/minelayer. Weisbach did not attack: 'the periscope motor failed several times immediately afterwards, I had to go to greater depths and could not approach any closer. The Nargen–Surop [mine] barrier is almost certainly in the position assumed previously. The entry boom gate is located just below Nargen.' Weisbach patrolled west of the mine barriers for the next two days, concluding that there was, 'nothing in sight beyond the barrier that makes forcing [it] seem desirable.' On the 21st, in a heavy sea, he observed two large formations of destroyers coming out of Revel' from south of Nargen: '[I] decided not to shoot … [*U.23*] was steering so unsteadily in the rough sea … that a safe approach could not have been made; secondly, the boats were travelling at a fairly high speed, separately, with extremely irregular gaps.'

That night, Weisbach headed west. Next morning, *U.23* again submerged to pass Bengtskär. The heavy swell had died down and visibility was excellent, but with a 'powerful mirage', caused by refraction. He was able to see a distant formation that disappeared west, whose details meant that: 'it could only be a battleship and two cruisers.' Smoke appeared: 'it was assumed that it was one of the three ships [coming back, I] turned about to reverse course. Whilst still turning, I noticed that the cloud of smoke was the almost black exhaust of a submarine, whose flag flying on the mast was clearly a British one. It … passed out of range towards Hangö.' Soon afterwards:

> … the three ships appeared again from the west, apparently in a staggered line with large gaps between them. *U 23* was almost in front of the centre one. As it was soon apparent that the ship furthest north only had two funnels, the approach was made towards this one [on the assumption that it was the battleship]. I contented myself with checking from time to time that the bearing of my target remained the same, with the periscope extended slightly.

> I only extended the periscope a little more shortly before the shot, and realised that I was not looking at a battleship, but a *Gilyak* class gunboat. As the cruisers were out of firing range, I decided to carry out the attack I had planned. At 1:58pm, I fired a torpedo set at 2m at a safe firing distance (300–400m), but it probably went under the target. As the periscope motor failed after the shot and simultaneously the boat began to fluctuate in depth, I remained in sight for some time after the shot, but as I had approached unseen did not come under fire. When I extended the periscope after 30 to 40 minutes, I observed shell impacts a few h[undred] m[etres] too short, whilst only the tops of the ships' masts could be seen in the direction of Hangö.

Weisbach decided to return to Danzig, as he had given away the presence of his boat and could see smoke from destroyers converging on his position from several directions. At 1:10pm next afternoon, *U.23* was east of Fårö. A submarine was sighted to starboard: 'Diving was carried out in this direction, whilst the boat sighted also appeared to be diving. After covering about four nautical miles … Neither the submarine nor a periscope was still visible.' Weisbach resumed course, reaching Danzig on the 24th.

Weisbach's target identification was generally poor, but he had spotted *E.1* or *E.9*, and later *Akula*, returning from patrol. All three vessels sighted on the 22nd were actually two funnelled-destroyers of the same class, on the daytime patrol. At 8:30am that morning, *Inzhener-Mekhanik Zverev*, *Inzhener-Mekhanik Dmitriev* and *Vnushitel'nyy* of 3rd Divizion had left Lappvik. At 2pm, the commander of *Inzhener-Mekhanik Dmitriev*, Kapitan 2nd Ranga Sergey Bardukov, wirelessed: '… attacked by a submarine in square 46, a torpedo passed under the stern.' Weisbach's periscope was sighted when it next popped up. *Inzhener-Mekhanik Dmitriev*'s gunners were alert after the previous attack, and opened fire with her 7.5cm guns. Ironically, if Weisbach had stayed on his billet for another day, he may have had a chance to attack *Avrora*, which left Lappvik for Revel' that morning. The 'cruisers' sighted on the 17th were almost certainly also the destroyer patrol, and were steering the same courses in the same positions.

His commander, Adam, was damning in his criticism of the patrol. He wrote that *U.23* should have immediately steered an interception course towards the sightings on the mornings of the 17th and 22nd. The charts showed that *U.23* could have reached an attack position in both instances. Of the torpedo attack, he wrote:

> The commander only noticed shortly before the shot that he was not facing a battleship, but a gunboat. This error should not have occurred, especially since the boat was equipped with a bifocal periscope (6x magnification). The commander was too cautious with the periscope. The shot at the gunboat should not have been taken, as this revealed the presence of the submarine. The commander knew that the Russian forces were carrying out their exercises with little caution near Bengtskär. He should therefore have given up his attack and been near Bengtskär the next day. … The commander completely failed in this extremely promising undertaking.

Behring was quick to act: 'Kapitänleutnant Weisbach has shown himself to be incapable of leading a submarine in offensive operations. Since he has also previously failed to exploit the most favourable prospects for an attack, I request that he be transferred and replaced by a more suitable officer.' Weisbach had not even attempted to pass the minefield. He had demonstrated the same pattern of indecisive manoeuvres on his previous patrol. Submarine success hinges on the abilities of the captain. Weisbach had come up short. Heinrich had him relieved of command and ordered Adam to take temporary command of *U.23*. Weisbach went to command the training boat, *U.1*.[5]

U.25's starboard engine broke down after leaving Danzig. It was helpful that *Augsburg* was in company. Her engineers machined a replacement bolt. *Augsburg* relayed orders from Behring not to pass the Central Position if the engine broke down again. The repairs were still underway when *U.25* headed into the Gulf. The crew finally completed the repair at 3pm on the 17th. *U.25* passed north of the German minefield that night. The next day Wünsche patrolled the area where *U.26* had made her attack on *Pallada*, seeing only distant smoke. On the morning of the 19th, it was time to attempt his breakthrough. After twice spotting *U.23* surfaced near the coast off Surop, he spent the morning looking for the gap in the Russian minefield, but quickly concluded that, 'it was not very promising and to try [instead] to go under the barrier.' Wünsche abandoned the first attempt. *U.25* was forced to dive too far west by patrols, and would be unable to complete the passage in darkness. Wünsche spent the 20th chasing distant smoke back on his patrol billet, but only sighted three ordinary steamers. The 21st was a bitterly cold day of high winds and heavy seas. When surfaced, ice began to encrust the decks. Patrolling was useless.

On the morning of the 22nd, there was a, 'calm sea, good visibility, frost… It was decided, as the sea had calmed down, to break through the barrier. 8am… After determining the ship's location from Pakerort and Surop Lighthouses, we set a course of 70° and approached the [centre of the] barrier [between Nargen and Rönnskär] to within about 6 miles.' Wünsche could make out smoke all around his position. At noon *U.25*, 'Went to a depth of 30m and sailed through the area of the suspected barrier at 80°, 2.4 knots.' Wünsche had no details about the exact position or make-up of the barrier. He was actually heading directly past nine rows of mines, moored at a depth of 5m. The mines were from 45 to 85m apart in each row. Whilst *U.25* was far below the mines themselves, she could foul the cables mooring them. If the cable became stuck, the results could be disastrous. He could not know it, but the chances of getting through without encountering at least one cable were actually quite low. However, Wünsche mentions no problems: '3:30pm. Went to 9m [periscope depth] after reaching [the far side of the barrier]. We could see Kockskär Lighthouse and the masts of a vessel [to the southeast]. No further details could be determined due to increasing dusk.'

Wünsche had successfully penetrated to the heart of the Russian defences directly between the fleet bases at Revel' and Helsingfors. The minefield was wide, but he had been cautious enough to go deep early and had crossed the full width of it whilst submerged. It soon began to snow. *U.25* submerged for the night. Before dawn next morning, Wünsche surfaced to charge, but an approaching vessel forced him to dive before it was complete. *U.25* spent the day patrolling the area south of Helsingfors, eking out a battery that was only part charged. He avoided the area off Revel' assigned to *U.23*. Wünsche made detailed observations of light vessel positions and the routes used by steamers, but saw no warships. He was suspicious of mines off Helsingfors, in an area that the steamers seemed to be avoiding. As the afternoon wore on the wind and sea rose. That night, Wünsche charged the batteries before diving. As

5 He later commanded *UC.3*, then *U.74*, both minelaying submarines. The latter was lost in May 1916 with all hands in the North Sea.

U.25 moved at low speed on the motors, the crew had a restless night: '... a sharp metallic sound followed by a sizzling noise like a mine or torpedo detonation is heard throughout the boat. Cause unknown. During the night until 6am another 8 such blows are heard at irregular intervals, sometimes louder and usually 2–3 in immediate succession.' A violent gale had blown in. The heavy seas resulted in the defences reporting a number of mines in the barriers exploding. Next day, the 24th, patrolling was impossible: 'No vessels or clouds of smoke in sight. Due to the swell, visibility was almost nil; remaining surfaced was not possible due to the risk of being seen.' The gale forced *U.25* to spend most of the day waiting it out at 20m. The next day the weather had calmed somewhat, but it was bitterly cold and snow fell. Wünsche saw only small steamers passing between Helsingfors and Revel'. Most steamer traffic was using channels within the northern skerries, avoiding open water, and naval patrols were absent. He made no attacks on steamers, for fear of spoiling the chance to attack higher value targets on future patrols.

U.25 was reaching the end of its endurance: 'As dusk fell, the return journey began and we steered through the mine barrier at a depth of 30m'. After two hours, *U.25* was through, once again without any problems. Next morning, the 26th, *U.25* headed out of the Gulf through fog and snow, getting a position fix near the lighthouse at Odenskhol'm and the mournful, abandoned wreck of *Magdeburg*. The weather cleared off Bengtskär to reveal the Russian destroyer patrol in the distance, but the trip back to Danzig was uneventful. Only on the morning of the 27th, Wünsche broke wireless silence to report: 'Have passed the barrier. Did not see the enemy behind. There may be a mine barrier in front of Helsingfors. Destroyers and merchant traffic near Hangö. Have begun return journey.' *U.25* arrived in Danzig on the afternoon of the 28th. His report was warmly received. Adam commented: 'On November 22nd the commander acted very boldly.' For his daring foray into the heart of the enemy defences, Wünsche received the Iron Cross, 2nd Class. The operation had brought glory for one commander and a ruined reputation for the other. Behring vented his disappointment at the lack of targets on Weisbach: '*U.25* does not appear to have had any opportunity to attack. This may have been due to the behaviour of *U.23*.'

Submarine sightings in the Russian defences had resulted in increased vigilance and potentially lost targets. On the 18th Essen reported that the, 'presence [of submarines] was discovered near Surop and between Nargen and the island of Vul'f.' The Surop sighting by the patrol boat *Vindava* may have been *U.23*, but the sighting off Vul'f was bogus. Kolomeytsev recalled *Admiral Makarov*, which had left harbour that day: 'Return immediately at high speed... Immediately go to the roadstead, beware of submarines.' Essen reported that a search: '... by destroyers, minesweepers and harbour steamers did not yield positive results. In the Surop Strait ... markers had been destroyed and removed.' Al'tfater recorded a split of opinions about the recent sightings within fleet command:

> ... a communications service boat supposedly saw a [submarine] boat in the Surop [minefield] entrance, and then in the Revel' roadstead. 9A [Essen] who was in Revel' at that time, immediately instigated a search with all available destroyers, but found nothing. Kolchak and Nepenin are absolutely convinced that there was no boat, but 9A believes that there were boats, because the engineering [mine] barrier in Surop was deactivated ... Personally, I am inclined to agree with Kolchak and Nepenin, because I consider the passage of a

submarine through Surop in a submerged state to be virtually impossible along the entire length of the fairway.

As the war went on it would become increasingly apparent that mines alone were not a very effective barrier to submarines. If Essen had been aware of the true situation, the alarm would have been extreme. Battleships and cruisers of the fleet frequented *U.25*'s patrol area on a regular basis for exercises in better weather.

Heinrich reported his conclusions to Pohl: 'All observations indicate that the Russian cruisers are mainly on the north side of the Gulf of Finland, and are probably steaming through the archipelago waters, emerging from the archipelago near Hangö.' This was a route that the Russians were routinely using for commercial traffic and small vessels, but the cruisers were sometimes still steaming directly between Lappvik and Revel' during daylight, albeit with destroyer escort. *U.23*'s early departure had caused Weisbach to miss *Avrora*, and both had not spotted *Ryurik* and *Bogatyr'* returning from an operation on the morning of the 20th. Drawing a firm conclusion from a limited set of observations, many made during very poor weather, with a defence on submarine alert, had caused Heinrich to underestimate the chances for successful attack.

The patrol reports prompted Heinrich to issue revised instructions on the 28th: '…after the conduct of a submarine commander did not meet with my approval. The forces permanently available in the Baltic are weak… Nevertheless, our activities must not be curtailed. … submarines despatched to the Gulf of Finland will attack Russian forces regardless of risk. Small torpedo boats and patrol craft should not be attacked, but, with these exceptions, all restrictions regarding attacks are withdrawn. I attach great importance to the destruction of Russian submarines, and I consider the destruction of a British submarine to be as important as that of a Russian armoured cruiser.' The perceived lack of targets identified by Wünsche resulted in instructions that made it unlikely that there would be another attempt to pass the Russian minefields: 'Commanding Officers … must weigh carefully what risks are to be taken from mines and booms. They are not to enter the approaches to Helsingfors and Revel'. In the very near future ice conditions will compel the Russian forces in Revel' to carry out practices to the west of the Nargen minefield.' Demonstrating activity to the Russians remained important: 'When a submarine has to leave her station to return home without being certain that she will be replaced with 24 hours, or that another German submarine is in the vicinity, she is to show herself at an appropriate moment, in order that her presence may be reported by the enemy.' One submarine was to be present in the Gulf of Finland at all times. *U.26* left Danzig on 26 November for the next patrol.[6]

Essen's mine offensive expands

Whilst *U.23* and *U.25* were in the Gulf of Finland, there had been a major new operation by the Baltiyskiy Flot. The battleship *Sevastopol'* was completing her trials. Essen used this to propose an expansion of the minelaying offensive. He argued that the powerful new dreadnoughts provided much greater security for the Gulf of Finland. Therefore, risking cruisers in offensive

6 BA:RM97 *U.23*, *U.25* KTB, RM49 Detachierten Admirals KTB; Firle, *Ostsee*, pp.246–248; РГАВМФ:Фонд 716, Опись 2, Дело 24, pp.71–91, Дело 13, pp.82–83, Опись 1, Дело 15, p.38.

Amur had rails internally for 250 mines. Armed with 5x12cm guns for defence, but speed only 17 knots. (Public domain)

operations was now acceptable. Essen's aim was that, 'all the approaches to the German ports … in the southeastern parts of the Baltic were to be mined, hindering any movement of ships in this region … basing of the enemy in Danzig, Pillau and Memel would also be hindered and the enemy would not be able to transport troops from the west to the above-mentioned ports.' The latter was sure to appeal to the army. Fan-der-Flit gave his approval.

Al'tfater wrote that the new plan was, 'conceived by the Admiral [Essen] and perfected by Kolchak and Cherkasskiy'. It envisaged large-scale minefields, for which destroyers were not suitable. In addition, only *Novik* had the range to reach distant areas. The surface minelayers, *Amur* and *Enisey*, would begin operations on the next period of moonless nights. Their maximum speed of 17 knots made them vulnerable, necessitating covering cruisers, along the lines of the plan originally proposed in September. The new plan integrated the expanded long-range submarine force to deter enemy patrols.

On 13 November, Essen issued the orders for the first operation to Laurence and Horton in Helsingfors. *E.1* and *E.9*, their refit complete, were to proceed, 'for offensive actions against German fleet in the Baltic, near Bornholm Island and to the west of it.' *Akula* would take position in the Gulf of Danzig, the limit of her operational range. All three would make themselves conspicuous, aiming to deter sorties by major German units. The relationship between the British crews and Essen was strengthened by the assignment of his only son, Leytenant Antoniy fon Essen, as *E.9*'s liaison officer.

Once the submarines were in position, *Amur* would sail under escort of *Ryurik*, *Oleg* and *Bogatyr'* to a position south of Gotland. Essen shifted his flag to *Tsesarevich*. Kerber raised his flag on *Ryurik* to command the operation. The inclusion of the powerful cruiser meant that the force should outgun any German cruiser force encountered. *Amur* would then detach to lay 240 mines in two separate fields during the night, on the route taken by vessels north of the shallow Stolpe Bank. This was a larger version of minefield 9N, originally allocated to *Novik*. She would then return to her escort at 8am next morning. If the cruisers encountered any weak enemy forces on the way, they were to attack. If the enemy force was superior, they were withdraw north, covering *Amur*, whilst she laid mines in the enemy's path.

Secrecy was paramount. The force would have to leave via the Gulf of Finland, as it was not possible for deep draught vessels to use any other routes. To mislead spies, it was announced that the cruisers would carry out gunnery practice in the Gulf on the 18/19th and that *Amur* was to lay a defensive field in the Gulf of Bothnia. Only the minimum number of officers knew the true nature of the operation. Minesweepers swept exit channels well in advance.

The plan was set in motion on the 15th, as soon as the gale that had also affected Behring's operations subsided. That morning, *E.1* and *E.9* left Helsingfors for their billet, splitting up to pass either side of Gotland. Here, the Norwegian merchantman saw *E.1* and reported her to *Augsburg*. *Akula* left Dagerort. She quickly sighted a nearby submarine in the rough seas. The emergency dive in shallow water caused her to strike the bottom. Damage to her propeller guards forced a return to dock for repair. Frustratingly, the submarine turned out to be *Drakon*, which had doubled back from her defensive patrol billet to seek shelter from the swell.

On the morning of the 17th, when the crew started *E.1*'s diesels, one of them was damaged. Laurence chose to press on with one engine, at reduced speed. The crew worked hard to make repairs, even lifting parts of the engine to access the interior whilst sat on the bottom during the next night. After 36 hours of toil, the engine was back in action. On the 19th, Laurence finally approached his objective, the narrow Kadet Rinne between Falster and the German coast. Four patrolling destroyers approached in a screen. Laurence dived to allow them to pass, 'but unfortunately found nothing behind them.' Laurence's Russian liaison officer, Leytenant Georgiy Chaplin, told Al'tfater that Laurence had ignored his advice to attack the destroyers. There was no patrol at the Kadet Rinne. Next day he found nothing except commercial shipping off the Sound. The engine problem had severely reduced his time on billet. That evening he left, returning the way he had come, having failed to make his presence on the billet known.

Horton had an uneventful run to his billet. *E.9* was approaching his destination off Arkona on the morning of the 17th:

> 1.43p.m. Sighted two funnelled cruiser through periscope to southward proceeding to northward on zig zag courses (Gazelle class?) Attacked her.
>
> 1.55. 500 yards [450m] 7pts on cruiser bow. [This was an ideal firing position, just ahead and to the side of the target]. Fired two torpedoes [from the bow tubes] (Heaters, controlling gear free) with no result.
>
> Both torpedoes broke surface badly directly after firing and presumably therefore ran cold. Cruiser must have observed torpedoes break surface for she commenced to swing towards me too quickly to allow firing a beam torpedo. Weather fine and clear. Slight swell, considerable lop ... Submarine lively. Submarine was reported horizontal 5 seconds before firing. But on actually firing bubble showed about ½° up by the bow.

Horton patrolled the Kadet Rinne and south of the Sound until his scheduled departure on the evening of the 20th, seeing commercial traffic and ferries, but no warships. He had also been unreported, despite his attack. The two submarines met off Bogskär on the morning of the 22nd. The Russian patrols were warned to prevent them being attacked and they returned to Lappvik with flags flying for recognition, as seen by *U.23*. When the reports reached London, Keyes commented that Horton must have underestimated the up angle. When torpedoes were fired at a significant upwards angle, they were likely to broach, then dive to the bottom. Churchill was blunter in his comments: '4 or 5 bad misses have been made'. The apparent depth keeping problems of the torpedoes resulted in queries from Laurence about their correct adjustment. The problems resulted in the despatch of a specialist, Engineer Lieutenant-Commander Edgar Groves, and two artificers. They arrived in February to carry out torpedo adjustments.

Gazelle and *Undine* were the only cruisers left in the western Baltic, greatly reducing the number of big ship targets. There were normally five destroyers south of the Sound, three torpedo boats in the Kadet Rinne and two further west in Fehmarn Belt. The cruisers took turns at Swinemünde. From here, they executed a daily 'show the flag' patrol past the Swedish and Danish coasts and back. Mischke's orders emphasised safety: 'During daylight always steam at high speed and on zigzag courses.' *Gazelle* left Swinemünde to head for the Swedish coast at 8.30am that morning. The rough sea concealed both *E.9* and her torpedoes. The course change had been a routine zigzag. *Gazelle* steamed on, oblivious to her escape. However, the zigzag had prevented a second attack. Heavy seas then reduced the meagre targets in the area even further. On the 18th, *Gazelle* had to shepherd the damaged *T.53* and *T.55* to Kiel. After briefly returning, she headed back to Kiel to coal on the morning of the 19th, whilst *Undine* was still cleaning her boilers.

Meanwhile, at noon on the 17th, Kerber assembled his force east of Nargen and briefed the orders for the operation to his captains. The timings and route were dictated by the 14-knot cruising speed of *Amur*. The vessels departed at 1.30pm, escorted by three destroyers of 6th Divizion. The lighthouses exiting the Gulf were lit as they passed, but Kerber then had those on the south side extinguished, to lead any watching German submarines into believing the force was headed west, not south. Kerber's force passed Odenskhol'm at 5pm, an hour after sunset. The routine night destroyer patrol was to remain in port until their return to ensure that the force could proceed and return without incident.

The force headed through the night east of Gotland. At dawn, *Amur* hoisted a false third funnel into place, making her profile appear more like that of a cruiser. The force skirted 30 miles south of Gotland, well out of sight of land, then after darkness fell, closed to within 20 miles of the southern end of Öland to get a position fix from the lighthouse there. *Amur* left to make the final run to Stolpe Bank.

The wind had picked up. The sea was breaking by the time she reached the target area. *Amur* turned to begin laying at 6 knots and opened the hatches in the stern. The heavy sea broke inboard. The crew laboured in water up to their knees to lay the mines from the port and starboard rails on the internal deck. To complicate sweeping and make the field more dangerous for different vessels, on one side the mines were laid at a depth of 5m and on the other at 3m. The work went off without a hitch. *Amur* returned to the rendezvous and the force returned the way it had come. None of the ships sighted anything beyond some distant smoke and lights that night. It was unlikely that the force was sighted. However, as a precaution, once east of Östergarn, *Ryurik* and *Bogatyr'* increased speed to 18 knots, aiming to ostentatiously arrive at Revel' after dawn next morning, the 20th, where they would be escorted in by 6th Divizion. The intention was that if any vessels had been sighted, this would be associated with the two cruisers and not a minelayer. Meanwhile, *Oleg* and *Amur* slipped quietly into Utö during the night, returning to Helsingfors on the 22nd. The elaborate precautions taken to ensure secrecy were a complete success. Despite the presence of both *U.23* and *U.25* in the Gulf during the exit and return of the force, no hint of minelaying or anything other than routine activity reached Germany.

Meanwhile, *Akula* completed repairs. Vlas'yev was to make a two-day patrol off Danzig. Like the British, he was to ensure that *Akula* was seen before leaving the billet. Danzig was pushing the limit of the fuel capacity. Vlas'yev secured additional oil in cans within the external ballast compartments, to top up the oil tanks during the patrol. *Akula* left Revel' on the 18th, but was held up by heavy seas in the Gulf of Riga. Vlas'yev finally reached the German coast off Rixhöft early on the morning of the 21st. Visibility was poor, with a gusty wind and grey sky. The lookouts saw nothing. Vlas'yev spent the night at anchor on the surface, as the submarine's shape prevented it resting on the bottom. Next morning, the last day of his patrol, he headed west, keeping well out of sight of the coast. At noon, a small steamer without a flag approached from the west. Vlas'yev submerged and steered to intercept. He fired a torpedo from one of the external bow frames. It missed, appearing to run under the bow. The steamer made off at speed. As he was due to leave, Vlas'yev surfaced to ensure that *Akula* was seen.

Kabelfischdampfer S.1 (*Generaldirektor Ballin*), a Neufahrwasser outpost boat, Leutnant zur See der Reserve Hugo Groening, was one of three boats 'fishing' for underwater cables. She was allocated the cable between Libava and Denmark. *Akula*'s torpedo was not seen in the choppy sea, but Groening reported, 'we sighted a submarine 800–1,000 meters from the ship. The submarine was half-surfaced … We mistook the boat for a German because of the two periscopes and it being side on to us. I considered it unnecessary to fire recognition signals, as the boat was submerged and therefore unable to send a reply. A short time later, the boat dived.' *Akula* was seen again, several miles away, when Vlas'yev re-surfaced. The small, shallow draught trawler had been an extremely difficult target, especially in the rough seas. A miss was to be expected. Groening made a routine wireless report of the sighting to Behring, who knew that this could only be an enemy submarine. Ironically, at almost the same time, *Amazone*, patrolling off Danzig, reported a torpedo attack close inshore. It was bogus, but added to the perception of heavy submarine activity. Heinrich ordered Behring to, 'Have Danzig Bay immediately cleared of [German] cruisers'. Vlas'yev obtained the reaction Essen wanted.

Mission accomplished, Vlas'yev headed back up the eastern side of Gotland. The weather worsened, with snowstorms and bitter cold. The rough sea caused the acid to spill from the batteries, making conditions below even more miserable. *Akula* spotted *U.23* returning to Danzig off Fårö. The lookouts on both boats had been alert, despite the weather. They were several miles apart and dived at about the same time. A blizzard forced *Akula* to anchor for an entire day off Dagerort, but Vlas'yev finally arrived at Utö on the 25th.

Whilst *Akula* was on patrol, Essen had sent out another minelaying mission. At 10am on the 20th, the Poludivizion (excluding *Sibirskiy Strelok*) headed out from Moon Sound across the Gulf of Riga, screened as usual by the first half of 2nd Divizion, with each of the three destroyers carrying 35 mines. That night they were to attempt again to lay minefield 2D. From 8pm, a strong easterly wind once again began whipping up heavy seas, rolling the destroyers in the swell. Lights repeatedly shone over the surface of the sea in the distance in the direction of both shore and sea, becoming brighter as the destroyers neared the target. They began laying mines in several separate lines over a seven-mile stretch. As they splashed off the sterns, a vessel could be seen in the distance, picked out by a searchlight. It would have been impossible to fight the guns and torpedoes in the conditions, but the crews stuck to the work until all the mines were laid, As they headed back, it was difficult to maintain speed in the heavy swell to ensure their return in darkness. The Poludivizion was now in serious need of repairs. On the 24th, it went to Helsingfors for a thorough overhaul and refit. *Lübeck* had been on patrol in the Bay that night and had been close, but the moonless night and poor visibility had concealed the Russian destroyers. The cruiser had used her searchlight to confirm the identity of three German steamers that night.

Novik's rudder repairs caused her to miss the last operation. As soon as she was out of dock, mines were loaded. Essen ordered Paletskiy to lay barrier 4N off the German coast south of Stolpe Bank, as soon as the weather cleared. On the morning of the 23rd, *Novik* departed Moon Sound in calm weather. As darkness fell *Novik* headed out to sea after passing inshore of the minefields off Vindava, then turned to cut through the sea to the German coast. A headwind blew up and began to raise a swell. The wait for good weather meant that the early part of night was now moonlit, but the cloudy sky helped reduce visibility. It was a bitterly cold winter night and the sea spray began to form ice on the bow, the mine apparatus and the mines themselves. By 9pm, *Novik*'s bow was cutting right through the waves ahead, rolling as she advanced, with her turbines pushing at a steady 24 knots to reach the distant target area. On all minelaying missions, tensions ran high. Graf recalled that:

> At about 11pm, the officer on watch saw a bright, white light straight ahead and reported it to the wardroom. We all ran up and did indeed see some kind of light ahead; then the commander, just in case, ordered the alarm to be sounded. One thing was strange: no matter how brightly the light shone, and no matter how fast *Novik* was moving, we still did not approach it. Soon, having looked closely at it, we were convinced, to our shame, that it was only Jupiter.

The waves reduced as *Novik* approached the lee of the German coast. The moon set, leaving a clear, cloudless starry night. Another light soon appeared. There was some uncertainty whether it was a shore light:

> At 1:15, we finally approached the designated location, turned to northwest and made 15 knots. The laying took place in very difficult conditions, since our stern was sometimes heavily flooded during the run, resulting in the rails and chutes being completely iced-up. It was very difficult to work: people were freezing, their feet were slipping, and those who were standing at the chutes even had to be tied on. All this greatly complicated the work, but the cheerfulness and calmness of the crew allowed us to carry out the task perfectly. We laid mines in separate banks, 10 in each, with intervals of one mile between each group. This way of working greatly extended the operation and kept the entire crew in a tense state for a long time, resulting in an uneasy feeling. The unpleasantness was further aggravated by the fact that the treacherous light was still visible, it sometimes seemed that it was moving and approaching us in the darkness, and then

> there was a great desire to jettison the mines quickly. Nevertheless, we held our nerve and accurately carried out the task.

Novik accelerated back to 24 knots, turned for home and was already back off the coast at Bakgofen at dawn, without having been sighted.

Essen was determined to keep up the pace of the offensive. With the Poludivizion out of action, the next operation was entrusted to 1st Divizion. These destroyers only had a small mine capacity. On the night of the 26/27th, *Vsadnik*, *Gaydamak*, *Amurets* and *Ussuriets* followed the usual route to lay a field of 50 mines. This was additional to those originally planned, close to the Russian border. The destroyers laid the mines 23 miles out to sea, intended to catch any vessels approaching Memel from the northwest. As with previous operations, they left in good weather, only to encounter heavy seas in the target area. They completed the mission unseen.

With the period of moonless nights now over, operations paused. Seven separate minefields, containing 740 mines, now contaminated German sea routes from the Stolpe Bank to Memel.[7]

7 BA:RM92 *Gazelle*, *Undine*, *Lübeck* KTB, RM99 *Generaldirektor Ballin* KTB, RM49 Detachierten Admirals KTB, RM28 KTB; РГАВМФ:Фонд 716, Опись 2, Дело 24, pp.71–93, Дело 13, pp.82–83, 201, Опись 1, Дело 15, p.40, 45, Фонд 418, Опись 1, Дело 3343, pp.105–108, 121; Pavlovich, *Operations*, pp.95–99; TNA:ADM137/271, pp.27–35; Меркушов, *Записки*, pp.284, 299–300; Гельмерсен, 'Заградительные', *Сборник 1*, pp.10–13; Графъ, *Новикъ*, pp.39–42; Томашевич, *операциях*, p.58.

8

'Naval warfare has lost its poetry': November to December 1914

German reactions to the underwater threat

The loss of *Friedrich Carl* had a profound impact. It temporarily brought German surface operations to a complete halt. Behring wrote to Heinrich on 19 November:

> My hope to see *Friedrich Carl* in action with ... Russian cruisers, fighting a straight fight man to man, chest to chest, will, sadly, never be realised. In my opinion, naval warfare in its current form with submarines, torpedoes and mines has lost its poetry.
>
> However, that cannot be helped, and one must accept it.
>
> I trust that your Royal Highness will be able to give me another armoured cruiser. If I could have some more destroyers also I should then be quite satisfied. I do not think it prudent to send the cruisers to sea again without destroyers. Conditions here are now much changed.

Behring was not alone in nostalgic romanticism for the era of gunnery as the decisive weapon at sea. Some were inclined to over-react to the shock of events such as the loss of *Pallada* and *Friedrich Carl*. Pohl was under pressure from the army to interrupt trade in the Baltic that supported the Russian war effort. The army had failed to deliver a knockout blow in the west and found itself bogged down in a war on two fronts. Pohl resisted, because of his perception of the magnitude of the underwater threat. His growing feud with Tirpitz and differences of opinion with his commanders over the offensive posture of the navy was heating up, as he describes in a letter to his wife:

> We have to lament a heavy loss in the Baltic Sea today. *Friedrich Karl* [*sic*] ran into a mine near Memel or was hit by a torpedo and then slowly sank. ... it is due to the rashness of the Fleet and Baltic Commanders, who wanted the 2nd Geschwader to go to Libava to bombard it. His Majesty refused this after I had presented my arguments. What would have happened if one or perhaps several of the battleships had been lost? I had expressly warned [Heinrich] of the submarine danger. This is proof of how right I was. Do not worry, the incident only argues for my approach of holding back. Tirpitz, with his theory of going out and attacking, can see where this leads. However, General v. Y. has also learned a lesson. Only

> yesterday, I had a conversation with him in which he asked me to disrupt trade between Gävle and Raumo in the Gulf of Bothnia. I refused, citing the submarine danger for the strong forces that I would then have to station off the Gulf of Finland…

Friedrich Carl sank precisely where *Thetis* had seen suspicious vessels in early November. Mines were therefore the obvious explanation, not torpedoes, but doubt lingered. Shipping heading for Memel was warned to approach from the south along the coast from Brüsterort. On the 18th, Heinrich telegraphed Behring: 'Please determine as soon as possible whether there are mines west of Memel. Report whether sufficient resources are available. This should not delay the cable [cutting] operation.' This was an odd priority. He began lobbying the High Command and Ingenohl to replace *Friedrich Carl* with the best of Rebeur-Paschwitz's three remaining armoured cruisers, *Roon*.

Behring responded: 'Means for rapid and accurate detection are currently unavailable, especially if cable work must not be delayed.' He later elaborated, 'The Neufahrwasser Hilfsminensuchdivision will have its new equipment in operation in a few days, which is significantly more suitable than the [current] heavy equipment due to its higher search speed. … Once the division is reasonably familiar with the equipment, I will have it search the areas west of Memel suspected of being mined. However, I would like to point out that casualties are to be expected during the clearance work due to the deep draught of the steamers. I am also currently not in a position to provide the division with any cover against enemy naval forces.' Heinrich had already dismissed the six minesweeper tugs at Swinemünde as, 'not very seaworthy.' The auxiliary sweeping units had been in existence for four months, but consisted of unsuitable vessels that could not sweep effectively. The absence of mines had bred complacency. Heinrich asked Ingenohl whether he could spare a North Sea Minensuchdivision, or 12 patrol boats to release 2nd Minensuchdivision temporarily from guard work in Kiel Bay.

Ingenohl gave a mixed response. He offered his oldest armoured cruiser, *Prinz Heinrich*, instead of *Roon* to the High Command. He could not spare any minesweepers or patrol boats, as he had a division already laid up for boiler cleaning. He offered Heinrich a destroyer flotilla to relieve 2nd Minensuchdivision, for which he was 'very grateful', but only after an operation on the 29th. The High Command ordered a compromise on the cruiser. *Friedrich Carl*'s sister ship, *Prinz Adalbert*, was ordered to the Baltic once Ingenohl's operation concluded.

Meanwhile, Heinrich left 2nd Minensuchdivision, a specialised minesweeping unit with 12 available boats, doing routine guard and contraband monitoring in Kiel Bay. Ten days after the loss of two ships, there had been no progress with even confirming the existence of mines in the Bay of Danzig. Vessels at Danzig had simply been patrolling to detect minelayers. As *Lübeck*'s experience proved, on a moonless night this was looking for a needle in a haystack with a blindfold on.

On the 27th, Heinrich sent a discussion paper to Behring, proposing that his surface forces should shift their base to Swinemünde: 'The presence of British naval officers in the Baltic Fleet and the presence of British submarines in the Baltic Sea seem to be stimulating the Russians to greater activity. Perhaps, however, the reason lies simply in the realization that the German forces operating against them are weak and that it is not possible to maintain a permanent, close surveillance of the Gulf of Finland. … With minelaying and submarine operations, they are actually becoming a nuisance to us.' He made enemy submarines, especially British, a priority target for submarine commanders next day. The irony was that the arrival of the

British submarines had actually delayed Essen's planned offensive. Recent intelligence reports suggested that there were up to four at Revel'. The recent submarine scare off Danzig and reports of submarines passing Gotland were no doubt on Heinrich's mind. It was this visible threat that pre-occupied Heinrich and Behring, not the hidden mine danger. Essen's strategy of asking his submariners to make their presence obvious to distract from minelaying was evidently a good one. Heinrich told the Admiralstab, 'The primary reason for the relocation of the base … is that the depth and weather conditions in the Bay of Danzig are considerably more favourable for enemy submarines than in the Bay of Pomerania, and that entering and exiting Neufahrwasser is always difficult for armoured cruisers, and not possible under all circumstances.' Planned dredging would alleviate access issues, but would make things more awkward in the short term. The concerns about the submarine threat drove Heinrich's conclusions, but there was also the unproven mine 'nuisance':

> The suspicion of mines has already prompted us to issue warnings for the approach to Memel. It would certainly be very desirable to have a minesweeping division determine beyond doubt whether Russian mines are actually present. However, we cannot be completely certain that <u>none</u> are present.
>
> We will have to accept the fact that the entire sea area east of 19°30' E, between 55°30' N and 55°50' N, [a wide area stretching from 25 miles west to 45 miles west of Memel] is suspected of being mined. It is to be assumed that, based on our announcement [requiring] approach [to Memel] from Brüsterort … the Russians will lay mines precisely on this line. Therefore, here too, we can only send ships behind a minesweeping division. This would mean permanently stationing a minesweeping division of the High Seas Forces in Pillau or Neufahrwasser. Given the limited combat strength of this minesweeping division, this would require an armoured cruiser and at least one small cruiser with destroyers to be based in Neufahrwasser [as a covering force].

The impression given is that Heinrich was unwilling to see his cruisers tied down covering minesweeping. Given his limited resources, this would preclude offensive action and potentially embolden the Russians further. His argument about not being able to prove that mines were not there is bizarre. Key routes needed sweeping as a priority to determine the extent of the danger, given available evidence. Rather than determine the extent of mining and sweep channels, Heinrich's approach going forward was simply to avoid them. The mine danger area that he outlined was notified to all naval forces in an intelligence briefing on 14 December.

Heinrich sent a staff officer to discuss the proposal with Behring. He concurred on the change of base. On 1 December, Heinrich informed the Admiralstab. Preparations for the move began. Adam's submarines and the Neufahrwasser Hilfsminensuchdivision would remain in Danzig. The former needed the shortest route possible to their billets in the north and were much less at risk of submarine attack. Behring had also suggested an attack on Mariehamn to regain the initiative as soon as *Prinz Adalbert* was available. On 18 November, intelligence had finally identified the presence of 'an older Russian submarine and a depot ship' there. Behring proposed a bombardment, and blocking the harbour exit using the mines that *Amazone* had brought to Danzig.

Meanwhile, the trawlers fitted with cable cutting equipment completed their work. On 23 November, they severed the two cables to Denmark in mid-Baltic. *Kabelfischdampfer S.3*

(*Senator Strandes*), Oberleutnant zur See der Reserve Heinz Stamer, had the most dangerous final mission, to cut the cable from Libava to Petrograd. On the afternoon of the 29th, he crept to within two to three miles of Steynort lighthouse. In high wind and rough seas, the crew located and dragged up the cable. They worked all night to insert a resistance block, which would be hard to locate and fix, until they were exhausted, deluged by each incoming wave. The stiff cable defeated them. They anchored for the night. Next morning, the cable had broken loose. They could not lift it, even with the engine at full power. However, they had done enough damage to stop it working and returned to Danzig.

With the work complete, they could now support the work of Hilfsminensuchdivision Neufahrwasser. However, on the 30th, Heinrich ordered Behring to, 'Temporarily abandon minesweeping operations near Memel.' Five of the trawlers were formed into the Division der Hilfsfahrzeuge (Auxiliary Division): *Generaldirektor Ballin*, *Senator Refardt*, *Oberbürgermeister Burchardt*, *Senator Strandes* and *Bunte Kuh*. They were to be equipped with improvised anti-submarine sweeps and explosive charges to 'fish' for submarines on the coast between Rixhöft and Swinemünde. German submarines were to keep east of this area. The vessels and their armament were hopelessly inadequate as an effective anti-submarine measure. Weidgen now had only six sweepers left, training with the new mine sweeps. He was to 'determine as soon as possible whether suitable shallow-draught steamers are available in Königsberg. If so, use them to determine whether there are any mines west of Memel.' It was a token gesture, not a minesweeping plan.

Anti-submarine patrols were also the focus in the western Baltic. Mischke had 60 laid up fishing drifters fitted out. The fishermen that had manned them were recalled from the front. They could fish when not required for patrol. The dangers facing Mischke's patrols in the busy waters of the western Baltic came to the fore at the end of November. In the early hours of the 23rd, the 808 GRT, Danish flagged steamer *Anglo Dane* was approaching the Sound with a cargo from Stettin to København. The moon had set. It was pitch dark. A crewman gives an account:

> … suddenly a ship without lights and at full speed was seen ahead of *Anglo Dane*. … a collision took place almost immediately. The prow of *Anglo Dane* penetrated about half a dozen feet [2m] into the hull of the torpedo boat; this cut the steam lines and steam streamed out. … Second Mate Bang … jumped to the torpedo boat immediately after the collision, and it was decided that two of the most seriously injured, the chief engineer and a stoker, should be brought on board *Anglo Dane* [the quickest way to a hospital]. They were scalded so terribly that large areas of their skin were hanging in sheets. A German ship's doctor accompanied them to København and tried to alleviate their suffering with morphine. The chief engineer [Torpedo-Obermaschinisten-Anwärter Karl Stange] died on the way here, the other [Torpedo-Oberheizer Richard Platschke] shortly after arrival.

Anglo Dane struck the similar sized *S.124*, Oberleutnant zur See Heinrich Metzger, of 7th Halbflottille, squarely amidships. The stoutly built steamer suffered little damage, but the lightly built destroyer suffered severe structural damage. The surge of live steam was devastating. In addition to the two men taken to *Anglo Dane*, one crewman was already dead, two badly injured and four less severely. The other two boats on watch, *T.97*, and the leader, *S.120*, were first on the scene. Kapitänleutnant Recke-Volmerstein, the unit commander, raised the alarm: '*S.124* rammed to starboard … First [aftermost] boiler room and forward engine room flooded. Main steam line broken. Leaks are under control. Boat at anchor. Towing currently impossible due to strong east wind. Send shipyard tugs.' The destroyer was likely to break up if towed, so it stayed put with a small guard until the sea calmed. On the 28th, the weather finally abated somewhat. Salvage vessels towed *S.124* into more sheltered water at Stevns Klint. On the 30th, severe weather was expected. In less than ideal conditions, the salvage tug *Norder* slowly towed *S.124* to Warnemünde, 110 miles away. *Undine* steamed ahead to lay an oil track to calm the waves. The strain proved too much. *S.124* broke in half and sank, with her bow and stern left sticking defiantly out of the shallow water, only a few miles short of the destination. In 1915, the wreck was salvaged, but was beyond repair and scrapped.

On 29th November, Ingenohl's 3rd Flottille arrived to relieve 2nd Minensuchdivision. It was available for two weeks. Heinrich used it for yet more anti-submarine patrols in the western Baltic, but the Minensuchdivision did no sweeping. There were now more minefields, covering a much wider area, of which the Germans knew nothing.[1]

Neutral trade and mining the Gulf of Bothnia

Trading in the Baltic settled into a new pattern after the disruption caused by the outbreak of war. The German stop and search regime approaching the Sound diverted considerable trade between Russia and her allies to a route that ran from the Swedish ports in the Kattegat, across the Swedish rail network to Stockholm, Gävle and Sundsvall, then across the Gulf of Bothnia to the Finnish ports of Raumo and Björneborg. The rail connections through Sweden to the Finnish border at the northern tip of the Gulf were under improvement, which was important to keep trade flowing when the Baltic and White Sea ports were iced-in.

For the Germans, Swedish iron ore was vital to their war effort. Much of this was shipped from Luleå in the Gulf of Bothnia and Oxelösund, south of Stockholm. Prior to the war, it had mostly arrived via the North Sea ports of Essen and Rotterdam. Stettin and Lübeck now handled most of this traffic, with the route crossing the Baltic from the southern tip of Sweden. On 13 October, Russian destroyers stopped the Swedish flagged steamer *Sydland* off the Åland Islands. The incident had caused alarm, even though she was released after her papers had been examined. German ore shipping companies appealed to Heinrich for protection, but he had none to give, simply reminding them to ensure that their vessels kept within the Swedish three-mile territorial limit whenever possible. All steamers were able to use Swedish territorial waters for much of their journey, making them inaccessible to all parties to the conflict. Trade in non-contraband goods continued with little interference in neutral flagged vessels.

Germany's dependency on Swedish iron ore also greatly handicapped any attempt by them to interfere with Baltic trade, despite the fact that Swedish goods and trade to and from Russia supported the Allied war effort. Sweden held a trump card, as any interruption to iron ore shipments would have a severe impact on the ability of German industry to sustain the war effort. Trade with Norway and Denmark, as well as their ability to source goods from further afield,

1 Pohl, *Aufzeichnungen*, p.88; BA:RM92 *Gazelle*, *Undine* KTB; RM28 KTB; RM49 Detachierten Admirals KTB, RM56 4.Torpedobootsflottille, 7.Torpedobootshalbflottille KTB, RM99 *Senator Strandes* KTB, RM2 Kriegsnachrichten; Firle, *Ostsee*, pp.247–252; *Østsjællands Folkeblad*, Havdrup, 24 November 1914; Anon., *Verlustliste No.13a*, p.63.

was also vital to sustain the German economy. For this reason, instructions to German warships were highly restrictive: '[searches] should only be carried out on Danish, Norwegian and Swedish ships in serious cases that can be justified by the commander. The commanders must bear in mind that there are political reasons for maintaining the neutrality of Denmark, Sweden and Norway, which is favourable to us. It follows that the examination of the ship's papers and the questioning of the crews on ships of these states, where appropriate, must be carried out in a friendly manner.' When patrols detained steamers for carrying contraband goods, they were sent to Swinemünde, where the German Prize Court had been established. However, after protests from their governments, they were often released.

There was a significant flare-up in late October. The Admiralstab had drawn Heinrich's attention to the use of neutral steamers to ship timber to Britain. It was thought that stopping this might cause British coalmines to cease production for lack of pit props. The guard vessels at the Sound began sending many steamers in to Swinemünde. The Swedish government lodged a complaint. The Admiralstab then informed Heinrich, 'that the Prize Law had been grossly violated, and declaring themselves to no longer be in a position to defend these repeated violations to the Foreign Office and the Imperial Courts of Justice.' The case of *Elida*, seized on 13 October, with a cargo of timber, was typical. The Prize Court found that timber did not meet the definition of conditional contraband. The steamer was released. The court's decision to deny compensation to the owners was then subject to further legal action. In May 1915, the decision was overturned on appeal. The German government had to compensate the owners for the detention.

On 19 November, these problems led Heinrich to write to Pohl: 'In the majority of cases it was not possible to search the holds of steamers held up in the Sound, on account of the deck cargoes. It is suspected that most of the steamers carrying worked timber, which is not contraband, had pit-props, rough timber, and other contraband in their holds … I therefore consider it most necessary to cancel the restrictions against searching Swedish steamers.' On the 23rd, Pohl persuaded the Foreign Office to declare all timber to be conditional contraband and drop the relaxed regime for Swedish steamers. The Swedes adapted by moving timber around the Baltic in shallow draught vessels that did not need to leave territorial waters.

Pohl continued to come under pressure to do something about the trade between Sweden and Finland. Intelligence indicated that lorries and machine tools were being shipped from the Swedish ports. Pohl suggested to both Heinrich and the army that minelaying would have a longer lasting impact on trade than a raid by surface vessels, proposing minefields off Raumo and Björneborg. The problem was that most of the trade was carried in Swedish vessels. Pohl consulted the Foreign Office, who placed some constraints on the operation. Heinrich was instructed to notify the Naval Attaché in Stockholm by wireless as soon as the mines were laid, so that Swedish ships in Finnish harbours could be warned before they sailed. Nevertheless, there was acceptance that some Swedish vessels would strike mines.

The short daylight hours meant that *Deutschland* could steam directly from Kiel to lay the mines, without an escort. Only six hours of full daylight remained in the area. Behring would meet her after the minelaying off Bogskär, and act as a wireless relay. On the afternoon of 3 December, *Deutschland*, with her new commander, Korvettenkapitän Hugo von Rosenberg, left Kiel. A gale blew up from the southwest off Bornholm. The converted train ferry's low mine deck aft flooded. Rosenberg had to turn back temporarily, heading into the wind and sea, whilst the crew built a barrier aft using timber and bagged coal, to keep out the sea.

On the 5th, *Deutschland* reached the Åland Sea in darkness. The crew manned the guns. Rosenberg increased speed to 15 knots for the most dangerous part of the mission. *Deutschland* encountered about 30 steamers whilst passing through the busy narrows into the Gulf of Bothnia. Rosenberg altered course for the northernmost target, Björneborg. Three pilots who knew these waters and the coastal landmarks were on-board to assist with navigation. Rosenberg began taking soundings as *Deutschland* approached land. The lighthouse was not working and light buoys were not in expected peacetime positions. Eventually, the steamer channel into the town's port of Mäntyluoto was located. *Deutschland* laid 120 mines in a meandering line offshore, at a depth of 3m, to catch the shallow draught steamers that worked on the route, then headed down the coast to Raumo. This was illuminated as if it was peacetime, making it easy to lay the last 80 mines, starting with a thick line across the northern approach. Heinrich's orders advised that the lightship in the southern approach should be sunk, after taking off the crew. As *Deutschland* neared it, two steamers arrived from the west. Rosenberg was sure that his minelaying had not been observed, so chose to pass by to avoid raising an alarm. The last few mines were laid at wide intervals in this approach. *Deutschland* left at high speed for the rendezvous with Behring and reached the Åland Sea next morning. Preparations made to disguise the ship as an armoured cruiser by erecting a dummy funnel and turret silhouettes forward and aft proved unnecessary. *Deutschland* passed the narrows into the Baltic without incident. On reaching Swedish territorial waters at Svenska Högarna after dark, Rosenberg wirelessed: 'Have completed task'. Behring was 15 miles to the south, with *Augsburg*, *Lübeck* and 20th Halbflottille, having left Danzig on the afternoon of the 5th. He relayed the message to Stockholm and Heinrich. Behring rendezvoused with *Deutschland* later that night and headed for his new base at Swinemünde. Once in safe waters, *Deutschland* detached to return to Kiel.

The consequences of the minelaying were almost immediate. On the morning of the 6th, the small Swedish steamer *Everilda* was approaching Mäntyluoto through rough seas, only hours after the mines had been laid. The first mate, Edvard Larsson, was on the bridge with the captain, C.E. Karlstrup:

> [He] took me by the arm, pointed straight out to starboard, and said: 'Take the binoculars and see if there isn't a mine floating there.' — 'Yes', I replied, 'it must be a drifting mine.' I immediately sent a man to the bow to look out, but I had barely given the order before we encountered an anchored mine, I don't think I'm exaggerating if I say that a quarter of the entire starboard side was destroyed with a thunderous blast, exactly at the bulkhead between the boiler room and the main hold. Everyone rushed to the boats, but before we could even hoist them out, *Everilda* listed about 45 degrees, and we were all thrown headlong into the water. She was going down, and it seemed like it took me forever to get to the surface again. That's when I was hit in the face and on my arms and legs by the large barrels of lime that were scattered on the surface.

Karlstrup, Larsson and four other survivors found themselves desperately clinging to flotsam in the icy water.

Luna, another Swedish steamer, was 6–7 miles away, outbound from Mäntyluoto to Sundsvall. She sighted an inbound steamer that suddenly heeled over. *Luna*'s captain, Adolf Landergren, immediately turned to render assistance, ordered full speed ahead and had the boats prepared for launch. In less than five minutes, the stern of the ship rose out of the water and she plunged to the bottom. *Luna* reached the scene and stopped in a field of floating deck cargo, from which desperate cries came. The crew later described the events:

> The lifeboats were launched and searched through the wreckage for the terrible screams. Four people were fished out by the starboard boat, all so badly injured that they immediately froze as soon as they came out of the water. The port boat rowed around for a while before two men were found on a piece of wreckage, who later turned out to be the captain and first mate … Only the captain was slightly conscious. …
>
> One by one the rescued were hoisted aboard *Luna*, after which they were carried down into the saloons and wrapped in blankets and quilts. They were unconscious by then.
>
> The four in the starboard boat had thankfully made it aboard *Luna*. [Then] *Everilda*'s captain had been taken up on deck and was about to be taken down, and they were just about to release the grip on the first mate's hands, which had convulsively closed around a knot in the port boat, when *Luna* was suddenly struck by a terrible explosion. A mine had exploded under *Luna*'s forepart, between the bow and the first cargo hatch, and its devastation was terrible. Both anchors flew up in the air, as did the bulwark and the deck hatches. … The engine crew came running up on deck in their light blouses. Immediately it became clear that *Luna*, despite her double bottom, was about to sink quickly. Everyone jumped into the boats, and those who had been rescued had to be left to their fate. A cook threw herself recklessly from the deck and ended up in a boat. As if by some miracle, she was not killed.

Landergren apparently hesitated to abandon the survivors: 'The last person I saw left on board *Luna* … was my colleague from *Everilda*. He was still lying on the deck with wildly opened, glassy eyes. I think he had lost his mind. It was my turn to leave the steamer, I went down a ladder, but found the boat [already] a good distance away, when the mate spotted me and rowed closer.' Only a couple of minutes after the first explosion:

> Captain Landergren had just taken his place in the lifeboat when a second mine exploded, this time below *Luna*. A cloud of smoke and steam enveloped the ship and before the lifeboats and their crew could get further than a couple of boat lengths away, *Luna* also sank into the depths and the unfortunates, who had already experienced a similar horror, drowned.

The salvage vessel *Assistans* and naval tugboat *Arkona* came out to tow the three lifeboats into harbour. They saw several mines at the surface. *Luna* had evidently drifted onto the mines in the strong wind blowing that morning whilst she was heaved to, but the second explosion may have been a boiler. Larsson had survived, but the other 17 crew of *Everilda* had been lost.

Rosenberg was wrong in believing that he had not aroused suspicion. A steamer was reported acting suspiciously off Raumo. The sinkings off Mäntyluoto suggested that this should be taken seriously. The port authorities immediately suspended all departures from Mäntyluoto and Raumo. Warnings were issued to all ports in the Gulf of Bothnia. That evening, a message arrived at the Mäntyluoto harbour office. All but two of the steamers bound for the two ports had turned back. The Swedish cargo and passenger steamer *Norra Sverige* was still expected next morning at Mäntyluoto. Fortunately, she had no passengers aboard; the *Västernorrland*

Left, *Norra Sverige*, centre, *Everilda*, bottom, *Luna* (*Hvar 8 Dag* 20 December 1914), right, *Everilda*'s only survivor, Edvard Larsson, soon after the sinking. (SM:SMK49424)

was also heading for Raumo. They were too far out for Swedish warships to reach in time and had no wireless. The Mäntyluoto harbour master went out next morning: 'At 4:50am I set off with 5 pilots in two motor boats towards the Säppi lighthouse … The weather was rainy, windy, with waves from the west-southwest… with the help of the pilots and lighthouse keepers, we began to keep an eye on the horizon. At 9:20am, the smoke of a steamer was spotted west of the lighthouse'. The harbour master ordered, 'the lighthouse keeper to start firing signal bombs to attract the steamer's attention, and I gave chase with the pilots in both motorboats towards the smoke.' The steamer came into sight: 'To attract attention to ourselves, we hoisted the pilot flag on the high mast of the boat, in the other motorboat we gave signals with the stern flag and fired shots with our guns. Ignoring us, the steamer continued its journey at full speed'. The motor boats fell behind:

> The steamer, which was recognised as *Norra Sverige*, apparently stopped its engines and hoisted the pilot flag … a little north of the place where the ships that had exploded the day before had sunk. I was … 1½ nautical miles from the steamer. … considering that we were on the edge of the mined area … I stopped the engines. Simultaneously, at 10:35am, an explosion was heard from the stern of *Norra Sverige* and a black column of smoke was visible. Two minutes later the steamer disappeared under the water, leaving nothing on the surface. After the explosion, I turned back to Säppi lighthouse.

The lethal nature of the mined area had evidently deterred any attempt to look for potential survivors, although a number of boats had come out from the harbour. The crew of 25 were all lost. It was a large crew for a small ship, due to the catering staff for the passenger restaurant. *Västernorrland* arrived safely at Raumo, missing the mines there by chance.

The mines had already sunk three Swedish steamers, totalling over 3,000 GRT, and cost the lives of 42 crew.[2] Essen reported to Fan-der-Flit that he was, 'sending minesweepers to locate the mine barriers, but it is difficult to say how successful this will be in the present stormy

2 *Everilda* (1882) 1,336 GRT, *Luna* (1905) 982 GRT, *Norra Sverige* (1875) 723 GRT.

weather.' This delayed departure, but meanwhile *Avrora* and *Diana* were despatched to survey a route suitable for the use of cruisers through the skerries, to exit into the Gulf of Bothnia east of Åland. *Minrep* and *Vzryv* were eventually able to depart through this route with *Grozyashchiy* as their depot. Kitkin was in command. On the 18th, they arrived in Raumo, sweeping the southern channel approach as they came in, finding no mines. On the 20th, Finnish shipping resumed trade from the port, although the northern channel where the suspicious vessel had been sighted remained closed.

Newspapers in Sweden initially attributed the losses to drifting Russian mines, although Landergren insisted to the journalist he spoke to, that the moored mines must have been carelessly laid by a German vessel. On 7 December, the German Naval Attaché in Stockholm advised Swedish shipping companies to suspend traffic with Finland. The German Ambassador informed Wallenberg that Germany had every right to lay mines off the enemy coast and had announced the intention to do so at ports where 'troops embarked and disembarked.' Exactly how this applied to undefended commercial ports such as Mäntyluoto and Raumo was debatable. There was no official admission of liability by Germany. The Swedes appear to have avoided making any official determinations of blame. Although some outrage was expressed initially in newspapers that no warning of the mining had been given, they highlighted a generous collection for bereaved relatives by German shipping companies, which, 'deeply regretted the serious damage caused by the sinking of the three Swedish steamers that hit mines in the Gulf of Bothnia. The participants feel even more deeply as it cannot be ruled out that German mines possibly caused the accident.' Mines had proved to be an effective, but less confrontational tool in disrupting commerce than direct action against Swedish vessels. Exploiting ambiguity about their origin could mollify outrage.

On the 18th Essen received intelligence that, 'there are several hostile light cruisers with the obvious task of intercepting Swedish steamships maintaining communications between Russian and Swedish ports [in the Gulf of Bothnia].' He ordered Kolomeytsev to take two cruisers through the skerries to patrol in the Gulf. Next day, Essen received a reply '... just before the intended departure time of the cruisers, [stating] that he was convinced of the operation's failure, and therefore could not take responsibility.' Essen finally had grounds to remove him: 'Since [Kolomeytsev] has previously shown a tendency to be unsuited to command, I consider it my moral duty ... to request the dismissal of the said Admiral ... and the appointment in his place of Kapitan 1st Ranga Bakhirev as acting commander of this brigade.' This was approved, and Bakhirev was soon promoted to Kontr-Admiral.[3] On the 23rd, *Admiral Makarov* and *Bayan* arrived in the Gulf of Bothnia. They patrolled until the 28th, but encountered no German forces, after which they remained in a support position at Lom in the skerries. Essen was frustrated at delays in sweeping. Although the weather was a major obstacle, it seems that reluctant pilots also played a part, which was solved by a cash grant. He also proposed to Fan-der-Flit, that laying a minefield in the narrow open sea passage giving access was the only way to protect the Gulf of Bothnia. He suggested entering into an agreement with Sweden to do so, as the western side lay in their territorial waters. Sweden refused.

On the 26th, *General Kondratenko* arrived to support the sweepers, as a rock had holed *Grozyashchiy*. Next day, they cleared a route out of Mäntyluoto, followed by the destroyer,

3 In September 1915, Kolomeytsev was given command of an inland lake steamer flotilla, well out of harm's way.

whose navigator charted the resulting channel. With goods piling up in the ports, Swedish shipping companies decided to resume sailings to Raumo on 29 December via the channel already back in use. However, the departing vessels returned 'after receiving information from official German sources, [that] the entire Finnish coast is now mined.' That day the sweepers worked with *General Kondratenko* in heavy seas to clear and buoy a channel through the mines in the northern channel at Raumo. It was tough work, with the buoys and weights pounding against the sides of the sweepers, and the crew, drenched by freezing waves, straining for all they were worth to control the mine trawls in heavy seas, rolling up to 40 degrees. They had tried to pick up a mine to prove its German origin, but the only one they dragged clear exploded when it hit a buoy. The weather moderated on the 31st. The sweepers completed work on the north channel and confirmed that there were no mines in the south channel. As the last mines laid were as much as 360m apart, it is likely that there were undetected mines close by. Another encounter with a rock holed *General Kondratenko,* and the minesweepers were in need of repairs after their battering by the sea. On 4 January, the force returned to Helsingfors, leaving local boats to finish marking out the channels. That day, the Russian Embassy in Stockholm announced that Mäntyluoto and Raumo were fully open. All vessels were directed to a position offshore, where a pilot would take them to the relevant port along safe routes. Trade slowly resumed, but: 'The Svea shipping company announces that steamer voyages to Finland will not resume until further notice, as the entire Finnish coast around the Gulf of Bothnia is considered to be infested with mines.' Svea had been particularly hard hit, losing both *Luna* and *Norra Sverige.*

The minefields were still there. On 15 January, the small Swedish steamer *Åhus* left Mäntyluoto, heading down the coast to Raumo to pick up a cargo. The ship, nine crew and two pilots failed to arrive. The weather on the 16th was atrocious. Damage from drifting ice was feared, but a search found nothing. Inevitably, mines dragged out of position or broke free of their moorings and drifted. The wreck was found in 2004, in 30m of water off Raumo. The damage is consistent with striking a mine.[4] The mines struck again on 21 January. The Swedish steamers *Drott* and *Birgit* had sailed in company for Raumo from Stockholm the day before. They had been warned of floating mines and had their lifeboats already swung out as a precaution. They arrived at the designated position to pick up their pilot, around 20 miles west of Raumo. Next morning no pilot boat showed up. They got underway once the shore was visible. Captain Sjösten was on the bridge of *Birgit*, following within hailing distance astern of *Drott*:

> [I] heard a loud bang and saw the bow of *Drott* explode into the air. The force of the mine was so severe that the ship's deck hatches and the lifeboats hanging on the side of the bow, as well as the ship's mast and rough timber, flew into the air in fragments. At the same time, a number of iron plates and engine parts that were cargo flew into the air. … The prow of the ship sank directly to the seabed and the crew of *Birgit* saw the *Drott*'s propeller rise up spinning in the air.

An off duty stoker on *Drott* was resting in his bed:

4 *Åhus* (1890) 341 GRT. A rumour that two Finnish skippers had sighted her striking a mine off Raumo on the 17th was reported weeks later in February. The skippers later denied the report, saying that their story about a ship blowing off steam in the area had been subjected to journalistic embellishment.

> When the impact happened, the deck lurched, throwing him up against the upper bunk and he fell to the floor. By then the room was already full of water and he floated upwards. Fortunately, the water lifted him to a topside passage, from which he was able to escape the room …he had badly injured his hands and face. … When the stoker had reached the deck of the ship, the others had already untied the ship's two [aft] lifeboats and most of them had jumped into the sea. Another stoker had remained in the engine room, where he had presumably died when the ship's second boiler exploded, which happened about a minute after hitting the mine.
>
> When the stoker had jumped from the deck into the lifeboat, which was already full of water and was already carrying about a dozen people, he saw a log in the distance and then jumped out of the boat and swam towards it. At that moment, the said lifeboat capsized and everyone in it fell into the water. However, four men and one woman managed to get to the keel of the capsized boat, from which they were then rescued.

Drott had sunk in less than 2½ minutes.[5] The other lifeboat had remained afloat. *Birgit*'s own boats quickly rescued as many of those in the water as they could, but five of the 18 crew drowned, including the captain, N.J. Smith and one of the caterers from the restaurant, Mrs. L. Stenkvist. The sinking was put down to an unlucky encounter with a drifting mine. Trade continued, but by the end of January sea ice was becoming too thick for the steamer traffic and trade came to a halt until the spring thaw. The ice destroyed the shallow minefields far more effectively than any minesweeper could. They caused no further problems, but had sunk over 5,000 GRT of Swedish merchant tonnage and cost nearly 60 lives. Trade in the Gulf had been disrupted for an entire month.[6]

Disastrous weather in the Gulf of Finland

The last Russian minelaying sortie had highlighted the need for *Ryurik* to receive a permanent repair to the damage received in August. The temporary repair left much of the fresh water storage unusable, making extended operations from base problematic. On 21 November, she went into dock. The next day, *Sevastopol'* finally joined the fleet at Sveaborg. A spell of atrocious weather now gripped the Gulf of Finland. By 29 November, a southwesterly was blowing at storm force. Essen had to move the battleships from the exposed anchorage at Sveaborg to shelter at the undefended anchorage on the opposite side of the Gulf, Paponvik Bay. Essen complained to Fan-der-Flit about delays in work to widen the channel into the sheltered, protected, inner Sveaborg anchorage. The new dreadnoughts could not enter at all and it 'constituted a major obstacle to the rapid exit of battleships to sea in case of need.' His hard worked destroyers on the patrol line in the Gulf of Finland had also taken a beating in recent weather. Essen set out new arrangements for the patrol, using vessels better adapted for harsh weather:

5 *Drott* (1900) 1,760 GRT.

6 BA:RM99 *Deutschland* KTB; Firle, *Ostsee*, pp.184–187, 215–217, 252–261; Anon, *The American Journal of International Law, Vol. 10, 1916* (New York: Cambridge University Press, 1916), pp. 916–921; *Dagens Nyheter*, Stockholm, 7–9, 16, 19, 30–31 December 1914, 4, 23, 29 January 1915; *Uusi Suometer*, Helsinki, 11 December 1914, 24 January 1915; *Hufvudstadsbladet*, Helsinki, 8, 12, 19 February 1915, Hamburger Fremdenblatt, 6 January 1915; Киреев, *Траление*, pp.48–52; РГАВМФ:Фонд 716, Опись 2, Дело 13, pp.201–203, 347–8, Дело 8, pp.215, 234.

> The present stormy and cold period makes it necessary to remove from patrol duty destroyers that require major or less extensive refits after intensive activity. For patrol duty in the western part of the Gulf [of Finland] in winter, I propose to assign steamers from the 2nd Partiya Traleniya, which are now being armed with 75mm guns and supplied with a wireless. Due to the slow speed of these ships, the patrol line will have to be moved inside the Gulf to the meridian of Odenskhol'm Island, leaving observation of the entrance to the Gulf only from coastal posts.

The minesweeping steamers had been recalled to Revel' on 28 November to be fitted out for their new duties. Repairs to *Ryurik* completed on the 30th. The weather finally abated somewhat and the battleships returned to Sveaborg on 2 December. With another dark moon period imminent, Essen's thoughts turned to further minelaying missions. Essen wanted to extend their range. Lacking fast minelayers, the solution was to use cruisers not just as escorts, but to lay the mines. He issued orders for minelaying rails and dropping gear to be urgently added to the decks of *Ryurik*, *Admiral Makarov*, *Bayan*, *Bogatyr'* and *Oleg*, later extended to *Rossiya*. Whilst the cruisers prepared for this new minelaying role, and the minelayers fitted out for patrol duties, the destroyers would have to keep working.

A new development was that the army had begun to take an interest in Libava. Parts of XIII Army Corps were now based there. On 1 December, Essen received new orders from Yanushkevich at STAVKA: 'To prevent bombardment of Libava it is necessary to place mine barriers in the sea at the points from which bombardment can be carried out. This measure is intended to ensure the safety of the troops'. Essen ordered Forsel' to complete a survey of the German minefield using the small boats in the port, to ensure that new mines could be safely laid. The eight small destroyers of 4th Divizion, which could only carry 10 mines each, were selected for the mission. On the 8th, they loaded their mines at the warehouses in Helsingfors. On the previous day, Essen also summoned Paletskiy, ordering him to prepare *Novik* to lay another minefield in the Bay of Danzig as soon as the weather was suitable. The 50 mines were loaded and prepared in Revel'. The destroyers then waited for a suitable break in the weather.

The days passed and the wind blew, keeping both destroyers and the Libava survey boats in port. On the 11th, it took a turn for the worse, swinging northwest, bringing an Arctic chill. Essen was becoming impatient. He issued orders for *Novik* and 4th Divizion to depart on the 12th. The latter were to hold at Moon Sound and proceed as soon as the survey at Libava was complete. Paletskiy queried the order, as the forecast was for a storm. There was a curt reply from Kerber: 'The observatory's predictions are favourable, go.' Paletskiy left Revel' at 4am. Graf writes:

> Although the weather was very breezy, we hardly rolled at all, thanks to a following wind. We … entered the Gulf of Riga. There the commander decided to test the strength of the roll on the courses on which we were to lay mines… *Novik* immediately began to roll violently, and when we turned broadside to the waves, she began to lay right over on her sides. The topmast immediately broke, the wireless net tore away, and the waves continually broke over the bridge. It became clear that there was no point in going any further that day, and we returned to Moon Sound.

4th Divizion on exercise, loaded with mines. This class of 11 destroyers carried 7.5cm guns fore and aft and 2x45cm torpedo tubes firing to either side. Rails for 10 mines, speed 26 knots. (Public domain)

The impact of the weather on *Novik* had been bad, but for the small destroyers of 4th Divizion it was worse. Six destroyers passed through the sheltered Finnish skerries from Helsingfors, emerging off Veksher Roads. They split into three pairs to head southwest across the Gulf to Moon Sound. Radiotelegrafist S. Lukashevich was in the first pair on *Lovkiy,* with *Moshchnyy*:

> Early in the morning of December 12, I transferred from *Vsadnik* to *Lovkiy* in Helsingfors to reinforce their wireless watch. My shipmate S. Doroshenko also transferred to *Letuchiy.*[7] … The Divizion commander [Kapitan 1st Ranga Leonid Ivanov] flew his pennant on *Lovkiy.* Whilst we were sailing through the skerries, we rolled comparatively little, but as soon as the overloaded and unstable destroyers left the Jussarö lighthouse [off the entrance to Veksher Roads], we began to roll violently and icy spray deluged us from the angry, stormy sea. The list reached over 30 degrees, and water [thrown up] from the bowsprit spar got into the first and second funnels, flooding the boiler room.
>
> The day was clear and visibility good. The wind moaned piercingly in the destroyer's rigging, and the topmasts of the destroyers, following in each other's wake, were sometimes hidden in the vast swells of water. Many of the crew suffered from the rolling, but everyone was in their place at action stations. The area of the Gulf of Finland, which we were crossing, was very often visited by German submarines, and therefore we had a speed of about 17 knots, keeping a distance of about 40–50 cables [four to five miles between each pair].

The next pair astern was *Ispolnitel'nyy*, Kapitan 2nd Ranga Edgar Dombrovskiy, and *Letuchiy*, Kapitan 2nd Ranga Lev Sakhnovskiy. The third pair was *Legkiy* and *Metkiy*. The meteorological office signalled the weather at that time: 'Northeast wind force 8, sea state 6.' The destroyers were ploughing through waves of 4 to 6m height, in bitingly cold gale force winds of up to 40 knots, driving freezing sea spray, steering a course across the swell from a following wind that increased constantly as they got farther from shore. Lukashevich continues:

> I had been in the forward crew quarters for about an hour, when several voices were heard through the hatch – '*Ispolnitel'nyy* has exploded!' Running quickly up the ladder to the upper deck, I saw the following picture.
>
> *Ispolnitel'nyy* was still floating capsized on the water; various wooden objects were floating around the sinking ship, and the crew, drowning and freezing in the icy water, was seeking salvation on them. On the keel loomed the figure of a sailor, manoeuvring along the red bottom and clapping his mittens. It was the stoker Besenkov, who was soon washed away by an oncoming wave.[8]
>
> At 12:56pm, *Letuchiy* made an unencrypted transmission on the wireless: '[To] destroyer *Lovkiy. Ispolnitel'nyy* was destroyed. Seven crew were saved." And four minutes later: 'Cause unknown. There was no explosion.'

7 Radiotelegrafist Sergey Doroshenkov per archive records.

8 Some of this detail must have been obtained later from *Ispolnitel'nyy*'s helmsman. The crewman is probably Mashinist 2nd Stat'i Dmitriy Bizhunov.

> Assuming that the destroyers were attacked by enemy [submarine] boats, the gunners, on the orders of the commander, rushed to the 75mm guns, since some of the crew, succumbing to panic, mistook floating objects for a periscope.
>
> However, the guns could no longer fire. They were frozen to their mounts from the muzzle to the breech, together with the trunnions, swivel and pedestal, as solid ice had formed on the gun platforms …

The evidence is contradictory about whether there was an initial explosion on *Ispolnitel'nyy*. Ivanov himself had not observed the incident. The commander of *Legkiy*, Kapitan 2nd Ranga Pavel Vil'ken, reported on arrival at Moon Sound that, 'on *Ispolnitel'nyy*, which was steering five miles ahead, an explosion with flame, smoke and a column of water was visible at 12.45pm. After one minute *Ispolnitel'nyy* sank. At 1pm, *Legkiy* and *Metkiy* approached the site of the sinking; together with *Letuchiy*, they rescued eight lower ranks. *Letuchiy* picked up seven [of these] and proceeded to its destination.' Meanwhile, *Lovkiy* and *Moshchnyy* had turned back. Lukashevich continues:

> When we approached the place where *Ispolnitel'nyy* sank at 20 cables [2 miles], *Letuchiy*, which was circling the spot, suddenly dove into the water with its bow in an unnatural way, and the stern collapsed up to the funnel, as if chopped off by a mighty swing of a giant axe. Everything was covered in black smoke and coal dust. None of us heard an explosion.
>
> The Divizion commander transmitted on the radio: 'move the destroyers away from the place where *Letuchiy* sank and do not approach it.' It was terrible to look at the perishing people and their desperate struggle with the enraged elements. They all hoped that we would save them, but the propellers began to boil, cutting through the leaden waters, and our flagship was the first to move away from the scene of the drama. *Letuchiy* sank, having stayed afloat for no more than 3 minutes. The signalman continued to signal something until the command bridge, where he was, began to sink into the water.
>
> For a long time we could see lone sailors on the crests of the waves, holding on to the fragments of the masts, planks and wooden gratings and fighting for their lives. They all died, with the exception of helmsman Karpov from *Ispolnitel'nyy*, who [had been rescued earlier when he] swam up to *Legkiy*, which saved him.[9] He had been in the water in the hellish cold for about 20 minutes…
>
> The division proceeded individually in zigzags. Soon the surviving six destroyers … entered Moon Sound.[10] On December 20, I returned to *Vsadnik*, but without my comrade, Radiotelegrafist Doroshenko.

Vil'ken reported, 'At 1.45pm *Letuchiy* was at a distance of 25 cables [2½ miles] from *Legkiy* and sank within 30 seconds. An explosion was not evident.' He assumed a submarine was responsible. Ivanov reported that, 'near the site of the sinking, I saw the moving conning tower of a submarine on the surface, which quickly disappeared from view.' He blamed the heavy seas for the lack of a rescue attempt. Ivanov reported the position of both sinkings in the middle of the

9 Name given as Vyadkazanov in signal by Ivanov.
10 Actually only four, as the final pair turned back much earlier. *Likhoy* had damaged the port propeller, docking at Helsingfors for repairs. Her partner, *Kryepkiy*, then went to Revel'.

Gulf, with the second six miles southwest of the first. The disaster cost the lives of 69 crew from *Letuchiy* and 72 from *Ispolnitel'nyy*.

Both Ivanov and Vil'ken jumped to the conclusion that a submarine had sunk the two destroyers in quick succession. Once in mind, the phenomenon of seeing the expected, in the form of conning towers and periscopes, gripped the crews. This seems to have motivated Ivanov to order his destroyers to leave. There had been a recent submarine sighting by destroyer patrols nearby. On December 7, *Vnushitel'nyy* reported an attack by an enemy submarine, seen diving two miles away. The report was false. There were also no submarines nearby on the 12th. It should have been obvious that an attack would have been almost impossible in the prevailing conditions. Nevertheless, Essen reported submarine attack as the probable cause: 'There is an assumption that *Letuchiy*, having sighted the submarine, tried to ram it and during the impact received such damage to the hull, that it sank itself.' He thought covert minelaying could also be to blame, but subsequent sweeping revealed nothing, effectively ruling this out. Neither Essen, nor Ivanov's reports mention the icing or flooding noted by Lukashevich. The *Lovkiy* class were top heavy and overloaded, especially after upgrade to 7.5cm guns. The mines on deck exacerbated this. The design featured a free draining, raised working deck, above the rounded hull. There were innumerable places for sea ice to collect both above and in inaccessible places below this deck. The extra weight, high above the waterline, was the final straw, making the small vessels critically unstable. This was almost certainly the cause of the loss of both destroyers. A mine may have exploded on *Ispolnitel'nyy* having broken loose, but it could have done so as the vessel was capsizing.[11] It had been imprudent to take these destroyers across the Gulf in the prevailing conditions, based on a false sense of urgency. It led to disaster, with plenty of blame to go round. Submarine attack was a convenient scapegoat.

Ivanov's destroyers and *Novik* sheltered off Vorms to weather a blizzard on the 13th. Next day, *Novik* returned to Revel' for repair with the only survivor of *Ispolnitel'nyy*. After a collision whilst being manoeuvred by tugs, her repairs put her out of action for two weeks. The weather continued to prevent surveying at Libava, so destroyer minelaying was deferred, and 50 mines were sent by rail. Forsel' was instructed to improvise laying these in the immediate approaches to the port using the small boats available, Essen later reporting, '... by December 17, minesweeping work had revealed the position of many lines of [German] mines, and then the port authorities began laying the mines sent by rail. The work of laying completed on December 27 ... placed in the most favourable places for bombarding Libava. Thus, the approaches to Libava are very difficult due to a continuous chain of enemy and our own mine barriers.' Ironically, Al'tfater had suggested this approach when Yanushkevich's orders were received. Essen reminded his superiors that should the Germans choose to sweep the mines, his orders prevented him from doing anything about it, making their protection somewhat illusory. On the 30th Essen reported that he would need to curtail destroyer activity drastically:

> The sending of destroyers now, to supplement the mine barriers laid, is made difficult by stormy weather and low temperatures, which cover the mines and their sinkers in a thick

11 The wreck of *Ispolnitel'nyy* was found in 2014, and *Letuchiy* two years later. Both are upright. The former is in poor condition. The visible parts of the latter are largely intact, with the hull poking up out of the sediment and the aft section buried.

> crust of ice. With the appearance of ice in Moon Sound, it will be necessary to abandon all departures of destroyers to the Baltic Sea south of Vindava.
>
> In addition, the constant heavy service of the destroyers has affected the condition of their engines and boilers, which require serious repair.
>
> In the coming days, considerations for the repair and completion of destroyers for combat activities in the spring should have paramount importance and therefore from the middle of January to the end of February only two groups (eight destroyers) will be at full readiness.

The minesweeping steamers would take up the slack on the patrol line. It would be down to the cruisers to keep up offensive activity in the Baltic.[12]

Essen's fight for resources and the third phase of the mine offensive

Essen had quickly suspected that *Friedrich Carl* had hit a Russian mine in November, but had no proof that his offensive was paying off. That day, several signals were intercepted and de-cyphered. *Friedrich Carl* transmitted one group in particular, repeated several times by other cruisers, 'tqf'. The *Magdeburg* signal book confirmed the meaning: 'Require immediate assistance'. The associated German map square corresponded with the minefield laid by the Poludivizion off Memel. Essen shared his conclusions off the record with Al'tfater, '...despite my request to include it in the report, [he] did not want to do this out of his modesty ... it could only be done when some kind of announcement was received from the Germans'. Despite Essen asking Al'tfater to: '... not tell anyone about this', on 24 November, he informed his opposite number at STAVKA, Kontr-Admiral Aleksandr Bubnov. Essen perhaps anticipated this unofficial leak. He needed all the help he could get to secure his supply of mines.

The initiative for the mine offensive had come from Essen. So far, his superiors had gone along with it. However, he was now deeply alarmed about his mine supply. Russia had declared war on the Ottoman Empire following a surprise naval attack on ports in the Black Sea on October 29. The Russian Fleet there significantly outnumbered the opposing German-Ottoman fleet. Nevertheless, their commander, Vitse-Admiral Andrey Ebergard, sent a telegram to the Naval Ministry on 11 November: 'In view of the rapid freezing of the Baltic Sea, I consider it necessary to transfer to the Black Sea everything possible to strengthen the Black Sea fleet, for example – submarines, guns, torpedoes, mines, machine tools, shells.' Al'tfater sought help from Bubnov to ensure that the request was refused at STAVKA: 'As you can see, the telegram is of such a nature that if it were possible to transport dreadnoughts by rail, then Ebergard would probably have asked for them to be sent to him urgently.' Yanushkevich ordered the transfer of 500 old pattern reserve mines to the Black Sea, on condition of replacement by spring with an equal number of new mines. Then, without any consultation, on 13 November STAVKA

12 РГАВМФ:Фонд 716, Опись 2, Дело 13, p.83, 121–126, 201–203, 279, 282, 347 and Дело24, pp.114, 123–127; С. Лукашевич, 'Гибель миноносцев „Летучий" и „Исполнительный" (Из воспоминаний о мировой войне на Балтморе)', *Морской Сборник № 8* (1934), pp.176–178; В. Блытов and О. Блытова, «Ветреные француженки» на службе России, < https://voenflot.ru/pomni/gibel-eskadrennogo-minonostsa-ohotnik>, retrieved 6 April 2025; Графъ, *Новикъ*, pp.46–50; Badewanne, *Ispolnitel'nyy* and *Letuchiy* <http://badewanne.fi>, retrieved 6 April 2025.

directed that all mine production should now go to the Black Sea. The ensuing correspondence demonstrated the fundamental lack of understanding that the Generals at STAVKA had of war at sea. When Essen became aware of the decision, he spelled out the consequences in his report of 27 November:

> [This decision] has caused me concern regarding replenishment of the required stock of mines by the spring of next year. The need for minefields in the present war at sea is extraordinary, since the enemy reduces almost all of his operations to laying minefields and working with submarines. Our main war plan, in view of the weakness of the fleet, is based, in part, on protecting the Gulf of Finland and the approaches to the capital, with a vast minefield, protected by all available means of the fleet. It is very difficult to say what state this field will be in by spring after the ice in the Gulf of Finland has cleared, but it is possible that some of the mines will be damaged and there will be a need to renew sections of the field and strengthen it.
>
> The possibility of Sweden's participation in the war may in the future create a need for new barriers in the area of the Åbo and Åland skerries, as well as off the coast of Sweden and in the Gulf of Bothnia.
>
> All this makes it necessary to use every effort towards the fastest possible production of mines and ensure their supply to the Baltic Fleet during the coming winter. I believe that before the opening of renewed navigation it is necessary to obtain 3,000 new mines and to continue their further production as intensively as possible.

Essen was relieved to receive an intelligence report from the Naval General Staff on 6 December: 'Via a person who has been transmitting reliable information… On 12 or 13 November, *Friedrich Carl* was destroyed in a minefield, with two-thirds of the crew killed.' He took the opportunity to report his own evidence and conclusions, 'to speak with confidence about the destruction of … *Friedrich Carl* on the mine barrier placed by the Poludivizion.' News of the sinking leaked to the press through the French Navy Ministry in Paris on the 12th. A Russian communiqué announced it on the 17th: 'The German first class armoured cruiser *Friedrich Carl* has sunk during her last voyage in the Baltic Sea. Two-thirds of the crew perished. About two hundred men were saved.' At last, Essen had confirmation of a major success for the mine offensive. Nevertheless, repeated appeals failed to resolve the mine allocations, so he raised it again in his report on 27 December to Fan-der-Flit:

> The forces of our enemy in the Baltic Sea exceed our forces by five times, whilst in the Black Sea our fleet has some advantage over the Turkish-German fleet. Finally, the climatic conditions of the Gulf of Finland force me to supplement the central barrier in early spring; it will suffer greatly from floating ice, which will not happen in the Black Sea. … under the given conditions, it is necessary that the needs of the Baltic Sea be satisfied first of all – needs that are caused by the threatening situation.

Essen's arguments finally succeeded. On 31 December, Yanushkevich amended STAVKA instructions to ensure, 'the distribution of replenishment mine stocks in both seas, with the aim of uniformly bringing them up to the requested standards [by Spring 1915].'

Meanwhile, Essen's next minelaying operation was the most ambitious yet. The aim was to lay four new minefields in, 'the approaches to Pillau, Danzig and Rixhöft and on probable routes north from Danzig into our waters.' Kerber would hoist his flag on *Ryurik* to lead it. Essen moved his staff to *Rossiya* to free his former flagship permanently for minelaying operations. If he went to sea for fleet operations, he would shift his flag and immediate staff to *Sevastopol'*.

Essen again used British submarines to deter German forces from putting to sea during the operation. On the 10th, they received their orders from him in Helsingfors. Laurence wrote that, 'I was told that two German armoured cruisers had been seen at anchor in Tromper Wiek and Prorer Wiek [bays on Rügen] also that a German gun boat patrolled the line Stevns Klint–Falsterbo and a light cruiser patrolled off Moens [Møns] Klint. A spin of the coin decided that *E.9* should look for the armoured cruisers and *E.1* for the gun boat and light cruiser.' The British submarines were to, 'attack any enemy's vessels that were seen. On 14th December if no attack had been made they were to show themselves to the coast lookout stations, so that the enemy should know of their presence.' The Russian spy network was providing accurate information about German patrols, but these were highly visible. However, the Rügen information was bogus. *Undine* had briefly anchored off Sassnitz on 27 November after escorting an icebreaker there, no doubt the source of the report, but this was a one off. The submarines departed next morning, through the skerries. The British were getting their first taste of the bitter Baltic winter. Merkushov saw the boats pass Veksher: 'due to the slight frost their sides were covered with icicles.' Laurence and Horton headed out to sea at Lappvik.

At 7am on the 13th, *E.1* arrived as planned off Stevns Klint to find nothing in sight. Laurence headed south towards Møns Klint. At 1.35pm:

> [I] sighted enemy's destroyer and dived to attack. The enemy was making large alterations of course but I succeeded in obtaining a position 600 yards [550m] on his beam, when I fired one torpedo, more with a view to letting him know of the submarines presence than with any hope of hitting. The torpedo missed. The destroyer remained in the vicinity for about half an hour, steaming at a high speed evidently hoping for an opportunity to ram.

Gazelle had been on patrol and had passed the spot a few hours earlier, noting, 'Cloudy weather … Rough seas and swell … Light rain showers.' The attack went unreported by the four patrolling destroyers of 7th Halbflottille, the prevailing weather conditions no doubt contributing. Laurence later dodged a small cargo steamer, which he wrongly concluded was towing an explosive anti-submarine sweep. When *E.1* surfaced to charge that night, the port propeller shaft fractured: 'As it was 400 miles to the nearest available Russian port and I had accomplished my purpose in letting the enemy know of our presence, I decided to proceed forthwith to Lapvick [*sic*].' In fact, for the second mission in a row, Laurence had gone unnoticed on his billet.

Horton's *E.9* found nothing except commercial vessels in the bays off Rügen on the 13th. He saw a destroyer later off Arkona, but too far away to attack. That evening: 'While charging port propeller blade carried away … vibration of steering shaft and worm was serious. Decided to proceed to patrol line West of Gotland.' Horton aimed to join *Akula* here, covering the minelaying against any attempt to cut it off via this route. The British submarine operation had so far been a washout.

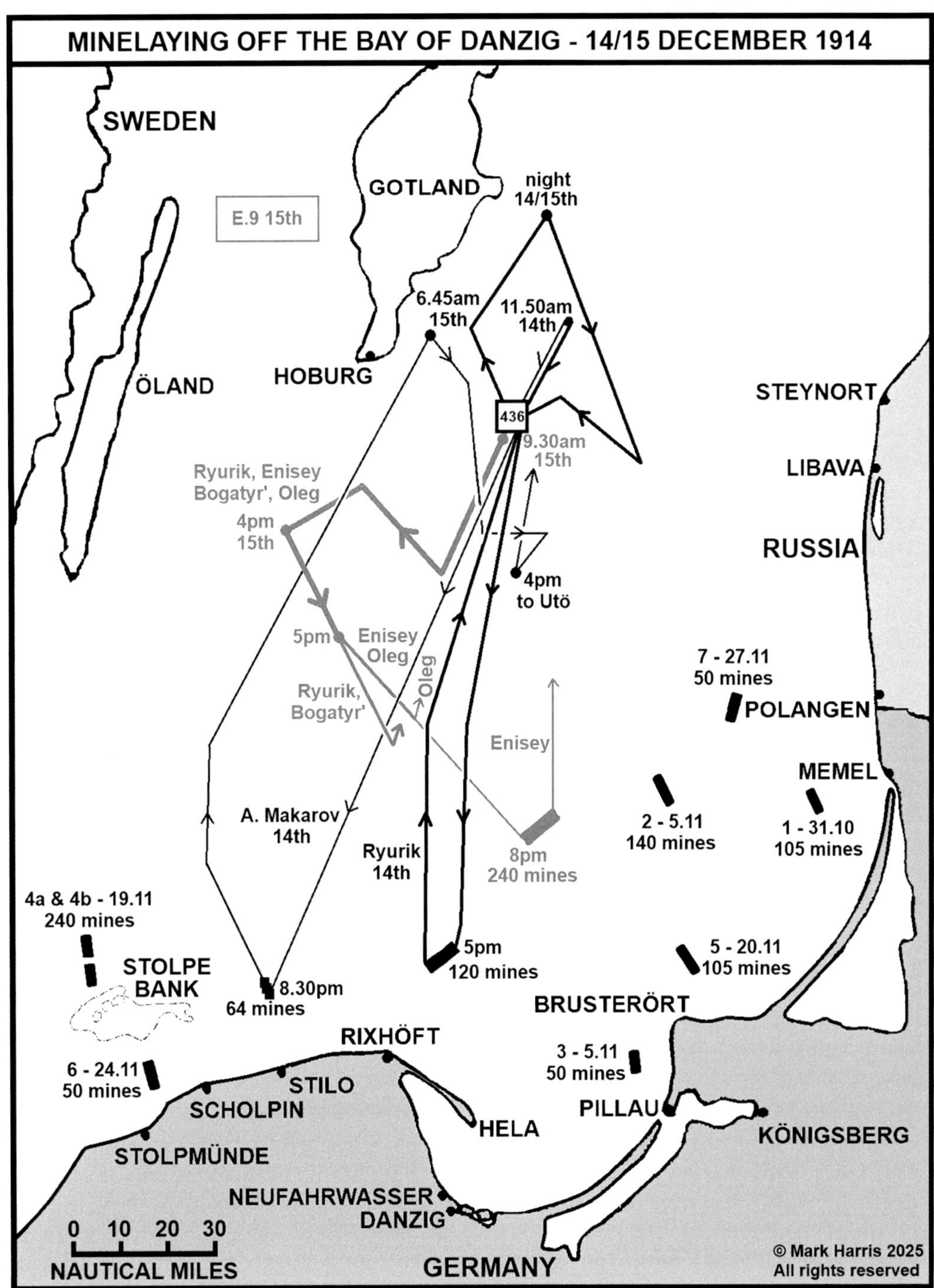
MINELAYING OFF THE BAY OF DANZIG - 14/15 DECEMBER 1914
SWEDEN
GOTLAND
E.9 15th
night 14/15th
ÖLAND
HOBURG
6.45am 15th
11.50am 14th
436
9.30am 15th
STEYNORT
LIBAVA
RUSSIA
Ryurik, Enisey Bogatyr', Oleg
4pm 15th
4pm to Utö
5pm
Enisey Oleg
Ryurik, Bogatyr'
Oleg
Enisey
7 - 27.11 50 mines
POLANGEN
MEMEL
A. Makarov 14th
Ryurik 14th
8pm 240 mines
2 - 5.11 140 mines
1 - 31.10 105 mines
4a & 4b - 19.11 240 mines
STOLPE BANK
8.30pm 64 mines
5pm 120 mines
5 - 20.11 105 mines
BRUSTERÖRT
RIXHÖFT
3 - 5.11 50 mines
6 - 24.11 50 mines
STILO
SCHOLPIN
HELA
PILLAU
KÖNIGSBERG
STOLPMÜNDE
NEUFAHRWASSER
DANZIG
0 10 20 30
NAUTICAL MILES
GERMANY
© Mark Harris 2025
All rights reserved

The minelaying force consisted of two groups. The first, with the furthest to travel, consisted of *Ryurik*, *Admiral Makarov* and *Bayan*. It was concentrated at Paponvik. *Ryurik* already had 120 mines loaded, the other two were to take 80 mines each from the auxiliary *Il'men'*. *Enisey*, *Amur*'s sister ship, would lay another 240 mines. She had been joined at Utö by *Bogatyr'* and *Oleg*, which would escort her. *Akula* would leave Utö for the covering position between Öland and Gotland. The two minelaying groups were to rendezvous in 'Square 436' off Gotland at 8am next morning. From there they would leave to lay their mines, first the three cruisers, then *Enisey* and her escorts. Early versions of the plan had the cruisers bombarding the German coast after laying their mines, but Essen decided against this, in favour of operational secrecy. The plan was to lay the most distant minefield no later than 2am. Even if the Germans detected the force approaching, they could return to the Gulf of Finland before dawn.

The weather that sank *Ispolnitel'nyy* and *Letuchiy* played havoc with the plans. It prevented the minesweepers from sweeping the exit channels. The force was due to sail on the 13th or 14th, after the British submarines arrived at their billets. A submarine or mines were suspected of involvement in the sinking of the destroyers, and *Bobr* had reported a submarine off Surop, although a search had found nothing. Kerber received the latest intelligence from Rusin: 'Early in the morning of 12 December in Kiel were: five dreadnoughts, six large warships, several small ones, 21 destroyers. All ships are taking on supplies. There are three submarines at the barrier. In Kiel, actions of the German fleet in the Baltic Sea are expected in the period from 12 to 15 December. In Kiel, special precautions have been taken for this period.' Despite the risks of atrocious weather, mines and submarines, Kerber decided that it was vital to get the minefields in place before the German fleet mustering at Kiel could reach the eastern Baltic.

The weather had prevented mine loading at Paponvik, and the gale was still blowing. However, in a lucky break, the wind shifted to southeast. Paponvik Bay offered shelter in this direction. Kerber confirmed departure of *Ryurik*'s group for noon on the 13th. This was later than planned, but would allow time for mines to be loaded. The force would still pass Surop after dark. He ordered *Bayan*, then *Admiral Makarov*, to load as many mines as possible before departure. Whilst this was underway, Kerber briefed his captains. More intelligence had come in, passed on by Volkov from the British Admiralty: 'Have information that the enemy is sending troops on transports and two cruisers to Danzig and Königsberg from western ports.' *Admiral Makarov* had only loaded 64 mines before time ran out. A blizzard now descended, but given the urgency of the tactical situation, Kerber proceeded, heading out at 16 knots. This made up for late departure and was a harder target for submarines. The cruisers stuck to the route used a couple of days earlier by *Bogatyr'* and *Oleg*, to reduce any risk of hitting mines. Kerber declined a suggestion by Essen that the auxiliary steamer *Mitava* precede his cruisers, as this would have reduced speed to 14 knots. The steamer would have acted as a barrier breaker, sacrificially hitting any mines in the path of the cruisers.

Kerber now received bad news from Utö. The blizzard and heavy swell prevented *Akula* and *Enisey* from leaving the harbour. The nearby *Kayman* had dragged her moorings and ended up on the rocks, but was recovered undamaged next day. Kerber was undeterred and ordered the Utö group to delay departure to the 14th. In the meantime, his group would go ahead and lay their mines, then return to the rendezvous to meet them. Worse followed. During the night, *Bayan* fell behind. Veys writes: 'The next morning the senior engineer came to me and reported that there was not enough coal for the voyage … The engineer was to blame for not calculating and receiving the coal [required] on the upper deck, but I was also to blame as the ship's commander, responsible for all mistakes on it. I had to inform [Kerber] and commenced the return journey.' This was a serious mistake. The round trip was around 1,100 miles. The high speed would have reduced the range of *Bayan* to less than 2,000 miles, but if the bunkers had been full, there would have still been a comfortable margin. It was evidently an uncharacteristic error: 'When I had to see Admiral N.O. Essen for the first time after this incident, he sympathetically regretted that I had not managed to lay mines.'

The plan had been for the three cruisers to keep in formation, taking turns to lay their mines. However, contingency plans and routes for splitting up were also in place. The mines on *Ryurik* were of the older 1909 pattern. They were dangerous to handle in complete darkness. Kerber decided that splitting up to lay *Ryurik*'s mines in the last light of dusk was a better balance of risk. At 11:50am, he notified Plen on *Admiral Makarov* and then pulled away at 18 knots.

The weather settled as the ships went south. The gloomy sky helped conceal the cruisers, with visibility of only four to six miles. *Ryurik* reached her target area near Rixhöft at 5pm, in the dwindling twilight. She slowed to six knots and headed inshore, laying her mines in six separate groups, making a barrier 5½ miles long. *Admiral Makarov* arrived at her destination north of Stilo in pitch darkness at 8:30pm. She laid the mines in three groups over 2½ miles, dodging to port between the laying of each group to make sweeping harder. The sea had been largely empty, just distant smoke by day and two steamer's lights during the night. That night the weather deteriorated and heavy rain set in. *Admiral Makarov* closed the shore near Hoburg lighthouse on Gotland. Her dead reckoning was spot on, confirming that the mines were exactly where intended, despite a long run with no position fixes.

At 3:35am on the 15th, Nepenin issued an alarming general signal based on directional wireless intercepts: 'The enemy was making signals by wireless at 12:45am squares 67, 68, 76, 77, 85, 86 call signs TU DU DV GU.' These squares were off the Gulf of Finland and just to the south of it. The call signs related to the powerful German dreadnought battleships *Markgraf* and *Kaiser*, *Gazelle* and an unidentified light cruiser. Coupled with the recent intelligence, this suggested a significant German fleet was now between Kerber's cruisers and their bases. Plen decided to skip the rendezvous, believing that Kerber would abandon the plan. The orders stressed the need for wireless silence, so he took *Admiral Makarov* south into open water to mark time. At 4pm, he began a run in to Utö to pass the indicated squares in darkness. Essen allowed Kerber to determine his own response to the intelligence, whilst preparing to offer support:

> I left Helsingfors on the battleship *Sevastopol'* together with the Brigada Lineynykh Korabley and destroyers of 6th Divizion for Paponvik Bay, from where I could go to sea at any time if I received a wireless message alert from Kontr-Admiral Kerber about the appearance ... of enemy forces ... on the approaches to Utö or the Gulf of Finland. At the same time, I gave all necessary orders for the readiness of minelayers and submarines for immediate departure to sea.

Kerber was unconvinced by the latest message, as it did not agree with messages intercepted by *Ryurik*'s own wireless room. He decided to continue the operation and marked time north of the rendezvous to await *Enisey*. The minelayer and her escorts had finally been able to leave Utö at 2pm on the 14th. Despite visibility of only six miles, they successfully rendezvoused with *Ryurik* at 9:30am next morning. As a precaution, Kerber led the force into open water to the southwest to mark time. At sunset, the force turned for the run in to the target area, northwest of Brüsterort. Once it was fully dark, *Enisey* broke away and the three cruisers left for Utö. At 8pm, *Enisey* turned northeast to begin laying mines in separate groups of 12 over a distance of 10½ miles. *Enisey* altered course to return via the Gulf of Riga. Her commander, Kapitan 2nd Ranga Konstantin Prokhorov, spent an anxious night. A string of lights kept approaching to port, forcing *Enisey* to take evasive action several times. Prokhorov maintained maximum speed for an extended run to ensure that he reached the Gulf of Riga in the darkness.

Kerber had successfully completed his second operation, despite the glitch with *Bayan*. He had kept his nerve under pressure. Both he and his commanders had overcome atrocious weather conditions. The weather had also been a friend, throwing a cloak over the entire operation. He had taken some risks, but had carefully weighed them, and had shown flexibility to complete the mission. There were now 1,164 mines in ten offensive barriers from Stolpe Bank to Memel. The Germans were still largely oblivious to their presence.

On the morning of the 16th, the cruisers reached Utö. Both British submarines were also limping home. Despite his damaged propeller, Horton patrolled west of Gotland on the 15th, but saw nothing. On the morning of the 17th *E.9* arrived at Lappvik. *E.1* had been just ahead of him, having returned the whole way on one engine. At 11:21am on the 16th, as he passed Bengtskär, Laurence was about to find out that Nepenin's message had not been entirely inaccurate. The Germans were off the Gulf of Finland.[13]

German reconnaissance and a tragic error

Essen had been concerned about the vulnerability of Åland and the skerries west of Hangö for some time. Heinrich had his own concerns that the Russians would base forces here and fortify the area. The tortuous access from the sea to the south made the area virtually inaccessible to German warships. The channels within the skerries provided a safe route for Russian ships almost all the way to Swedish waters. With the winter imminent the area received a new focus, as it normally only briefly froze over. Russian forces based here would be able to begin operations before those in the Gulf of Finland.

U.23's report of Russian armoured cruisers off Bengtskär focussed attention on whether the Russians were using the channel here to enter the skerries to the west. *U.26* arrived on 28 November, after being shepherded as far as Östergarn by the naval collier *Edmund Hugo Stinnes 4*, an encumbrance of dubious benefit. Berckheim had intended to, 'observe the north coast for two days, especially the entrances to Hangö and Ekenäs.' The unreliable port engine quickly broke down. The weather was atrocious. Berckheim had seen nothing: 'Since the starboard engine is not working properly, and there are always rattling noises at low speeds, I decide – also influenced by the weather – to abort the operation and head for Gotland. Surface running is out of the question, as staying on the conning tower is almost impossible even when heading into the seas.' *U.26* left to limp home next morning, buttoned down, alternating between the unreliable

13 РГАВМФ:Фонд 418, Опись1, Дело398, p.5, Фонд 716, Опись 1, Дело 15, p.32–40 and Опись 2, Дело 13, pp.159, 118–119, 203, 279–282, 313, 353, Дело24, p.131; Pavlovich, *Operations*, pp.100–107; TNA:ADM137/271, pp.37–46; Меркушов, *Записки*, pp.304–305; Гельмерсен, 'Заградительные', *Сборник 2*, pp.90–97; BA:RM92 *Gazelle*, *Undine* KTB, RM56 4.Torpedobootsflottille KTB; Вейс, «Баян», p.42.

engines. On the evening of the 2nd, Berckheim finally reached Danzig and went straight into the docks. Repairs put *U.26* out of action for a month. *U.A* had been scheduled to replace her, but was also docked for repairs after a collision escorting *Senator Strandes*. Fundamental problems with her machinery soon led to her withdrawal to Kiel, putting her out of action for months.

On the evening of the 9th, *U.25* was ready for action, and left for Bengtskär. There was no superfluous surface escort. Good weather on departure vanished as Wünsche headed north. *U.25* arrived at the billet on the morning of the 11th, making only eight knots in the heavy swell. Once dived, it was almost impossible to maintain a steady depth. The next day was worse. Far to the east, the Russian destroyer disaster unfolded. Most of the day was spent submerged riding out the gale. The weather on the 13th was impossible, with storm force gusts of up to 50 knots: 'Due to a snowstorm and rising seas, visibility was inadequate, sometimes only 1 nautical mile. Nothing in sight during the day … Dived to 20m.' Wünsche had surfaced as little as possible to top up the battery since arriving. He had no chance of spotting Kerber's cruisers heading out that night. It was remarkable that he had maintained position this long, but on the morning of the 14th, 'It was decided, since the weather forecast was poor with a falling barometer, and no position fixes had been available for three days, to abort the patrol and head for [shelter at] the northern tip of Gotland. When the weather forecast improves, the advance will recommence.' Off Fårö, the weather moderated. That evening, Wünsche surfaced to use the wireless to update Adam. The message was transmitted several times, as there was no acknowledgment. Nepenin's direction finders must have picked up these transmissions. Reception must have been patchy, with garbled call signs transforming the solitary submarine into a veritable fleet. As the operator was being thrown around by heavy seas at the time, his Morse was probably not at its best.

The weather calmed on the 15th. Wünsche informed Adam that he was heading back to his billet. He saw nothing that day in the poor visibility as *Enisey*'s group headed south across his path to join *Ryurik*. At 11:25am next morning, *U.25* was heading slowly east at periscope depth, four miles off Bengtskär. The wind had picked up again, and the sea was choppy. Visibility remained poor between snow flurries: 'A dark object was sighted astern to port, at a distance of approximately 2–3 nautical miles, which was not close enough to make out. It was identified as a submarine maintaining an easterly course, by steaming towards it with the rudder hard to starboard. Kept turning further and steered to approach by the bow.' Seven minutes after commencing his turn, Wünsche was in position: 'Torpedo fired with depth setting reduced to 1.5m at about 2–300 m. The track could not be observed in the rough seas. Shortly after the shot, the boat seemed to be intending to dive into the depths. After two minutes, the periscope was used, but nothing more was seen of the enemy submarine. However, no detonation was heard, only a violent disturbance along the boat's passage was observed.' Wünsche saw nothing more for the rest of the day.

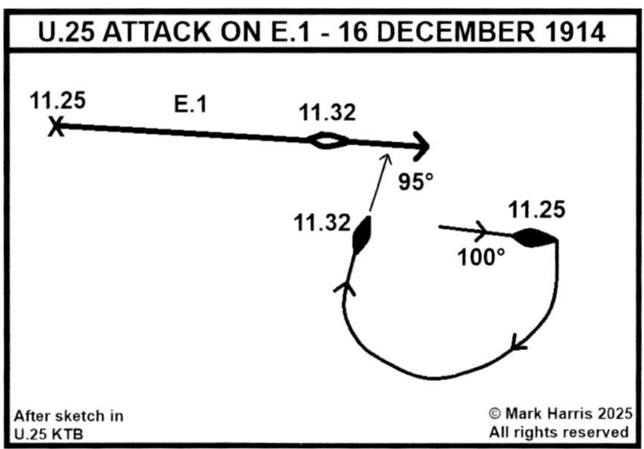

His target had been *E.1.* Chaplin wirelessed immediately after the attack that 'one [torpedo] passed very close.' Laurence simply reported, '… we were attacked by a German submarine who fired two torpedoes. Both were avoided by the use of the helm. Dived and proceeded submerged.' The track had been mistaken for two torpedoes. Laurence remained submerged for two hours to clear the area. On arriving at Lappvik later that day, he was ordered to head to Helsingfors for repairs. Essen spoke to him, and reported to Fan-der-Flit that: 'One of the torpedoes passed close to the submarine and only the chance sighting of a periscope and an immediate turn saved the submarine from destruction.'

Wünsche does not say why he only fired a single torpedo at a high priority target. It is likely that in the heavy sea, whilst making a tight turn, the crew had only been able to set the shallow depth setting on one torpedo, which was essential for any chance of hitting. Despite a prodigious effort by Wünsche and his crew, Adam's commentary was downbeat and confined to technicalities: 'Previous tests and experience with shallow firing have shown that torpedoes and their engines quickly fail when the sea is very rough.' For his part, Merkushov was left to reflect ironically about *E.1*, 'What a shame! An Englishman can only make nine knots of surface speed due to a machinery malfunction, whilst our veterans, when their engines are in perfect order, can only make eight knots. An Englishman complains that he can't go any faster, but for most of us, nine knots is an unattainable dream. Everything in the world is relative!'

Meanwhile, Heinrich had been in discussion with the Admiralstab about Behring's proposal to attack Mariehamn. They were unenthusiastic. Mariehamn was an undefended port. Bombardment simply because of the presence of a submarine would invite a response against cities like Memel. They considered limited mining ineffective, with hundreds needed for an effective barrier. Further discussion was postponed until after the *Deutschland* operation.

On 8 December, Behring's new flagship, *Prinz Adalbert*, arrived in Swinemünde, escorted by *T.97* and *G.134*. These joined 20th Halbflottille. These six destroyers were of limited range and barely adequate as escort for the cruisers. They now had an even longer journey to the operational areas compared to Danzig. Behring's existing force arrived the same day, after escorting *Deutschland*. The High Command refused to bring 4th Flottille up to strength, leaving it with just nine boats.[14] Everyone wanted more. Next day, Heinrich refused a request from Ingenohl to get *Prinz Adalbert* back for a raid on the British coast.

Behring took *Augsburg* to Kiel to confer with Heinrich. An operation to confirm whether the Russians were fortifying the Åland Islands and prepare for subsequent battleship bombardment and comprehensive mining of Mariehamn was agreed. Intelligence from the Stockholm Embassy had indicated that fortification had begun and British officers had been reported there. To reduce risk during the initial reconnaissance, the ships were not to proceed into the islands. Heinrich wanted all navigational marks in the area, as well as any installations at Bengtskär, Lågskär and Bogskär destroyed. Submarine operations were to continue to focus on the entrance to the skerries at Bengtskär, but also determine whether the channel at Utö was in regular use. The submarines were to stay west of Revel'.

Behring returned to Swinemünde and his force left on the night of the 15th. The cruisers formed a wide scouting line with *Augsburg*, *Lübeck* and *Thetis* passing east of Gotland and *Amazone* heading west of the island. Behring followed 12 miles behind with *Prinz Adalbert*, escorted by the six destroyers of 20th Halbflottille.

On the 17th, the hospital ship *Imperator*, colliers *Otto Hugo Stinnes 9* and *Oberpräsident Delbrück* took position off Hoburg to provide logistical support. Off to the north, the sea was calmer than it had been recently, but there was a cold northerly wind blowing in rain and snow

14 *S.122* finally replaced the lost *S.124* on 23 January 1915.

squalls. At 2am that morning, after passing Gotland, *Amazone*, which was too slow to risk in enemy waters, was detached to head back down the west side of Gotland, carrying out commerce warfare on the way. *Augsburg* broke away to make a high speed run into the Åland Sea, aiming to surprise any patrolling Russian destroyers, before conducting the reconnaissance of Mariehamn and the nearby anchorages. *Lübeck* and *Thetis* took up a covering outpost line, off Utö and the shallows off Dago respectively. From 9am onwards, Russian wireless activity spiked upwards.

Meanwhile, *Prinz Adalbert* and her escorting destroyers took position south of Bogskär, zigzagging as a precaution against torpedo attack. *G.134* and *T.97* closed the island. A cutter went ashore. The crew found a long deserted lighthouse gutted by fire, but managed to find some kerosene barrels in the cellar to smash open. *G.136* circled the island. It was deserted.

At 9am, *Augsburg* arrived off Mariehamn, having seen only commercial shipping. Horn's task was to identify navigational marks for the bombardment and sketch the shoreline of the main island, Åland. He concluded that small islands concealed both Mariehamn, and the anchorages in the inlet east of the island, from any areas accessible to deep draught warships. There were no significant landmarks to assist in correcting indirect fire either, even if aircraft could be used for spotting. The bombardment looked good on paper in Kiel, but made no sense on the ground. Rosenberg was on-board to assess the scope for mining. This offered good prospects for blocking the inlet east of the main island, but not for blocking Mariehamn itself. The coastal observers on the island identified a *Gazelle* class cruiser and raised the alarm by wireless at 9:20am. *Beluga* got underway to attack, but *Augsburg* was too far away. Horn took about an hour to complete the survey, made his report and left, unaware of the submarine's presence.

Whilst the objective had been a wash out, *Lübeck* made a valuable discovery. The rain had stopped and visibility was excellent. Halm closed the skerries to fix his position, and investigate Utö. He spotted a number of smoke clouds near the island, which he reported to Behring. As *Lübeck* closed, around 11am: 'It was observed that vessels were leaving Utö between the skerries. ... The lookout in the crow's nest (Fähnrich z. S. [Heinrich Riensberg]) initially mistook them for steamboats and later definitely identified them as submarines. Eventually, they were confirmed as such from the bridge, after their disappearance had been clearly observed by diving and prior to this, by white clouds of smoke, which could only have come from gasoline fumes. Five submarines were definitely identified (probably a sixth), which dived one after the other immediately after leaving port.' Riensberg thumbed through his copy of Weyer and identified them as resembling *Akula*. He also spotted another vessel resembling *Khrabryy* coming out. The whole thing looked like a well-rehearsed response to a threatened attack. By noon, Halm: 'deemed [it] necessary to abandon the outpost line immediately and break off at high speed on a southerly course.' As *Lübeck* accelerated to 20 knots, minutes later orders came in from Behring for a general retirement, *Augsburg* having confirmed that her reconnaissance was complete. The ships retraced their course, led by *Prinz Adalbert*, with the other cruisers covering astern.

At 1am on the 16th, Essen had already ordered the 2nd Divizion of submarines at Utö to be prepared to take up positions in the Gulf, as part of the general alert in expectation of a German attack based on wireless intercepts. They had been sheltering from the recent storms. The four submarines, *Alligator*, *Drakon*, *Kayman* and *Krokodil* headed out of harbour. They moored in the fairway to the despatch vessel *Sputnik* ready for a quick exit. *Khrabryy* was nearby as base protection. Kerber's cruisers, which had just returned from their minelaying mission, left Utö that evening for Revel'. Essen wanted them back to coal urgently. *Akula* also left to take up a position off Gotska Sandön by dawn.

At 9:40am next morning, smoke appeared to the south, but the watchers assumed that it was *Enisey* returning. They raised the alarm fifteen minutes later. Even from 23 miles away, it was obviously a German advance. There was a delay ordering the submarines out. They got underway forty minutes later, heading out in line ahead. Once out of the fairway, they turned to make a direct approach and then dived to attack. The observation post kept up a steady stream of reports, identifying both light cruisers, with *Lübeck* correctly identified as a *Bremen* class in the crystal-clear air, although the closest she came was 16 miles. By the time Halm left, the submarines were four to five miles away from his position. They surfaced and headed to their assigned patrol positions, in case the Germans returned.

E.9 had arrived at Lappvik that morning. With reports of German warships pouring in, Horton was not prepared to sit things out, despite the boat's mechanical problems. He asked Leytenant Essen to send a signal to fleet headquarters: 'The commander of the submarine *E.9* requests permission to go to sea for 51 hours to attack the enemy.' The Essen family name signing off the signal certainly did no harm. Permission came back at 7:45pm for a two-day patrol. Horton headed out immediately for a position 15 miles east of Gotland, hoping to strike any vessels heading in or out of the Gulf.

In contrast, the response from the destroyers returning to watch at the mouth of the Gulf after the recent storm was unimpressive. At 5pm, the leader of the duty patrol from 3rd Divizion signalled: 'Due to floating mines and large swells, *Bditel'nyy Vnushitel'nyy Burnyy* anchored Hangö.' This earned a rebuke from Essen for the Divizion commander: 'Extremely dissatisfied with the inaction of 3rd Divizion, I demand that four destroyers immediately go on patrol. Go to sea and stay west of … [German] minefield.'

Meanwhile, *Akula* had passed the German force unawares as it approached in the darkness. On the morning of the 17th, Vlas'yev arrived at Gotska Sandön. He spent the day keeping watch on the surface, just out of sight, east of the island. The position was well chosen. At 3pm, as the sun was setting, five columns of smoke approached from northeast. *Akula* dived to attack. As they closed, the target, identified as a *Gazelle* class light cruiser, altered course, having apparently got a position fix from the island, and passed four miles away. Vlas'yev surfaced. The sea remained calm, but it began to snow. By 7pm, it was completely dark and the steady wind had raised a swell. The chance of attack at night was slim, especially in the prevailing weather, but Vlas'yev stayed on the surface, keeping watch with his first officer, Michman Konstantin Terletskiy. Suddenly, the helmsman, Rulevoy Botsmanmat (Coxswain) Ivan Paste called out as something emerged from a snow squall to the north: 'Ship to starboard! Twenty – twenty-five cables! [over two miles] It's on a closing course!' Vlas'yev ordered the boat to dive. Before going below, he wiped the snow from the periscope. On reaching the control room, he had second thoughts. It would take three minutes to complete the dive. The snow had obscured the periscope already. Vlas'yev turned to Terletskiy, 'There is only one option: we need to get back to the bridge, trim the boat down in the water and command from above. The helmsman will stay here. Let's go!' With only the end tanks flooded, *Akula*'s hull would submerge, but leave the conning tower above water. The ability to fire the external side-mounted torpedo frames in these circumstances was one of their few advantages. In the weather, the Germans should not spot the small target. The hull would be submerged and steady within a minute. The waves were crashing over the exposed bridge, which was now close to the sea. As they slammed into the tower, water poured down the hatch. It was in danger of upsetting the trim, or worse. Vlas'yev ordered Terletskiy to close it. Helm orders had to be shouted down an open ventilation valve.

The crew of *Akula*, late 1914. Kapitan 2nd Ranga Sergey Nikolayevich Vlas'yev seated at centre, Michman Konstantin Filippovich Terletskiy to the viewers left. (Public domain)

The snow continually masked the cruiser. It emerged, just over a mile away and somewhat ahead. It was a long shot; Vlas'yev fired a two-torpedo spread from the external frames.[15] There was no explosion. The cruiser disappeared in the snow, heading south. Vlas'yev reported that: 'The probable reasons for the failure are the following: poor aim due to limited visibility, an intermittent snowstorm, and the fact that, having remained up top, we had to give most of our attention to not being washed overboard by the breaking waves – at the moment of firing I barely managed to keep hold of the rail.' Vlas'yev commended the crew for their performance in the difficult conditions, especially, '… Michman Terletskiy, an outstanding officer in all respects, deserving special recognition in his service for his knowledge, character and abilities.' *Akula* returned to Utö next morning. The increasing swell also forced the four 2nd Divizion submarines back into harbour. *Drakon* and *Kayman* had remained out at their billets overnight in the hope of getting in an attack at dawn.

E.9 reached Gotland at 3pm. The visibility was poor and Horton headed back north that night. Just before *E.9* arrived back at Lappvik on the afternoon of the 19th, the port shaft finally seized up completely. A diver went down, 'who reported one blade left on port propeller and also that shaft casing had opened out and jambed [*sic*] the shaft.' Horton limped back to port through the skerries. Both of the British submarines were once more out of action.

Ultimately, only *Akula*, pre-positioned on the return route, had been able to attack. The Germans were unaware of her presence in the difficult conditions. If they had been carrying out an extended operation, it would have faced much greater danger of torpedo attack on the second day. In the circumstances, Vlas'yev had made the most of the fleeting opportunities. His first sighting was *Prinz Adalbert* with her destroyer escorts. The torpedo attack was on *Augsburg*, at the western end of the retiring cruiser line.

15 Merkushov says six torpedoes, which would be all four frames plus the two internal bow tubes.

On the 17th, as the operation played out to the west, *U.25* spent an uneventful day patrolling off Bengtskär. The forward hydroplane began sticking, making depth control awkward. Next morning Wünsche decided to head east to Russarö. At 12:30pm, this brought him into contact with the patrol line:

> Three destroyers with four funnels – *Gromyashchiy* Class boats – come into view, proceeding at high speed to cross ahead of *U.25*'s course. Proceed on the old course of 60°, believing that this offers the most favourable prospects for attack.
>
> When transitioning from quarter line to line ahead, the leading boat steered to approach bow on. Due to the rapid succession of course and formation changes, the periscope had to be shown more frequently and for longer periods to deliver the attack.
>
> 1pm. [Our] boat was seen at this point, as the leading destroyer turned sharply towards *U.25* and fired several salvos. Went to a depth of 15 meters; judging by the sound of the propellers, the destroyer moved away from the boat.
>
> After five minutes, the periscope was shown. The boats were about 1,000 meters away … to port astern. A salvo was fired, proceeded again to 15 meters reversing course to 240°.

U.25 had encountered the duty patrol of 5th Divizion north of the German minefield, led by *Dostoynyy*, which Wünsche had correctly identified. There had recently been a flurry of submarine sightings in the Gulf of Finland, by three different patrolling destroyers, including *Dostoynyy*. A number of mines had broken loose in the weather and been destroyed. They were probably the cause of the alarms. However, the incidents no doubt put lookouts on alert. The Divizion commander, Kapitan 2nd Ranga Aleksandr Razvozov, had attacked, preventing Wünsche from firing: 'At 1.30pm *Dostoynyy* saw a submarine nearby, at 3 cables [550m] opened fire, attempted to ram, it managed to dive and disappear.' The next afternoon, Wünsche finally abandoned the patrol when his remaining periscope lens fogged-up. The other was already out of action with a short circuit.

Behring's force had continued through the night of the 17/18th towards Swinemünde. At 3:42am, *Thetis*, at the eastern end of the cruiser scouting line, was mid-way between Gotland and Rixhöft. Two white lights appeared to port. Her new commander, Korvettenkapitän Walter Hildebrand:

> Turned towards the light, repeatedly made recognition signals with the searchlight. No answer; the vessel is moving away at high speed on a southeasterly course. Illuminated and pursued… It is obvious that the vessel has not extinguished the white light. Suspicion arose that the vessel is intending to drag *Thetis* onto mines. Therefore, the vessel ahead is followed to starboard. The vessel turns starboard on a course of south by east. To cut her off, the vessel was followed two points ahead to port. *Thetis* closed in. 4:7am: Made recognition signal with funnel [whistle]. No answer. Vessel illuminated with searchlight. Dimly visible, black – not grey – steamer. Steamer has a gun on-board. A shot was fired across the bow of the steamer to force it to stop. The steamer readies the gun and opens fire.

A small shell struck the rail outside the bridge of *Thetis*, wounding three nearby crewmen, two of them seriously. Hildebrand gave the order to return fire. *Lübeck* had observed the play of lights to the east. Those on the bridge now heard: 'First a partial salvo, then 6–7 full salvos.' At point blank range, the 10.5cm salvoes from *Thetis* had a devastating effect on the small vessel caught in the searchlights. Hildebrand continues:

> Twice fire was suspended, assuming that resistance had been broken. The steamer was enveloped in smoke. Since the steamer continued firing, re-opened our fire until 4:20. It was then determined that the vessel was the steamer *Ruth*, Stockholm.

With resistance evidently crushed and the target on fire, Hildebrand stopped, and launched *Thetis*'s cutter to rescue survivors. He signalled Behring: 'fishing trawler *Ruth* sunk by gunfire because repeated recognition signals went unanswered and the vessel opened fire. Personnel taken on board. The vessel is burning and sinking.' Minutes after they were rescued, the steamer sank. However, the survivors were German naval ratings. The vessel was actually *Senator Strandes*, on her anti-submarine patrol. Her gun was an obsolete 3.7cm revolver cannon intended for anti-personnel use at close range. Eight of the crew were unaccounted for, presumed dead, including the commander of the unit, Leutnant zur See der Reserve Charles Hamilton. Five of the survivors were wounded. One of these later died of his wounds.[16] The cutter scoured the area for more survivors for an hour, whilst *Thetis* swept it with searchlights, but no more were found. Later that afternoon, Behring reported that: 'Based on the interrogations [of survivors] conducted so far … Hamilton initially correctly identified *Thetis* as a German ship, but then apparently concluded that he had identified an enemy submarine, which was making an incorrect identification signal, and opened fire. The steamer apparently made recognition signals, but these were not seen by *Thetis*.' The explanation is unsatisfactory, but perhaps Hamilton thought the submarine was working with a larger vessel, which had him cornered. For obvious reasons, the incident was not publicised. *Senator Strandes* was a long way offshore, but was free to operate widely in search of submarines. It was an avoidable accident, with forces left ignorant of each other's presence in the same area at night. A few days later Heinrich ordered that the patrols continue, but keep within 20 miles of the coast.

Behring's force returned to port that afternoon, followed by *U.25* on the 21st. The intelligence from the Stockholm Embassy had been wrong. Behring abandoned thoughts of an attack on Mariehamn. He now advised the destruction of the newly discovered submarine base at Utö as soon as possible.[17]

16 *Senator Strandes* (1911) 192 GRT. Cuxhaven steam trawler, requisitioned 14 August 1914. Casualties per *Thetis* KTB. Published sources incorrectly list two dead. Casualties reported in *Verlustliste* erratically, often years later. No explanation found for being reported as *Ruth* of Stockholm in archive material. Use of a covert false Swedish trawler identity is possible. This would put enemy submarines off their guard and allow a Q-ship style ambush at close range.

17 BA:RM97 *U.26*, *U.25*, RM28 KTB, RM92 *Prinz Adalbert*, *Lübeck*, *Thetis*, RM3/2857 Reichsmarineamt; Firle, Ostsee, pp.263–272; TNA:ADM137/271, pp.40–46; РГАВМФ:Фонд 716, Опись 2, Дело 13, p.215, 229, 282, Дело 24, p.143, Дело 8, p.111; Меркушов, *Записки*, pp.306–307; Ю. М. Стволинский, *Конструкторы подводных кораблей: Документальные рассказы о создателях советского флота морских глубин* (Ленинград: Лениздат, 1984), pp.186–188; Томашевич, *операциях*, p.63; Gröner, *Band 8/1*, pp.217, 219; Anon., *Verlustliste No.15*, p.2, *16*, p.11, *18*, p.3, *25*, p.22, *109*, p.6, *117*, p.7, *149*, p.8, *163*, p.4; Гельмерсен, 'Заградительные', *Сборник 2*, p.98.

9

Success and failure: December 1914 to February 1915

Russian mines and the German surprise attack on Utö

The small German steamer *Stadt Lübeck* left Danzig on 20 November bound for Lübeck, with a cargo of lumber.[1] The steamer and her crew of 11 never arrived. The only evidence of her loss was a cargo crate and a lifebuoy that washed up on the Gotland coast over the following months. The weather had been good, making the loss inexplicable. The Russian minefield off Stolpe Bank, laid by *Amur* a few days earlier, was the only minefield possibly in her path, but her loss here remains speculation.

There was no great alarm, but three German steamers then went missing in a short space of time. On 16 December, the small steamer *Lebbin II*, with a crew of 14, left her namesake town on the island of Wollin, near Swinemünde, bound for Königsberg, with a cargo of cement. On the 17th, *Elsa Hugo Stinnes 15*, with a complement of 18, left Neufahrwasser bound for København with a cargo of sugar. On the 18th, *Stockholm* left Lübeck, bound for Königsberg, with a cargo of cement. All three disappeared, with over 40 crew.[2] On the 22nd, Stettin shipping owners contacted Heinrich, to ascertain whether there was any danger. He responded: 'No warnings for shipping between Lübeck or Stettin and Königsberg.' The Gribel Company was unimpressed. They forwarded details of the three ships overdue and requested escorts as: 'We have received reliable reports that British naval officers in Helsingfors claim to have been off Swinemünde with their submarines some time ago. We fear that British submarine activity is continuing on our coast and that the loss of the missing steamers … is due to this.' Heinrich ruled out escorts, and was dismissive in a letter to Behring: 'there is some unrest about security on the [German] coasts. However, only two steamers have been reported overdue so far. It cannot be ruled out that they have fallen into enemy hands or encountered drifting mines. I request that appropriate measures be taken to calm our shipping; … all steamers arriving in Swinemünde should be interrogated … regarding their observations. … I request that a patrol service by the destroyers under your command is established along the coast … and assume … that a permanent security service has been established in the Bay of Pomerania with the boats of the Swinemünde

1 *Stadt Lübeck* (1884) 351 GRT.

2 *Lebbin II*, ex-*Hans Kyvig*, ex-*Itzehoe* (1905) 539 GRT; *Elsa Hugo Stinnes 15* (1912) 1,752 GRT; *Stockholm* (1878) 806 GRT.

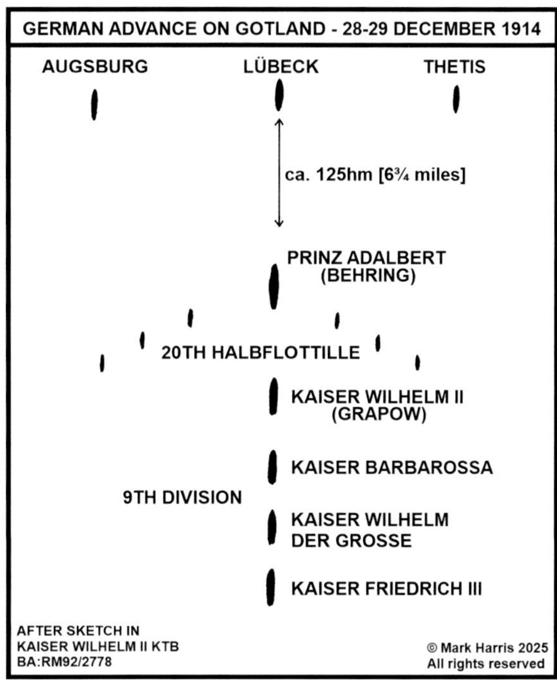

Hilfsminensuchdivision.' There was no mention of minesweeping.

Heinrich focussed on dealing with submarines at source. He accepted Behring's proposal to attack the newly discovered submarine base at Utö. However, he wanted first to make an ostentatious advance to Gotland with battleships, to convince the Russians that these were still being deployed as operational support. On the 23rd, he approached Ingenohl, who agreed to lend Grapow's four old battleships of 9th Division, which were exercising and refitting at Kiel. The orders state that there had been no sightings of submarines in the western Baltic for weeks, with no mention of mines. The High Command duly approved the plan.

Grapow would command. On the evening of the 26th, he left Kiel, passing the western Baltic narrows in darkness and keeping out of sight of land. At 2pm next afternoon, he rendezvoused with Behring's force just north of Oder Bank. The force advanced towards Gotland at a leisurely 13 knots. Around 2pm next day, the scouting cruisers sighted land. Grapow had: 'Hoburg Lighthouse on the starboard beam, 5 miles. Visibility of the southwest coast of Gotland … is good. Until nightfall, vessels will steer northward so close to the coast that observation from land is certain, and in this respect, the demonstration can be considered assured.' Once it was dark, the ships retraced their routes home. The seas grew rough next day, so the destroyers detached early to Danzig to shorten the journey, with *Thetis* as escort. This meant they ran the gauntlet of several undiscovered minefields. By the morning of the 30th, all ships were back in port. Behring's three cruisers passed just north of the undiscovered minefield laid by *Amur*. The operation was too low key to draw attention and had no discernible impact. Apart from routine directional wireless contact, it seems to have passed unremarked by the Russians. Their intelligence focussed on the appearance of dreadnought battleships in Kiel, a more obvious point of concern. They were there for exercises.

Whilst returning past Bornholm, 9th Division picked up a capsized lifeboat. It bore the name of *Elsa Hugo Stinnes 15*. The Admiralstab were approached by the Stettin based Gunstmann shipping company about all four overdue steamers. On the 29th, Heinrich received orders: 'The earliest possible identification of mine danger areas by m[inen]s[uch]d[ivision] appears urgently necessary in order to warn shipping, and as far as possible, eliminate the mine threat, as well as to confidentially provide German shipping with specific safe routes.' It had been six weeks since the suspicion of Russian mines off the German coast arose. The signs had multiplied since then. However, Heinrich and Behring's obsessive focus on the presence of the British continued to focus activity on submarines. The Admiralstab had finally made mines and their threat to German trade an issue.

Heinrich ordered sweeping of the coastal track between Danzig and Pillau. He grudgingly issued guidance to the shipping companies: 'Since some shipping losses in the Baltic Sea seem to have caused concern in the shipping community, which I do not share, since reports of the enemy are lacking, I recommend the following sea route to ships bound for Königsberg: North of the Stolpe Bank in deep water to the Hela meridian. Then head for Hela ... and continue close to land to Pillau. These routes are to be kept secret for security reasons. Please have the shipping companies instruct all steamer captains to telegraph all observations of suspicious vessels made during the voyage to [me] in Kiel upon arrival at their destination, as well as to send their track chart.' His instructions were unlikely to allay anxieties. Routes were unlikely to remain secret, once many skippers knew of them.

Behring received permission to proceed with the surprise attack on Utö. Heinrich suggested a date over Orthodox Christmas, 8/9 January. He wanted at least one submarine covering off the Gulf of Finland, preferably two. This was a problem. *U.23* had left for Bengtskär, but had encountered bad weather and been forced to turn round with engine trouble off Dago. A thorough overhaul was going to take weeks. Unreliable engines and machinery problems had now put all four submarines of 5th Halbflottille out of action.

Behring, impetuous as ever, was determined to move as soon as *U.26*'s repairs completed. At 4pm on 3 January, his force left Swinemünde and Danzig, heading out under the cover of darkness. Within hours, a gale blew in a blizzard of snow from the southeast. It was pointless to continue. Behring postponed the attack and ordered all surface vessels back to port. *U.26* slogged on through the weather and heaving seas. Next day, Berckheim had to take shelter west of Gotland in the lee of the island. Once the sea moderated, he headed to his billet off Bengtskär, arriving on the evening of the 6th.

At 3.30am on 4 January, the German steamer *Latona* was passing Scholpin about 10 miles offshore. The steamer *Apollo* was nearby. Those on the bridge saw an explosion. Within a minute *Latona* sank. *Apollo* could see no survivors from her 12 crew.[3] The disaster was reported when she docked, early on the 6th. At night, mines were suspected, rather than a torpedo. The six boats of Swinemünde Hilfsminensuchdivision, Kapitänleutnant der Reserve Walter Bertenburg, left Stolpmünde, with orders to sweep the reported position. At 9am, they found the minefield laid by *Novik* on 24 November. Some mines were only 1½m below the surface, significantly less than the draught of the sweepers. Sweeping was difficult, as the trawls kept snagging on a wreck, but a Russian mine was identified.

At 1.30pm, Oberleutnant zur See der Reserve Hans Hoffmann's *Suchboot A* (*Binz*), was about 350m to port of the divisional leader, *Suchboot B* (*Hohenzollern*), Oberleutnant zur See der Reserve Leopold Fritsch. Suddenly there was:

> ... a dull bang, accompanied by heavy smoke and flames that enveloped [*Suchboot B*] from the bow to the funnel, as high as the mast. Immediately afterwards, thick white clouds of steam, caused by a boiler explosion, erupted around the stern. ... after a few seconds, only debris remained floating on the water. ... The mine hit the ship on the port side at the forward transverse bunker and also detonated the gun ammunition. ... *Suchboot A*, *C*, and *D* immediately launched lifeboats to rescue any survivors.

3 *Latona* (1905) 649 GRT.

Hohenzollern (1907), a 98 GRT excursion vessel and tug working around Stettin before the war. (Author's collection)

> Fritsch, who was standing on the bridge beside the division commander, was thrown into the air, fell back into the gaping coal bunker, was pulled down with the ship, fought his way to the surface, and grabbed a lifebelt, which, despite being wounded himself, he pushed over the head of Matrose Proeck, who could not swim. He then swam towards boat *A*, losing his strength; Vermessungsgast Ritzdorff from boat *A* jumped overboard, swam to him, and effected his rescue.

After searching for survivors, the boats returned to port. Bertenburg and 14 crew were killed. Nine had been rescued, four with wounds. Oberheizer Paul Gliwa died later that day from multiple injuries and burns. The wrecks of *Latona* and *Suchboot B* were located in 2002, lying just 250m apart.

The disaster confirmed the worst fears about the suitability of the auxiliaries for sweeping. Heinrich reassigned both Hilfsminensuchdivision solely to patrol duty. Behring requested use of a regular Minensuchdivision and hastened the collection of small shallow draught 8t motor boats to back them up, as he thought they would be far more suitable to search for mines.

The probable loss of all four missing steamers on mines was finally impossible to ignore. Heinrich warned all shipping companies through official channels of, 'a serious danger to public shipping between Stolpe Bank and the coast'. The warning instructed owners not to use this route and reminded them to follow the recent route guidance. The authorities feared that the Russians would lay more mines, once they were aware the Germans had found the existing minefields, so the warning was not made public. Charts of recent voyages were examined to identify safe routes. None of this was a substitute for minesweeping. The 2nd Minensuchdivision headed for Stettin that night, not to sweep mines, but to lay up in the yards for a major refit. There were now no minesweepers available. On the 9th, Ingenohl contacted Heinrich, because the Admiralstab directed him to negotiate the transfer of a North Sea Minensuchdivision. Heinrich replied, 'The allocation of a second M.S.D. of the High Seas Forces was neither requested nor suggested by me, as I can, if necessary, wait for the completion of the known clearance work until the [2nd] Division, which is undergoing repairs in Stettin, is completed … However, if a second M.S.D. can be assigned to me from there shortly after January 12th, … I would of course be grateful.' He comments in his war diary, 'How the Admiralstab considers it to realistically be feasible to search a steamer route approximately 100 nautical miles long for mines will be inquired at a later opportunity. For the time being, the matter is not urgent, as no M.S.D. has been assigned to the task.' Heinrich's stubbornness in not taking the threat seriously is hard to understand. That day, a boat and a buoy from *Stockholm* washed ashore on the east coast of Gotland. The wreck of *Lebbin II* was identified in 2002 by its bell, in the coastal track, at the location of *Admiral Makarov*'s minefield. The other three wrecks of the missing steamers are yet to be located.[4]

Meanwhile, Behring had received a forecast of fine weather for the 6th. His ships left Swinemünde and Danzig at 5pm for the operation against Utö. The two groups met northeast of Bornholm and then advanced up the east coast of Gotland. The plan was an audacious one. The attack force would arrive off Utö at dawn. *Augsburg* would be in position to scout to the east and *Lübeck* to the west. *G.134* and *T.97* would deploy their mine sweeps and advance up the approach. The rest of 20th Halbflottille and *Thetis* would advance 1,400m behind in support. *Prinz Adalbert* would follow, but only as far as her 8m draught allowed. If there were no mines, the destroyers would advance into the harbour, destroying any vessels present and bombarding the harbour facilities. If defending batteries fired, *Thetis* and *Prinz Adalbert* would suppress them first. Behring hoped that surprise would catch the defences off guard. Hildebrand had discretion to abort the attack at any point.

Before dawn on the 8th, the force arrived off Utö. The weather was bad, but Behring pushed on: 'drifting snow temporarily obscured visibility. However, the obstruction was not great enough to justify immediately calling off the attack, especially since the sea was relatively calm and the wind was light.' The destroyers deployed their sweeps, but progress was slow. They parted twice as 'the destroyer commanders lack practice in operating the sweep, but mainly due to the fact that … the kites … got stuck in the shallows.' As there were no mines, and nearly two hours had been lost, Hildebrand decided to press ahead without sweeping. The destroyers zigzagged ahead of *Thetis*, sounding regularly. Snow fell heavily, obscuring visibility. When the depth unexpectedly dropped to 8m, Hildebrand stopped. Behring spotted *Thetis* reversing course ahead and assumed she had lost her bearings. He signalled the abort code for the operation. Ironically, the snow was thinning. Ehrhardt on *G.133* had just spotted Utö lighthouse, just over five miles away, as the sun came up. He signalled *Thetis*, but the reply was to retire. Behring had decided that the delays had cost the operation the element of surprise. The force returned through a vicious winter gale, passing west of Gotland for shelter, arriving back in Swinemünde on the afternoon of the 9th.

Heinrich was not happy: 'It is not entirely clear from the war diaries why the raid was not carried out with S.M.S. *Thetis* and 20th Halbflottille. The element of surprise for an operation against Utö has been lost.' Behring hoped that his early withdrawal had avoided detection, or that the Russians would suspect minelaying rather than a raid. He proposed returning in a few weeks, once any alarm died down, using a barrage breaker to steam ahead and light cruisers only. The depth appeared too shallow for *Prinz Adalbert* and minesweeping.

U.26 returned early from patrol on the 10th. Berckheim and his crew had a miserable two days in snow and fog off Bengtskär, with visibility at times less than 200m. They had seen nothing except *Augsburg*. Problems with both engines had been the final straw. Freezing sea

4 Older sources assume loss of all four in the *Amur* minefield. *Stockholm* and *Elsa Hugo Stinnes 15* could also have been lost in the *Novik* or *Admiral Makarov* minefields that sank *Latona*, *Lebbin II* and *Suchboot B.*

ice around the main hatch had required five minutes of hammering to clear before the boat could dive. Ice also fouled the periscopes and could take up to 15 minutes to melt after diving. Patrolling in these conditions was not just pointless, but dangerous.

On the afternoon of the 16th, Heinrich received more bad news: '[German] Steamer *Grete Hugo Stinnes 8* carrying coal from Harburg [Hamburg's port to the North Sea] to Danzig in 55°25'N. 19°E. struck a mine and sank on the night of the 14/15th at 1:20am.' The steamer had been sailing in line behind two others. Seven minutes after the first explosion, there had been a second. The ship then sank in just ninety seconds. There was safety in numbers. Captain J. Jülfs of the German steamer *Hector* received recognition for his decision to go back to save all 18 crew. The steamers had kept especially far out to sea to a point north of Hela and encountered the mines laid by *Enisey* a month earlier.[5]

Russian mines had now probably sunk seven German steamers, as well as *Friedrich Carl* and *Suchboot B*, within the space of two months. There had still been almost no action to deal with mines, which had obviously been widely laid in the eastern Baltic. Heinrich adjusted his guidance. Steamers were to keep north of Stolpe Bank, but not too far north, staying south of 55°15' N. The impression was one of a situation out of control. The Admiralstab contacted Heinrich again. The Lübeck Chamber of Commerce had written to them on the 13th: 'private insurers are no longer accepting insurance to Königsberg and Danzig. It is presumed that Russian fishing boats have scattered mines in that area. ... shipping in Königsberg and Danzig is seriously alarmed by the total losses [of ships and their crews] that have occurred, and its continuation in the future is therefore seriously in doubt..' The result was that, '... consideration is being given to halting sea transport of grain and flour between Königsberg and Lübeck/Stettin. Due to the threat to these essential staple foods a prompt statement is respectfully requested as to ... which approach routes ... have been searched for mines and whether they are considered safe by the [Baltic] Naval Command.' Heinrich responded: 'Based on the route maps of a large number of merchant steamers, I consider the route Hela Rixhöft at a distance of 5 nautical miles from the coast, then north of Stolpe Bank, to be safe until further notice, apart from the normal wartime risk. Searching the routes for mines has not yet begun. The route in question would require approximately 20 completely quiet days, assuming a minesweeping division is available.'

The yard work on 2nd Minensuchdivision had been due to complete by the 12th. It was now expected to take until the end of the month. Half of the boats in 4th Flottille were also refitting by turns at this time. It is incomprehensible why the same approach was not taken with the minesweepers. There was no follow through to secure a division from Ingenohl.

Heinrich focussed instead on new opportunities for offensive operations. He ordered Behring to improve the mine clearing equipment and training of 20th Halbflottille to be better able to sweep the way into enemy bases. On the 12th, he warned him: 'The Russians are probably aware of the panic that has arisen in Stettin shipping circles. They will also know that Swinemünde is the cruiser group's new base. ... The route to and from Swinemünde could be blocked. ... precautionary measures when approaching and departing appear necessary; the cruisers should be screened ahead by destroyers ... with their sweeps out.' His fear was justified, but the solution inadequate.[6]

5 *Grete Hugo Stinnes 8* (1911) 1,551 GRT.
6 BA:RM5/5275, RM28 KTB, RM92 *Lübeck*, *Kaiser Wilhelm II*, *Thetis* KTB, RM62 Hilfsminensuchdivision Swinemünde KTB, RM49 Detachierten Admirals KTB, RM56

Russian preparations for winter and an advance into the western Baltic

Whilst Heinrich was beset with problems, Essen was delighted with the outcome of the last mining sortie. On 18 December, he wrote to Fan-der-Flit:

> Under the direct supervision of my Chief of Staff, Kontr-Admiral Kerber, two important operations … were carried out. The execution of the second operation, which owed its success, despite the very difficult conditions, to the command of Kontr-Admiral Kerber, provides grounds for petitioning Your Excellency to award [him] with a promotion … advancing him to Vitse-Admiral. The latter … seems extremely desirable with regard to the possibility of replacing me if necessary, since he will then be the most senior of all the flag officers commanding in the Baltic Sea.

As well as anointing a potential successor, Essen was preparing the ground for winter and a new campaign after the spring thaw. There were personnel and organisational changes. Kolomeytsev had gone and Shtorre was dismissed. He had been seriously ill for some time. Essen planned for Kolchak to take a more direct role leading destroyer operations. With his protégé Bakhirev now commanding 1st Brigada Kreyserov, Essen reorganised the reconnaissance force. *Ryurik* would now lead the faster vessels in 1st Brigada. The four older, slower cruisers went to 2nd Brigada. By 5 January, all four of the new dreadnoughts had joined the fleet. This was a step change in firepower. It increased the main gunnery broadside of 30.5cm guns in the fleet from 16 to 64. However, the new battleships would need to work up to combat efficiency, both individually and as a unit, once the spring thaw came. See Appendix VII for the revised organisation.

The fleet was already preparing for the winter freeze. Essen wanted to make sure that his forces started the new campaign season in a high state of mechanical efficiency. Conditions were already too difficult for effective submarine operations off the bases, as Berckheim found. The older submarines of 1st Divizion withdrew from Utö to Veksher on 6 December. The rest followed on the 22nd. Behring would have found a deserted anchorage at Utö. The observation post had not sighted the Germans, although the direction finding stations picked up their wireless off the Gulf.

The three submarines at Baltiyskiy Port stayed put. In theory, this would allow them to carry out local defence in the spring when the ice began to retreat. These miniature novelties had already demonstrated unreliable engines and a tendency for battery fires. Their near worthlessness had earned them the ironic designation, 'Saviours of the Fatherland'. More usefully, once repaired, the British submarines would be available for long-range missions from Revel'.

One of Essen's biggest challenges was the freezing of the Gulf of Finland. This eventually locked the fleet into its bases, unable to intervene in less icy waters to the west and south. The Germans were unaffected, as the southern Baltic did not freeze. As the ice retreated in spring,

20.Torpedobootshalbflottille KTB, RM97 *U.26* KTB; Firle, *Ostsee*, pp.271–276; Gröner, *Band 4*, pp.75–77, *Band 6*, pp.86–87; *Hamburger Echo*, Hamburg, 15 March 1915; *Hamburgischer Correspondant* 23 February, 23 March, 10, 17 June 1915; podwodnedziedzictwo, < https://www.podwodnedziedzictwo.pl/wrak-lebbin-ii-czyli-betonowiec-kolo-leby/>, retrieved 29 April 2025; РГАВМФ:Фонд 716, Опись 2, Дело 24, pp.95–98, Дело 13, pp.287, 329, 330; Dziedzictwo historyczne na dnie Bałtyku, <https://dziedzictwo-historyczne-na-dnie-baltyku.pl/latona/>, retrieved 16 May 2025; Anon., *Verlustliste No.16*, p.10.

Poltava, one of the four new dreadnoughts. Armed with 12x30.5cm guns in four triple turrets, 8x12cm guns and 2x45cm underwater torpedo tubes on each side. Hull protected by 22.5cm armour, speed 23 knots. (Public domain)

this gave the Germans greater access, whilst the Russian Fleet was still in thick ice. It was an ideal time to land on the Russian coast.

Essen's concerns were greatest in relation to the Finnish Åbo skerries west of Hangö and the demilitarised Åland archipelago. The area had become vital, providing the fleet with protected fairways to multiple points of egress, bypassing any attempt to blockade the Gulf of Finland with mines or submarines. Essen proposed a plan to fortify and protect these areas. There was currently almost no military presence. Positions, '... on the flank of probable landing routes to Finland ... would allow us ... to carry out effective surveillance of the entrances to the Gulf of Finland and the Gulf of Bothnia, and to continue to combat enemy attempts to deprive the fleet of access to the open sea, thereby protecting the southwestern and western coasts of Finland from the landing of significant forces.' He wanted Kapitan 1st Ranga Otton Rikhter, commander of *Slava*, to lead a new command in the Åbo–Åland skerry position. As well as ships, this would have four new defensive batteries and a battalion of naval infantry to man defensive positions. There would be no fortification of the Åland Islands because of treaty obligations, but preparatory work setting up more communications posts and dredging channels would be undertaken, to allow fast troop deployment if threatened. By 17 January, Rikhter arrived to set up the new base at Åbo, with gunboats *Khrabryy* and *Grozyashchiy*, auxiliary minelayer *Il'men'* and two transports. *Beluga* had arrived on the 9th, to over-winter. At the end of January, four minesweepers, *No. 7*, *No. 2*, *No. 9* and *No. 11* were sent from Revel' to keep the route to Sweden clear throughout the winter. The Russians continued to innovate in their mine clearance. These were some of the first sweepers equipped with a 'fortral'. This had seen its first test in October. It was a bow trawl, a primitive forerunner of the paravane, which worked by pushing mines off to the side, away from the hull. Once proved effective, it was also fitted to cruisers. More warships were to arrive in the spring, including *Slava*, *Tsesarevich*, *Diana*, *Avrora* and a division each of destroyers and submarines.

Ezel' was also vulnerable on the southern approach. It was vital for flank defence, the security of Moon Sound, direction finding and seaplane operations. Essen once again requested a detachment of militia to guard Ezel' against raids. Previous requests had been unsuccessful. Fan-der-Flit finally agreed, and they came under Essen's orders.

Work also began at Russarö on an island battery to protect the approaches to Hangö. The Naval Ministry procured 23.4cm guns from America to arm it. Work to complete the Revel' fortress defences and improve the Sveaborg fortress defending the fleet base at Helsingfors, with guns transferred from the far east, went ahead after considerable lobbying by Essen.

The Tenth Army had responsibility for the coast south and west of Riga and were concerned about potential landings at major ports. They had proposed to Sixth Army that destroyers and submarines would be better employed during the winter defending Libava, along with a 15.2cm gun battery, supporting the modest troop presence there. An increase in coastal observation and wireless stations was also proposed, with the existing naval ones brought under army control. The fleet were already completing four new directional wireless stations over the winter at the southern tip of Ezel', Lyuzerort, Vindava and Libava. The last thing they needed was subordination to, or interference from, army wireless stations. For Sixth Army, the navy was there to defend their patch. As Al'tfater put it: 'I think that the Dvinsk district is mixed up in a thing that is not its business.' On 28 December, General-Leytenant Georgiy Raukh, the new Chief of Staff of Sixth Army responded by dismissing all of these proposals:

> The deployment of guns by the fleet at Libava does not seem strictly necessary, due to the fact that Libava, … has absolutely no significance for operations at sea and its defence does not feature in the tasks set for the Baltiyskiy Flot … the … coast is not a military objective for our enemy either.
>
> As for sending our destroyers and submarines to Libava and basing them there, this also seems unpromising due to the above-mentioned reasons, as well as the fact that the entire southeastern corner of the Baltic Sea … has been mined by us on such a large scale that any serious movement of enemy ships and transports here is out of the question.

Whilst Raukh's arguments held true for troop landings, the arguments betray the lack of interest in wider concerns by Sixth Army. Heinrich and Behring had demonstrated a fixation with Libava. However, marooning destroyers and submarines there over the winter was not a good strategy, as it would have been impossible to either get them out or reinforce them until the ice in the Gulf of Finland broke up. When it came to making use of Libava, this was too little, too late. For the navy to invest in turning Libava back into an operational base would have required a much more significant commitment of troops to defend the frontier around Memel. Placing some mobile batteries would have been a more realistic approach by Tenth Army to offer resistance to deter future attacks, rather than warships or fixed naval gun batteries.

Winter soon closed in. On 7 January, Merkushov noted that in Helsingfors, 'Frosts have begun, 10–13° Réaumur [minus 13–16°C]. There are no winds, so the sea is quickly covered with a thick ice sheet.' By the 12th: 'Winter has finally come into its own, covering the entire Gulf of Finland with an ice sheet; under its protection, the Baltiyskiy Flot has the opportunity to carry out the necessary repair work on ships and give its personnel a rest.' As had been planned, the submarines and most of the destroyers went into refit. The auxiliary minesweepers took over the guard patrol. 1st Brigada Kreyserov, *Novik*, the Poludivizion and the British submarines remained at Revel' to support them, whilst the body of the fleet over-wintered in Helsingfors.

Ships could still leave port with the aid of icebreakers. However, on the 11th Essen reported to Fan-der-Flit, 'The freeze that has begun off the coast of the Gulf of Finland will soon severely restrict the freedom of ships to leave their bases, and I fear that our enemy, taking advantage of this circumstance, will decide to undertake some form of operations off our coast in the Baltic Sea.'

Intelligence reports confirmed the withdrawal of Behring's force from Danzig to Swinemünde. From here, they could advance through unmined waters east of Bornholm to the northern Baltic and via Cape Arkona to Kiel. Essen was determined to defy the winter weather and maintain the momentum of his offensive: 'With the onset of the new moon and moonless nights [in mid-January], I decided to carry out another operation to lay mines in the western part of the Baltic Sea, on the communication routes with the ports of Swinemünde and Kiel, for which it seemed essential to pass beyond the island of Bornholm, the straits on both sides of which had to be assumed to be under continuous enemy control.' The fleet would advance into the western Baltic for the first time.

Kontr-Admiral Vasiliy Kanin would command the operation. He led the fleet's minelaying force. The efficiency of Kanin and his mine specialists had underpinned all of the mining work to date. It was the first time Kanin had taken a role leading an offensive operation. Timirëv, who had recently joined the staff of the fleet, writes that:

> He did not have singular outstanding abilities like Kolchak, Kerber and many other subordinates of Essen, but he was undoubtedly an intelligent person and an excellent manager, with great service and technical experience. In addition, he possessed to the highest degree the quality of maintaining the best relations with the most diverse types of people. A man of restraint, affable, and undoubtedly having a large reserve of common sense, Kanin gradually won the position of the first adviser, and even a friend, to Admiral Essen. This circumstance often caused clashes between him and Kerber, who could not reconcile himself to such an intrusion into his domain as Chief of Staff … Kerber was perhaps the only person with whom Kanin failed to establish good relations, despite all his adroitness. It was felt that they were two rivals, and that a struggle between them for power, for preponderance in the fleet, was inevitable.

This was Kanin's opportunity to shine after Kerber's own recent successes. *Rossiya*, *Oleg* and *Bogatyr'* formed the minelaying detachment, each with 100 mines. Kanin raised his flag on *Rossiya*, which Essen vacated for the operation. Kolchak, the operational mastermind behind the offensive, remained on the flagship, as did other members of the fleet staff, including Rengarten's code breaking team. Bakhirev would cover the operation with the other three cruisers of 1st Brigada. The cruisers left Revel' in separate groups on the two nights prior to the raid, pushing through the thin ice. They loaded the mines on the way from *Amur*, at an isolated roadstead near Örö. They then passed through the skerries to Utö. Here Kanin briefed the commanders.

Minesweepers swept a channel out of Utö the day before departure, as a precaution after the recent detection of German vessels in the area. On the night of the 12th, the force departed. Bakhirev's cruisers took the lead, followed at a distance by Kanin's minelayers. The weather next morning was calm, with unwelcome good visibility. The cruisers steamed east of Gotland, keeping clear of shipping lanes. At 4pm on the 13th, the six cruisers closed up and turned west at 14 knots towards Bornholm. In the event of discovery, the contingency was to lay all of the mines east of Bornholm. As they had seen nothing, Kanin opted to proceed with the plan. Once darkness fell, *Rossiya* increased to 16 knots and pulled away. This was the fastest the ship could steam without glowing coal embers from the funnels attracting attention. *Rossiya* had the longest

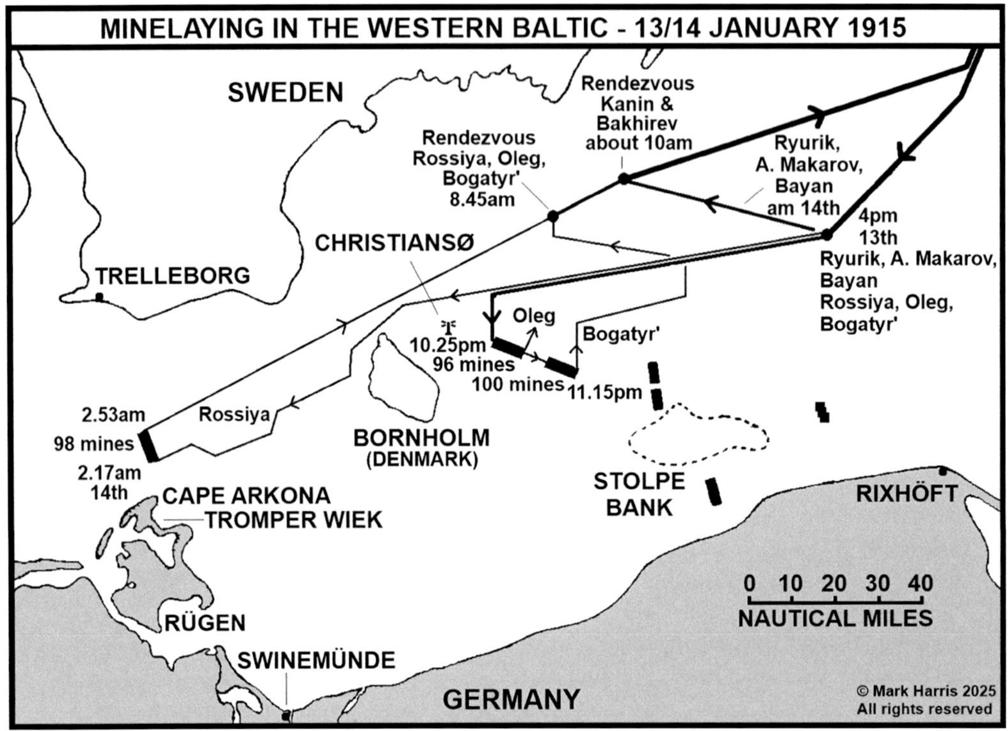

journey that night. She had been chosen for her large bunker capacity, allowing a sustained high speed, despite a 1,000 mile round trip. Essen describes the situation: 'The weather conditions were not favourable for breaking through the probable patrol near Bornholm, since the night was clear and the sky free of clouds at times, but the cruiser passed without encountering any enemy ships near Bornholm, although German wireless messages that were received and decoded indicated the presence of cruisers and destroyers beyond Bornholm.' The codebreakers were evidently hard at work.

Rossiya passed north of Bornholm, after getting a position fix from the lighthouse on the tiny Danish island of Christiansø. North–south steamer traffic west of Bornholm was heavy. *Rossiya* had to alter course more than once to keep a distance. Kanin apparently had second thoughts, believing that it was impossible that the big cruiser had escaped detection. There are a number of different accounts about exactly what happened. Kapitan 2nd Ranga Leonid Larionov writes that the doubts originated with *Rossiya*'s commander, Kapitan 1st Ranga Nikolay Podgurskiy. Merkushov says that Kanin, 'ordered a return course to lay the mines in another place, provided for this very eventuality. But as soon as the senior navigator commanded "starboard", A.V. Kolchak, who had come up to the bridge, addressed the admiral. "Your Excellency, are we really not going to fulfil the main task? We are so close to the goal!" This was enough, and Kanin ordered a return to the original course.' Whatever the exact details, all accounts agree that Kolchak encouraged Kanin to push on. As *Rossiya* approached Arkona, the destination, Essen writes that, 'it became clear from a received German wireless message that an enemy cruiser was in the area of the proposed minefield.' The recognition codes indicated *Undine*. Kanin decided to turn immediately to lay the mines two miles short of the intended position. At 1:30am on the 14th, *Rossiya* turned to starboard, slowed to 12 knots and began laying five separate, staggered groups of mines northwards for the next seven miles. The crew also launched a number of dummy periscopes, rigged up from small boat spars. The aim was to delay the sweeping of the minefield, by implicating a submarine for any sinking in the area. Two mines were retained, to drop in the path of any pursuit.

To everyone's relief, nothing appeared. *Rossiya* increased to 16 knots and retraced her course. Those off duty retired to the wardroom to toast success and the New Year, as it was 1 January in the Russian calendar. Merkushov writes that Kanin toasted Kolchak: 'Aleksandr Vasil'yevich! Thank you very much. Thanks to you, we were able to complete our main task.' It is perhaps more important that the remark was reported than whether it was made. It linked Kolchak to Kanin's success. For several hours, another vessel, feared to be *Undine*, steered a similar course, seeming to attempt signalling by light. Kanin decided to ignore them to maintain secrecy. Eventually the vessel turned away.

Meanwhile, once it was dark, Bakhirev had broken away to return to his 4pm position, to hold in place overnight. *Bogatyr'* and *Oleg* headed on in the wake of *Rossiya*. After getting their position from Christiansø, they turned for their minelaying run. At 10.25pm, *Oleg* laid 96 mines in five clusters. Twenty minutes later *Bogatyr'* laid her mines further east. The cruisers had to dodge encounters with other, unidentified vessels. At 8:45am next morning, Kanin's three cruisers rendezvoused northeast of Bornholm. They soon met Bakhirev and the force made an uneventful return to Utö. The crews had laid the mines without a hitch, apart from four of *Oleg*'s mines, damaged on loading. The modern 1912 pattern mines were very safe to handle, as they featured an internal timer and hydrostatic arming mechanism that was not affected by the elements.

Undine had been in the area. She was on watch off the Sound, and received orders to take over the escort of an important new floating dock north of Stolpe Bank. *D.10* and two auxiliaries were escorting it from Danzig. *Undine* passed south of Bornholm heading to the rendezvous during the night. The signal made to her from Swinemünde does refer to return via Arkona. *Undine*'s wireless acknowledgment would have sounded close to *Rossiya*, but she could not have been the vessel steering a similar course.

On the 17th, Essen summarised the success to date: 'I can only explain the recent failure on the German side by the extremely difficult navigation conditions created by our systematic mining of the approaches to German ports. Intelligence and private information, which is not yet fully reliable, indicate that not only was *Friedrich Carl* sunk … but also several light cruisers and over 12 steamships, which disappeared without a trace on the way to German ports.' A somewhat rosy assessment, but the last mission had added a deadly trap on routes heavily used by both Behring's warships and those operating from Kiel.[7]

7 РГАВМФ:Фонд 716, Опись 2, Дело 24, pp.177–180, Дело 13, pp.322–326, 382–384, 389–392, Дело 11, p.298, Дело 8, p.217, 242, Дело 37, pp.2, 12–13, Опись 1, Дело 15, pp.41–42; Меркушов, *Записки*, pp.301–320; Киреев, Траление, pp.33, 62; Гельмерсен, 'Заградительные', *Сборник 2*, pp.107–112; Pavlovich, *Operations*, pp.107–112; Тимиревъ, *Воспоминанія*, p.21; А.Д. Федечкин, 'Участие броненосного крейсера «Россия» в активных минно-заградительных операциях в 1914–1915 гг.', in *Елагинские Чтения, Выпуск VIII* (Санкт Петербург: Федеральное архивное агентство Российский государственный архив Военно Морского Флота, 2016), pp.61–68; BA:RM92 *Undine* KTB.

'A sad state of affairs'

Heinrich was searching for ways to reinvigorate offensive operations. Intelligence indicated a resumption of trade in the Gulf of Bothnia and production in Libava's factories. On 19 December, Heinrich ordered *P.L.19* to Königsberg, primarily to bomb these factories. He thought an airship might also help locate mines off Memel. After waiting for a break in the weather, *P.L.19* arrived on the 25th. Adverse weather aborted several attempts to bomb Libava. On 10 January, Heinrich chased apparent inaction. He wanted confirmation of intelligence received. This mentioned guns being emplaced, the entrances being re-opened and submarines in the harbour: 'I am very keen that the operation take place as soon as weather permits.'

On 12 January, Heinrich sent a paper to Behring, proposing two new operations. He contacted Ingenohl, seeking support from 5th Geschwader. The first proposal was to use *Augsburg* to, 'Launch a vigorous strike against enemy trade and the Swedish contraband trade in the Gulf of Bothnia.' The rest of Behring's force would cover from south of the Åland Sea. The second was, 'Renewed bombardment of Libava to destroy the industrial facilities, primarily the barbed wire factory.' Behring's destroyers would first need to have mastered minesweeping: 'There is a considerable mine threat off Libava. It is reasonable to assume that it is lowest for the approach from the North. From there, it should be possible to advance the battleships to fire at a range of 100 hectometres [just over six miles].' There was an option to combine both operations for maximum impact.

Behring responded that the plans were 'worthwhile and promising.' He requested three light sweeps to equip his destroyers, but was sceptical whether they would be 'suitable for mine clearance operations at all', even after training. He proposed fitting out a steamer as a barrier breaker instead. Typically, such vessels were filled with a cargo that would help them stay afloat. This would steam the planned route into Libava on the night before the attack, accompanied by *D.10*, manned by volunteers.

Ingenohl confirmed the availability of two of Grapow's battleships. Heinrich told Behring to take the required sweep gear from the laid up 2nd Minensuchdivision and loaned *S.129* and *S.131* for the duration of the operation, which was to take place within two weeks. On the 14th, *U.25* left Danzig to survey the intended approach and report traffic along the coast north of Libava, with orders to return by the 18th. Wünsche spent three days investigating the coast from Steynort to within sight of Libava, following the 20m line to keep clear of the known German mines to the west. He flew British colours to confuse anyone who caught sight of *U.25*. On his second visit, he got a clear view of the harbour and saw five steamers and two sailing ships. Apart from fleeting searchlights seen at night, there was no sign of traffic on the coast. Crucially for the proposed operation, there were no mines. On the return, he received a warning about the newly discovered *Enisey* minefield. He had already passed it for the third time. *U.26* and *U.23* had also done so on their last patrols.

On the 16th, Heinrich shared his plans with the Admiralstab, and requested a barrier breaker. The vessel Behring had hoped to use was not available until February. The Kaiser approved the plan, subject to bombardment only of 'militarily important' targets, and ensuring 'security against the danger of mines.' The Admiralstab authorised the naval contract collier *Otto Hugo Stinnes 9* as a barrier breaker.

On the 18th, Behring arrived at Kiel for discussions. That afternoon, he had an interview with Heinrich about the failed Utö operation. It was an uncomfortable meeting. Heinrich wrote that, 'The difficulties of an operation in the archipelago waterways become fully apparent. … It was a mistake that [Behring] had not embarked on one of the destroyers or on *Thetis* instead of remaining on *Prinz Adalbert*, from which he could not oversee the situation.' Grapow then joined them. Heinrich presented his detailed plan for the upcoming operation. This combined the two proposals, with the bombardment following the advance into the Gulf of Bothnia. All of Behring's surface forces would take part, with *U.25* and *U.26* covering to the east. Swedish vessels carrying contraband to Finland were to be sunk after their crews were removed. Heinrich left the two Admirals to discuss his proposal and present their views in the morning. Grapow was deeply unhappy. He thought the sinking of Swedish prizes was politically explosive. Behring suggested switching to attack the Russian warships reported in the area, but Grapow thought the plan was 'dangerous for the forces of [Behring] as well as for his own.' He was even less enthusiastic about the bombardment, believing a full Minensuchdivision was required for mine security, despite *U.26*'s findings. When Behring confirmed that only three of his destroyers were trained in sweep use, covering a width of only 160m, Grapow indicated that he would, 'request that [the bombardment] be abandoned.'

The three admirals reconvened next morning. Given the Kaiser's directions about safety, since Grapow was convinced that his battleships were in danger, the bombardment was a non-starter. Heinrich broke the news that the Admiralstab had indeed directed that Swedish vessels must not be sunk: 'for political reasons and due to ongoing special negotiations.' Adam had reported that *U.25* was unavailable due to defects and had reservations about the safety of operations in the northern Baltic after *U.26*'s last patrol. Grapow expressed concerns about rumoured Russian minelaying in the Åland Sea. This meant entry and exit via Swedish waters. Bringing prizes out this way would be controversial. Behring again suggested an attack on warships instead. Grapow objected as, 'if the 5th Geschwader was forced to come to the aid of [Behring], both could be placed in a very unpleasant situation.' Heinrich retired to make his decision and spoke on the telephone to Behncke, who advised dropping operations against Swedish commerce altogether. Regardless of the merits of the proposed operation, this episode epitomises the mire of unresolved issues that bedevilled any attempt at decisive action. High Command agreed operations in principle, but hedged them with risk mitigations that derailed operational implementation. Commanders brought together from different chains of command had irreconcilable priorities.

Heinrich handed over new orders to Behring that afternoon. These confirmed that the commerce raid on the Gulf of Bothnia was 'abandoned'. *Lübeck* and *Thetis* were to head to Kiel for delayed refits. Submarines were restricted to waters south of Gotland due to the icing problems. The priority for them was comprehensive refit to ensure that they were mechanically reliable in the spring. Reconnaissance operations were to continue: 'As soon as possible, taking advantage of any favourable weather conditions, *Augsburg* is to conduct an exploratory raid with four destroyers to the southern entrance of the Åland Sea. Movements with *Prinz Adalbert* and the remaining four destroyers are left to your discretion.' Behring left after a frustrating two days, but this last sentence left him a tantalising window of opportunity. Heinrich's entry in his war diary about the discussion had been clear that the operation to bombard Libava was also 'abandoned', but his written orders were less explicit.

Behring was back in Swinemünde on the 20th. As the weather was good, he immediately issued orders for the new operation, at a conference with his senior officers next morning, using his entire force. The 22nd dawned bright and sunny. *Augsburg* and four of Ehrhardt's destroyers left mid-morning, passing north of Bornholm, then up the west side of Gotland overnight, to arrive on the evening of the 23rd off the Åland Sea. They would raid it that night, entering through Swedish waters to avoid any mines. *Prinz Adalbert* left at mid-day, escorted by *G.132*, *T.97*, *S.129* and *S.131*. Behring headed up the east side of Gotland, to a support position south of the Åland Sea, to rendezvous with the returning *Augsburg*. Colliers *Oberpräsident Delbrück* and *Edmund Hugo Stinnes 4* would rendezvous off Hoburg on the 23rd, covered by *U.26*, to allow coaling next day.

By midday on the 23rd, Behring was east of Östergarn. He confided his thoughts to his war diary: 'The clear weather … makes an operation against Libava, similar to that [previously] planned … appear promising. The concerns … regarding the mine threat appear less significant for a single ship than for a squadron. … it would be necessary to head for Steynort, whose sounding would probably be possible, and then set a course for Libava on the 20-meter line. Navigational security would be provided by a destroyer anchored off Steynort. Execution during the night, so that the bombardment position would be reached by the time sufficient light arrived, allowing for maximum surprise.' The combination of his desire for action and frustration with recent losses and reverses seems to have driven him to test the 'left to your discretion' clause in his recent orders to the limit. At 4:15pm, as the light failed, *Prinz Adalbert* turned round and ordered her escorting destroyers to form astern. He sent no message to Heinrich, or anyone else.

Back in Danzig, Adam contacted Heinrich that evening. Behring had not briefed him about the current operation and he had no written orders, just a wireless message to despatch *U.26*. Heinrich filled in the background, noting in his war diary: 'This request proves that the Admiral's command approach failed in this case.' He had already spoken to Behring about his lax control over the forces at Danzig.

Prinz Adalbert obtained an exact position fix by closing Faludden lighthouse in southern Gotland. Behring then headed directly towards the 20m line, five miles off Steynort. From here, he would follow the route used by *U.25* to the bombardment position just north of Libava. Success required precise navigation in darkness. By 2:30am on the 24th, by dead reckoning, the force was 22 miles from the coast and stopped. The orders for the advance and bombardment were reasonably complex, referencing an attached sketch, and were now distributed. *T.97*, *S.129* and *S.131* formed a line 400m (440m) ahead of *Prinz Adalbert* and broke out their mine sweeps. *G.132*, commanded by Röder, formerly of *V.26*, went ahead at 15 knots to get into position as the mark boat off the coast. Once the destroyers were ready, the force set off at 10 knots.

Röder reached the coast, confirmed his position, shifted to the correct spot, about a mile away, and then placed two white lights on the starboard side of the bridge, shining west. It was 5am. Röder was about to give the order to drop the anchor when a crewman called his attention to port. A vessel emerged from the inky gloom to the north. *Prinz Adalbert* should have been at least 20 minutes away. The vessel looked like a big destroyer, possibly Russian. Röder ordered action stations. The crew rushed to bring the guns and torpedoes to the ready. The vessel crept closer. Three funnels were made out, then three small vessels ahead of her. It had to be *Prinz Adalbert*, but the signal lights were pointing the wrong way. The crew quickly shifted them to the port side.

Oberleutnant zur See Eberhard von Prittwitz und Gaffron commanded *T.97*, at the southern end of the sweeping line. His plot indicated arrival at Steynort at 5am. The crew began taking regular soundings. Within minutes, these gave just 6m. This was not a problem for *T.97*, but most certainly was for *Prinz Adalbert*. Each sounding was relayed by megaphone to the senior officer, Oberleutnant zur See Georg Fett, in the centre boat, *S.129*. Fett took no action, exasperating Prittwitz. After the last sounding, he added, 'We cannot possibly lead *Prince Adalbert* onto the mud!' The words were barely out of his mouth when the seaman on the sounding line called out, '4 meters of water to starboard.' Another meter and *T.97* herself would be in trouble. Fett answered, 'Your sounding cannot be right, we have enough water here and besides you would be able to see the white lanterns of *G.132*.' This was too much for Prittwitz. He ordered, 'Stop all engines! Hard to starboard!' Prittwitz now made out the outline of land. He called over to Fett, 'Even if I can't see 132, I can still see the coast right in front of me.' *S.131* at the northern end of the line turned hard to starboard. Fett finally lit the red warning lantern at the stern of *S.129*.

Kapitän zur See Andreas Michelsen of *Prinz Adalbert* had retired to rest. He gave orders to wake him at 5am when the watch changed, to take command half an hour before arrival off the coast. His first officer, Korvettenkapitän Günther von Zerboni di Sposetti, was in command on the bridge. The navigating officer, Kapitänleutnant Paul Cleve, was plotting progress in the chart house. He had previously been navigating officer of *Yorck*. She had sunk on German mines in November after a disastrous navigation error, for which Cleve was held responsible, along with *Yorck*'s captain. Zerboni visited the charthouse at 4:20am. Cleve and Oberstuermannsmaat Krüger had carefully annotated the chart with the numerous changes in course and speed needed to stay astern of the minesweepers. Zerboni looked at the chart, but failed to notice that the plot implied that she would arrive at the coast half an hour early. Cleve did not point it out to him. Twenty minutes later the sounding machine measured 30m, indicating that the turning point was coming up. At 5am, the watch was relieved. The new officer of the watch, Oberleutnant zur See Walrad Albat, ordered the helmsman, Obermatrose Seemann, to make a slow turn southwards to adjust position on the centre of the sweeping line ahead. The change of watch delayed the next sounding until 5:04am. The depth had only dropped to 27.5m. Puzzled, Cleve ordered the next sounding after the ship had advanced another nautical mile, which would take 6 minutes. Kapitänleutnant Paul Troll had just relieved the officer in charge of the lookout watch and was giving orders to his lookout posts over the ship's telephone. Behring came up to the bridge. Troll heard him call out, 'There is a vessel!' Troll dropped the phone, ran to the starboard wing of the bridge and looked through his binoculars where Behring was pointing. He could dimly make out a vessel to starboard, where no German vessel should be. He immediately pointed it out and shouted: 'Attention combat watch!' As he did so, the seaman arrived with the latest sounding and relayed it to Cleve. It was 12m. *Prinz Adalbert* was close to grounding. Cleve rushed out of the charthouse, shouting: '12 meters sounded. Hard to starboard!' Immediately Albat gave the order: 'Starboard 30!' As he did so, a shudder ran through the ship. Seemann hauled the wheel round, encountering strong resistance until it hit the stops at the maximum rudder angle. More shudders continued to run through the ship, as she gradually came to a halt, with the propellers churning uselessly aft. *Prinz Adalbert* was stuck fast off the enemy coast with an unidentified vessel close by to starboard. It was 5:14am.

Albat immediately ordered, 'Stop all engines! Midships!', then, 'Engines full astern!' Matrose Grulich at the engine room telegraphs rang up maximum astern power as Seemann hauled the wheel back. *Prinz Adalbert*'s propellers churned away, but she would not budge. The sweepers ahead had turned to starboard. Ironically, *S.129* now exposed her red light. There was relief as the mystery vessel to starboard showed two white lights. It was *G.132*.

Michelsen had been getting dressed when the ship grounded. On reaching the bridge, he ordered the engines stopped. As the light began to grow, the faint outline of the coast appeared. *Prinz Adalbert* had made landfall too far to the north. Sounding round the ship confirmed that she had grounded amidships with a slight list to starboard. The bow and stern were in deeper water. Flooding was not serious, but had affected a number of the compartments in the double bottom. It was only spreading very slowly.

After lightening the ship by lowering the boats and pumping fresh water overboard, Behring ordered the destroyers to assist. As the engines went full astern: '... an attempt was made to have *G.132* tow the stern to starboard and *T.97* push the bow from port to turn the ship and push it off the shallows.' It was worse than useless. A broken towline wrapped round the starboard propeller shaft. The starboard engine had to stop.

Things looked bleak. The nearest ship powerful enough to pull *Prinz Adalbert* off by brute force was hundreds of miles away in Kiel. The crew began ditching coal from side bunkers over the side. Gercke now suggested that the destroyers steam in as close as they could, passing in formation at top speed so that the churning wash from their propellers would rock the ship and displace the ooze around the hull. The destroyers passed the starboard side, as *Prinz Adalbert* went full astern on the two remaining engines. She would not move. As the light grew, Steynort Lighthouse began making repeated recognition challenges. *Prinz Adalbert* bluffed a reply. It would not be long before the Russians sent out ships. The destroyers tried again. To Behring's relief: 'the ship is lifted by the resulting sea and frees itself'. *Prinz Adalbert* had been stranded for almost two hours.

At 5:35am, *Augsburg* was heading back out of the Åland Sea, having seen nothing, when an alarming message from Behring arrived: '*Prinz Adalbert* aground on a shallow [at Steynort].' Horn immediately headed for the position. Heinrich received the same message a few hours later. His reaction was unsurprising: 'Completely incomprehensible how the ship got there.' Another message from Behring came in minutes later: 'Double bottom partially leaking. 200t of water in the ship, but out of danger, heading for Swinemünde.'

Flooding stabilised at a manageable 350t and no assistance was required. Behring cancelled further operations and the separate forces retraced their outward routes. The colliers returned to port, as they were no longer required. Another command muddle now surfaced. *U.26* set off for the Gulf of Bothnia, to carry out attacks on warships and commerce. Adam had ordered Berckheim to do so, once his escort task was completed. Heinrich saw a copy of the orders that afternoon. He immediately countermanded them, as this was inconsistent with his instructions and discussions with the Admiralstab. This was more evidence of poor command control by Behring. *U.26* returned to Danzig. Later that evening, Heinrich ordered *Prinz Adalbert* to head directly to Kiel for repairs, as the dock there was the only one in the Baltic that could accommodate her.

At 1:55am that night, the 25th, *Augsburg* passed 14 miles from Christiansø. Horn was in the charthouse when, 'a very violent detonation occurred on the starboard side adjacent to Boiler Room Three. The ship briefly rose amidships and whipped back strongly at both ends, bow and stern.' Horn went immediately to the bridge, ordering: '"Steady, slow ahead." Shortly thereafter, I received the message: "Rudder failure."' The steering gear that ran to the steering engines had jammed. Ehrhardt's four destroyers were keeping touch, following in line astern in the darkness. *G.133* was about 50m away, when there was '... a violent detonation on *Augsburg*. A high, black cloud of smoke rose on the starboard side ... *Augsburg* gave three short blasts with its siren, which *G.133* repeated. … The Halbflottille destroyers reversed course, causing *G.133* and *G.136* to collide, and *G.136*'s stem to be rather severely deformed.'

Stoker Klein was in Boiler Room Three, 'I was just about to get some air under the port fan engine rotor [which drew air into the boiler room] when there was a bang and I was thrown into the air in the darkness. When I regained my footing, I tried to escape through the door to the companionway, but I couldn't open the door because it was jammed shut by the warmed water that had come in. The next moment, the water crashed over my head, and I was sucked upwards through the ash chute. Once at the top, with great difficulty, struggling to breathe, I managed to open the armoured hatch and escape.' The boiler room had filled almost instantly, killing eight crew at their posts. Only one other man who had been standing at the door escaped. Almost everything in the ship jumped violently upwards, including people. Five crew were injured. Everything breakable smashed. The wireless net crashed down, along with the forward rangefinder.

The crew manned the hand steering wheel below decks, above the rudder, to get the ship back under control. Horn realised that *Augsburg* was slowly turning to port, despite steering a steady course by compass. The compasses had failed. Horn ordered a full stop until damage was under control. Grassmann wrote, 'Under the energetic, prudent leadership of the First Officer, Kapitänleutnant Gernot Goetting, the "heart" of the ship, and … Marineoberingenieur [Karl] Klein, the damage control team, together with the crew of the next endangered boiler room, worked for hours behind blazing-hot boilers, constantly doused and soaked by the water … to save Boiler Room Two.' *Augsburg* had a 3° list to starboard. This was largely corrected by trimming and counter-flooding. There was 600 tons of flooding, increasing the draught forward by a metre. Horn reported that 'the measures taken by the First Officer were impeccable.' The timber shores and leak plugs in the bulkheads allowed the pumps to keep the water down in the boiler rooms fore and aft of the hit. Ehrhardt reported the situation to Behring. It had been fifty minutes since the explosion: 'Hit by mine 002 Beta 9. Boiler Room 3 full of water. No danger at present.' The attack in darkness and lack of any torpedo track, with no wind to ruffle the calm water, convinced Horn that a mine had been the cause. *G.133* managed to pick out the site of the explosion with her searchlight: 'a patch of yellow foam'. Ehrhardt led his destroyers to *Augsburg* across this spot, now presumed safe. A mine laid by *Oleg* just 12 days earlier had been responsible. Behring's entire force had passed through the area on the way north.

The newer light cruisers were heavily compartmented and big enough to enable damage to be localised from a single underwater hit. Their relatively shallow draught placed less strain on bulkheads than the deeper draught armoured cruisers and battleships, making it easier to shore up and control leaks. Despite the devastating blast, by 3:25am, *Augsburg* was stabilised and ready to move off. Horn ordered Ehrhardt to place two destroyers ahead with their sweeps out and got underway at 5 knots. *G.133* went ahead to navigate. It was 90 miles to Swinemünde. Ehrhardt ordered *G.132* and *T.97* to join him. Behring had already detached them to return to Swinemünde. *Prinz Adalbert* was approaching Arkona, with *S.129* and *S.131*. He immediately turned east to close *Augsburg* on receiving Ehrhardt's report.

At 9am, *G.132* and *T.97* joined the escort. Three hours later, four Swinemünde auxiliaries and two tugs arrived. *Oberpräsident Delbrück* approached during the morning. With plenty of vessels to screen *Augsburg*, Ehrhardt ordered *G.134* and *G.135* to break off and coal from her along the way, to fill their near empty bunkers. Meanwhile, salt water had contaminated the feed to *Augsburg*'s remaining working boilers: 'During the morning, the main engines had to be shut down several times because the boilers were priming due to the high salt content, meaning the available steam was only sufficient to keep the bilge pumps running. At 12:30pm, abandoned the ship's own engine for power and took a tow from [*G.133*].' Ehrhardt, 'was able to tow at [revolutions for] 12 knots, giving 6 knots over the ground. Apart from a few minor hiccups, I towed *Augsburg* to within a mile of ... Swinemünde, where we arrived at 6:30pm.' Docking revealed a 70 square metre hole in the hull.

Meanwhile, far to the west, *Gazelle* was on routine patrol that day, shuttling between the Sound, Møn, Trelleborg and Arkona. Mysing was zigzagging at 16 knots. There was almost no wind and a calm sea. At 2:39pm, *Gazelle* was at the end of a leg from Trelleborg to Arkona. Suddenly, there was an explosion at the stern, which lifted, then slammed back down, throwing crew and objects to the deck. The cause was quickly apparent, a torpedo:

> Shortly after the detonation ... the periscopes of a submarine came into view [at 500m] on the starboard beam. It was being fired upon by the forward guns. The periscopes vanished for a very short time and then came back into view ... astern. A portion of the boat's surface, approximately 10–15 meters long and about 40cm high, also emerged from the water. This boat was now being fired upon by the aft guns. ... a hit was clearly observed amidships [at 2,000m] below the periscope. ... Immediately afterwards, the stern appeared, quickly disappeared again, and a swirling of water was seen.

Almost immediately: 'The periscopes [of a second submarine] came into view about 15° ahead on the starboard bow [300m away] and moved forward on the bow to the port side. It was fired upon by the forward guns.' Mysing now arrived on the bridge:

> I had just retired and was in the bunk room of the sea cabin during the explosion, and I was thrown against the ceiling by the shock. At first, I passed out. I was then hastily bandaged by the ship's doctor and went to the bridge. There, the Nav[igating] Officer reported to me: "Submarine in sight, ahead to starboard." I then gave the order: "All ahead full, ram submarine." I did not see any periscopes myself, but I attribute this to my head wound (my eyes were temporarily clogged with blood, and there was numbness in my head caused by the impact).

Since the rudder was not responding, the ship was steered by reducing power on one of the engines. The second submarine disappeared. The 10.5cm guns had fired about 60 rounds. The gunnery officer had to stop some wild shooting at black dots that he identified as diving ducks, although he also confirmed the hit on the submarine through his binoculars.

Mysing maintained full speed to clear the danger area. He headed into shallower water at Tromper Wiek bay on Rügen. The explosion had broken the mainmast, wrecked the wireless net and damaged equipment. It was impossible to send a wireless message. As well as Mysing himself, five crew were injured. Damage control parties were fighting the flooding aft. The aftermost steering compartment had flooded instantly, killing the two crewmen in it. Watertight doors were closed, but it was impossible to stop the flooding in the second compartment, which had to be abandoned. Although the next bulkhead was leaking, the damage control parties got it shored up, and the pumps were able to keep the water down. Flooding spread in the compartments above the severely damaged armour deck. The stern sank almost 2m into the water, and the bow rose about 1m upwards, but despite 700t of flooding, *Gazelle* was not in danger of sinking. The engines had been unaffected by the explosion, but at 3:39pm the starboard engine began racing. It was evident that the propeller had fallen off the shaft. The engine was shut down and speed reduced on the port engine, leaving the ship locked into a slow turn to starboard. Ten minutes later the port propeller dropped off. *Gazelle* was dead in the water. In desperation, Mysing launched the steam pinnace to tow the ship. It was hopelessly underpowered. Mysing hailed a passing steamer. This proved to be the Swedish ferry *Konung Gustav V*. Her captain agreed to a tow. However, whilst she manoeuvred into position, Mysing was relieved to see German destroyers coming into sight at around 6pm. He dismissed the ferry with thanks.

At 3pm, the observation station at Arkona had reported, 'Apparently several submarines, light cruiser firing in all directions.' This was followed by, '*Gazelle* apparently intends to run aground here.' By 3.30pm, *Gazelle* was close enough to the observation post to get a coded message through by searchlight, reporting the torpedo hit and damage. Heinrich ordered Wieting to send two destroyers from the Sound to assist. He sent *T.113* and *S.123*. Behring was to send any available destroyers. Thanks to Ehrhardt's foresight coaling his destroyers, he was able to send *G.132*, *G.134* and *G.135*. Behring reached *Augsburg*, which obviously needed no further assistance. Due to the submarine danger, Heinrich ordered *Prinz Adalbert* into nearby Swinemünde. Behring released *S.129* and *S.131* to assist *Gazelle*.

Röder was the senior destroyer officer with *Gazelle*. He secured *G.132* to starboard and *G.134* to port, in order to be able to steer the ship with their engines. *G.135* prepared to tow ahead. *S.129* arrived and took the five wounded men for treatment in Swinemünde. The injured Mysing stayed with his ship. The other destroyers arrived to assist with navigation and an anti-submarine screen. The formation set off at 7 knots at 8pm. Despite *G.135* having to drop her tow with a rudder failure, at 5am next morning, the destroyers guided *Gazelle* into Swinemünde. Fortunately, the weather had stayed calm, with just a sprinkling of snow. Röder had done a consummate job organising the salvage, showing the good seamanship previously displayed rescuing the crew of *Magdeburg*.

Gazelle had run into the minefield laid by *Rossiya*. There were no submarines near the area. There is a possibility that she had engaged one or more of the periscope decoy floats that *Rossiya* had deployed at the minefield, or the whole thing may have been the result of overwrought imaginations. The day had claimed two victims, but the disasters were not over yet.

P.L.19 had made another failed attempt to reach Libava in adverse weather on the 19th. Her highly experienced commander, Hauptmann August Stelling, now left to take command of the new *P.L.25*. He was relieved by Oberleutnant a.D. (Retired) Ernst Meier, who had been commanding the small *P.L.6*. This vessel had proved unsuitable for patrol work and been taken out of service on 27 December.

The calm weather on the 25th finally gave a window for attack. At 4:20am, *P.L.19* took off from Königsberg, with a mixed bomb load of 50kg and smaller bombs, totalling 275kg. To reduce weight, there was a minimum crew aboard, and no wireless equipment. Low cloud forced the airship to navigate at less than 1000m. By 9:30am, the crew sighted the distinctive lake just south of Libava. The passage through the freezing air caused problems, as her civilian engineer, Doktor Rotzoll relates: 'there was 200–300kg weight of hoarfrost, which had formed thick crusts (3cm) everywhere… the ship had holes in the propeller plane next to the gangway on both sides … there was one about the size of a hand. … We had already observed pieces of ice flying from the propellers against the hull, and these pieces of ice had caused large cracks in the gangway lining.' The forward gas-venting valve also refused to close properly. With the target in sight, the problems were manageable. Meier pressed on. The cloud forced the airship to come in low to bomb Libava at 600m. Obermaschinistenmaat Zimmermann was manning the engines: 'At about 9:50am, attack on Libava. All bombs away. Fired upon by the shore batteries, machine guns, and rifles. At about 10:13am, the attack ended, and we began our return journey. … The blast of air from each individual bomb was clearly noticeable when it exploded.'

With the load greatly reduced by fuel consumption and the release of the bombs, the airship rose into the clouds. It looked like the loss of gas was not going to be a problem. It was actually hard to keep the airship down. Zimmermann was relieved: 'We went out to sea, heading for home. Joy, satisfaction, and pride on every face.' However, the strain of the ice on the propellers had evidently taken its toll on the engines. Rotzoll continues:

> … half an hour into our return journey, the main bearing of the starboard propeller burst at an altitude of 800 meters. At that time, the ship was experiencing severe downdraft. … she fell very quickly at first, later more slowly, and at an altitude of 300m, after considerable dropping of ballast and a steep [almost vertical] upward tilt, she almost succeeded in breaking her fall. Then the port engine also failed, no longer receiving fuel due to the tilt, and now, despite frantic dropping of ballast, the ship fell down to the water. The impact was not very severe. … After a single gentle dip, the gondola remained suspended [in the air] close to the water and only gradually came to rest at the back end.

The *Russkoye Slovo* reported on the raid:

> … airship No. 19 emerged from the fog above the city. It was flying so low that the officers and crew sitting in the gondola could be seen. … the first bomb … fell on a pile of scrap iron in the Becker factory. The second bomb fell near the freight depot, the third near the railway bridge, and the fourth on the roof of a house. In total, the Germans dropped nine bombs without causing any damage to the city. Nobody was killed.

Next day Essen reported:

> The Zeppelin bombarding Libava was damaged and alighted 15 miles south of Libava. The auxiliary vessels sent after it under the command of Kapitan [2nd Ranga Apollinariy] Nikiforaki and Yurkovskiy closed in and fired at it with small arms. After several return shots from rifles, the crew surrendered. Having taken the prisoners onto the vessels, they tried to tow the zeppelin, but due to the difficulties encountered, they could not do this, and the zeppelin was destroyed.

It had taken the two small steamers just over two hours to reach *P.L.19*. The wrecked airship was set alight after the tow failed. It is unsurprising that the Russians concluded that the large amount of rifle fire directed at the low flying airship by border guards had brought it down, but it had no effect on the outcome. There is no mention of any anti-aircraft weapons in Russian accounts. Unsurprisingly, the seven prisoners seem to have done nothing to deepen their humiliation by contradicting the Russian version of events. It is unclear whether Zimmermann knew that they were being shot at until after his capture. When the airship failed to return, Heinrich ordered boats out from Neufahrwasser to search. Two days later the Russians announced the shooting down in an official communiqué.

The disastrous sequence of events had crippled Behring's forces, leaving him with no available cruisers. In view of the torpedo attack, Heinrich immediately suspended exercises by battleships in Kiel Bay and confined all large ships to port. The news of the attack off Arkona further spooked the shipping companies. The train ferry service between Sweden and Germany was briefly suspended. Heinrich issued new orders directly to Adam to redirect efforts to an anti-submarine patrol west of Bornholm, but he currently had no submarine to send to it. He was also coming under pressure to hand his submarines over for an impending campaign of unrestricted commerce warfare in the North Sea and Atlantic, as submarines were critically short to support it.

Behring was unconvinced by *Gazelle*'s report of submarine attack. The facts did not add up, such as the absence of torpedo tracks in the calm water. He recommended sweeping Arkona for mines. Six boats of 2nd Minensuchdivision were finally available. They were assigned to Behring. On the 30th, they began sweeping, supported by the Swinemünde auxiliaries. On 1 February, they cleared the first Russian mine.

On 26 January, the Kaiser read the summary of the previous day's events from the Admiralstab. The full-page of woe devoted to the Baltic came on top of a growing realisation that a battle had been lost at Dogger Bank in the North Sea. Hopman reflected on the mood at Headquarters: 'The future of our navy, and thus mine, looks bleak. … It's now a sad state of affairs with our Baltic forces.'[8]

The conference in the castle

By 2 February, Heinrich considered it safe enough to bring *Prinz Adalbert* to Kiel for repair. Behring headed out next morning, heavily screened by 20th Halbflottille. The minesweepers of 2nd Minensuchdivision swept ahead as it passed where they working at Arkona. On the morning of the 4th, Heinrich convened a conference at Kiel Castle. His Deputy Chief of Staff, Korvettenkapitän Martin Hosemann and his assistant, Kapitänleutnant Otto Betz attended. Michelsen and Gercke accompanied Behring, whose war diary gives a formal account of the meeting:

> [Heinrich] explained to [Behring] that he could not spare him a reproach of the most serious nature. … it was not in accordance with his intentions that [Behring] abandon the northward advance on 23 January … This course of action, combined with the failure to report his intentions … was so undisciplined that it could lead to [his] dismissal from post and the initiation of court-martial proceedings against him. [Behring] is asked to state whether he

8 BA:RM28 KTB, RM49 Detachierten Admirals KTB, RM97 *U.25*, *U.26* KTB, RM92: *Prinz Adalbert*, *Yorck*, *Augsburg*, *Gazelle* KTB, RM56 20.Torpedobootshalbflottille, 4.Torpedobootsflottille KTB, RM117 Marine-Luftschiffe der Kaiserlichen Marine, *P.L.6*, *P.L.19* KTB; Stoelzel, *Ehrenrangliste*, p.171; Hopman, *Leben*, pp.552–556; Firle, *Ostsee*, pp.276–282; Anon., *Verlustliste No.18*, p.2, *20*, pp.13–14, Grassmann, 'Augsburg', pp.201–202.

recognizes his actions as wrong. He acknowledges that he acted incorrectly from a military perspective, but requests that court-martial proceedings be initiated to clarify the matter. Heinrich requests that he should decide this.

After discussing the likely cause of the damage to *Gazelle*, Heinrich outlined the revised basis for future operations:

> The plan is that [Behring], who is to be stationed in Swinemünde, will establish patrol lines for cruisers from this port around Bornholm, effectively abandoning the eastern Baltic. The submarine patrols already planned between Sandhammaren and Adlergrund will continue. Danzig will remain the submarine base.
>
> … Once 2nd Minensuchdivision has completed operations in the area north of Arkona, it will work the area between Bornholm and Adlergrund (Rønne Bank). Kiel Hilfsminensuchdivision will carry out the clearance of the mines near Stolpe Bank, with aircraft to support it. [Behring] will remain in overall command, and his deputy, in the event of leave, will be Kapitän Michelsen.

Next day, Behring responded in writing to Heinrich. He gave a detailed defence of operating under the 'freedom of action' granted, in both the guidance given on appointment, and in the order for the last operation. However, he acknowledged:

> The mere fact that the operation, which I had independently planned and scheduled, ended in failure proves me wrong. Ultimately, I feel personally responsible for the failure of the signal transmission to *G 132*, for the indecisiveness of the minesweeper commanders, and for the error in the command of S.M.S. *Prinz Adalbert*, which caused the grounding. Experience has long taught me that I cannot place the same demands on the personnel or material of the ships and vessels under my command as I can place on ships of the first battle line. If I did not allow myself to be deterred from initiating a venture on my own that required very high performance, then I must bear the consequences if it failed.
>
> Furthermore, there was nothing to prevent me from informing Your Royal Highness of my plan in a timely manner by means of a wireless report. I am aware that, due to this omission, the accusation of unmilitary conduct is justified against me.
>
> In view of these facts, which coincide with a three-month period of ill fortunes in war, I expected Your Royal Highness's displeasure.

Michelsen echoed Behring's reference to personnel weaknesses. In his report, he criticised his first officer, Zerboni, as having, '… paid too little attention to the navigation of the ship.' Cleve had, 'shown serious errors of confidence and decision-making.' He had admitted responsibility for the grounding, but felt that it was reasonable to have relied on a warning from the destroyers. Cleve left *Prinz Adalbert* two months later, but remarkably, later had two more short appointments as a Navigating Officer. Michelsen criticised Fett for ignoring Prittwitz's warnings as, 'absolutely unbelievable.' However, the destroyers had little experience of sweeping, making reliance on them a gamble.

Heinrich had ceded control of the eastern Baltic and adopted a purely defensive stance with the meagre forces that remained seaworthy. *Prinz Adalbert* and *Augsburg* were out of action until the spring. As well as being out of favour with Heinrich, Behring was also in poor health. On the 7th, Heinrich granted him a four week leave, 'due to his intestinal complaint, to enable recuperation and to take a spa cure.' Michelsen was left in command. That day, *Lübeck* and *Thetis* completed their refits. They carried out exercises west of Bornholm, offering some cover to the minesweeping at Arkona. *U.26* made an uneventful patrol off Bornholm from 3–13 February, during which she lost one of her hydroplanes. Berckheim returned to Danzig for repairs and a major engine refit. *U.25* was still undergoing hers. As soon as *U.23* completed repairs on 19 February, she went to the North Sea to join the commerce war. Submarine patrols were over until spring.

Gazelle had been patched up by 18 February. However, repairs were estimated at over six months duration. On the 22nd, the Reichs-Marine-Amt decided that *Gazelle* would not be repaired, in view of the age of the ship and the level of damage. Both external propeller shafts and the rudder were missing. There was extensive internal structural damage to the hull. The engineers considered a mine, rather than a torpedo, to be responsible, but *Gazelle*'s officers continued to insist on submarine attack. She was decommissioned and hulked, with armament and equipment removed. This left Mischke with just *Amazone*, *Undine* and *Panther* to support the destroyer patrols in the western Baltic. 20th Halbflottille was temporarily assigned to allow his destroyers to carry out much needed refits.

Mines were still a threat, and were no respecters of neutrality. On 20 February, the German minefield in the Great Belt claimed a victim. The Norwegian steamer *Bjerka* strayed into it with a cargo of coal, approaching her nearby destination. The crew got into the boats before she sank. They were quickly picked up. A few days earlier, there was news of corpses and a log from another Norwegian steamer, *Nordkyn*, washed up at Rixhöft. She had been heading from Bergen to Königsberg, with a crew of 11, carrying herring. The last log entry was passing Christiansø on 24 January. She almost certainly hit a Russian mine.[9]

The priority was to restore navigational security before the spring thaw and the renewal of hostilities, but progress was slow. 2nd Minensuchdivision finished their work around Arkona and moved to investigate reports of mines south of Bornholm. The converted steamer *Answald* arrived at Swinemünde to join the hunt on 13 February. Her two seaplanes made tentative attempts to spot mines from the air. By the end of the month, the search wound up, with nothing found, since there were no mines here. The Kiel Hilfsminensuchdivision arrived on 19 February to work from Stolpmünde on the coast eastwards, having been equipped with shallower draught boats. By the end of the month, they only managed to declare it clear as far as Scholpin. The Neufahrwasser auxiliaries kept up patrols on the declared safe routes to restore the confidence of the shipping companies. At the end of February, the Swinemünde Hilfsminensuchdivision was disbanded and the boats transferred to the other two divisions. The personnel were to form a new unit. Although Heinrich had been sceptical, Behring's idea of using motor boats to search for mines was a good one. Two steamers, *Inkula* and *Indianola*, were being prepared to act as carriers and depots for six boats each. However, the new unit would not be available for use until

9 *Bjerka* (1914) 620 GRT, *Nordkyn* (1875) 268 GRT.

Gazelle in dry dock, showing mine damage at the stern, 3 February 1915. (Public domain)

the spring. The swathe of Russian mines in the eastern Baltic was untouched. Many minefields were undiscovered. Meanwhile, the Russian fleet continued their work.[10]

Defying the ice

Essen was determined to keep up offensive operations for as long as the ice permitted, both mining and long-range submarine patrols, but the British had been out of action for some time. On 21 January, *E.9* completed repairs. The dockyard had cast a new propeller, but on the day it was completed, long awaited stores and replacement parts, including a spare propeller, finally arrived from Britain, via Arkhangel'sk in the Arctic. At 9:30am on the 24th, Horton departed Revel' for a patrol in bitterly cold weather. The icebreaker *Petr* carved a path ahead of him through many miles of ice choking the Gulf.

10 BA:RM5/4046, RM49 Detachierten Admirals KTB, RM28 KTB; *Aftenposten*, Oslo, *Arbeidet*, Bergen, 17 February 1915; *Nidaros*, Trondhjem, 21 February 1915; Firle, *Ostsee*, 282–284.

That morning Steynort observation post sent out the alert that a cruiser had run aground there. Essen immediately ordered the Poludivizion to head to the area to attack any vessels that came to its aid. They were to order Horton to spend time in the area before proceeding to his patrol billet. *E.1*, which had just completed replacing her broken shaft, as well as 2nd Divizion, were to prepare for sea to reinforce them.

At 5:35pm, the destroyers caught up with *E.9* and passed on the new orders. Two hours later the force finally emerged into open sea, after 75 miles in the ice. *Petr* returned to Revel'. The destroyers went ahead and would reach Steynort before dawn. It was not to be. At 10pm, the news that the cruiser had already departed resulted in their recall. *E.9* did not receive the message. Horton pressed on. He arrived at the scene of the grounding next day to find nothing. *E.9* investigated up and down the coast until the afternoon of the 26th. Concluding that the cruiser was gone, Horton headed for the western Baltic.

E.9 arrived off Stevns Klint on the 28th, having been careful to avoid being seen on the way. There was plenty of commercial traffic, but only a single destroyer. Next morning, conditions were more promising off Møns Klint. Horton decided to attack. There was a heavy swell, making depth keeping difficult, but this would conceal his periscope and torpedo. Three destroyers heading to the Sound passed too far off. *E.9* closed in to the route they had used. Another approached. Within ten minutes, Horton was in the perfect position to attack, 600 yards [550m] away and slightly ahead:

> 3.32 … Fired bow torpedo. Observed torpedo to be running well for about 150 yards [m] and the destroyer to be keeping a steady course. Dipped to avoid detection. At the correct moment after firing – 45 to 50 seconds – heard the unmistakeable noise of torpedo detonating.
> 3.36 Rose to 17 ft [periscope depth]. Found destroyer had disappeared.
> 3.37 Observed another destroyer 1½ miles approaching from the Northward. She appeared to be very much on the qui vive as I turned to give her a beam torpedo. She turned directly away from me at right angles and making a considerable detour, passed through the spot where first destroyer was last seen, at high speed.

More destroyers turned up to search the area. They were very alert. There were no more opportunities to attack. That night *E.9* began the return journey:

> … very cold North wind and rising sea. Spray froze as it struck and bridge became a mass of ice. Experienced considerable difficulty in keeping conning tower hatch free of ice. Found it necessary to keep a man continuously employed on this work. Bridge screen immovable, ice about 6 inches [15cm] thick on it. Telegraphs frozen.

The only way to get rid of the ice was to dive to the bottom and wait for it to melt. Next day, there were frequent snowstorms. On the afternoon of the 31st, *E.9* reached Utö. An icebreaker was summoned to lead the way back to Revel'. Merkushov wrote that, 'The British complain that navigation in the Gulf of Finland has become almost impossible due to continuous ice fields up to one foot thick, and they have had great difficulty in reaching Revel'.' That day Essen noted, 'the appearance of solid ice floes 6 to 12 inches thick throughout the Gulf of Finland.' In his report, Horton commended all three of his officers, including Leytenant Essen, for, 'resource

E.9 after arrival at Revel' on 1 February 1915. Ice encases the bridge screen and forward part of the conning tower. *E.1*, moored next to the depot ship, *Rynda*, is comparatively ice-free. (Public domain)

and cheerfulness under novel and at times trying conditions.' His father was delighted with the results of the operation, and recommended that the entire crew receive medals for the successful attack. Horton received the Order of St. Anna, and the rest of the crew lesser awards. Both he and Laurence already had a St. Vladimir for their breakthrough into the Baltic. In a futile attempt to keep their presence secret, the Admiralty requested no announcement.

Unfortunately, there had been no success. Horton had attacked *S.120*. She had been late leaving for the Sound guard that morning, chasing after three boats of 8th Halbflottille. Suddenly there was a: 'Water whirlpool and shortly thereafter heavy detonation near the boat. Boat undamaged. Suspected grounding of a torpedo fired by a submarine, as the water at the detonation site is dirty. I searched, found nothing. I did not see a submarine.' Horton's torpedo had dived to the bottom. It exploded just 50m off the starboard bow, throwing up a 2m column of dirty water.

All three of his torpedoes fired in the Baltic had failed to run correctly. The 'second destroyer' was *S.120* coming back to investigate. The attack caused limited concern, as the evidence was ambiguous, but it joined a steady stream of other reports of torpedo attacks in Kiel Bay, the Sound and on steamers east of Bornholm. All of them were bogus, but continued disruption to fleet exercises and trade confidence resulted.

The Russian intelligence network was now providing Essen with daily reports on the coming and goings in all of the German Baltic ports. Whilst they also contained inaccurate local rumours, they were largely accurate as to ship movements. Reports at the beginning of February correctly identified the safe route directly north from Danzig. This coincided with a gap in the Russian minefields. On the next period of moonless nights, Essen was determined to foul it. He lobbied to include *Andrey Pervozvannyy* and *Imperator Pavel I* in support positions for his ongoing offensive: 'clashes become more and more likely, especially since the enemy will eventually understand that leaving their adversary's mining of its own waters without counteraction is hardly permissible.' With the growing strength of the fleet and coastal defences, as well as the lack of any uncommitted German troops to mount a seaborne operation, Fan-der-Flit considered the risks acceptable. He recommended the proposal to STAVKA. Grudging approval arrived just too late for the next operation, but with a debilitating caveat: 'all measures must be taken to ensure that these ships do not expose themselves to the risk of a combat encounter with significantly superior enemy forces.'

On 7 February, Tenth Army made an enquiry: 'The command of the Dvinsk District reports that in the near future operations are planned against Memel and the coastal strip adjacent to it. … is it possible to expect any assistance from the fleet and naval aviation in these operations.' The onset of winter made a positive response impossible. Essen proposed a range of options that the fleet could take to support the army, if they postponed the operation until after the spring thaw. This included the deployment of shallow draught vessels to use in the lagoon beyond Memel. The only immediate support was more mining of the Bay of Danzig, already in plan. The whole idea was 'postponed indefinitely', after Tenth Army's positions further south in Ostpreussen became the target of a German offensive launched that very day.

The next minelaying plan called for the force to concentrate at Utö. *Novik*, with 50 mines, and the four destroyers of the Poludivizion, with 35 each, would lay the mines in the target area north of Danzig. Kolchak would command. Bakhirev, with 1st Brigada Kreyserov, excluding *Bayan*, which was refitting, would provide cover from a position south of Gotland. *Oleg* and *Bogatyr'* would each load 100 mines as backup if the weather prevented the destroyers from minelaying. *E.1* would carry out the covering deterrent patrol in the Western Baltic.

At 8am on 9 February, *E.1* followed *Petr* out of Revel', through the ice to Utö. Within four hours there was a: 'Strong S.W. wind, shipping heavy spray which froze immediately, rendering C[onning] T[ower] hatch and all gear on bridge immovable.' Laurence ordered the breaker to lead them in to Baltiyskiy Port until the weather improved. Next morning the wind had dropped. *Petr* led *E.1* out to sea. However, *E.1*'s mechanical gremlins struck again before reaching the billet. On the 11th, east of Bornholm, a mistake in drill after an engine component failed put the port engine out of action. With the bow torpedo tube cap badly damaged by ice, Laurence decided to abandon the patrol. *E.1* limped back to Utö on one engine. On the 13th, Laurence ran into thick ice eight miles from the island. *E.1* was stuck fast for over 24 hours waiting for assistance. *Petr* arrived next day and towed *E.1* back to port. Repairs would take several days.

The southerly wind opened a window for the minelaying mission, but thick ice driven into the Finnish skerries forced changes to the plan. *Novik* dropped out. If the destroyers were unable to return to the Gulf, they might have to overwinter in Mariehamn. Since *Novik* ran only on fuel oil and there was no storage there, she would be immobilised. The cruisers now left directly from Revel', whilst the Poludivizion would be led through the ice to Baltiyskiy Port by icebreaker *Tsar' Mikhail Fëdorovich*, which would carry the mines to load there. On the 11th, the forces moved to their departure points and loaded their mines. Graf writes:

> It was a real winter day [at Baltiyskiy Port], with a frost of (-)8°R [-10°C] and a light south wind, which pressed all the ice to the northern shore of the bay. ... suddenly, during the day, it also began to break-up, and large slabs of ice ... floated to the exit. ... [The destroyers] had to immediately weigh anchor and, manoeuvring, let the ice floes pass between them. ... The slightest touch of the ice floes on the side of the *Kondratenko* split it in two places along the waterline, with two cracks forming: one was more than a foot [30cm] long, and the other about 5" [13cm]. However, they managed to patch them up...

The destroyers had been due to leave that night, but in view of the navigation hazard, Kolchak delayed departure until the next morning. Next day, the destroyers were at times brought to a standstill by thick ice, but finally they got free of it and reached the next waypoint at Tagelakht Bay off Ezel'. Kolchak was behind schedule to rendezvous with Bakhirev in the open sea west of Memel at 9am next morning, the 13th. He used the wireless to send a message, only to receive a shocking reply.

The day before, Bakhirev's cruisers had left Revel', heading out through the ice floes down the swept channels for open sea. There were frequent squalls and snowstorms, blotting out landmarks. The ice also made it hard to take soundings, as it kept breaking the sounding lead lines. Navigational accuracy inevitably suffered. Starshiy Leytenant Nikolay Kryzhanovskiy, the navigator for the Brigada, was on the bridge of *Ryurik*, which was following *Admiral Makarov* at the head of the line:

> At 3:30am, sleet began to fall and the horizon was obscured by a blizzard. ... At 4:02am *Admiral Makarov* altered course 10° to port ... a weak light was glimpsed from the [Fårö] lighthouse ahead. At 4:07 [Bakhirev] ordered course 160 [30° to port]. *Ryurik* now felt a light blow. Speed was reduced [from 16] to 12 knots. A lighthouse then appeared ahead, shining like a searchlight. Immediately "hard-a-port" ordered. Then a second blow followed. We stopped the engines. I measured the distance to the lighthouse with a rangefinder – 21 cables [just over two miles]. There was no bank or shoal [marked on the chart] in this place.

The navigational challenges had resulted in the Brigada being eight miles closer to Fårö than planned. *Admiral Makarov*'s navigator escaped sanction, particularly as no shoal was marked. The reason for plotting a course close to Gotland was lingering fears that the Germans had laid mines west of Ezel', fed by continuing reports of mines washing up. *Admiral Makarov*'s shallower draught left her unaffected. *Ryurik* had struck ground, but her momentum carried her clear. Essen later reported the damage: 'most of the double bottom compartments, part of the lower bunkers and Boiler Room Three compartment were flooded ... a total of 2,400 tons of water.' The boiler room crew were able to prevent a steam explosion by damping the fires before the compartment flooded. Fortunately, the rocks only pierced the boiler room itself, although other bulkheads distorted. The flooding increased *Ryurik*'s draught by 1.3m. Bakhirev cancelled the operation. Kryzhanovskiy later recalled, 'The boats had already been swung out on the davits ... But Koronat [Bakhirev] held firm. The men worked like devils to save the ship and *Ryurik* cautiously made it to Revel'. The soul of this rescue was Koronat. In my opinion, this was the greatest manifestation of his character and courage.' At 6:30am, with the flooding under control, Bakhirev set course for Utö, making just 6 knots to avoid straining the bulkheads. The cruisers met icebreakers at Utö. They reached Revel' on the evening of the 15th, after nearly three days of agonising progress. Due to her extra draught, *Ryurik* had to anchor west of Nargen, where Essen boarded to examine the damage for himself.

Kolchak had received the news at 5am on the 13th. The weather was good. He was determined to press on without cruiser cover. His destroyer commanders concurred. At 8am the force headed south down the coast, soon clearing the remaining ice floes, then headed out to sea as usual south of Vindava. Although Essen sent a wireless cancelling the whole operation at 11am, he quickly granted Kolchak discretion to continue. At 1am next morning, the 14th, the force was approaching their objective. Graf writes, 'The night was clear, starry, with a complete calm. However, just at the moment when the Poludivizion began to turn [east] to begin laying mines, a thick fog appeared completely unexpectedly.' The destroyers switched on their stern lights immediately, except for the second in line, *Sibirskiy Strelok*. As a result, *Okhotnik*, following astern, lost sight of her. She began laying mines as planned, ordering *Pogranichnik* astern of her to follow suit. They passed a fairway marker during laying. There was hope that this marked the German safe channel. Meanwhile, Kolchak fell back on the contingency agreed for accidental separation. To avoid fouling the path of the other destroyers with mines, he turned *General Kondratenko* north, followed by *Sibirskiy Strelok*, and laid the mines away from the planned return track. The destroyers retired and met up again off Lyuzerort. They anchored for the night in Tagelakht Bay to avoid moving at night through the ice. They then dodged their way back to Revel' through the floes, reaching harbour at 8am on the 16th.

Essen reported that enemy vessels had been at sea during the retirement and alluded to an encounter with 'some cruiser', which was not seen because of the poor visibility. The directional stations seem to have been picking up German signals in the northern Baltic. There were actually no German warships active east of Bornholm.

Just 30 minutes after the Poludivizion arrived, the weather changed. Essen reported that. 'This morning a northeast wind began to blow and ice began to appear from the north, which is why I believe that in the coming days the departure of ships from the Gulf of Finland will be extremely difficult and it will be necessary to cancel further operations until more favourable conditions.' The minesweeper patrols at the mouth of the Gulf had to be withdrawn with the help of icebreakers. An attempt to mount another operation to the Bay of Danzig on 18 February with *Admiral Makarov*, *Oleg* and *Bogatyr'* had to be abandoned. Thick ice stopped the cruisers at Surop. Essen ordered all active vessels into refit. There were concerns after the recent attack on Libava by *P.L.19*, that the fleet, immobilised in the ice, could suffer attack by German airships. As a precaution, all ships in harbour received a ghostly camouflage of whitewash.

Nevertheless, Essen could not relax. The fleet had to be ready for a renewal of the action. *Ryurik* was vital to the fighting power of the cruiser force. Repair was only possible in the large dry dock at Kronshtadt. After being pulled into the harbour at Revel' and examined by divers, *Ryurik* was patched up, and had equipment removed to reduce her draught to make the

Rossiya at Helsingfors, iced in and whitewashed, early 1915. The bow has a fortral fitted. Note sentry boxes on deck and ice. Armed with 12x15.2cm guns on each side and one each at bow and stern, with 15x7.5cm guns in various positions. 20cm hull armour, speed 19½ knots. (Public domain)

journey possible. On 2 March she began an epic five day journey through the thick ice in the Gulf, preceded by two icebreakers, *Ermak* and *Tsar' Mikhail Fëdorovich*. Once docked work proceeded round the clock to repair the hull, expected to take about six weeks. The cruiser actions had shown the weakness of the main armament of the other armoured cruisers, with a broadside of just two 20.3cm guns. Essen gave orders for alterations to *Gromoboy* to receive two additional guns on the centreline, allowing effective four-gun salvo spotting at long range. There was no easy solution for the two *Bayan* class.

Essen made a five-day tour of the skerries south of Åbo on the icebreaker *Bore*. This was his biggest worry regarding the spring thaw. Guns had finally arrived for batteries. Essen examined the key locations and gave orders for temporary batteries on wooden bases to cover the construction of permanent concrete emplacements at Örö and Utö. When guns became available, two additional batteries at skerry entrances further west would follow. Essen arranged for a mobile troop force ready to transfer to Åland, should there be a threat of attack. He proposed additional new plans for the development of a permanent destroyer base within Moon Sound.

For the Baltiyskiy Flot, the war was on pause until the spring thaw. The last operation brought the total number of offensive mines laid to 1,598, in 16 minefields from Arkona to Memel. Four warships and eight steamers had already hit them. Kerber had already been promoted to Vitse-Admiral for his part in the success. Now Kanin was also promoted, with seniority backdated to the same day, bringing their rivalry into even sharper focus.

On March 8 Essen issued a general order, with a distribution of medal awards: 'The ship crews of the active fleet worked well, with complete dedication, in the difficult conditions of autumn and winter sailing, carrying out patrol duty, sweeping enemy mines, setting up minefields, cruising at sea and protecting the coast. Constantly exposed to danger from enemy mines and submarines and risking being destroyed by a stronger enemy, many crews and individual enlisted men demonstrated examples of courage and valiant performance of duty.' The next day, the Tsar arrived to inspect the fleet. Timirëv described the visit: 'The sovereign visited *Rossiya* … and then rode in a car across the ice past the entire fleet, enthusiastically greeted by the endless cries of "Ura"'. The gloomy expectation that an overwhelming German attack would crush the fleet was gone. The contrast with the recriminations in Kiel could not have been starker.[11]

11 TNA:ADM137/271: pp.49–61; РГАВМФ:Фонд 716, Опись 2, Дело 37, pp.85–91, 160, Дело 91, pp.12–13, 38–39, Дело 14, pp.87–94, Опись 1, Дело 15, p.55, Фонд 418, Опись1, Дело3343, p.135; BA:RM56 4.Torpedobootsflottille KTB; Меркушов, *Записки*, pp.330, 333–334; Pavlovich, *Operations*, pp.113–117; Гельмерсен, 'Заградительные', *Сборник 2*, pp.113–126; Тимиревъ, *Воспоминанія*, pp.23, 171–172; Kan. 2 p. Н.Н. Крыжановскій, 'Адмиралъ Михаилъ Коронатовичъ Бахиревъ и его современники', *Морскія Записки, Vol. XXI, № 58* (1963), p.67. Графъ, *Новикъ*, 57–62.

Epilogue

Any basis of comparison of the Russian and German fleets at the opening of the campaign would have concluded that Germany would be able to control the Baltic with ease. However, it ended with German forces abandoning the eastern and central Baltic after suffering disproportionate losses. Furthermore, Russian mines were widespread, disrupting a number of trade routes.

This poses a question about the underlying reasons for an outcome achieved with relatively limited means. The answer lies in inspired leadership and the use of an asymmetric strategy. The key to Russian success was the way in which they used the limited means at their disposal. However, maintaining the disruption to German control would face future challenges.

In 1914, there were three basic means to exert naval power. The surface fleet with its attendant force of torpedo vessels, the submarine and mine warfare. The Baltiyskiy Flot was not in a position to seize control of the Baltic with a traditional surface fleet naval action. The overwhelming advantage in numbers and combat power of the German surface fleet made this impossible. The basic strategy of defending a key position far from German bases was sound. If Pohl's 1914 plans had been implemented, it would also have been unlikely that Scheer's lone squadron could have sustained any attack on the Central Position. Even if the Germans committed a larger force, it would have potentially faced serious losses from an integrated defence with mines, submarines and destroyer attacks. It would also not have been possible to sustain operations in the Gulf of Finland without capturing a base of operations there. The challenge of keeping a large fleet coaled this far from their bases would have been insurmountable. As time passed, the task became harder as the Russian defences strengthened. However, this also meant that the Germans had almost unchallenged control of the Baltic outside the Gulf of Finland. The German operations in the first two months had no impact on this basic situation. Behring's appetite for tactical risk also backfired spectacularly with the loss of *Magdeburg*, to the lasting woe of the German war effort.

The second means to exert naval power was the submarine. The handful of spectacular successes of submarines early in the war created a panicked response amongst many, especially in the absence of effective anti-submarine weapons. The introduction of submarines to attack into the depth of the Russian defences scored a striking success against *Pallada*, but the Russians responded by adapting their patrol patterns and tactics, avoiding further losses. Submarines were a weak point in the Russian naval inventory, because of the limited capabilities of their available vessels. The arrival of the small British submarine force changed this, and had an impact out of all proportion to its size. However, their impact was largely psychological. Submarines fired seven British, four Russian and five German torpedoes at warships during the campaign, hitting only *Pallada*. Once warships are alert for submarines and the right screening and zigzagging tactics are used, they become difficult targets. Destroyers and smaller vessels are naturally difficult to hit. The German vessels targeted only observed three real attacks, one Russian and two British. This handful of real attacks reinforced the bogus sightings created by over-wrought imaginations and occasional sightings of real submarines in transit.

In the Baltic, a more fundamental factor caused the Germans to over-react to the submarine threat. They displayed a contemptuous disdain for their Russian naval opponents. This serious error in assessing their operational capabilities opened up the opportunity for Essen to exploit. The appearance of the British seemed to play into the German admirals' underlying belief in Anglo-Saxon superiority, crediting a handful of British officers with leading a dramatic invigoration of Russian offensive activity. This bore no relation to reality, but submarines, and especially British submarines, became an almost obsessive focus for Heinrich and Behring, diverting resources to unproductive activity. The idea that bombarding their perceived bases was going to suppress their activities was fanciful. Gunnery was not an antidote to the submarine.

This brings us to the final means of asserting naval power, the mine. If the surface fleet and submarines were weaknesses for the Russian fleet, mines were their strength. They were fundamental to Essen's offensive and defensive tactical and strategic doctrine. Heinrich and Behring completely lost sight of this, despite knowing Russian technical capabilities. Mines were the enablers of the Russians asymmetric advantage. However, this was not a technological advantage, but an operational one. The Russian mines were highly effective, but so were those of the Germans.

Whilst mines did the damage, the creation of a trained force and the strategy to deliver them offensively at scale was where the true advantage lay. Essen's ambitious plan for his mine offensive delivered the tactical surprise needed to break the stalemate. Heinrich failed to grasp the gravity of the situation until it was too late. Essen's vision for strategic mine warfare determined the outcome of the campaign. The plan combined placement at key transit points with stealth in execution. However, it went further and employed misdirection. Essen encouraged the German's to focus on submarines. His orders emphasised the need to attack and make their presence known. Obtaining torpedo hits would be a bonus, but the submarine's key role was misdirection and deterrence, going as far as the use of dummy periscopes alongside mines for extra effect. Heinrich and Behring took this bait enthusiastically and became the architects of their own defeat.

The results finally became impossible to ignore in January, especially after Behring's final operation. The impression created by mysterious disappearances of steamers, and fear of submarines, amplified the very real menace created by widespread mining in the central and eastern Baltic. The result was the withdrawal of the remaining German naval forces to the western Baltic and a dramatic loss of confidence by commercial shipping. Heinrich failed to organise minesweeping effectively to resolve the issue.

However, these plans and operations did not arise from individual actions. Essen himself was not a great planner. He could be impetuous. His true talent was in leadership. The subordinates around him also had their flaws, but Essen created a team from his disparate subordinates that was much more than the sum of its parts. From the bitter ashes of defeat against Japan, he had created a fleet that had the operational capability and the right people to seize the opportunity presented. Achieving this whilst constrained in a strategic straight jacket, imposed by generals who had little understanding of naval matters is all the more remarkable.

Heinrich's leadership had not risen to the challenge. The odds were heavily stacked against him when it came to resources. They ebbed and flowed in unpredictable ways, often leaving him struggling to sustain activity with inadequate and obsolete resources. Any move towards a decisive use of force by him quickly dissipated when it came to operational commitment. This flowed inevitably from the competing agendas in the byzantine German command structure and the different appetites for risk within it. The opposing parties constantly undermined each other with the Kaiser. Nevertheless, Heinrich's failure to recognise and act on the mine danger was a serious and avoidable error.

Two timeless lessons emerge from the management of the campaign. The first is never underestimate an opponent. Heinrich mistook a posture of strategic defence for inaction. This was complacent. Even a cursory assessment of Essen's capabilities and record showed the danger. The second lesson is to thoroughly understand the capabilities of new weapon systems and embed effective counter-measures in tactical doctrine. Both sides had not integrated the impact of advances in submarine capabilities, despite their awareness of them. However, for Heinrich and Behring, a misdirected response to the problem also left them exposed. Their failure to anticipate, plan for, and respond to Russian minelaying was their undoing.

However, looking to the future, the ability to turn disruption to something more permanent would need more resources. The Russians had received limited but useful operational assistance from their British allies so far. In November, Admiral Fisher became First Sea Lord. He held a fervent belief that the Baltic could be the key to Germany's defeat by seizing naval control there, cutting off the supply of resources to Germany from Scandinavia. He had already commissioned the construction of a 'siege fleet', with shallow water capabilities designed to precipitate a break through into the Baltic, bringing Denmark into the war on the side of the allies. However, this was a scheme intended to come to fruition in early 1916 and would have to navigate competing interests. For now, his focus was on clearing the Belgian coast, whilst Churchill was focussing on a new plan to knock Turkey out of the war at the Dardanelles. The Baltiyskiy Flot would have to hold their positions in 1915 largely with their own resources.

With her armies and fleet deadlocked in the west, 1915 saw the German High Command look east for a decisive breakthrough in the war. The Baltic coast would inevitably draw the attention of both armies. The German fleet would respond to play its part, setting the scene for major actions, as the Baltiyskiy Flot resisted its push to restore control over the Baltic.

Appendix I

Organisation of the Baltiyskiy Flot, 27 July 1914

Based on General Order Number 12 of 1914 by Kerber.[1]

BALTIYSKIY FLOT (BALTIC FLEET)
Commander: Admiral Nikolay fon Essen
Chief of Staff: Kontr-Admiral Lyudvig Kerber
1 armoured cruiser: *Ryurik* (fleet flagship), 1 destroyer as tender: *Pogranichnik*[*]

SQUADRONS FOR ACTIVE OPERATIONS
1-ya Brigada Lineynykh Korabley (1st Battleship Brigade)[†]
Vitse-Admiral Baron Vasiliy Ferzen
4 battleships: *Andrey Pervozvannyy, Imperator Pavel I, Tsesarevich, Slava*

Razvedochnyy Otryad (Reconnaissance Detachment)
1-ya Brigada Kreyserov (1st Cruiser Brigade)
Kontr-Admiral Nikolay Kolomeytsev (commander of Reconnaissance Detachment)
4 armoured cruisers: *Gromoboy, Admiral Makarov, Pallada, Bayan*, 1 destroyer: *Novik*
2-ya Brigada Kreyserov (2nd Cruiser Brigade)[‡]
Kontr-Admiral Pëtr Leskov
1 armoured cruiser: *Rossiya*, 3 cruisers: *Bogatyr', Oleg, Avrora*

1-ya Minnaya Diviziya (1st Mine Divisional Group)
Kontr-Admiral Ivan Shtorre
Poludivizion Osobogo Naznacheniya (Special Purpose Half-Division), 3 destroyers:[*]
Sibirskiy Strelok, Okhotnik, General Kondratenko
1.Divizion (1st Division), 8 destroyers: *Ussuriets, Finn, Amurets, Moskvityanin, Dobrovolets, Vsadnik, Gaydamak, Emir Bukharskiy*

1 РГАВМФ:Фонд 418, Опись 1, Дело 308, pp.22–23, Фонд 719, Опись 1; К.Г. Житкова, Н.Н. Нордмана (eds), Российский Императорский флот 1914 г. (Санкт-Петербургъ: И.Д. Сытин, 1914), pp.86–88; Киреев, *Траление*, pp.8–9.

2.Divizion, 8 destroyers: *Donskoy Kazak*, *Zabaykalets*, *Kazanets*, *Strashnyy*, *Steregushchiy*, *Turkmenets-Stavropol'skiy*, *Ukrayna*, *Voyskovoy*

4.Divizion, 8 destroyers:[1] *Ispolnitel'nyy*, *Legkiy*, *Lovkiy*, *Letuchiy*, *Likhoy*, *Moshchnyy*, *Metkiy*, *Kryepkiy*

Brigada Podvodnykh Lodok (Submarine Brigade)

Kontr-Admiral Pavel Levitskiy

1 destroyer as tender: *Molodetskiy*, 1 torpedo boat as tender: *Poslushnyy*

1.Divizion Podvodnykh Lodok (1st Submarine Division), 4 submarines: *Akula*, *Makrel'*, *Okun'*, *Minoga*

2.Divizion Podvodnykh Lodok, 4 submarines: *Kayman*, *Krokodil*, *Alligator*, *Drakon*

Uchebnyy Otryad Podvodnago Plavaniya (Submarine Training Detachment), 3 submarines: *Peskar'*, *Sterlyad'*, *Beluga*

Morskaya Partiya Traleniya (Minesweeping Group)

Kapitan 2-go Ranga Pëtr Kitkin

1 ex-gunboat as leader: *Grozyashchiy*

7.Divizion as 1.Otdeleniya (1st Section), 8 torpedo boats: *No.214*, *No.215*, *No.216*, *No.217*, *No.218*, *No.219*, *No.220*, *No.222*

2.Otdeleniya, 4 auxiliary minesweepers: *Iskra*, *Plamya*, *Patron*, *Yakor'*

3.Otdeleniya, 6 minesweepers: *Cheka* (ex *No.132)*, *Vzryv*, *Minrep*, *Zapal*, *Provodnik*, *Fugas*, 2 auxiliary steamers

FORTIFIED POSITIONS AND RESERVES

Morskaya Krepost' Imperatora Petra Velikago (Naval Fortress of Emperor Peter the Great)

Vitse-Admiral Aleksandr Gerasimov

Sea defence of the Naval Fortress

Otryad Zagraditeley (Minelaying Detachment)

Kontr-Admiral Vasiliy Kanin

6 minelayers: *Amur*, *Enisey*, *Ladoga*, *Narova*, *Onega, Volga*

Defence of Revel' approaches and anchorage

1-y Rezerv Otryad (1st Reserve Detachment)

1 battleship: *Imperator Aleksandr II*, 1 training ship: *Petr Velikiy*, 1 cruiser: *Diana*, 2 despatch vessels: *Voyevoda*, *Posadnik*

Flank Skerry Position

2-ya Minnaya Diviziya (2nd Mine Divisional Group)

Kontr-Admiral Aleksandr Kurosh (commander of Flank Skerry Position)

3.Divizion, 8 destroyers: *Vnimatel'nyy*, *Vynoslivyy*, *Vnushitel'nyy*, *Burnyy*, *Inzhener-Mekhanik Zverev*, *Inzhener-Mekhanik Dmitriev*, *Bditel'nyy*, *Boyevoy*

5.Divizion, 9 destroyers: *Gromyashchiy*, *Stroynyy*, *Rastoropnyy*, *Dostoynyy*, *Del'nyy*, *Deyatel'nyy*, *Razyashchiy*, *Storozhevoy*, *Sil'nyy*

6.Divizion, 1 destroyer: *Vidnyy*, 5 torpedo boats: *Retivyy*, *Rezvyy*, *Podvizhnyy*, *Prochnyy*, *Prytkiy*

Otryad Kanonerskikh Lodok (Gunboat Detachment)
6 gunboats: *Bobr*, *Sivuch*, *Gilyak*, *Koreyets*, *Khivinets*,¶ *Khrabryy*¶

Sluzhba Svyazi (Communication Service)
Kapitan 1-go Ranga Adrian Nepenin
1 destroyer: *Leytenant Burakov*, 6 torpedo boats: *No. 104*, *No. 119*, *No. 120*, *Porazhayushchiy*, *Prozorlivyy*, *R'yanyy*

SVEABORG PORT AND FORTRESS DEFENCE

Svodnyy Rezervnyy Divizion Minonostsev (Combined Destroyer Reserve Division)
1 destroyer: *Iskusnyy*, 5 torpedo boats: *No. 128*, *No. 129*, *No. 142*, *No. 212*, *No. 213*

KRONSHTADT PORT AND FORTRESS DEFENCE

2-y Rezerv Otryad (2nd Reserve Detachment)
Kontr-Admiral Aleksandr Sapsay
5 training ships: *Voin*, *Vernyy*, *Rynda*, *Afrika*, *Dvina*

Notes

* *Pogranichnik* also operated with Poludivizion Osobogo Naznacheniya.
† Kerber lists as 2nd Brigada, with the new battleships forming the 1st, but as they were delayed the existing Brigada remained the 1st.
‡ Until Leskov appointed on 29 July 1914 this was 1-y Rezerv (1st Reserve) Brigada Kreyserov. *Diana* added after completing major refit, 28 August 1914.
‖ 4.Divizion initially attached to support minelayers in Sea Defence of Naval Fortress.
¶ *Khrabryy*, *Khivinets* assigned to guard submarine anchorage.

Appendix II

Major warships of the Baltiyskiy Flot[1]

Class	Launch	Type	Official Displacement Tonnes	Main battery size cm / length in calibres	Secondary battery size cm / length in calibres	Waterline Krupp Armour mm	Torpedo tubes cm / mines	Range miles @ cruising speed knots	Maximum speed knots
Sevastopol', Poltava, Petropavlovsk, Gangut	1911[*]	Battleship	23,370	12x30.5/52	16x12/50	225	4x45 / -	1,625 @ 13	23
Imperator Pavel I, Andrey Pervozvannyy	1906–7	Battleship	18,290	4x30.5/40 14x20.3/50	12x12/45	216	2x45 / -	2,100 @ 12	18
Slava	1903	Battleship	14,630	4x30.5/40	12x15.2/45 8x7.5/50[†]	194	2x45 / -	1,970 @ 10½	18
Tsesarevich	1901	Battleship	13,320	4x30.5/40	12x15.2/45 8x7.5/50[†]	250	2x45 / -	2,805 @ 11	18
Imperator Aleksandr II	1887	Battleship	10,170	2x30.5/30 1x20.3/45[§]	10x15.2/45[‡] 4x12/45	171[¶]	-	4,440 @ 8	14
Petr Velikiy	1872	Battleship	9,950	4x20.3/45[§]	20x15.2/45[ǀ] 12x7.5/50 4x5.7	136[¶]	-	2,900 @ 10	12½
Ryurik	1906	Armoured cruiser	17,200	4x25.4/45 8x20.3/50	20x12/50	152	2x45 / -[**]	4,000 @ 10	21

1 Житкова/Нордмана, *флот*, pp.2–21; Ю.В. Апальков, *Боевые корабли русского флота 8.1914г-10.1917г Справочник* (Санкт-Петербург: Интек, 1996), pp.18–39, 85–88; Л.Г. Гончаров and Б.А. Денисов, *Использование мин в мировую империалистическую войну 1914–1918 гг.* (Москва Ленинград: Военмориздат НКВМФ СССР, 1940), pp.151–155; Сергей Евгеньевич Виноградов, *Броненосец "Слава". Непобежденный герой Моонзунда* (Москва: Эксмо, 2011), Глава 5, Кампания 1914 г.; Stephen McLaughlin, Russian & Soviet Battleships (Annapolis: United States Naval Institute, 2021), pp.1, 32, 295; РГАВМФ:Фонд 902, Штаб начальника бригады линейных кораблей эскадры Балтийского моря (1911-1914), Опись 1, Ед.Хр. 150, Фонд 716, Опись 1, Дело 15; Алексей В. Скворцов, Крейсеры «Диана», «Паллада», «Аврора» (Санкт-Петербург: ЛеКо, 2005), Глава 9; Алексей Дмитриевич Федечкин, 'Проблемы перевооружения крейсеров «Россия» и «Громобой» в 1915—1916 гг.', Военно-Исторический Журнал (2022), <http://history.milportal.ru/problemy-perevooruzheniya-krejserov-rossiya-i-gromoboj-v-1915-1916-gg/>, accessed 26 April 2024; В. Хромов, *Крейсер "Олег". Морская коллекция N 1 (2006)* (Москва: Моделист-конструктор, 2006), p.7; В. Хромов, *Канонерская Лодка «Храбрый». Морская коллекция N 11 (2005)* (Москва: Моделист-конструктор, 2005), p.10; Алексей В. Скворцов, 'Канонерские лодки Балтийского флота «Гиляк», «Кореец», «Бобр», «Сивуч»', *Гангут № 35* (2003), pp.3–26.

Class	Launch	Type	Official Displacement Tonnes	Main battery size cm / length in calibres	Secondary battery size cm / length in calibres	Waterline Krupp Armour mm	Torpedo tubes cm / mines	Range miles @ cruising speed knots	Maximum speed knots
Admiral Makarov, Pallada, Bayan	1906–7	Armoured cruiser	7,960	2x20.3/45 8x15.2/45	20-22x7.5/50	175	2x45 / -**	2,100–2,450 @ 14	21
Gromoboy	1899	Armoured cruiser	13,480	4x20.3/45 22x15.2/45	4x7.5/50	152	2x45 / -	3,825 @ 9	18
Rossiya	1896	Armoured cruiser	13,270	22x15.2/45‖	15x7.5/50	155¶	- / -**	5,700 @ 12	19½
Oleg	1903	Protected cruiser	6,500	12x15.2/45	8x7.5/50	Deck only	2x38.1 / -**	2,400 @ 14	21
Bogatyr'	1901	Protected cruiser	6,500	12x15.2/45	12x7.5/50	Deck only	2x38.1 / -**	2,760 @ 12	23
Avrora	1900	Protected cruiser	6,810	10x15.2/45	20x7.5/50	Deck only	- / -	2,500 @ 11	18½
Diana	1899	Protected cruiser	6,810	8x12/45‡	20x7.5/50	Deck only	- / -	2,980 @ 11	19
Gilyak, Bobr, Sivuch	1906–7	Gunboat	980	2x12/45	4x7.5/50	-	- / 60††	1,100 @ 9	12
Koreyets	1907	Gunboat	980	2x12/45	8x7.5/50	-	- / 60††	1,100 @ 9	12
Khivinets	1905	Gunboat	1,380	2x12/45	8x7.5/50	-	- / -	2,070 @ 9	11
Khrabryy	1895	Gunboat	1,760	2x20.3/45 1x15.2/45	5x4.7	97¶	1x45 / -	900 @ 10	14½
Grozyashchiy	1890	Gunboat‡‡	1,830	-	6x4.7	61¶	- / -	995 @ 8	13
Voyevoda	1892	Torpedo Gunboat§§	420	2x7.5/50	-	-	- / -	2,800 @ 10	18
Posadnik	1892	Torpedo Gunboat§§	420	1x10.2/60 1x7.5/50	-	-	- / -	1,640 @ 10	18
Amur, Enisey	1906–7	Minelayer	3,250	5x12/45 2x7.5/50	-	-	- / 250	3,200 @ 12	17
Volga	1905	Minelayer	1,740	4x4.7/45	-	-	- / 230–277	2,200 @ 8½	13½
Ladoga	1865	Minelayer	6,200	4x4.7/45	-	-	- / 1,080	1,520 @ 9	12
Narova	1873	Minelayer	4,550	4x7.5/45	-	-	- / 658	1,600 @ 10	11½
Onega	1875	Minelayer	4,600	4x7.5/50	-	-	- / 300	2,800 @ 9	13

Notes

* Dates of joining fleet: *Sevastopol'* November 22 1914, *Poltava* December 19 1914, *Petropavlovsk* January 4 1915, *Gangut* January 5 1915.

† 12 additional 7.5cm on *Slava* and *Tsesarevich* at main deck level in most sources removed when war broke out or just before.

‡ When war broke out *Diana* refitting, awaiting new 13cm main armament. On 28 August 1914 joined fleet after temporary rearmament with 12cm guns shown. In mid-October replaced with 10x15.2/45 from *Imperator Aleksandr II*.

§ All five 20.3/45 removed from *Imperator Aleksandr II* and *Petr Velikiy* end of August 1914 for coastal battery.

‖ *Rossiya* had 4x20.3/45 in most sources removed to coastal batteries when war broke out, soon replaced by additional 4x15.2/45 from *Petr Velikiy*.

¶ Thickness of actual armour: *Imperator Aleksandr II* 356mm compound (steel-iron), *Petr Velikiy* 356mm wrought iron, *Rossiya* 203mm nickel steel, *Khrabryy* 127mm nickel steel, *Grozyashchiy* 127mm steel.

** Rails added for mines, December 1914; *Ryurik* 500, *Admiral Makarov* 150, *Bayan* 150, January 1915; *Oleg* 150, *Bogatyr'* 150, *Rossiya* 300

†† *Gilyak* class had to remove 7.5cm guns if more than 40 mines carried.

‡‡ *Grozyashchiy* was non-combat auxiliary when war broke out.

§§ Re-rated as despatch vessels 1907.

Ships received anti-aircraft guns from commencement of hostilities; mix of 4.7, 6.35 and 7.5cm calibre. These and 4.7cm guns used for saluting not listed.

Appendix III

Torpedo vessels of the Baltiyskiy Flot[1]

Class	Launch	Type	Official Displacement Tonnes	Guns cm / length in calibres	Torpedo tubes cm / mines	Range miles @ cruising speed knots	Maximum speed knots surface / submerged
Novik	1911	Destroyer	1,280	4x10.2/60	8x45 / 60	1,470 @ 21	36
Okhotnik, Pogranichnik, Sibirskiy Strelok, General Kondratenko	1905–6	Destroyer	750	2x10.2/60 2x4.7	3x45 /42*	2,220–2,400 @ 12	25
Emir Bukharskiy, Dobrovolets, Moskvityanin, Finn	1904–5	Destroyer	660	2x10.2/60 1x3.7	3x45 / 20	1,020–1,150 @ 12	25
Amurets, Ussuriets, Vsadnik, Gaydamak	1905	Destroyer	720	2x10.2/60 1x3.7	3x45 / 20	1,270 @ 10	25
Ukrayna, Voyskovoy, Turkmenets-Stavropol'skiy, Kazanets, Steregushchiy, Strashnyy, Donskoy Kazak, Zabaykalets	1904–6	Destroyer	710	2x10.2/60 1x3.7	2x45 / 7	1,105 @ 10	25
Inzhener-Mekhanik Zverev, Inzhener-Mekhanik Dmitriev, Bditel'nyy, Boyevoy, Burnyy, Vnimatel'nyy, Vnushitel'nyy, Vynoslivyy	1905–6	Destroyer	460	2x7.5/50	3x45 / 16	960 @ 12	27
Iskusnyy, Ispolnitel'nyy, Kryepkiy, Legkiy, Leytenant Burakov,† *Lovkiy, Letuchiy, Likhoy, Metkiy, Molodetskiy, Moshchnyy*	1905	Destroyer	410	2x7.5/50	2x45 / 10	1,000–1,200 @ 14	26
Gromyashchiy	1904	Destroyer	430	2x7.5/50	2x45 / 20	1,200 @ 15	26
Vidnyy	1904	Destroyer	430	2x7.5/50	2x45 / 16	1,000 @ 14	26

1 Житкова/Нордмана, *флот*, pp.8–37; Апальков, *флота*, pp.42–84, 89–103, 182–183; Гончаров/Денисов, *мин*, pp.151-155; Ю.Г. Степанов and И.Ф. Цветков, *Эскадренный миноносец «Новик»* (Ленинград: Судостроение, 1981), pp.24, 110; Рафаил М. Мельников, *Эскадренные миноносцы класса Доброволец* (Санкт-Петербург: Истфлот, 1999), pp.70–71; Siegfried Breyer, *Soviet Warship Development, Volume One: 1917-1937* (London: Conway Maritime Press, 1992), p.49; Томашевич, *операциях*, pp. 221, 254, Приложения 12; Harris, *Submarines*, pp.316–318.

Class	Launch	Type	Official Displacement Tonnes	Guns cm / length in calibres	Torpedo tubes cm / mines	Range miles @ cruising speed knots	Maximum speed knots surface / submerged
Sil'nyy, Storozhevoy, Stroynyy, Razyashchiy, Rastoropnyy, Del'nyy, Dostoynyy, Deyatel'nyy	1905–7	Destroyer	390	2x7.5/50	2x45 / 18	800–900 @ 15	26
Prytkiy, Prochnyy, Podvizhnyy, Porazhayushchiy,† *Poslushnyy, Prozorlivyy, Retivyy, Rezvyy, R'yanyy*	1899–1901	Torpedo Boat	240	2x7.5/50	2x45 / 10	664 @ 13½	27
No. 214, No. 215, No. 216, No. 217, No. 218, No. 219, No. 220, No. 222	1902–3	Torpedo Boat	150	2x4.7	2x45 / -	500 @ 12	26
No. 212, No. 213	1902	Torpedo Boat	200	3x3.7	2x38.1 / -	1,200 @ 12	24
No. 128, No. 129, No. 142	1896–7	Torpedo Boat	120	2x3.7	2x38.1 /-	550 @ 10	21
No. 120	1894	Torpedo Boat†	120	1x3.7	3x38.1 / -	550 @ 10	19
No. 119	1894	Torpedo Boat†	120	2x3.7	3x38.1 / -	550 @ 10	14
No. 104	1893	Torpedo Boat†	80	1x3.7	2x38.1 / -	475 @ 15	19½
HMS *E.9*	1913‡	Submarine	677	-	5x45 / -	2,600 @ 12½	15 / 10¼
HMS *E.1*	1912‡	Submarine	677	-	4x45 / -	2,600 @ 12½	15 / 10¼
No. 1, No. 2, No. 3	1914§	Submarine	35	-	2x45 / -	150 @8	8 / 6
Akula	1908	Submarine	380	-	8x45 / -	1,900 @ 9	11½ / 6½
Kayman, Krokodil, Alligator, Drakon	1908	Submarine	420	-	6x45 / -	1,100 @ 8½	9 / 7½
Makrel', Okun'	1907	Submarine	140	-	4x45 / -	760 @ 7	9 /5
Minoga	1908	Submarine	120	-	2x45 / -	960 @ 8	10½ / 4½
Peskar', Sterlyad', Beluga	1904	Submarine	110	-	1x45 / -	450 @ 7½	9 / 6

Notes

* *Okhotnik* class removed aft gun and torpedo mounts if more than 24 mines carried.

† *Leytenant Burakov* and *Porazhayushchiy* re-rated as despatch vessels 1912 and 1913 respectively, maximum speed 21 knots. Also *No.104* 1909, *No. 119* and *No. 120* 1912.

‡ Arrival dates in Baltic: *E.1* 17 October 1914, *E.9* 18 October 1914.

§ *No.1*, *No.2* and *No.3* commissioned September 1914.

Guns of 7.5cm and smaller on anti-aircraft mounts fitted after outbreak of war on many boats.

Appendix IV

Major German warships serving in the Baltic[1]

Class	Launch	Type	Official Displacement Tonnes	Main battery size cm / length in calibres	Secondary battery size cm / length in calibres	Waterline Krupp Armour Mm	Torpedo tubes cm / mines	Range miles @ cruising speed knots	Maximum speed knots
Braunschweig, Elsass	1902–3	Battleship	13,208	4x28/40	14x17/40 18x8.8/35	225	6x45 / -	5,200 @ 10	18
Wittelsbach, Wettin, Zähringen, Schwaben, Mecklenburg	1900–1	Battleship	11,774	4x24/40	18x15/40 12x8.8/30	225	6x45 / -	5,000 @ 10	17–18
Kaiser Wilhelm II, Kaiser Barbarossa, Kaiser Wilhelm der Grosse, Kaiser Friedrich III	1896–1900	Battleship	11,233	4x24/40	14x15/40 14x8.8/30	300	5x 45 / -	3,420 @ 10	17
Kaiser Karl der Grosse	1899	Battleship	11,097	4x24/40	18x15/40 12x8.8/30	300	6x 45 / -	3,420 @ 10	17
Wörth, Brandenburg	1891–2	Battleship	10,013	4x28/40 2x28/35	8x10.5/35 8x8.8/30	340*	3x45 / -	4,300 @ 10	16
Blücher	1908	Armoured cruiser	15,842	12x21/45	8x15/45 16x8.8/45	180	4x45/ -	6,600 @ 12	25
Yorck	1904	Armoured cruiser	9,533	4x21/40	10x15/40 14x8.8/35	100	4x45 / -	4,200 @ 12	21
Friedrich Carl, Prinz Adalbert	1901–2	Armoured cruiser	9,087	4x21/40	10x15/40 12x8.8/35	100	4x45 / -	5,000 @ 12	20

1 Gröner, *Band 1*, pp.36–42, 72–80, 127–138, 169–170; *Band 3*, pp.176–179; *Band 4*, p.36; BA:RM92 *Kaiserin Augusta* KTB.

Class	Launch	Type	Official Displacement Tonnes	Main battery size cm / length in calibres	Secondary battery size cm / length in calibres	Waterline Krupp Armour Mm	Torpedo tubes cm / mines	Range miles @ cruising speed knots	Maximum speed knots
Freya, Victoria Louise, Hertha, Vineta, Hansa	1897	Protected cruiser	5,660	2x21/40	6x15/40 3x8.8/35 11x8.8/30	Deck only	3x45 / -	~3,500 @ 12	19
Kaiserin Augusta	1892	Protected cruiser	6,056	10x15/35†	2x10.5/45 2x10.5/40 2x8.8/45† 4x8.8/35† 4x3.7	Deck only	1x35 / -	3,240 @ 12	21
Graudenz	1913	Light cruiser	4.912	12x10.5/45	-	60	2x50 / 120	5,500 @ 12	27½
Strassburg, Stralsund	1911	Light cruiser	4,564	12x10.5/45	-	60	2x50 / 120	5,820 @ 12	28
Magdeburg	1911	Light cruiser	4,535	10x10.5/45‡	-	60	4x50‡ / 120	5,820 @ 12	24‡
Augsburg	1909	Light cruiser	4,362	12x10.5/45	-	Deck only	2x45 / 100	3,500 @ 14	26½
Lübeck	1904	Light cruiser	3,265	10x10.5/40	-	Deck only	2x45 / -	3,800 @ 12	23
Undine	1902	Light cruiser	2,706	10x10.5/40	-	Deck only	2x45 / -	4,400 @ 12	21½
Amazone, Thetis	1900	Light cruiser	2,659	10x10.5/40	-	Deck only	2x45 / -	3,560 @ 12	21½
Gazelle	1898	Light cruiser	2,643	10x10.5/40	-	Deck only	2x45/ -	3,570 @ 10	20
Panther	1901	Gunboat	977	2x10.5/40	-	-	- / -	3,400 @ 9	13½
Rügen	1914	Minelayer	1,894 GRT	2x3.7	-	-	- / 153	1,700 @ 15	16
Deutschland	1909	Minelayer	~4,200 2,847 GRT	4x8.8/40 2x5	-	-	- / 420	?	16½
Hertha	1905	Minelayer	1,221 GRT	2x3.7	-	-	- / 130	815 @ 15	16
Odin	1902	Minelayer	1,137 GRT	2x3.7	-	-	- / 130	850 @ 15	16
Prinz Sigismund, Prinz Adalbert, Prinz Waldemar	1893–1899	Minelayer	700 GRT	2x3.7	-	-	- / 80	?	13
Primus	1907	Minelayer	297 GRT	-	-	-	- / 60	?	8
Delphin	1906	Tender	450	4x8.8/35	-	-	-	3,210 @ 7	11½

Notes

* Thickness of actual armour 400mm Harvey Steel.

† *Kaiserin Augusta* rearmed over 6–8 August for gunnery training as above, removing 2x15/35 and 8x8.8/30 shown in most sources. 4x15/35 replaced with 2x8.8/35 and 1x8.8/45 over 17–19 August. Remaining 6x15/35 removed 30 October 1914.

‡ *Magdeburg* had two deck torpedo tubes as torpedo trials ship in place of 2x10.5cm. Design speed of 27½ knots unattainable, as centre turbine removed after long-standing problems. Most sources show armament and speed as designed.

Appendix V

German torpedo vessels serving in the Baltic[1]

Class	Launch	Type	Official Displacement Tonnes	Main battery size cm / length in calibres	Torpedo Tubes cm / mines	Range miles @ cruising speed knots	Maximum speed knots surface / submerged
S.31, S.32	1914*	Destroyer	802	3x8.8/45	6x50 / 24	1,100 @ 20	34
V.25, V.26, V.27	1914†	Destroyer	812	3x8.8/45	6x50 / 24	1,080 @ 20	36
V.180, V.183, V.186	1910	Destroyer	666	2x8.8/30	4x50 / -	1,170 @ 17	33½
S.176, S.177, S.179	1910	Destroyer	666	2x8.8/30	4x50 / -	1,025 @ 17	32½
G.174, G.175	1910	Destroyer	700	2x8.8/30	4x50 / -	920 @ 17	31½
V.156, V.157, V.158, V.159, V.160	1908	Destroyer	558	2x8.8/30	3x45 / -	1,895 @ 17	31
V.150, V.151, V.152, V.153, V.154, V.155	1907–8	Destroyer	558	2x8.8/35	3x45 / -	1,895 @ 17	30
S.138, S.139, S.140, S.141, S.142, S.143, S.144, S.145, S.146, S.147, S.148, S.149	1906–7	Destroyer	533	1x8.8/35 3x5.2	3x45 / -	1,830 @ 17	30
G.132, G.133, G.134, G.135, G.136	1906	Destroyer	412	4x5.2‡	3x45 / -	1,060 @ 17	27
S.126, S.127, S.128, S.129, S.130, S.131	1904–1905	Destroyer	371	3x5	3x45 / -	1,080 @ 17	28
S.125	1904	Destroyer	355	3x5	3x45 / -	?	27½
S.120, S.121, S.122, S.123, S.124	1904	Destroyer	391	3x5	3x45 / -	1,500 @ 17	27½
T.113	1902	Destroyer	330	3x5	3x45 / -	1,225 @ 17	29
S.102§	1901	Destroyer	315	3x5	3x45 / -	1,020 @ 17	27½
S.91, S.93, S.94, Sleipner§	1899–1901	Destroyer	310	3x5§	3x45 / -	830 @ 17	26½
D.10	1898	Destroyer	310	5x5	2x45 / -	2,120 @ 14	27
D.6	1889	Destroyer	300	3x5	3x35 / -	2,310 @ 14	22½
Carmen	1886	Destroyer	249	3x5	3x35 / -	1,940 @ 14	20½

1 Gröner, *Band 2* pp.31–54; *Band 3* pp.26–32, 48, BA:RM56 20.Torpedobootshalbflottille KTB.

Class	Launch	Type	Official Displacement Tonnes	Main battery size cm / length in calibres	Torpedo Tubes cm / mines	Range miles @ cruising speed knots	Maximum speed knots surface / submerged
S.58, S.60, S.63, S.65[§]	1891–2	Torpedo Boat	132	1x5	-[‖] / -	1,580 @ 12	20
T.46, T.47, T.49, T.50, T.51, T.52, T.53, T.54, T.55, T.56, T.57	1889–1890	Torpedo Boat	127	1x5	-[‖] / -	2,160 @ 10	21½
T.39	1887	Torpedo Boat	94	1x5	-[‖] / -	2,050 @ 10	20
T.27, T.28, T.30	1886	Torpedo Boat	83	1x5	-[‖] / -	2,040 @ 12	19
U.23, U.25, U.26, U.32	1913–1914	Submarine	669	-[¶]	4x50 / -	7,620 @ 8	16½ / 10
U.A[**]	1914	Submarine	270	-	3x45 / -	900 @ 10	14 / 7
U.3, U.4	1909	Submarine	421	-[††]	4x45 / -	3,000 @ 9	11½ / 9
U.1	1906	Submarine	238	-	4x45 / -	1,500 @ 10	10½ /8½

Notes

* Completed on 9 August and 10 September respectively.

† Completed on 27 June, 1 August and 2 September respectively.

‡ *G.135* had 1x8.8/35 and 2x5.2. Others given the same: *G.133* 8 November, *G.132*, *G.136* 28 November, *G.134* 16 January 1915. *G.135* 2x5.2cm replaced with additional 8.8/35 16 January 1915.

§ Until war broke out *Sleipner* (ex-*S.97*) tender to imperial yacht. All torpedo boats and destroyers with original numbers less than 114, including *Sleipner*, were re-named with T letters 4 September 1914: *Sleipner* became *T.97* and the other boats substituted T for S. 1x5cm replaced by 1x5.2cm on *T.97*, 16 January 1915.

‖ 3x35 tubes on these boats had been replaced with minesweeping gear.

¶ *U.25* alone had 1x8.8/30.

** Norwegian Navy's *A.5*, fitting out at Kiel when war broke out. Requisitioned 5 August, commissioned 14 August as *U.0*, renamed *U.A* 28 August.

†† 1x3.7 added late 1914.

Appendix VI

Organisation of German naval forces in Baltic at commencement of hostilities[1]

OSTSEESTREITKRÄFTE (BALTIC SEA FORCES)
Oberbefehlshaber (Commander-in-Chief): Grossadmiral Prinz Heinrich von Preussen
Chief of Staff: Kapitän zur See Paul Heinrich

Küstenschutzdivision der Ostsee (Coastal Defence Division of the Baltic)
Kontreadmiral Robert Mischke (appointed 2 August)

Available on declaration of war

2 light cruisers: *Augsburg*, *Magdeburg*, 1 gunboat: *Panther*, 9 destroyers: *Sleipner*, *Carmen*, *S.91*, *S.93*, *S.94*, *S.102*, *S.143*, *V.186*, *D.10*[*] 2 submarines: *U.3*, *U.4*

Commissioning at Danzig (all 4 August)

1 protected cruiser: *Freya*,[†] 3 light cruisers: *Undine*,[‡] *Thetis*,[‡] *Gazelle*[‡]

Commissioning at Kiel

2 light cruisers: *Amazone* (2 August),[‡] *Lübeck* (12 August),[‡] 4 minelayers:[|] *Prinz Waldemar* (2 August)[¶], *Prinz Adalbert* (3 August), *Deutschland* (4 August), *Prinz Sigismund* (14 August), 3 destroyers: *S.127* (5 August), *V.25* (8 August), *V.26* (8 August), 1 submarine: *U.A* (14 August)

Neufahrwasser vorpostenboote (outpost boats)

4 requisitioned trawlers, ready by 23 August

Hilfsminensuchdivision Neufahrwasser (Auxiliary Minesweeping Division)

7 requisitioned trawlers fitted with mine sweeps, ready by 3 September

Hilfsminensuchdivision Swinemünde

6 requisitioned tugs fitted with mine sweeps, ready by 7 August

Auxiliaries in Swinemünde

4 blockships – requisitioned merchant ships prepared for blocking ports: *London*, *Rhein*, *Elli*, *Viandra*, (mid-August)

1 BA:RM60-II KTB; Gröner, *Band 3*, pp.176–179; Firle, *Ostsee*, pp.41, 52–53, 76, Tabelle 3.

Auxiliaries in Kiel

12 vorpostenboote – outpost boats, 3 sperrbrecher – requisitioned merchant ships used for ensuring channels were clear of mines, 3 naval colliers, (dates various)

Artillerieschule Kiel (Gunnery School)

1 protected cruiser: *Kaiserin Augusta* (6 August)

U-Bootschule Kiel (Submarine School)

1 torpedo boat: *T.27*, 1 submarine: *U.1* (11 August)

MARINESTATION DER OSTSEE (BALTIC NAVAL STATION)

Vizeadmiral Gustav Bachmann

Hafenflottille Kiel (Harbour Flotilla)

1 minelayer: *Primus* (3 August)**, 1 tender: *Delphin*, 4 torpedo boats: *S.58*, *S.60*, *S.63*, *S.65*

Hilfsminensuchdivision Kiel

requisitioned trawlers and boats fitted with mine sweeps, ready by 9 August

Notes

Dates in brackets are commissioning dates for vessels activated from reserve or requisitioned from civilian use, otherwise available 1 August

* *D.10* served as leader boat for the submarines.

† *Freya* decommissioned after accidental flooding, 28 August. Recommissioned as stokers training ship at Kiel, 12 September.

‡ Light cruisers mobilised from reserve only completed maintenance repairs and crew training between 21–24 August.

‖*Rügen* added 24 August.

¶ *Prinz Waldemar* returned to civilian use 15 September, no actual use as minelayer.

** *Primus* returned to civilian use 28 December 1914.

Appendix VII

Change in organisation of the Baltiyskiy Flot, 23 December 1914[1]

1-ya Brigada Lineynykh Korabley (1st Battleship Brigade)
Kapitan 1-go Ranga Arkady Nebolsin*
4 battleships: *Imperator Pavel I, Andrey Pervozvannyy, Tsesarevich, Slava*
2-ya Brigada Lineynykh Korabley (2nd Battleship Brigade)
Kontr-Admiral Andrey Maksimov†
4 battleships: *Petropavlovsk, Gangut, Sevastopol', Poltava*
1-ya Brigada Kreyserov (1st Cruiser Brigade)
Kapitan 1-go Ranga Mikhail Bakhirev‡
3 armoured cruisers: *Ryurik, Admiral Makarov, Bayan*, 2 cruisers: *Oleg, Bogatyr'*
2-ya Brigada Kreyserov (2nd Cruiser Brigade)
Kontr-Admiral Pëtr Leskov
2 armoured cruisers: *Gromoboy, Rossiya*, 2 cruisers: *Diana, Avrora*

Notes
* Nebolsin, commander of *Imperator Pavel I*, had replaced Ferzen on 29 October 1914, promoted Kontr-Admiral 11 February 1915.
† Maksimov had been in post since 2 August 1914
‡ Bakhirev replaced Kolomeytsev 21 December 1914, promoted Kontr-Admiral 6 January 1915.

1 РГАВМФ:Фонд 716, Опись 2, Дело 13, p.315, Дело 1, pp.15, 25.

Bibliography

Archival Sources

Bundesarchiv, Freiburg (BA)
RM2 Kaiserliches Marinekabinett
RM3 Reichsmarineamt
RM5 Admiralstab der Marine / Seekriegsleitung der Kaiserlichen Marine
RM8 Kriegswissenschaftliche Abteilung der Marine (Marinearchiv)
RM28 Oberbefehlshaber der Ostseestreitkräfte der Kaiserlichen Marine
RM49 Befehlshaber im Flottenbereich der Kaiserlichen Marine
RM51 Geschwader und Gruppen der Kaiserlichen Marine
RM56 Torpedobootsverbände der Kaiserlichen Marine
RM60-II Küstenschutzdivision der Ostsee der Kaiserlichen Marine
RM62 Minensuchverbände und Räumverbände der Kaiserlichen Marine
RM92 Schwere und mittlere Kampfschiffe der Preußischen und Kaiserlichen Marine
RM93 Leichte Kampfschiffe der Preußischen und Kaiserlichen Marine
RM97 Unterseeboote der Kaiserlichen Marine
RM99 Hilfskriegsschiffe der Kaiserlichen Marine
RM117 Marine-Luftschiffe der Kaiserlichen Marine

Государственный архив Российской Федерации (ГАРФ)
Фонд 110, Штаб отдельного корпуса жандармов

Российский государственный архив Военно-Морского Флота (РГАВМФ)
Фонд 418, Морской Генеральный Штаб г.Петроград (1906-1918)
Фонд 479, Штаб Командующего Флотом Балтийского Моря г.С.Петербург (1908-1917)
Фонд 485, Штаб Начальника 1-й Бригады Крейсеров Балтийского Моря (1911-1917)
Фонд 716, Морской Штаб Верховного Главнокомандующего (Ставка) (1914-1917)
Фонд 719, Штаб Начальника 2-й Бригады Крейсеров Балтийского Моря (1914-1918)
Фонд 902, Штаб начальника бригады линейных кораблей эскадры Балтийского моря (1911-1914)

The National Archives, Kew (TNA)
ADM137/271: Baltic Sea Operations, Docketed papers, 1914, 1915

ADM137/2067: Commodore (S) War Records, Volume I. Reports of proceedings of submarines attached to HMS Maidstone, 1914

ADM186/620: Naval Staff Monographs Volume XI: Home Waters – Part II September and October 1914

Published Official Histories

Corbett, Julian, *History of the Great War based on official documents – Naval Operations – Volume 1* (London: Longmans, Green and Co., 1920)

Corbett, Julian, *History of the Great War based on official documents – Naval Operations – Volume 2* (London: Longmans, Green & Co., 1921)

Firle, Rudolph, *Der Krieg zur See 1914–1918 – Der Krieg in der Ostsee Band 1* (Berlin: Mittler & Sohn, 1921). A highly partisan account to be used with caution.

Groos, Otto, *Der Krieg zur See 1914–1918 – Der Krieg in der Nordsee Band 1* (Berlin: Mittler & Sohn, 1920)

Pavlovich, N. B. (Translated Rao, C. M.), *The Fleet in the First World War (Flot v Pervoi Mirovoi Voine) Volume 1: Operations of the Russian Fleet* (New Delhi: Amerind Publishing Co. Pvt. Ltd., 1979)

Rollmann, Heinrich, *Der Krieg zur See 1914–1918 – Der Krieg in der Ostsee Band 2* (Berlin: Mittler & Sohn, 1929)

Винтер, Е., 'Балтийский флот в периол начала мировой войны', in *Военно-морская комиссия по исследованию и использованию опыта войны 1914-1918 гг. на море, Сборник № 1* (Петроград: 10-я Государственная Типография, в Главк. Адмиралтействе, 1920), pp.1–31.

Винтер, Е., 'Период крейсерских походов и ожидания генерального сражения, на центральной позиции', in *Военно-морская комиссия по исследованию и использованию опыта войны 1914-1918 гг. на море, Сборник № 2* (Петроград: Государственное издательство, 1922), pp.179–258.

Гельмерсен П., 'Заградительные операции Балтийского флота у германского побережья в 1914–1915 г.г.', in *Военно-морская комиссия по исследованию и использованию опыта войны 1914-1918 гг. на море, Сборник № 1* (Петроград: 10-я Государственная Типография, в Главк. Адмиралтействе, 1920)

Гончаров Л.Г. and Денисов Б.А., *Использование мин в мировую империалистическую войну 1914–1918 гг.* (Москва Ленинград: Военмориздат НКВМФ СССР, 1940) To be used with caution. Some operational details and associated dates are unreliable and not supported by primary sources.

Киреев, И. А., *Траление в Балтийском море в войну 1914–1917 гг.* (Москва, Ленинград: Военмориздат НКВМФ СССР, 1939)

Новицкий, Виктор, 'Критический разбор плана операций на Балтийском море', in *Военно-морская комиссия по исследованию и использованию опыта войны 1914-1918 гг. на море, Сборник № 2* (Петроград: Государственное издательство, 1922), pp.56–84.

Петров, Михаил Александрович, *Морская оборона берегов в опыте последних войн России* (Ленинград: Военной типографии Управления делами Наркомвоенмор и РВС СССР, 1927)

Петров, Михаил Александрович, *Подготовка России к мировой войне на море* (Москва, Ленинград: Государственное издательство РСФСР, 1926)

Томашевич, А. В., *Подводные лодки в операциях русского флота на Балтийском море в 1914-1915 г.г.* (Москва, Ленинград: Военно-Морское Издательство, 1939)

Фирле, Р., (Translated Гельмерсен, П.В. and Тимонова, А.В., ed. Ралль, Ю.), *Война На Балтийском Море, Том I* (Москва: Государственное Военное Издательство Наркомата Обороны Союза Сср, 1937) Russian translation of Firle, used for editorial notes only.

Эмме, В., 'Период крейсерских походов и ожидания генерального сражения, на центральной позиции', in *Военно-морская комиссия по исследованию и использованию опыта войны 1914-1918 гг. на море, Сборник № 2* (Петроград: Государственное издательство, 1922), pp.127–178.

Published Contemporary Sources

Anon., *Amtliche Kriegs-Depeschen nach Berichten des Wolff'schen Telegr.-Bureaus – Band 1* (Berlin: Nationaler Verlag, 1915)

Anon., *Geheime Marine Verlustliste* (Berlin: Kaiserliche Marine, published periodically 1914–1915)

Anon, *Lloyd's Register of Shipping 1914-1915, Volume II – Steamers* (London: Lloyd's Register of Shipping, 1914)

Anon, *The American Journal of International Law, Vol. 10, 1916* (New York: Cambridge University Press, 1916)

Churchill, Winston S., *The World Crisis 1911–1918* (London: Odhams Press Limited, 1939)

Gilbert, Martin, *Winston S. Churchill: Volume III Companion Part 1, Documents July 1914–April 1915* (London: Heinemann, 1972)

Graf, H. (Translated Anon.), *The Russian Navy in war and revolution from 1914 up to 1918* (Munich: R. Oldenbourg, 1923). Translation of *На „Новикъ"*. Useful for English readers, omits some sections and translation somewhat clumsy.

Grassmann, Werner, 'Die brave alte "Augsburg"', in Mantey, Eberhard von (ed.), *Auf See unbesiegt, Erlebnisse in Seekrieg erzählt von Mitkampfern, Band 2* (München: J.F. Lehmans, 1922), pp.195–205

Hoetzsch, Otto, *Die Internationalen Beziehungen im Zeitalter des Imperialismus, Band 5 / Band 6* (Berlin: Reimar Hobbing G.M.B.H, 1934)

Hopman, Albert (ed. Epkenhans, Michael), *Das ereignisreiche Leben eines "Wilhelminers": Tagebücher, Briefe, Aufzeichnungen 1901 bis 1920* (München: de Gruyter, 2004)

Keyes, Roger J. B., *The Naval Memoirs of Admiral of the Fleet Sir Roger Keyes – The Narrow Seas to the Dardanelles 1910–1915* (London: Thornton Butterworth, 1934)

Pohl, Hugo von, *Aus Aufzeichnungen und Briefen während der Kriegszeit* (Berlin: Karl Siegismund, 1920)

Preussen, Prinz Heinrich von, 'Der Vorstoss S.M.S. "Blücher"', in Mantey, Eberhard von (ed.), *Auf See unbesiegt, Erlebnisse in Seekrieg erzählt von Mitkampfern, Band 1* (München: J.F. Lehmans, 1922), pp.32–38

Promber, Otto, *Im Kampf uns Vaterland 1914* (Stuttgart: Loewes Verlag Ferdinand Carl, 1915)

Scheer, Reinhard (Translated Anon), *Germany's High Sea Fleet in the World War* (London: Cassell and Company Ltd., 1920)

Stoelzel, Albert (ed.), *Ehrenrangliste der Kaiserlich Deutschen Marine, 1914-1918* (Berlin: Thormann & Goetsch, 1930)

Valentiner, Max, *Der Schrecken der Meere: Meine U-Boot-Abenteuer* (Zürich, Leipzig, Wien: Amalthea-Verlag, 1931)

Wieting, Franz, *Der Ostsee Krieg 1914–1918* (Berlin: Gustav Braunbeck G.m.b.H., 1918)

Wieting, Franz, 'Torpedobootsfahrten in der Ostsee', in Mantey, Eberhard von (ed.), *Auf See unbesiegt, Erlebnisse in Seekrieg erzählt von Mitkampfern, Band 1* (München: J.F. Lehmans, 1922), pp.64–73

Вейс, А.К., 'На крейсере «Баян» в годы Первой мировой войны', *Гангут № 44* (2007), pp.34–55

Граф, Г.К., (ed. Емелин, А.Ю.), *Императорский Балтийский флот между двумя войнами. 1906–1914* (Санкт Петербург: «БЛИЦ», 2006)

Графъ, Г., *На „Новикѣ", (балтійскій флотъ въ войну и революцію)* (Мюнхенъ: Р. Ольденбургъ, 1922)

Дудоровъ, Контръ-адмиралъ Б.П., 'Вице-адмиралъ А. И. Непенинъ', *Морскія Записки, Vol. XVIII, № 51*, pp.31–66, *№ 52*, pp.16–38 (1960)

Житкова, К.Г., Нордмана, Н.Н. (eds), *Российский Императорский флот 1914 г.* (Санкт-Петербургъ: И.Д. Сытин, 1914)

Крыжановскій, Kan. 2 p. Н.Н., 'Адмиралъ Михаилъ Коронатовичъ Бахиревъ и его современники', *Морскія Записки, Vol. XXI, № 58* (1963), pp.57–71

Лукашевич, С., 'Гибель миноносцев „Летучий" и „Исполнительный" (Из воспоминаний о мировой войне на Балтморе)', *Морской Сборник № 8* (1934), pp.176–178

Тимиревъ, Контръ-Адмиралъ С.Н., *Воспоминанія Морского Офицера Балтійскій Флотъ Во Время Войны И Революціи (1914 – 1918 Г.Г.)* (Нью Іоркъ: American Society for Russian Naval History, 1961)

Newspaper and Periodical Archives

Aftenposten, Oslo; *Arbeidet*, Bergen; *Dagens Nyheter*, Stockholm; *Die Presse*, Thorn; *Hallesche Zeitung*, Halle; *Hamburger Echo*, Hamburg; *Hamburger Fremdenblatt*, Hamburg; *Hamburgischer Correspondant*, Hamburg; *Hufvudstadsbladet*, Helsinki; *Hvar 8 Dag*, Göteborg; *Nidaros*, Trondhjem; *Østsjællands Folkeblad*, Havdrup; *Uusi Suometer*, Helsinki; *Либавская мысль*, Либава; *Новое Время*, Санкт-Петербург

Secondary Sources and Other Reading

Beesly, Patrick, *Room 40, British Naval Intelligence 1914–1918*, (London: Hamish Hamilton, 1982)

Björklund, E., 'Det Ryska anfallsföretaget mot Sverige år 1914' (Stockholm: Svensk Tidskrift, 1936)

Breyer, Siegfried, *Soviet Warship Development, Volume One: 1917-1937* (London: Conway Maritime Press, 1992)

Chalmers, W.S., *Max Horton and the Western Approaches* (London, Hodder & Stoughton, 1954)

Greger, René (Translated Gearing, Jill), *The Russian Fleet 1914-1917* (London: Ian Allen, 1972)

Gröner, Erich, *Die deutschen Kriegsschiffe 1815-1945. Band 1–8* (Koblenz: Bernard & Graefe Verlag, 1982-1993)

Harris, Mark, *Harwich Submarines in the Great War: The first submarine campaign of the Royal Navy in 1914* (Warwick: Helion & Co., 2021)

Lambert, Andrew, *The British Way of War* (New Haven and London: Yale University Press, 2021)

Lambi, Ivo Nikolai, *The Navy and German Power Politics, 1862-1914* (Boston: Allen & Unwin, 1984)

Marder, Arthur J., *From the Dreadnought to Scapa Flow, Volume 1 – The road to war 1904-1914* (London: Oxford University Press, 1961)

McLaughlin, Stephen, *Russian & Soviet Battleships* (Annapolis: United States Naval Institute, 2021)

Rössler, Eberhard, *Die Torpedos der Deutschen U-Boote* (Herford: Koehler, 1984)

Wilson, Michael, *Baltic Assignment – British Submarines in Russia 1914–1919* (London: Leo Cooper, 1985)

Амирханов, Л.И., *Морская крепость Императора Петра Великого* (Санкт-Петербург: Иванов и Лещинский, 1995)

Апальков, Ю.В., *Боевые корабли русского флота 8.1914г-10.1917г Справочник* (Санкт-Петербург: Интек, 1996)

Баширова, Л.В., 'Строительство Морской Крепости Императора Петра Великого (1913–1914)', in *Война и оружие, Новые исследования и материалы Труды Третьей международной научно, практической конференции, 16–18 мая 2012 года, Часть I* (Санкт Петербург: ВИМАИВиВС, 2012), pp.81–89

Вести Лисьего Носа, Выпуск № 16 (352) 30 августа 2023 года

Виноградов, Сергей Евгеньевич, *Броненосный крейсер "Рюрик". Флагман Балтийского флота* (Москва: Эксмо, 2010)

Виноградов, Сергей Евгеньевич, *Броненосец "Слава". Непобежденный герой Моонзунда* (Москва: Эксмо, 2011)

Виноградов, Сергей Евгеньевич and Федечкин, А.Д., *Крейсера «Адмирал Макаров», «Паллада», «Баян»* (Санкт-Петербург: Галея Принт, 2006)

Горлова, Д.В., 'Установление англо-русских военно-морских связей накануне Первой мировой войны', in *Первая мировая война, Версальская система и современность* (Санкт Петербург: СПбГУ, 2014), pp.198–210

Ерофеев, Ю.Н., *Аксель Берг. ЖЗЛ. Жизнь замечательных людей* (Москва: Молодая гвардия, 2012)

Кикнадзеб, Владимир Г., *Невидимый фронт войны на море. Морская радиоэлектронная разведка в первой половине XX века* (Москва: Русский фонд содействия образованию и науке, 2011)

Козлов, Денис Ю., 'Записка Е. Ф. Винтера о «шведском походе»', in И. А. Тихонюк (ed.), *Великая война 1914-1918: Вып. 6* (Москва: Квадрига, 2017), pp.107–118

Козлов, Денис Ю., '"Новик" против "Magdeburg", август 1914 года', *Гангут № 104*, (2018), pp.23–46

Мельников, Рафаил М., *Броненосные крейсера типа «Адмирал Макаров» (1906-1925)* (Санкт-Петербург: М.А. Леонов, 2006)

Мельников, Рафаил М., *Эскадренные миноносцы класса Доброволец* (Санкт-Петербург: Истфлот, 1999)

Мельников, Рафаил М., *Минные крейсера России. 1886-1917 гг.* (Санкт-Петербург: М.А. Леонов, 2005)

Меркушов, Василий Александрович, (ed. Лобыцын, В.В.), *Записки подводника 1905–1915* (Москва: Согласие, 2004)

Новиков, Виктор and Сергеев, Александр, *Богини Российского флота. «Аврора», «Диана», «Паллада»* (Москва: Коллекция; Яуза; ЭКСМО, 2009)

Партала, М.А., 'Рифы и мифы острова Оденсхольм. К истории захвата секретных документов германского флота на крейсере «Магдебург» в августе 1914 г.', *Защита информации. Инсайд. № 13*, pp.84–90, *№ 14* pp.80–86 (2007)

Партала, М.А., Симонов, Д.Н., 'Радиоразведка Русского императорского флота на Балтийском море: история создания', *Защита информации. Инсайд. № 1* (2005), pp.90–96

Скворцов, Алексей В., 'Канонерские лодки Балтийского флота «Гиляк», «Кореец», «Бобр», «Сивуч»', *Гангут № 35* (2003), pp.3–26

Скворцов, Алексей В. *Крейсеры «Диана», «Паллада», «Аврора»* (Санкт-Петербург: ЛеКо, 2005)

Степанов, Ю.Г. and Цветков, И.Ф., *Эскадренный миноносец «Новик»* (Ленинград: Судостроение, 1981)

Стволинский, Ю.М., *Конструкторы подводных кораблей: Документальные рассказы о создателях советского флота морских глубин* (Ленинград: Лениздат, 1984)

Федечкин, А.Д., 'Участие броненосного крейсера «Россия» в активных минно-заградительных операциях в 1914–1915 гг.', in *Елагинские Чтения, Выпуск VIII* (Санкт Петербург: Федеральное архивное агентство Российский государственный архив Военно Морского Флота, 2016), pp.61–68

Хромов, В., *Канонерская Лодка «Храбрый». Морская коллекция N 11 (2005)* (Москва: Моделист-конструктор, 2005)

Хромов, В., *Крейсер "Олег". Морская коллекция N 1 (2006)* (Москва: Моделист-конструктор, 2006)

Эмме, В., (Винтер, Е.Ф.), 'Балтийский флот в начале Первой мировой войны', *Гангут № 102*, (2017), pp.31–52

Эмме, В., (Винтер, Е.Ф.), 'Балтийский флот в начале Первой мировой войны', *Гангут № 105*, (2018), pp.38–64

Эмме, В., (Винтер, Е.Ф.), 'Балтийский флот в начале Первой мировой войны', *Гангут № 107*, (2018), pp.27–54

Electronic Sources

Åselius, Gunnar, 'Military and Strategy (Sweden)' 1914–1918 International Encyclopedia of the First World War (2017), < https://encyclopedia.1914-1918-online.net/article/military_and_strategy_sweden>

Badewanne, <http://badewanne.fi>

Buss, Holger, Survey Report, Elbing IX, <http://files.mikrokopter.de/Gezeitentaucher/(EN)_ELBING_IX.pdf>

Divesport Вспомогательно-потрульное судно SS "Worms" <https://divesport.blogspot.com/2018/10/ss-worms.html>

Dziedzictwo historyczne na dnie Bałtyku <https://dziedzictwo-historyczne-na-dnie-baltyku.pl>

Fog of War, Armoured cruiser Pallada, <https://digimuseo.fi/en/exhibitions/sodan-sumua/>

Stichting Maritiem-Historische Databank, <https://www.marhisdata.nl/>

podwodnedziedzictwo, < https://www.podwodnedziedzictwo.pl>

Блытов, В. and Блытова, О., «Ветреные француженки» на службе России, < https://voen-flot.ru/pomni/gibel-eskadrennogo-minonostsa-ohotnik>

Наша Лиепая, <https://nashaliepaja.lv/1914-god.-vtoraya-bombardirovka-libavy.html>

Федечкин, Алексей Дмитриевич, 'Проблемы перевооружения крейсеров «Россия» и «Громобой» в 1915—1916 гг.', Военно-Исторический Журнал (2022), < http://history.milportal.ru/problemy-perevooruzheniya-krejserov-rossiya-i-gromoboj-v-1915-1916-gg/>

Форум Журнал Кортик, <https://kortic.borda.ru>

Index

Page numbers in *italics* refer to illustrations